THE COMPLETE MACHINE-HOUR RATE SYSTEM FOR COST-ESTIMATING AND PRICING

by

Spencer A. Tucker, P. E.

President

Martin & Tucker, Inc., Management Consultants

and

Managing Director

Profit Planning & Management Institute

The Chase Manhattan Bank Building
Little Neck, N.Y. 11362

PRENTICE-HALL, INC. Englewood Cliffs, N. J.

to

Lambchop

Prentice-Hall International, Inc., *London*
Prentice-Hall of Australia, Pty. Ltd., *Sydney*
Prentice-Hall of Canada, Ltd., *Toronto*
Prentice-Hall of India Private Ltd., *New Delhi*
Prentice-Hall of Japan, Inc., *Tokyo*
Prentice-Hall of Southeast Asia Pte. Ltd., *Singapore*
Whitehall Books, Ltd., *Wellington, New Zealand*

Tenth Printing . . . . . August 1987

Library of Congress Cataloging in Publication Data

Tucker, Spencer A
The complete machine-hour rate system for cost-estimating and pricing.

1. Price policy. 2. Cost accounting. I. Title.
HF5417.T83 658.1'55 74-23238
ISBN 0-13-160721-9

Printed in the United States of America

By Spencer A. Tucker

Successful Managerial Control by Ratio-Analysis
McGraw-Hill Book Company, New York, 1961

Cost-Estimating and Pricing with Machine-Hour Rates
Prentice-Hall, Inc., Englewood Cliffs, N. J. 1962

The Break-Even System: A Tool for Profit Planning
Prentice-Hall, Inc., Englewood Cliffs, N. J. 1963

Pricing for Higher Profit: Criteria, Methods, Applications
McGraw-Hill Book Co., New York, 1966

The Complete Machine-Hour Rate System for Cost-Estimating and Pricing
Prentice-Hall, Inc., Englewood Cliffs, N.J., 1975

Creative Pricing for the Printing and Allied Industries
North American Publishing Co., Philadelphia, 1975

Respective Foreign Translations:

Japanese translation of *Successful Managerial Control by Ratio Analysis*
Charles E. Tuttle Co., Tokyo, 1964

German translation of *Successful Managerial Control by Ratio Analysis*
Verband für Arbeitsstudien REFA E.V., Darmstadt, Germany, 1966

Control de Gestion (Método de Los Ratios)
Editorial Hispano Europea, Barcelona, 1968

L'évaluation des Coûts et la Détermination des Prix par la Méthode THM
Entreprise Moderne D'édition, Paris, 1965

Break-Even-Analyse: Die Praktische Methode der Gewinn-Planung
Verlag Moderne Industrie, Munich, 1966

El Sistema del Equilibrio: Instrumento para la Planificacion de las Utilidades
Herrero Hermanos Sucs., Mexico City, 1966

Winst en Winstplanning
Samson Uitgeverij Bv, Holland, 1968

Politica de Precios
Ediciones Deusto, Bilbao, Spain, 1971

ABOUT THE AUTHOR

Spencer A. Tucker, P.E.

President of Martin & Tucker, Inc., Management Consultants, the author has in 33 years of professional practice served more than 400 companies in the U.S., Canada, Mexico, Western Europe, and the Orient in matters of profit planning, profit evaluation, production methods and work standards, and cost-estimating.

As Managing Director of Profit Planning and Management Institute, he has personally conducted 86 workshop sessions for top and middle management. More than 4,300 executives have been trained in his profit-planning concepts, tools, and techniques.

The author of six books and more than 300 articles in professional journals and trade magazines, Dr. Tucker is a Registered Professional Engineer in New York, twelve other states, and two Canadian provinces. He is the only non-accountant to be awarded the Lybrand Gold Medal from the National Association of Accountants, the highest award of the accounting profession. A second singular honor is being the only U.S. recipient of a grant from the Ottawa government to improve profitability in Canadian converting industries.

Dr. Tucker, who holds graduate degrees in industrial engineering and business administration, was awarded an honorary Ph.D. to recognize the original contributions made through his professional practice.

Foreword

Sound and reliable economic data for making pricing decisions and other related economic judgments are mandatory regardless of the country's economic weather. Whether the barometer shows a climate of inflation, deflation, boom, bust, material shortages or abundances, a businessman must have the ability to measure the benefit of meeting, beating or withdrawing from prevalent and/or competitive prices. And once he has the order booked, he must know which is his lowest cost production method from among those available to him.

If management has rational cost data available, it is able to make these and other decisions and thus generate additional profit from both the market area and from internal operations.

While this might seem like the best of all possible worlds, it is realistically attainable by the use of Dr. Tucker's practical methods which are so well presented in this book. What is important are his concepts which prove the invalidity and real dangers of the traditionalist's full costing approach and his ways of utilizing data to give management knowledge about its company which it never knew before. For example, a large company testing to see whether it should discourage small-order transactions, discovers that this is the very activity which generates the most profit with a minimum use of facility time, working capital, etc. Before the Tucker MHR System, that company was influenced by the notion that being a small-order "house" conveyed a negative image.

I have been involved in analyzing make-or-buy projects, justifying capital equipment acquisitions, determing the relative profitability of products, product lines, customers, facilities, etc. Invariably, when *proper* direct-cost data were used (in a backtesting exercise) the previous decision based on traditional data, would have been reversed. And when I refer to *proper* direct-cost data, I do not mean the accountant's approach to the separation of direct and period costs. Generally, that technique considers the various costs as wholly direct and wholly period in behavior. As Dr. Tucker stresses, analysis of cost behavior and its subsequent separation should be a team effort comprised of various specialties within the company. Thus, he emphasizes the need to extract the direct cost components of *mixed* expenses.

The author succeeds in getting across the idea that a company which uses production facilities of any type should look at itself (for purposes of measuring economic benefits) as being in the business of selling the time of its facilities. Tucker's Machine-Hour Rate System is indispensable as the measuring benchmark and this book on the subject is the first, and to my knowledge, the only one which gives complete instructions in constructing and using MHR. His book describes the reasoning, the rationales and provides sufficient criteria for development and installation. Unlike some authors who are in professional practice, Tucker does not hold back. The book is complete and supported with models which he develops to show variations in application and implementation.

This book should be read by people from top management down to the technician who is charged with obtaining details. And I might add that this applies to the smallest and the largest company, from those with a single product line to those in a multi-product business.

One of the most important pluses, and one which I have used with great success, is the author's description of the "backtesting" technique. Besides reviewing historic mistakes and indicating exactly where corrective action should be taken, it is the strongest foundation for determining market intelligence for future strategy and the most defensible guideline for generating the maximum return on total capital employed.

Marvin M. Eisner, *Comptroller,*
Bag Division
Union Camp Corporation

Preface

The underlying requirement for profit decisions is cost. This refers to future costs: when a matter arises for which an answer is needed, *the decision is in progress* and has not been made. Thus, I consider that the parameters of decision making deal with future data, a major component of which is *future costs.*

In cost estimating, pricing, profit planning, justifying capital expenditures, testing proposed alternative actions, *ad infinitum,* cost is the crucial factor. Unfortunately, cost muddling is where the profit trouble starts, since management can select from a large array of all kinds of costs, cost systems, cost concepts, cost formulas, cost allocations, *ad nauseum.*

Not being a multi-professional, the manager is helplessly in the hands of cost practitioners who spoon-feed him information. He may question but is unable to analyze. So he accepts since he has little alternative in the face of an intensively-technical rationale defensively presented in support of a specific method. Without a technical board of arbitration constantly in session, management is victimized or rewarded (either way accidentally) by the specific cost method employed.

When the word *cost* is used, there should be the implication of dimension and specific value. Yet, depending on the training, previous and current experience of the coster, the company gets numbers related to *one* particular method of costing from a host of possibilities. Therefore, in profit measurement or other data quantification, the resulting "bottom line" or final decision number is subjective and dependent on one body of opinion which is inadvertently prejudicial.

Cost then is not cost in the sense that everyone is talking about the same number. Under this arbitrary environment, costs don't stand still!

I have performed numerous experiments on the same model to prove the point: I have presented a set of cost, revenue and other required data to a group of technically-trained cost accountants and/or analysts with the request that they calculate product costs and profit. The model data pertained to a company in an industry familiar to the entire group. In *every* instance, *everyone* doing this exercise produced *different* costs and profits for the *same* product selling price!

Appalling is hardly the word that expressed my feelings after one of these cost clinics or roundtables. Frustrating is a better one.

Yet, the costers are really not at fault. Each of them is a product of his previous education and experiences. Each applied the method he was taught or the method he believed in; each was able to argue effectively in its defense. This same defensive rationale aggressively articulated on-the-job, is a method management uses for testing the limits of the coster's understanding and posture. More psychological than technical!

High product quality, excellence of production equipment, good labor relations, high productivity, and fine market acceptance, are not panaceas for profit! Wholesale dilution of economic value could be destroyed by the accident of *who* developed the cost data, *who* is doing the profit analyses, *who* is doing the pricing, and where and how they learned their methods and where and how they received their experiences.

Imagine if you will, the actual results of annual operations in a business enterprise as might be generated with alternate costers employed during the same year. Profits then can become more a function of how costs are developed and reflected instead of what they could be by the proper projection of cost data. Profits then become the result of accident, not plan, and *cost systems* compete against each other, instead of *companies.*

HOW COME?

The "how come" syndrome then becomes verbalized, viz: "How come we earned less profit than last year when this year's sales revenue was higher?"; "How come we kept our machines 30% busier than last year and produced fewer profit dollars on the bottom line?"; "How come we sold more physical units than in the previous period and made less profit in this period?" The "how come" question is a strong clue to what parameters of operation were used as profit panaceas, i.e., facility activity, revenue levels, material usages, units of output, labor utilization, etc. Invariably (as demonstrated in the book), expensive facilities are kept busy, the company gets the poorer orders and loses the good ones. Profits, if any, are made by the accident of having the lowest price in the company's markets enough of the time at a sufficiently high enough volume.

COST UNLIMITED

Once it is recognized that costers generally make some alterations in applying classical cost formulas, one can conclude that there are practically as many costing methods as there are costers. Who is right? Which is correct? In the most elementary of calculations, the "right" cost is required in order to find the "right" profit of a given sales transaction. It is obvious then that there could be a myriad number of "profits" ascribed to an identical sales value—ranging from a bad loss to a high profit. Which should and does management believe? More importantly, how does management use the numbers and how badly can it be misled?

RITES ARE WRONG

Cost determination as a part of profit planning abounds with formulas and rituals resembling early, primitive tribal rites. The activity is tantamount to the practice of sorcery and witchcraft, where the witchdoctor, with mask and bones, dances around the tribal fire and divines the magic cost from which a magic price is set. To produce consistent profits, the magical qualities of this price must consist of: its attractiveness to buyers (competitive compatibility); a profit generator for the seller; a minimum use of critical facilities, materials and skills; a minimum of supportive working capital; a minimum of storage space; etc. Who could ask more of such a price?

The ritual requires another "professional": the sorcerer. He does the planning in this tribal cost/price environment. He states in a grandiose manner what will happen in the future period in the tribe's enterprise: the usages of all facilities; the degree of intermix between products, customers, materials and facilities; the amount and variety of joint or common facility usages; the product/sales mixture; and most critically, a forecast of sales revenue in the coming year. And mind you, he thinks he is able to do this for the latter even though his customers' sales forecasts (and therefore, purchasing needs) are either non-existent, shaky or casual. Truly, the sorcerer is a man to cherish! For all seasons?

Unfortunately, witchcraft methods don't work; the evil spirits are not exorcised as they take over the tribe's profit structure. Such practices mislead; problems are postponed which ultimately must be faced; and instead of getting the maximum potential profit from every situation and time period (regardless of a current economic condition), drives for an adequate return on total capital employed degenerate into a strange set of business practices, viz: keeping raw material suppliers in business; keeping facilities busy; being charitable to customers (with inadvertently low selling prices); paying commissions to the seller's salesmen (even for loss-producing transactions, of which the seller is unaware); contributing to the community's landscaping; etc.

Ironically, the supporting paper work underlying these traditional methods is gigantic. Worse yet, when these data are reduced to computer printouts, there develops an unwarranted degree of credibility which almost obviates the need to question the bases of the magical assumptions. After all, in addition to professional costers, don't we have systems and procedures experts, programmers and software analysts? Too often this entire effort boils down to *automating the confusion* and organizing what is arbitrary, traditional and obscuring.

In an unbelievably complex business environment with an almost infinite number of interweaving variables, there is no place for the traditional approach to profit planning. Conditions demand clear, unclouded, provable, rational data—logically developed, easily traceable, securely understood, and simple to implement. Anything less leads to insecurity and decision making by instinct and impulse.

THE VARIABLES

The day has long passed when the market would accept a price based on a seller's marked up material and labor cost or on his total unit or "full" costs. Competition has seen to that! Today, the seller is faced with the dual and coexisting tasks of pricing competitively and also recovering the investments in his facilities. Earning a return on capital investment is a direct function of profit generating; volume in itself is no panacea for profit.

These goals can be accomplished if pricing is profitable and volume is adequate within the limits of a seller's scarce factor, viz: machine time, working capital, storage space, supply of critical skills, etc. Pricing is profitable only if there is enough margin between *costs* and prices.This is not as casual as it sounds because the major question raised (and solved) in this book is: "What kind of costs?"

Estimating direct labor and materials usually poses no special problem because of their ready identifiability with the product or job order. But these are only a portion of the total cost package that must be considered in cost estimating and price evaluating. The other not-so-clear costs are more difficult to get because of the great number of interweaving variables in manufacturing and in the marketplace, viz: the order quantities; the ratios between preparatory and run times; the broad, ever-changing product mix, not always produced on the same machines (common or joint facilities); the volatile sales mixture with changing customer classes, territories, volume levels; competitive responses; etc. No wonder managements resorted to magic formulas as industrial life became more complex.

The reader will find in this book, that the rational way to pre-determine costs of a prospective order is really not that complicated. He may have to kill a few sacred-cow prejudices, but once he has buried the witchdoctor, the logic and objectivity will shine through for his acceptance.

MACHINE-HOUR RATES

The term Machine-Hour Rates (MHR) is not new. There are many traditional systems which carry this or similar names. Unfortunately, most of them still carry the same conceptual errors which continue to mislead their users and at the same time (ironically), give them a false sense of security. Even with a set of rational MHR's, management often pays little attention to the estimating function, regarding it as some form of routine number exercise. It must be realized that, in effect, poor estimating is a giveaway of pieces of the company.

The author has pioneered the re-conceptualizing and refinement of the basic MHR approach so that it became a solid basis for pricing and price evaluating, in addition to its non-pricing applications. He started by simplifying the accounting ambiguity and confusion and established it as a non-accounting marketing device. Manufacturing and marketing criteria made the technique understandable to practical business managers as demonstrated in workshops conducted by the Profit Planning & Management Institute.

The MHR technique given in this book is the result of a professional experience developing, installing, testing, correcting and cross-checking thousands of MHR installations in a variety of industries and company sizes.

PRICING DYNAMICS

This book shows management how to obtain the most profit out of every pricing situation consistent with the use of production facilities and employment of capital. The book does not cover the legal implications of pricing because methods rather than policy is the subject stressed. Nor is there an attempt to go deeply into economic theories. The book covers pricing from the individual company's point of view as a vital part of its profit-planning. It accepts the market as an existing fact of life and emphasizes making the most out of the market rather than trying to change it.

The author recognizes that existing market prices are the result of a mixture of prices contributed by the community of competitors serving the market, and that the forces of demand and competition exert a more powerful impact on prices than any one company's pricing method. Economic theories of prices, markets, competitive behavior, and the like, indicate the existence, and to an extent, the direction and location of the nonprice factors bearing on the pricing task. However, these theories do not provide measurements of intensity and so simply remain theories for the economists to debate. As such, the derivation of these theories is beyond the scope of this book. However, some of these laws of economic behavior are immediately applicable and can be used effectively to improve the profits from pricing. Therefore, wherever applicable to specific and practical problems discussed in this book, they are presented, demonstrated, and used.

No businessman can price successfully and in depth without a knowledge of his costs, competitive prices, market demand, and ideally, a basis for predicting competitors' behavior and especially their reaction to price change. Out of the interplay of these variables in any immediate pricing situation, there is always one best decision and optimum price available to the seller with the right tools.

Traditional cost and pricing methods are confused by both accounting and economic dogma, each competing with the other and both vying for management acceptance. This leaves management in the unenviable position of being a technical arbitrator, of trying to unscramble an answer out of the muddle of impractical theory and technical gobbledegook. Worse yet, the practice of erecting prices traditionally based on arbitrary costs denies the existence of market demand and competition. This could cause the company to lose business on the one hand, and make it impossible to measure the profit contributions (if any) of the business they do get from such pricing, on the other.

While the internal tangible factors about a seller's company are methodized into a pricing format, the external, intangible, unpredictable factors of the marketplace cannot be methodized as finite measurable elements. Only clairvoyance, extrasensory perception, radar, and a highly polished crystal ball could begin to accomplish that objective. Pricing methods spelled out in this book suggest approaches that can be used for different businesses, once the external factors have been estimated by the pricer. The methods presented can be thought of as a systematic attack on price, pricing, and pricing decisions within the volatile framework of rapidly changing external conditions.

All other things being equal, if a market price for an article was based on an individual seller's cost, then there would be as many market prices for that article as there are sellers. Obviously, only the seller with the lowest cost would get the order and he would continue to get this business until he exhausted his capacity. The fact is that a market price is not directly identified with one cost, one selling price, or one seller. The "going" price is instead a mixture of demand and the price-offering community of all the sellers in that market. That is why no one price can provide the same amount of tangible benefit to all sellers who are capable of producing the article. The measurement of economic value to the seller of meeting a market price depends on what he uses for cost. If he uses traditional cost, he might wind up taking business he shouldn't and vice versa. If he disregards market price and builds his own price from his traditonal cost, he denies the existence of competition and gets work only when his traditional cost produces a price at or below the market. Getting business on this basis can contribute to profit or not, but traditional data will never say which. But if the seller uses *tangible, identifiable cost,* only then does he have an objective measure of what meeting a market price will contribute to his profit, to his return for the use of facilities, to the return on his capital employed.

CONTENT

In preparing material for this book, I wanted to illustrate and apply my concepts and techniques to the most complex segment of industry. In this way, I feel that the book will render a more effective service to a greater number of readers and users. Experience has shown that since these concepts work in complex areas, they will work universally.

Books which advertise how-to techniques are sometimes shallowly illustrated, weakly demonstrated and poorly explained. This has the effect of leaving the reader frustrated and with countless unanswered questions as to how this or that technique should be modified or adapted to fit his specific company needs.

This book offers an in-depth presentation of the concepts and techniques in step-by-step fashion. Sufficient criteria are given to allow and encourage the user to adapt the systems to his company. Section VI gives a set of blank forms (of the type used throughout the book) to make system development and implementation convenient and rapid. The reader should have little difficulty making the transition from book to effective system. Such is the intention of this text.

The book is divided into six Sections:

Section I is concerned with the basics of profit planning. Comprising seven chapters, this Section starts by describing the industry model selected for discussion throughout the book. It goes on to explore the part that proper costs must play in the price decision. The reader is next exposed to a detailed examination of how dangerous traditional costs can be and how the prevalent cost methods are constructed. From this, the reader can see clearly the invalidity of these practices and will resolve (hopefully) not to consider using them. The author believes firmly that the ancient methods must first be analyzed and understood and then tested and discredited without equivocation, before he can get people to be open-minded about rational concepts and methods. Chapter 4 tackles the question of rational costs and develops data essential to the proper measurement of profit contribution. Following this introduction to direct costs, the reader is shown how to separate costs into their proper behavior categories: time-related and volume-related. These are then applied in cost-volume-profit (cvp) analyses, and to the identification and profitability of the company's product mix. Chapter 6 introduces the Break-Even System and how this technique is used for solving product mix problems. The Section closes with the chapter on using the Break-Even System for day-to-day proposal evaluations and analyses of alternative courses of action.

Section II starts by introducing the specific model company for which a Machine-Hour Rate System (MHR) is developed and constructed. In the next seven chapters, the reader is given detailed step-by-step instructions for developing such a system. Each chapter is concerned with a major constructional step. And for each step there are clear-cut reasons why certain procedures are used. Just as important, each procedure contains criteria for each decision so that the reader can make alterations that more specifically apply to his particular company.

Section III presents in four chapters, a complete MHR System for each of four different companies. Again, the purpose is to indicate how some of the variables of operation can be handled differently, even though the MHR concept remains the same.

Section IV puts it all together to give the direct cost of the product or order. Cost is the product of the rate of cost (MHR) and the hours of usage. Chapter 19 therefore, discusses the role of production standards and illustrates and explains how standards should be developed. A crucial part of the demonstration is the recognition and use of the time parameters of operation. Once the need for standard time is established, Chapter 20 presents a variety of cost estimates for products/orders, using MHR and production standards and shows how problems connected with each of them are solved. These problems are typical of the seller/buyer gyrations as regards changes in quantity, price, transaction costs, making concessions to customers, etc.

Section V deals with pricing and price evaluating. These are the techniques which must be learned after the basic direct-cost procedures have been established with MHR. Those readers who already have good direct-cost data and equitable production standards can go right to this Section for an understanding of pricing dynamics and for an acquisition of pricing "methods" which may be of interest. Chapter 21 deals with the anatomy of price: a tie-in between the external, strategic market forces and the internal profit structure. This is "required reading" for the novice and even experienced pricer. Next is presented the basic economic evaluator: contribution pricing. Here, we give the reader the how-to of getting the profitability characteristics of his activity segments: product-line, etc. And for those who are forced to "follow" an established industry price list, we give the "goes" and "no-goes." Part of this chapter is also devoted to explaining the contribution pool concept, an exercise in economic psychotherapy which once and for all firmly establishes the validity of the basic profit concept. And for a control of pricing quality, we present the basic form of the contribution log. Chapter 23 builds on basic contribution measurement to develop the contribution level per hour of facility time (or per unit of any other scarce factor in the company, viz: critical materials, skills, etc.) as a further basis of comparing the relative worth of alternative order bookings. Just as important, it provides management with the most rational basis for evaluating the returns they are obtaining for the use of their facilities. This CPH technique is also applied to pricing quantity differentials and is used to expand the data of the basic contribution log.

The next chapter relates external price to facility investment so that price acceptances are made with this vital requirement in mind. If the motive for a business enterprise is to earn a desired rate of return on its total capital employed in the business, surely pricing must give effect to this, but at the same time must learn to live within market price levels. Pricing for return on capital therefore should not be an attempt to dictate prices but rather must serve as an internal financial tool to indicate cumulatively to what extent booked prices are fulfilling capital return needs. This ingredient becomes a further addition to the contribution log, serving as an additional quality evaluator. Chapter 25 presents a target pricing plan with procedures for recognizing different rates of return for different kinds of cost, viz: raw materials cost vs. machine running cost. Whole target, mini-target and break-even price schedules are developed for use in various industry situations. The last chapter demonstrates and explains how to measure the quality of pricing and the overall results of operating. Here, the unique concept of "backtesting" is presented which serves as a means of reviving previously rejected work, but more importantly, provides the company with a quantification of market intelligence in its various profitability or activity segments. This step is crucial to the success of the pricing activity since it sets the practical floor on price levels. Management information profitability reports are developed for product-lines, customers, salesmen, end-use, etc. The chapter ends with the pulling together of all company data into direct-cost statements which are free of the arbitrariness and indefensible assumptions of conventional absorption statements. Besides presenting several direct-cost formats, the final exhibit shows a unique approach to a direct-cost operating statement and ties this in to its equivalent conventional statement. Reconciling data are given to recognize the separate needs of sound internal profit information and external reporting for tax purposes.

Section VI consists solely of a set of installational forms which the reader can use, with little change, for developing his own MHR system.

SUMMARY

If a manufacturing enterprise sold just one product, in only one size, made it on its only machine, sold it to its one and only customer, and used the same amount of capital and storage area each time the product was made—cost determination would be relatively simple. But even under this model of simplicity, the traditional costing approach would ignore the external ingredients of market demand and competition. It is extremely rare to fit even the smallest manufacturing company into the above set of conditions because of all the interweaving variables of product mix, common facilities, customer classes, end-use, etc. Just one typical modern transaction defies profit analysis by traditional means. One might just as well invent costs and make pricing decisions by reference to changing hemline lengths or according to sunspot activity.

Good accounting practice doesn't necessarily result in good profits. Accounting is the process of recording past events; profits deal with the future using a set of pre-determined (future) costs. The costs in themselves will determine which direction profit planning will take, assuming there is adequate information from the marketing areas. True, historical data are a useful source of information, but unless we expect the future to be exactly the same as the past in all respects, these data cannot be used as the basis for profit planning. If they are so used, management will bog down in a vast number of variance mechanisms as product mixes, sales forecasts and market assumptions do not conveniently come to fruition.

While such practices may qualify as academically-good accounting theory, they also have the danger of obscuring the facts and clouding the dynamics of the company's *economic personality*. The MHR technique presented in this text does not require constant, expert accounting knowhow simply because the system deals with arabic numbers. What it does need is intelligence, common sense, a business man's outlook, a firm knowledge of workers, materials, equipment and an in depth knowledge of the marketplace and the company's competitors.

Spencer A. Tucker

Acknowledgments

I am happy to acknowledge the work of many talented individuals who read parts of the manuscript and offered advice and suggestions. Among these are:

E.C. Blake, Assistant Controller, Packaging Corporation of America, Evanston, Ill.; Paul O. Branding, Divisional Manager, St. Regis Paper Co., St. Louis, Mo.; J.F. Brumback, Division Industrial Engineer, Hoerner Waldorf Corp., St. Paul, Minn.; P. Durrant, Comptroller, Dominion Envelope Company Ltd., Don Mills, Ontario, Canada; Marvin M. Eisner, Comptroller, Union Camp Corporation, Wayne, N.J.; H.C. Haroun, President, Pakwell Paper Products, Portland, Oregon; J.J. Kelly, Secretary-Treasurer, Lewis Business Forms, Jacksonville, Fla.; Z.S. Kolley, Operations Control Manager, Rolph-Clark-Stone Ltd., Bramalea, Ontario, Canada; D.P. McNelly, Division Manager, St. Joe Paper Co., Rochester, N.Y.; William H. McManus, Executive Vice President, Envelope Manufacturers Association, New York, N.Y.; E.C. Merkle, Managing Director, National Flexible Packaging Association, Cleveland, Ohio; D.R. Russell, Vice President, Sonoco Products Company, Hartsville, S.C.; Edward S. Shorkey, Director of Marketing, Continental Can Co., Greenwich, Conn.; Harvey Stern, Controller, Jeffries Banknote Company, Los Angeles, Calif.; Wallace Stettinius, President, The William Byrd Press, Inc., Richmond, Va.; Dwight E. Wheeler, Director, Rexham Corp., Charlotte, N.C.

For typing the manuscript, I wish to thank Racheal Gallant and Catherine Dragotta for their devoted attention to difficult details. And finally, for the most exacting task of proofreading, I thank Catherine Dragotta again, and my sons Harry J. Tucker and Michael M. Tucker.

Contents

SECTION II. DEVELOPMENT AND CONSTRUCTION OF THE DIRECT-COST MACHINE-HOUR RATE SYSTEM

SECTION III. MODEL MACHINE-HOUR RATE CONSTRUCTIONS

Exhibits

SECTION I

Elements of Profit-Planning Data

Chapter 1

Selecting the Industry Model

To find a proper industry candidate, one which would test severely the limits of my concepts and techniques, a separation was made between companies which mass produce and those which provide a custom or "job shop" service to their customers. Examples of the former are: manufacturers of radio and TV sets, appliances, automobiles, household wax, cosmetics, etc. These are typical products which are catalogued, available from industrial lists, advertised, appear on supermarket shelves, etc.

Examples of job shop manufacturing are: machine shops, foundries, wood cabinet contract plants, fabric cloth converting, printers, packaging converting manufacturing, etc. Most of these enterprises function as secondary or tertiary sources of supply in that their products do not reach the ultimate consumer without further change or addition made by the manufacturers which follow. Thus, a cosmetic manufacturer mass produces cosmetics which are packaged in folding cartons produced by a custom converter to rigid customer requirements.

What characterizes the differences between both is that the mass production company manufactures to stock in anticipation of orders, whereas the job shop converter manufactures on demand directly to his customers' specific requirements. The mass producer anticipates his output and plans his volume in advance. He knows what production costs he will incur, he plans where his products will be sold, what the expected price levels will be, etc. Thus, a manufacturer of standard roller bearings knows, by reference to trend data and current information on devices which use his bearings, approximately how many bearings of standard size and types he can expect to sell during a period. And usually, such items are listed in standard industrial catalogs with a published price and discount structure. Sales are, in effect, pre-priced; costs are similarly pre-determined at standard rates, stemming usually from economic lot quantity techniques. Cost and price structuring is relatively uncomplex, although this is not to say that market prices are ignored. Costs are easily identified with products and kept current using variance techniques. Prices are published and ostensibly not subject to negotiation on each order or transaction.

At the other extreme, the job shop or converter enjoys none of this economic simplicity. He has no standard product that he can plan to make in a pre-determined quantity and pre-determined cost and price. In fact, he usually has no product that he offers for sale because he cannot identify his output until he receives an order. In addition to the cosmetic manufacturer needing cartons, the converter also supplies cartons (as ordered) for packaging toys, meat products, etc., typically made on the same set of converting facilities.[1]

Thus, the primary commodity or product the job shop offers for sale is service, viz: usage of his production facilities and the various skills of his technical people. These services are then variously applied to fulfilling the requirements of his customers' specific orders, after the converter has cost-estimated and priced an inquiry and has emerged as the successful bidder.

But this is a gross oversimplification of job shop characteristics. The major internal economic problems facing the converter are: first, the comparative difficulties in predicting and/or estimating future costs of customers' orders. The second is the lack of pricing benchmarks and the continual pressures of competitive bidding in the presence of unknown future costs, future activity, future product mix, future usage-mix of facilities.

In mass production manufacturing, the plant can set up a production line to make x number of units on specific equipment at readily traceable costs and against established selling prices. Not so the job shop: since he doesn't know for what to set up a line until he receives the order, he is unable to make cost pre-determinations. And until he gets the order, he cannot plan price or profit. Consequently, he attempts to pre-determine costs on a different dimension. Instead of building a cost-estimating system on little-known orders, he constructs it on each of his service or facility centers that he regularly offers for sale, and unitizes these costs by the hour. Thus: a machine shop costs its engine lathe for $20 per hour; a corrugated container costs its printer-slotter at $27 per hour; a printer costs his 4-color offset press for $36 per hour; etc.

This switch from product costs to facility-hour cost estimating does not really solve the problem for converters because of other characteristics which they all have in common. First, is trying to predict the number of hours each facility will operate in the coming period. This information is usually required in order to reduce annual facility costs to an hourly basis. Second, are costs in a converter's plant which are not directly traceable to, nor identifiable with, a specific facility. In the "all-inclusive" hourly facility cost concept (strongly opposed by the author) each cost, even if wholly unrelated to any facility, viz, administrative salaries, real estate taxes, etc., must be allocated or apportioned to facilities. The bases or factors for accomplishing this distribution are myriad, and by a large variety of persuasive arguments can be equally defended by their advocates. This consequent *indefensibility* plus the lack of objectivity in relation to specific facilities, makes all such allocation methods arbitrary and misleading.

By far however, the major issue which abuses management's attempts to earn an adequate return on total employed capital, is the entire notion of building costs (and thus the converter's profit structure) on an estimate or projection of future activity. This is an exercise in continuously repetitive but inadvertent grandiosity. For what may not be realized in performing this annual ritual is a structuring of the profit function around the foretelling of the future. For example, a folding-carton plant attempts to project annual facility hours in order to arrive at a "full" hourly cost for each of their converting facilities. The dynamics of operation include: the use of paperboard of various types, grades and finishes which are converted into cartons which package tooth paste tubes, hair lotions, sliced bacon, toys, hardware items, etc.; these are printed by various techniques, in different colors, sizes, styles, etc., in an almost infinite variety. Annual facility hours are then projected by one favorite method or another, none of which can possibly reflect what will occur in the next 12 months. How can this job shop possibly be this clairvoyant in stating how customers' orders will make use of his facilities, when his customers are not that certain of their own annual volume, future price levels, growth of their competition, product acceptances, etc.?

1 Common or joint facilities.

The converter may blithely estimate that a press, which is used partially for running cosmetic orders, will operate 3000 hours in the next 12 months. But a major cosmetic customer is unable at this same instant, to predict how well his marketing efforts on behalf of a new exotic hair lotion will come to fruition. Surely then, the converter has only the vagaries of the market and no objective basis for future activity projections that he tries to use to generate profits.

AIMED AT THE JOB SHOP

The focus of the techniques in this book will be the customer job shop or converting operation since it offers the greater challenge for cost estimating, price evaluating and profit planning. The distinguishing characteristics of this large segment of the gross *international* product are:

1. *No proprietary product.* While some job shops may have developed a product to use excess facility time, this practice is usually the exception to the rule. Production facilities are devoted to processing a variety of items for other enterprises.
2. *Relatively high fixed investment in facilities.* A tough task for the profit manager: focussing his return on this fixed capital by being dependent on the vagaries of his customers' transactions and how these will use his equipment.
3. *Wide processing mixture.* No rigid sequence of operations. Varying use of alternate methods and facilities. Typically, many jobs of differing sizes, quantities, shapes, specifications, etc., are often run on the same equipment—at different costs and prices.
4. *Common or joint facilities.* One piece of production equipment can process, at different times: a myriad number of similar items for different customers; a variety of different items for the same customer; or any combination thereof. Identification of costs with a specific order, item or customer becomes a difficult task.
5. *Unpredictability of facility usages.* Without a proprietary product line, the job shop cannot plan the activity or timing of their facilities. Obviously, he is completely dependent on the plans of his previous, present and prospective customers.
6. *Competing for facility time.* Inactivity or relatively high levels of activity affect end costs. High capacity operations can bottleneck critical facilities resulting in cost variances different from that estimated. The net result can be a large variance in period profits.
7. *Unknown future specifications.* At one point in time, a machine may produce a low-profit item. And at another time, the same machine-hour can be processing a high-profit order. Manufacturing is done to customers' very specific requirements—facts which are not known in advance. Production cannot be geared to making products in anticipation of orders since there are no parameters which can even remotely guarantee the generating of a volume.
8. *Vagaries of market/customer demand.* Demand depends on how well the job shop's customers accept their products and how well they exploit and implement it. This leaves the converter in the position of having to take whatever comes—surely a weak base for planning.
9. *Unpredictable competition.* Job shops have competition for their services, whether they sell \$50,000 or \$50 million annually. Unless the job shop has a well-structured, sophisticated, competitive intelligence system, the job shop cannot predict the reactions of their competitors to pricing. Obviously then, the price level is another factor affecting the ultimate activity of the converter.

JOB/CUSTOM SHOP SUMMARY

Regardless of whether the job shop processes paperboard into folding cartons, polyethylene film into lawn clean-up bags, steel rods into valve parts, or pig iron into special castings, they have all of the above nine characteristics in common. As converters, their business is selling facility time (and other services), not someone else's raw material which they convert.

Typically, this converting time (facility-hour) represents the major investment in the enterprise, on which the company should be targeting its profit return. To the extent that this facility time is intelligently cost estimated and rationally priced is what determines the converter's optimum product mix (and facility mix) and maximum possible profits.

Chapter 2

The Role of Costs in Profit Planning

Business enterprise is organized for the purpose of making a profit. As its level of profits is raised, a company has the opportunity to recuperate the money invested in its facilities. The risk of capital investment is taken in the hope of generating enough sales income gradually to pay off the investment, meet expenses and have enough money left over as a fair return for the investment risk taken.

Sometimes sales income is a reflection of what price leaders and competitors do; in other cases it is based directly on a markup above the figures on the cost sheet. And perhaps prices may even be reached by instinctive estimate. In any case, knowledge of costs and of how to use them is one of the most powerful competitive tools in the present razor-sharp industrial economy. Some companies have modern *cost-reduction* programs but use *cost-estimating* systems so antiquated they actually drain off some of the profit potential.

A cost-estimating system worth anything must reflect accurately and currently all changes in the company so that management may price effectively in its markets, channel its sales effort for maximum profits, enhance profitable facilities, discard unvirile facilities, and plan for expansion. Management must know its costs while the events in manufacturing are current, not "after the fact" when the events have become ancient history. A proper cost-estimating system must be able to predict in advance, within close limits, the ultimate costs of running an order.

For pricing, however, costs are only the starting point. Since competition and customer demand must be considered, selling prices rarely have a rigid relationship to cost. Pricing is more an overall total-product planning task where management analyzes the possible courses of action, balances one against the other and then selects the one which promises to be the most advantageous. For the selling effort, management must key sales effort not only to the most favorable markets but also must peg these efforts to the most profitable company facilities so that the invested capital is made as productive as possible. No matter from what areas profits ultimately are produced, the basic function of a cost-estimating system is to help management operate at a profit.

WHAT ARE COSTS?

For a company to operate profitably, expenses must be properly identified, classified, reported and allocated to the various products so that the customer pays for these in the selling prices, leaving a fair return to the owners. Of course, where "competition sets the price" the profit return may not be so attractive, but the manufacturer who enters into this type of transaction should enter with full knowledge of his own cost "floor" even though he sells this cost at someone else's price level. The traditional cost systems leave much to be desired in these marginal situations, since there is a lack of advance measurement of the cost floor and often companies find themselves selling below their actual out-of-pocket costs.

While, in general, selling prices of certain products are not established on the basis of production costs, the total aggregate selling price of a firm's products over a period of time must exceed the total cost of making those products. Within a specified period there are many fluctuations in cost and selling price, because of the nature of the particular product, the time of year, the customers' demands. A proper set of cost data skillfully used will allow the manufacturer to exploit such factors to his own advantage and thus obtain a greater gap between total costs and sales income. Of course, costs on the estimating sheet must be a reflection of rational costs, or the manufacturer will lose the good orders and get poor ones.

But what are costs? How are they identified? What do we do with them?

A cost or an expense is generated in every molecule of a company's geography, on every square inch, from every act and activity—during each second of the company's life. Costs never stop being born while the company is breathing although some costs grow at different rates than others. Indeed, costs, which are created in myriad ways, never remain static. In one second, a plant incurs labor, depreciation, and occupancy costs, and each of these costs acts in varying degree on every aspect of the company's economy.

A cost is born when a lathe is purchased; another when a switch to operate it is thrown. Direct costs are incurred in production: when a setup is made, bar stock is loaded, a piece turned or a product inspected. Costs also enter in: when the floor is swept, the tool crib attendant issues a tool, a grinder is repaired, or when the supervisor checks a dimension on a print.

Some costs are quiet and proceed unobserved: rental is paid, interest expense is paid, depreciation expense purrs along 24 hours per day, 365 days per year. Other costs are generated outside of the factory: a salesman knocks on a prospect's door, the manager counsels the foreman, an invoice is typed, a pack of estimating blanks is ordered.

All these costs, to some measurable degree, have to be estimated. First, however, all cost must be reduced to the same dimension; that is, all cost elements have to be considered "by product," or "by order." Here is where we encounter the first difficulty, because incurred costs are not paid for "by product."

Rent is paid for space, by the month; payroll is paid for human labor, by the week; material is paid for per lot, by invoice; and depreciation is paid for ownership of machinery, by the year. Nowhere in manufacturing enterprise, where converting of raw materials is being performed and where, in effect, plant and machine time is being sold, can all expenses be imputed to each individual manufactured product. Some expenses are incurred in blanket form, and it is the task of the manufacturer to segregate them and apportion them to products so that they may be recovered without overpricing, but leaving enough room for a reasonable profit.

COSTS ESSENTIAL

It is vital that management know intimately the ingredients and behavior of product costs in order to price products most advantageously within the turbulent environment of competition, vagaries of demand, and product mix. Then a company can accelerate cost recovery, evaluate proposals to change selling prices, segment the market to gain advantage of the different layers of customer demand, select most profitable business when capacity is limited, determine the price at which to refuse an order, distinguish between volume which adds to the peaks and that which creates bottlenecks, and determine which work to abandon when more attractive opportunities are available.

Even though costs generally do not determine prices, costs for pricing purposes are essential both for measuring the profit contribution of the selling transaction and as data for inter-product comparisons and rankings. Costs for pricing require both estimates of future cost magnitude and behavior and study of the profit structure of the firm.

Knowing what the costs are becomes essential when prices for products have to be determined. Naturally, a company that has a good costing system will tend to give costs a greater emphasis in its pricing policies than a company that is not so fully acquainted with the costs of its products.

COST-PRICE RELATIONSHIPS

In a buyers' market, the customer and not the seller determines the price. Regardless of sellers' prices, the buyer in the long run will determine what the price will be and how much will be accepted at any price. Therefore, only after a price acceptable to the buyer is reached does the question of cost enter the picture. Then the question for the seller is: Can the product be made and sold at a cost which will leave a profit satisfactory to the seller? This measure of the profit contribution of the sale transaction is the starting point in formulating a pricing attack.

If the demand for products is low, prices are lower than if demand is high. It's as simple as that. Therefore, the price that a buyer is willing to pay for a product will not be necessarily related to what the product costs the manufacturer. The price will instead depend on what the buyer will have to pay for it elsewhere. Costs only indicate the minimum sales price at which costs will be recovered; they do not show the profit margin that the market is ready to accept. That's why selling prices rarely have a rigid relationship to cost. What buyers pay for a product need not bear a direct relation to what it costs any seller to make.

From the customer's point of view, a successful price is one which makes him buy. From the seller's viewpoint, a successful price is one which produces a profit. While the buyer is not interested in the seller's cost, the seller must know his own costs and have some idea of competitors' prices. Reconciling (balancing) these two elements for the seller leads to a policy of successful pricing.

Cost plays an important but limited part in pricing. It indicates whether the product can be made and sold profitably at any price. But it does not indicate the amount of markup or markdown on cost which will be accepted by buyers.

Where selling prices are established in a market and an individual company has practically no latitude for independent pricing, proper costs allow measurement of profit contribution which leads to a decision to sell at the prevailing price or to withdraw. Most important, proper costs serve to guide management in the design of the most profitable product mix and in determining how much cost can be incurred without sacrificing profit.

However, when a company is a price leader in its industry and can pursue a policy of independent pricing, pricing can be tied to a target profit markup on cost expressed as an objective return on its total capital employed. Often this technique is employed for pricing a brand new product, whether the company is a price leader or not.

On the other hand, when a company is neither a price leader nor follower but rather operates with others in a highly competitive market (converter), it can maximize its profits by a judicious balance of cost, volume, prices, and product mix phased in with the external influences of the marketplace.

RESULTS OF INADEQUATE COSTS

A company that does not know the cost of making, selling, and distributing its own products is like an unguided missile. It may take off, but nobody knows where it will land. So it is with cost systems. A company manufactures products, but if it cannot predict what the products' sales will contribute to its profits, it is in the dark and must wait until the operating results are published. This is management "after the facts" and is surely too late for guiding pricing; the lack of profits is a fact, and a rigid pricing precedent may have been set in the company's markets.

Yet numerous companies operate on the basis of poor cost information—which, of course, may be at one and the same time a source of delight to their competitors as well as a major headache to them because of the necessity of now having to meet lower prices. That doesn't mean that companies which use poor costing methods have poor production methods. It does mean that regardless of methods or the degree of plant streamlining, product costs are not an effective guide to pricing.

Poor costs for pricing purposes have led some managements to push the wrong product or product line, drop the wrong product, extend excessive service to the wrong customer or market, and make a host of other profit-draining mistakes. Frequently, a desired profit may amount to only a few pennies per product. It follows, therefore, that a loss of merely these same pennies can mean failure to operate profitably. Errors in pennies can be the result of inaccuracy and sloppy recordkeeping, but they can also be caused ultimately by an improper segregation of costs of widely differing behavior patterns. Usually, the latter type of error accounts for most poor operating results.

Management decisions are divided into two basic groups: short-term and long-term. Probably the large majority of day-to-day management decisions are of short-run nature; pricing decisions represent most of these. Costs, similarly, have a short-term as well as a long-term nature, but unfortunately these different behaviors of costs are not too often taken into consideration either in classic cost accounting or in the process of pricing. Thus, pricing practices in many instances fail to relate the short-term decision to the short-term cost.

BASIC INFORMATION REQUIRED

Not all costs are incurred necessarily in one total in the budget. Some, such as material, are incurred with the volume of output, per piece if you will. Other costs, such as machine depreciation, are incurred annually. Some costs are more identified with the productive effort than others. Direct labor is usually considered a manufacturing cost, whereas executive salaries are classified as a non-manufacturing cost.

The vital point to bear in mind is that changes in price will change volume output; while some manufacturing costs will vary directly with this change, other manufacturing costs will vary somewhat disproportionately to the output change. On the other hand, it is possible for some nonmanufacturing costs to vary or remain fixed with the change in volume output. With the exception of sales commission, it is rare for a nonmanufacturing cost to vary directly with changes in output.

Completed costs, whether budgeted by production center or products, should be assembled and summarized separately so as to disclose the various elements of material, labor, factory overhead, administrative overhead, and the like.

To be valuable for profit planning and pricing purposes, any cost system has to be flexible enough to provide the information required at different times as a response to changing conditions. A cost system represents only an assembly of facts presented in an orderly manner for the purpose of obtaining some predetermined answer. Consequently, a cost system must be uniform and consistent for the individual company. If the methods used in organizing the data are changed, the results will also differ. For this reason, the cost of a product may never be a single, precisely calculated figure; it is a figure obtained to fulfill a specific function in a company, whether for pricing, profitability determinations, or control. That is why it is of the utmost importance to decide before organizing any cost system, what will be the purpose of the system and which objectives the company will try to reach with it.

FUTURE COSTS ESSENTIAL

What kinds of costs are required for profit planning and pricing? Surely raw accounting costs will not do because they are historical and do not indicate what future costs are likely to be. Costs for pricing deal with the future. Current or past information may not provide a proper basis for pricing measurement nor for profit projections unless we are willing to assume that what has happened in the past will happen in the future—with respect to product mix, volume levels, price levels, customer actions, competitive responses, and all other interrelated variables of operations.

Product costs used for determining pricing actions must be based on *expected* purchase costs of raw materials, labor wage scales, and other expenses to be incurred. Products and manufacturing may be divided basically into those which are made to order and those which are made in anticipation of future orders. The first group can be characterized as custom or job shop operations; the second as mass produced in predetermined lot sizes or catalog type. The job shop effort has to wait until orders are placed. The second type of manufacturing proceeds on a planned rate of output without regard to specific orders. For either type of manufacturing category the need for predictable future costs is essential.

Besides knowledge of production costs, information about development, promotion, marketing, and distribution costs is needed. Development costs may be related to a product, to a product line, or to a period in which there is expected a general development program. Promotional costs include advertising and selling costs, whether applicable to a product line, a territory, or a market.

Historical and "standard" costs provide only a *guide* to current or future costs. When costs of material, labor, facilities, and services change, costs previously recorded have to be restated in dollars having the same purchasing power as the dollars in which the selling prices are being quoted. One of the deficiencies in the use of costs for pricing is the inclusion of the depreciation expense based on the original or acquisition cost of the capital asset in use. This deficiency calls for a "price level" adjustment on the acquisition cost so that it will reflect current dollars. Current dollars in an inflationary economy have lower purchasing power than original dollars. Thus the depreciation expense would have to be inflated to make provision for the future replacement of assets in current dollars.

Information on product cost must be regularly presented to management for consideration of selling prices and the constant question of deciding what to do about meeting, beating, or withdrawing from competitive prices. The planned cost, rather than the past costs, is the deciding factor, so that management can know in advance the relative profit contributions of the various products that it is planning for present and future markets.

COST-ESTIMATING

Cost-estimating for pricing purposes may be defined as the process of calculating the expected cost of articles to be produced when past experience does not provide the historical cost of identical items produced under identical conditions.

All pricing problems have both long- and short-range components. While fixed costs must be considered to provide a complete recovery of expenses at the end of a given period, the short-range impact also must be given consideration. Both long- and short-range volume differentials in cost must be available to permit accurate pricing decisions.

Product costs based upon normal volume and mix of facilities are not sufficient for short-range pricing. The term "short-range" refers to any period in which there are costs that do not change with volume. This period is characterized by the stability of fixed costs and the fact that the industrial manager usually cannot adapt his productive capacity to take advantage of sudden increases in the demand for his product, nor can he substantially change his production costs overnight.

Academic approaches to product costing state that every price should cover the "full" cost of the product. Yet, the amount of overhead apportioned to a product is never precisely measurable, and there are always degrees of interpolation existing between even the closest allocation bases. Customers are not interested in the seller's allocation basis or the amount of projected activity expected, nor in that of his competitors. Allocations are done for the information of the seller and should not be done for the benefit of the customer.

Because of this "unitizing" of period costs, the actual amount carried by each unit or product cannot really be known until after the number of units have been produced—at the end of the period. That's why the getting or losing of a particular order may in itself affect the cost of filling it—as well as affecting the cost of all other units produced.

CLASSIFICATION OF COSTS

Costs may be classified into period (fixed) and direct (out-of-pocket), manufacturing and nonmanufacturing, controllable and noncontrollable, common and separable, cash outlay and sunk, identifiable and general, order-related and facility-related, etc. In costs for profit planning and pricing purposes, management must know which costs vary with volume and which do not. Thus, when management is considering additional volume which will not involve additional facilities to produce, fixed costs may not be included in such a proposal, and the contribution made to profits from this volume increment would be the difference between the incremental direct costs and the revenue. In other cases, if the volume increment being proposed requires additional equipment, both fixed as well as direct costs have to be considered.

In other instances, it may be helpful to know the direct charges incurred by the product apart from the general and administrative costs, which are not related directly to the product. The use of these cost classifications will be discussed in detail in a later chapter.

After costs have been identified and categorized, they must be reported in a form suitable for convenient evaluation and application. Costs take different forms, change at different rates, and occur at different places in the company's geography. Reporting methods must take these characteristics into consideration. One would not report the cost of machine depreciation in the way purchase of a lubricant is reported.

OTHER USES FOR COST DATA

A proper cost system also helps determine which machines or production centers in a plant are the most profitable. This consideration is important since it enables management to reflect this profitability in its sales emphasis. Inaccurate, illogical cost information can result in sales emphasis channeled in the wrong direction, applied to the poorest products or markets. In some cost systems, the level of materials costs becomes the sole guide to prices, even though a product may be produced on expensive facilities. Sales of this type make the manufacturer a jobber of someone else's raw materials instead of a merchandiser of his production facilities, thus diluting the profit return on capital equipment.

In a multiproduct company, proper costs also help determine which products will be manufactured, in what quantities, in what volume, on which facilities, and for what markets. Costs show the relationship of profitability of facilities or products to the marketing costs required to promote and sell the products.

Costs are also essential for the planning of expansions, whether in terms of equipment, markets, product lines, sales territories, or the like. In planning for the longer term, management must compute the expected results of a future course of action. Proper costs and cost separation are essential for applying the break-even technique to company operations and to the analysis of cost-volume-profit relationships.

For the shorter term, proper costs separated into their fixed and direct elements will give the out-of-pocket as well as the break-even point of specific orders, facilities, market areas, and the like. This procedure enables management to attract work to use unfilled capacity or to fill out a product line. However, the acceptance of this type of work requires discretion to avoid causing bottlenecks in the plant or occupying facilities at a time when more profitable work is available in the immediate future.

MANAGEMENT'S ATTITUDE TOWARD COST INFORMATION

Executives tend to underrate or overemphasize the importance of costs in pricing. Some dismiss costs by an attitude of "competition sets the price." Others overplay the importance of costs by rigidly adhering to the notion that costs determine prices. Costs, competition, and demand all must be considered in the pricing decision. In some cases, costs may have little direct effect on prices. In other situations, prices may tend to establish costs. Even when costs have little immediate influence on pricing, they are essential for evaluating such internal proposals as which products to push, which to drop, which to innovate, etc.

Successful competitive pricing is not simply a process of assigning an economic value to the item being priced. Nor is it just a matter of following competitive prices of the same or similar items. Even if either or both of these procedures succeeded in generating sales, the revenue could be profitless at best or loss producing at worst.

Obviously, cost is a primary factor in pricing decisions. No matter how a price is arrived at in the management inner sanctum, that price should be compared with its cost before posting in the marketplace. While this procedure may appear to be obvious and basic to profit control, a surprisingly large number of managements believe that any mistake made by neglecting this comparison can be compensated for later by increases in volume.

Chapter 3

Pitfalls of Using Traditional Cost Data

The cost of a product is not necessarily an exact, specific sum. Its amount depends on concurrent manufacture of other products and on the activity of the facilities involved in its production. Cost determination is based on many variables, not the least of which is allocation of overhead cost to the product. Usually, when an executive inquires about the cost of a specific product, or order, he is given figures developed by the orthodox accounting approach. This figure is not useful for internal managerial decisions and it tends to be inadequate for profit planning and pricing purposes.

COST-ESTIMATING FORMULAS

The key to the cost-estimating puzzle is the way period or fixed expenses are allocated, unitized, and charged to the individual product, order or facility. The direct product costs, such as direct labor and direct materials, pose no special allocation problem. These costs are generated with the manufacture of the product and do not exist if the product is not made. These costs are part of a group called direct or out-of-pocket costs. The period portion of direct costs is not variable directly with the product but rather changes in total with overall company output. These *period variable* costs are not traceable to a specific product, viz: sales clerical salaries. There are also the fixed period costs which remain constant over the short term, generally considered to be a one-year operating period. These costs are not identifiable in any manner with the product, viz: real estate taxes. These expenses are incurred at the same amount irrespective of volume and exist regardless of the booking of any order or group of orders.

Over the years, myriad formulas have cropped up, each claiming to be the best way of allocating period expenses to the product or order so that each carries "its proper share," "pulls its own weight," is "fairly charged." Cost-estimating became hampered by unnecessary complications and illogical theories. Short cuts, formulas, magic numbers, factors, and percentages confused the cost-finding process and generated tons of paper work. Often these methods arose out of a need for quick quotations; many managements never recognized product costing as a science. Once the idea of the magic number became implanted, it was hard to pry loose, especially if management was able to point to a profit figure on a recent operating statement.

Unfortunately, the use of the magic number does not *find* costs, it *forces* them. Period costs get spread with a bulldozer, filling in holes and leveling peaks. Management is victimized by the current short-cut formula in use and alternately rides the peaks of profit and the valleys of loss as the formula approaches or departs from actual costs.

TRADITIONAL COST-ESTIMATING METHODS

The following is a list of current methods being used to estimate product costs. Two products are shown for each example for comparative purposes. In all cases, the two products are the same and are made by the same company. Product 1 is produced on slow, old, inexpensive facilities; Product 2 is manufactured on fast, modern, expensive equipment. An understanding of these methods will assist the reader in the analysis of current pricing methods given in a following chapter:

METHOD A: *Total Overhead Costs Applied on the Basis of Direct Labor Cost*

Item	Product 1	Product 2
Direct material	$ 9.00	$ 9.00
Direct labor	8.00	3.00
Overhead = 150% of direct labor	12.00	4.50
Total cost	$29.00	$16.50

Comment: Method A assumes a direct relationship between overhead costs and direct labor costs. It is perfectly possible for low-labor items to require massive overhead expense support, and vice versa. This method will undercost expensive work, such as Product 2, and overcost work requiring a higher amount of direct labor, which may be true of work produced on slow, old equipment, as in Product 1. The effect is to keep the expensive facilities very busy, especially those on which the unit direct labor cost is low. In some instances, this method has led to overtime, multiple-shift operations and even to a duplication of facilities. When profits do not provide the expected objective, the tendency is to secure volume by "desperation pricing" in order to avoid excess idle capacity. Frequently, this desperation pricing results in selling below out-of-pocket costs. This method victimizes the user to the extent of his direct labor content in any product; product mix becomes customer dominated and not seller controlled; the company generates a great amount of unprofitable volume; and usually any profit is made by accident and not by plan.

METHOD B: *Total Overhead Costs Applied on the Basis of Direct Labor plus Direct Material Costs*

Item	Product 1	Product 2
Direct material + direct labor	$17.00	$12.00
Overhead = 33 1/3% of direct material + direct labor	5.67	4.00
Total cost	$22.67	$16.00

Comment: Method B assumes a direct relationship between overhead costs and the sum of direct materials and direct labor costs. There may not be any sensible relationship between overhead expense and the amount of raw materials used in the product. Raw material content can be very high and the cost of facilities used to manufacture the product can be very low, so that the product becomes overloaded with overhead expense because of its inherently high material-cost content. Naturally, the reverse is also true. In other cases, the labor and materials can both be low or high.

This method is a compounding of illogical relationships, the overhead being assigned by two elements of direct cost, both of which may vary considerably without having any real appreciable effect on the overhead actually incurred. Orders having the lowest combination of materials and labor wind up with the least overhead charge. This practice limits volume on expensive facilities where most of the company's investments exist if the material cost is a large portion of product cost. The method also victimizes the user as in the foregoing Method A, but to an even greater extent because of the interplay of cost with a changing product mix. For example, if Product 1's material and labor cost of $17 had a different mixture, say, $16 for material and $1 for labor instead of what is shown above, then the one-third for overhead could be far too much. If the proportions were changed in the other direction, the one-third could be too little. If Product 2 had a different breakdown, say $2 for material and $10 for labor, the distorting effect of the one-third overhead charge would be even more serious because of the nature of Product 2's facility cost.

METHOD C: *Total Overhead Costs Applied on the Basis of Direct Material Costs*

Item	Product 1	Product 2
Direct material....................................	$ 9	$ 9
Direct labor....................................	8	3
Overhead = 100% of direct material..................	9	9
Total cost....................................	$26	$21

Comment: Method C, similar to Method A in the sense that only one cost factor is used as the allocation base, makes product cost the accident of the material content. In this case, even though both products are made on facilities which differ considerably in capital cost, the method assumes that the incurred overhead is the same. Products made at high speed on expensive equipment will not be charged with much overhead if the material cost in the product happens to be low. In the reverse case, products which make little use of capital facilities and incur little overhead cost will be charged with a great amount of overhead cost if the material in the product happens to be high. This method is very simple to compute and use, but its valid application is limited to bulk materials industries such as forgings, cement, sugar, paint, bread, and the like. In these cases, this method is applied on a weight instead of a dollar basis. For example, if a brass foundry produces 800,000 pounds of castings per month of uniform style and weight and the overhead expenses for the month are $80,000, the *overhead per pound* is 10 cents. Thus, the overhead cost estimate for a casting weighing 5 pounds would be 50 cents. If however, the foundry's products are *not* uniform and it produces a variety of castings which vary in weight, shape, and style, requiring all manner of coremaking, this method becomes inequitable. Under this circumstance, the simple but heavy casting will be overcost, and the complex but light casting will be undercost.

METHOD D: *Total Overhead Costs Applied on Unit of Product Basis*

Item	Product 1	Product 2
Direct material....................................	$ 9	$ 9
Direct labor....................................	8	3
Unit overhead....................................	5	5
Total cost....................................	$22	$17

Comment: In Method D, the expected output is divided into the total budgeted overhead to get the cost per unit. Here we are assuming overhead costs of $100,000 per year and output at 20,000 units per year, or $5 per unit. This method is a more direct method of charging overhead cost—but only in severely limited cases. It can be used only where one product is made or where products are few, closely related, and have some common denominator such as weight or volume. Examples of industries where the use of this method may be considered safe, but still not logical, are the shoe industry and the mattress industry, where the size is standard and the grades held fairly close. In the above case, the illogical effect shows up by assigning as much overhead to one product as to the other in spite of the wide gaps between their use of facilities and actual incurrence of overhead costs.

METHOD E: *Overhead Applied on the Basis of Conversion Costs*

Item	Product 1	Product 2
Direct material	$ 9.00	$ 9.00
Conversion costs:		
Direct labor	8.00	3.00
Direct manufacturing overhead	2.00	7.00
Period overhead = 125% of conversion cost	12.50	12.50
Total cost	$31.50	$31.50

Comment: Method E assumes that overhead costs vary directly in accordance with direct conversion costs and is similar to Method A, in which only the direct labor was used as the basis of allocation, except that some direct overhead is charged directly to products and the balance to be allocated is only the period or fixed component of overhead. This refinement does not change the logic, only the numbers. Consider the above case where the sums of direct labor and direct overhead are both $10. Does this mean that the depreciation expense for the equipment (a period fixed cost) is the same for both products? Does it mean that the space occupied, and thereby the real estate taxes (another period fixed cost), for each piece of equipment used for the two products will be the same? Certainly there could be substantial differences which might lead to vastly different total product costs. This method is an attempt to divorce material as one of the bases of allocating overhead and is a step in the right direction. This method also recognizes that those overhead costs which are directly identified with a piece of equipment (and thence with the product) should be charged directly without the necessity for an arbitrary allocation. This is creditable and another step in the proper direction. Other rationales for this method include one which recognizes the process of conversion as the service being sold and thereby attempts to apportion fixed overhead in accordance with the respective capital investments in each product. Again, the desire to assign value to a product based on investment levels is sound, but only if the various layers of capital and their respective degrees of risk are considered. But this method amounts to a blanket average and is not specific enough.

METHOD F: *Manufacturing Overhead Applied by the Machine-hour Rate Method* [1]

Item	Product 1	Product 2
Direct material	$ 9.00	$ 9.00
Conversion costs:		
Direct labor	8.00	3.00
Manufacturing overhead	4.00	10.00
Total manufacturing cost	$21.00	$22.00
Nonmanufacturing cost = 10% of manufacturing cost	2.10	2.20
Total cost	$23.10	$24.20

1 Spencer A Tucker, *Cost-estimating and Pricing with Machine-hour Rates,* Prentice-Hall, Inc., Englewood Cliffs, N.J. 1962.

Comment: A machine-hour rate is the cost of operating one production center for one hour in the processing of orders or products. Some machine-hour rate plans include only manufacturing costs; others include nonmanufacturing costs as well. The machine-hour rate, then, is a *rate of conversion cost.* For example, assume that Product 1 has to pass through just one piece of equipment in its process. If this machine carries a machine-hour rate of $2 (manufacturing cost only) and Product 1 uses that machine for 2 hours, the conversion cost is then 2 hours at $2 per hour or $4. If Product 2 also requires processing through one machine for 15 minutes and its machine-hour rate is $40, obviously its conversion cost is 0.25 X $40 = $10. The machine-hour rate method is the most equitable way of allocating overhead since the apportioned overhead cost reaches the product cost by way of the facilities used. In this way overhead is charged by the way it is incurred and where it is incurred, instead of where the impact of overhead incurrence is obscured. This method, however, includes only manufacturing cost in the conversion cost rate, leaves the nonmanufacturing cost to be allocated by percentages, and may or may not be equitable depending on the specific company and its product characteristics. For example, in some industries one product may require much more or much less nonmanufacturing support than a fixed percentage on manufacturing cost would yield. The following two methods show the logical refinements of the machine-hour rate method.

METHOD G: *Total Overhead Costs Applied by the Machine-hour Rate Method*

Item	Product 1	Product 2
Direct material	$ 9	$ 9
Conversion costs:		
Direct labor	8	3
Total overhead	5	18
Total cost	$22	$30

Comment: Method G is similar to Method F with this exception: the conversion rate is all-inclusive of manufacturing and nonmanufacturing costs; nonmanufacturing costs are not applied by a percentage of another total. In Method F, total overhead costs were shown to be $6.10 ($4.00 + $2.10) for Product 1 and $12.20 ($10.00 + $2.20) for Product 2. When the machine-hour rate is all-inclusive, the total overhead costs are $5 and $18 respectively, indicating a possibly greater cause-and-effect relationship between each product and the amount of nonmanufacturing overhead charged. Even though this method shows a greater degree of refinement, we have to go one step further before it can be used for profit planning and pricing.

RECOMMENDED COST-ESTIMATING METHOD

A method which is presented in detail later is discussed briefly here to provide a comparison:

METHOD H: *Period and Direct Overhead Costs Applied by the Machine-hour Rate Method*

Item	Product 1	Product 2
Direct material	$ 9.00	$ 9.00
Direct conversion costs:		
Direct labor	8.00	3.00
Direct overhead (facility)	3.40	9.80
Direct overhead (order)	0.40	2.10
Period direct costs	1.60	1.80
Period fixed costs	1.10	1.90
Total cost	$23.50	$27.60

Comment: In Method H, overhead is applied to products through the medium of the cost of facility usage, as in the previous two methods, but with the exceptions that (1) the machine-hour rate is an all-inclusive overhead rate and (2) the costs which behave differently are treated differently. This method is known as the two-part machine-hour rate system wherein a machine-hour rate is expressed in the direct cost per hour and the "full" cost per hour. Thus, a machine-hour rate for a given production center could be $36.75 "full" cost, of which $22.45 is the direct-cost component. Since the fixed costs are reflected in "full" costs by an assumed rate of expected activity, the "full" costs, even though they may represent the result of cause-and-effect relationships, are nonetheless arbitrary because of the unknown element of future activity. If the marketplace is not ready to accept such a "full" cost (since it represents only the projections of one manufacturer without reference to competitive price levels), management is faced with a reduction in its price if it wishes to get the order. In this event, it is essential that management know its *floor* on cost—its *out-of-pocket cost* level. This method of cost-estimating provides simultaneously both out-of-pocket and "full" costs. A word of explanation is in order regarding the two types of direct overhead charges shown. The direct overhead (facility) refers to those charges which are incurred directly by a machine, such as electricity for operating, machine supplies which vary directly with volume, and the like. Direct overhead (order) represents those overhead charges which are incurred by the order, such as freight out, salesman's commissions, and any other direct-order charge which requires no statistical allocation.

SUMMARY OF THE EIGHT COST METHODS

Obviously, great differences exist among the eight methods illustrated:

Total costs estimated	Product 1	Product 2
Method A	$29.00	$16.50
Method B	$22.67	$16.00
Method C	$26.00	$21.00
Method D	$22.00	$17.00
Method E	$31.50	$31.50
Method F	$23.10	$24.20
Method G	$22.00	$30.00
Method H (recommended)	$23.50	$27.60

Which cost is correct? Regardless of whether management intends to use estimated costs for pricing or for other internal decisions, the cost method must produce a reliable number. It should be clear from this comparison that much damage can be done to the firm's profit objective as well as to the market price levels if illogical cost methods are used as the basis for price. Yet it has been the author's experience that all these methods are used by groups of competing companies serving the same markets. Often, then, a company gets the order which it thinks is profitable solely on the basis of the cost method used. One can look at this situation as competition based on cost-estimating methods rather than on the basis of individual company quality, performance, and modern processing methods.

SUMMARY

When a manufacturer offers a product for sale he is really offering to make his services, facilities, and technical knowledge available to his customers. Ideally, the customer should pay for a portion of each of these items so that the manufacturer gets back all the costs he has incurred. The industrialist experiences risks of operating his business by investing capital in machinery, buildings, inventory, labor force, and other factors of production. Against these risks, the manufacturer balances his profits and the selling prices that should bring in the expected revenues. When estimated costs are wrong, regardless of the pricing method used, anticipated profit contributions shrink and/or orders are lost.

The seller must apportion the various categories of cost to products or to facilities which produce his output. Direct costs which vary with volume are identifiable with, and traceable to, output and call for no special allocation to products. The allocation of fixed or period costs to products requires the use of one of a great number of allocation bases, each of which has some degree of logic but is nonetheless arbitrary. The contention that a given allocation method is the "right one" is indefensible because of the lack of direct, traceable relation between the cost and the product. This attempt to unitize time costs can victimize the manufacturer and distort the basis on which prices are decided. In a multiproduct business, the use of magic numbers for cost estimating distorts information needed for analyzing the product mix and facility usage.

Later chapters will suggest rational approaches to cost estimating for pricing purposes and will apply them in specific situations where there are the volatile interplays of costs, volume, prices, profit, product mix, facility usages, market forces, and competitive behavior. The pricing technique will show how these operational variables can be quite different from company to company and from one situation and time to another situation and time.

Chapter 4

Rational Costs and the Profit Structure

As was seen in the previous chapter, cost is not cost in the sense that everyone is talking about the same number. That is, all people don't mean the same thing when they refer to it. The cost of an identical order can vary all over the lot depending on who calculated the cost, what magic formula he used, who developed the formula, and where the developer learned it.

NEEDED: A COST WHICH STANDS STILL

The use of the word cost implies a tangible, factual dimension. But if this number moves around for the same transaction as a result of different development methods, then no reliable profit measurement can be made. Omitting fixed costs for the moment, if an item costs $8 and is sold for $10, the profit is $2. If the measurement of the $8 cost is anything but rational, the profit is obscured, the profit could be artificially translated into a loss, and management is misled.

The need to *allocate* rather than to *identify* costs keeps the job shop in a quandary in its attempt to identify and quantify its sources of profit. Exhibit 4-1 shows the dilemma of a folding-carton company which tries to make this analysis. Each of the four methods, A through D produces a different cost, which must therefore produce a different profit *measurement.* Which is correct and how should management perform its planning on the basis of these data?

As we will see, by using the correct approach, we can find a cost which stands still regardless of volume fluctuations and other interweaving variables, from which rational economic measurements can be made.

THE PROFIT STRUCTURE

Not all costs change in proportion to revenue, and profits do not change in proportion to either costs or revenue. Not all costs change at the same rate and in the same way. Neither is each element of cost affected by the same cause in the same way. Some costs change directly with volume, such as direct labor and material. Some costs remain constant with volume, such as real estate taxes and machine depreciation (assuming no capital additions within the operating period). Some costs change in step fashion with volume, such as supervisory expense and some types of office clerical salaries.

THE GOAL: What annual profit is earned in each of the following folding-carton product lines?

DATA	ANNUAL TOTAL	PRODUCT LINES: Food	Cosmetics	Garment
Sales	$6,000,000	$2,000,000	$2,000,000	$2,000,000
Costs	5,400,000	?	?	?
Profit	600,000	?	?	?

THE PROBLEM: What method should be used to allocate costs to product lines for profit measurement?

	Food	Cosmetics	Garment
A. Annual machine-hour method?			
Allocated costs	$1,600,000	$2,800,000	$1,000,000
"PROFIT"	400,000	(800,000)	1,000,000
B. Annual tons consumed method?			
Allocated costs	1,800,000	600,000	3,000,000
"PROFIT"	200,000	1,400,000	(1,000,000)
C. Annual revenue generated method?			
Allocated costs	1,800,000	1,800,000	1,800,000
"PROFIT"	200,000	200,000	200,000
D. Annual pieces produced method?			
Allocated costs	2,300,000	2,400,000	700,000
"PROFIT"	(300,000)	(400,000)	1,300,000

EXHIBIT 4-1: A Major Stumbling Block in Profit Planning How to allocate costs for profit determinations?

This is why a given increase in revenue will not necessarily cause the same increase in profits. As a matter of fact, it is possible for an increased revenue to produce a loss where before the increase a profit existed. In the following tabulation, the original selling price for an annual volume of 100,000 units is $28 each; then management is persuaded that it could get a volume increase of 30 per cent by reducing the price per unit to $21:

Item	Original conditions	Volume increased 30%
Units sold	100,000	130,000
Direct cost per unit	$10	$10
Annual period cost	$1,500,000	$1,500,000
Annual direct cost	1,000,000	1,300,000
Total cost	$2,500,000	$2,800,000
Selling price per unit	$28	$21
Annual revenue	2,800,000	2,730,000
Pretax profit or (loss)	$ 300,000	($ 70,000)

This result could occur when management did not know how the specific cost ingredients of its profit structure behaved in response to volume. Naturally, not all companies will respond to the same price and volume change in the same way. The way each would react is a function of its specific profit structure—its economic personality.

This type of response occurs in companies making a single product as well as in those making several products. In cases where multiproducts are made on common or joint facilities, decision making is based on guesswork, not fact, unless management has a clearcut picture of the behaviors of its costs. The specific nature of costs makes the prediction of profits at different volumes impossible by the use of classical profit-and-loss statement as a base. In the case of a company producing more than one item, usual in most manufacturing enterprises, a change in sales volume or revenue may or may not contain the same proportions of the various products. The presence of different amounts of various products made and sold is known as *product mix* or sales mixture. This product mix does not conveniently stand still. It changes in response to prices, to actions of the competitive community, and to demand. Unless management reflects in its pricing actions the likely effect of product mix changes and their consequent impact on the costs generated, the company could be sailing into dangerous waters.

PROFIT ANALYSIS

Analyzing profit and examining the behavior of the cost, price, and product mix ingredients which cause it is vital to the management of any business at any time, to say nothing of its absolute necessity in planning the pricing action.

Changes in profits come in two basic ways: changes in revenue and changes in cost. Obviously, the revenue change comes from the combination of changes in prices and volume. If more than one product is being made and sold, however, the revenue and cost changes are each affected by the product mix, i.e., the volume of product related to its specific price and cost. Obviously, not all products carry the same profit margins nor are they always sold in the same proportions. Therefore, the net change in profits is the result of the interplay of all factors. In short, changes in selling prices cause changes in product mix, which cause changes in revenue and volume; these, in turn, cause changes in costs in a never-ending cycle. Only a comprehensive analysis can show the effect of all the forces.

EFFECT OF VOLUME

If all costs varied or were controllable with the physical volume of production, the total cost to make and sell would vary directly with volume and therefore the cost and profit of each product unit would remain the same. For example, if 200,000 units cost $2,000,000 to make and sell, and if 300,000 units cost $3,000,000 to make and sell, it is obvious that each unit costs $10. But because of the presence of typical constant or fixed expenses, which are incurred only with the passage of time, it is impossible for such a direct proportion to exist. Fixed expenses do not vary with volume, and in the typical manufacturing enterprise, these expenses usually remain constant throughout the operating year from a volume level of zero output up to the level of operation for which they were intended.

Considering these fixed expenses as time or period costs leads to this simple comparative analysis for the same company:

Type of cost	200,000 units sold	300,000 units sold
Volume (out-of-pocket, direct) costs........	$1,000,000	$1,500,000
Fixed (constant, period, time) costs.........	1,000,000	1,000,000
Total costs..............................	$2,000,000	$2,500,000
Unit "full" costs.........................	$10.00	$8.33

Volume in itself exerts a dual pressure on profits. It affects both the revenue and the unit costs. As the number of units sold drops, revenue falls and unit costs rise. If both factors are present and worsening, costs and revenue soon meet and losses begin. The above analysis is simple once the separation of volume and time costs has been accomplished. But in a multiproduct company experiencing the usual changing product mix, profit analysis is complicated if not impossible using conventional profit-and-loss statements.

PRICE-CHANGE PROPOSALS

Evaluating proposals to change selling prices is a task faced frequently by management. Often management is confronted with questions of obtaining additional volume from other markets if its normal prices are reduced. Unless proper data are available, management might agree to such a reduction and achieve a poor result, or it might be misled into turning down such a proposal and deprive itself of an increased profit opportunity. The solution to the problem is available from an analysis of the company's profit structure. Let's say that a company is attempting to predict what additional profits will develop from a 40 per cent increase in unit sales volume. The use of traditional profit-and-loss data for both the original sales level as well as for the 40 per cent increase would show (product mix and prices assumed constant):

Type of cost	Original sales level $1,000,000	Sales level increased to $1,400,000	Increase, %
Direct labor costs	$250,000	$ 350,000	40
Direct material costs	300,000	420,000	40
Factory overhead costs	200,000	280,000	40
Selling, general, and administrative costs	150,000	210,000	40
Total costs	$900,000	$1,260,000	40
Pretax profit	$100,000	$ 140,000	40
Profit return on sales, %	10	10	0

When management approaches profit and cost behavior in this manner, it is making the following incorrect assumptions:

1. That all costs change in the same way with a change in revenue. Above analysis shows that since revenue increased 40 per cent, every cost in the company also increased 40 per cent.
2. That all costs change in the same way with a change in volume of units sold. The analysis also shows that since volume of units sold increased 40 per cent, every cost in the company also increased 40 per cent.
3. That all revenue dollars carry the same "profit," i.e., that the same 10 per cent profit is earned on all sales.
4. In particular, that the same 10 per cent profit is earned on any sales increase above $1,000,000.

If the additional 40 per cent volume had to be priced 10 per cent lower in order for the company to book it, management might be prompted to turn it down. Its reasoning would be that since the same 10 per cent profit would be made on this incremental volume as well as on the original volume, the additional volume would be profitless after the 10 per cent price decrease. Decisions on this type of traditional data could deprive a company of legitimate sources of profit.

	ORIGINAL SALES REVENUE	SALES REVENUE INCREASED 40%	INCREMENTAL SALES REVENUE
	$1,000,000	$1,400,000	$400,000
Direct (oop) Costs:			
Direct Labor	250,000	350,000	100,000
Direct Materials	300,000	420,000	120,000
Factory Overhead	125,000	175,000	50,000
Selling, General & Administrative	25,000	35,000	10,000
TOTAL DIRECT	$700,000	$980,000	$280,000
Period (fixed) Costs:			
Factory Overhead	75,000	75,000	0
Selling, General & Administrative	125,000	125,000	0
TOTAL PERIOD	$200,000	$200,000	0
TOTAL COSTS	$900,000	$1,180,000	$280,000
Pre-tax profit	$100,000	$220,000	$120,000
Profit %	10%	15.7%	30%
Profit-Planning Data:			
Contribution	$ 300,000	$ 420,000	$ 120,000
PV	.30	.30	.30

Effect of Increment:

1. Increase in Revenue = 40%
2. Increase in Volume = 40%
3. Increase in Profit = 120% or $120,000

EXHIBIT 4-2: Analysis of the Profit Structure (c-v-p) (product mix and prices assumed constant)

INCREMENTAL PROFIT

Exhibit 4-2 shows what a proper analysis would look like. In this tabulation, volume and time costs are separated. The fixed cost portions of the Factory Overhead and Selling, General, and Administrative cost categories have been extracted and held constant over the volume increment. (Of course, this assumes that the company has the available capacity to produce this increment.)

Only the direct costs are shown to move with volume changes. In other words, the direct costs are the only costs identified and traceable to the volume increase. The fixed costs incurred only by time period remain constant.

Thus, while profit is 10 per cent at the original sales level, it increases to 15.7 per cent because of the "spreading" of the fixed costs over a greater revenue. Because the only costs incurred specifically to produce the additional 40 per cent volume are the direct costs, the profits on just the incremental portion alone are 30 per cent. This contradicts the traditional notion that the same profit is earned on all revenue dollars, and shows management that, if necessary, a 10 per cent price decrease on this portion can be made without wiping out incremental profits.

Exhibit 4-3 shows how a proper analysis can show the effect of a 10 per cent price reduction on this 40 per cent volume increment. Here the various classifications have been condensed into direct and fixed segments. Since prices on just the 40 per cent volume increment have been reduced 10

	ORIGINAL SALES REVENUE	SALES VOLUME INCREASED 40%	INCREMENTAL SALES REVENUE
	$1,000,000	$1,360,000	$360,000
Direct Costs	700,000	980,000	280,000
Period Costs	200,000	200,000	0
TOTAL COSTS	$900,000	$1,180,000	$280,000
Pre-tax profit	$100,000	$180,000	$80,000
Profit %	10%	13.2%	22.2%
Contribution	$300,000	$380,000	$80,000
PV	.300	.279	.222

Effect of Increment:

1. Increase in Revenue = 36%
2. Increase in Volume = 40%
3. Increase in Profit = 80% or $80,000

EXHIBIT 4-3: Analyzing Effect on Profit Structure (product mix constant and prices reduced 10% on the 40% volume increment)

	ORIGINAL SALES REVENUE	INCREMENTAL REVENUE (new mix)	COMBINED REVENUE
	$1,000,000	$400,000	$1,400,000
Direct Costs	700,000	440,000	1,140,000
Period Costs	200,000	0	200,000
TOTAL COSTS	$900,000	$440,000	$1,340,000
Pre-tax profit	$100,000	($40,000)	$60,000
Profit %	10%	(10%)	4.28%
Contribution	$300,000	$ (40,000)	$ 260,000
PV	.30	(.10)	.1857

Effect of Increment:

1. Increase in Revenue = 40%
2. Increase in Volume = 63%
3. (Decrease) in Profit = (40%) or ($40,000)

EXHIBIT 4-4: Analyzing Effect on Profit Structure (prices assumed constant; product mix of increment changed)

per cent, the revenues for the combined sales as well as for the increment have been reduced to give effect to this price change.

Since the incremental volume of units remain the same, the direct costs are the same as those shown in the previous exhibit. And, of course, since the time costs are not readily discontinued or adjustable with revenue, the fixed costs remain the same. The data show that even if prices were reduced 10 per cent on just the incremental portion, profits for that portion would be 22.2 per cent, further discrediting the traditional approach to uniform profit-making.

A further calculation inserted on this exhibit because of its vital nature in pricing is the figures for the *contribution.* Contribution measurement is one of the pivotal factors and will be discussed at length throughout the remainder of this book. The dollar amount of contribution is obtained by subtracting the direct costs from the revenue. While the example shown develops contribution from annual data, the major use of this figure comes when management is developing unit prices.

Rather than using profit, which is the result of intermixing volume and time costs, i.e., identifiable and nontraceable costs, the contribution figure is preferable to use as a measurement of economic value because it is the result of subtracting two tangible, nonarbitrary, identifiable amounts: The contribution amount is the sum left over from revenue after paying the out-of-pocket costs and is used to pay the fixed expenses with the overage equal to profit.

Not all incremental business is profitable as shown on the previous two exhibits. Of course, this will not be apparent without the availability of sound cost information. As an example, the company is offered a piece of business representing a 40 per cent increase in sales volume but did not have the costs of producing that business separated between its period and direct costs. Many job shops don't consider the possible effects of blindly booking substantial increases in revenue. The syndrome of "we'll make it up on volume" still persists. And so does the notion that "we must keep machines busy" is a panacea for profit. Exhibit 4-4 shows what could happen by booking the 40 per cent volume increment on hunch or instinct.

This type of analysis is crucial in the pricing function, especially on a unit-by-unit basis in a multiproduct operation. Besides its use in pricing, profit analysis is vital for profit-planning and decision-making in all areas of the enterprise, as later chapters will show. First and foremost must come the separation of costs into their respective behavior categories.

These examples have been presented to show the importance of sound profit analysis in guiding pricing decisions. Obviously, there are other pricing considerations, such as competitive reactions and market demand, which must be recognized.

Chapter 5

Classifying and Applying Basic Cost Data

For the determination of profit at any time, at any volume, at any price level, and for any condition of product mix, proper cost classification and analysis are required. As we have said, some costs vary closely with changes in volume, whereas others remain unchanged in total amount regardless of changes in sales activity or production volume. Costs which change with volume are usually called *direct* costs and those which don't over the short term are called *fixed* costs. When fixed and direct costs are scrambled together into a total unit cost, it is impossible to relate volume to costs; hence, pricing and other decisions are weakened. This problem can be resolved by obtaining costs that have been divided into their fixed and direct elements. Then the effect of volume becomes immediately apparent. When these segregated data are applied to segments of the profit structure, sources of profit as well as areas of strengths and weaknesses are revealed.

DIRECT COSTS

In profit planning and pricing, direct costs are also known as out-of-pocket costs, since it is these costs which are incremental to the decision to make and sell and which require outlay of immediate cash to support. One test of a unit direct cost is whether it is readily discontinuable or whether it will not exist if an order is not booked.

Direct costs may be said to include those costs which the product incurs unit by unit in any area of the company. These will include such obvious costs as productive labor and electrical energy charges at production centers, as well as charges directly incurred by the order, such as materials, sales commissions, royalties, freight out, etc. The major criterion of a direct cost is that it be traceably and tangibly generated by, and identified with, the specific product being made and sold.

While there are some direct costs which vary directly or almost automatically with volume, there are some direct costs which increase with volume but not in direct proportion.

PERIOD VARIABLE COSTS

Profit planning decisions must be based on a knowledge of the specific behavior of various costs used in the enterprise. The first task is to separate from total costs, and then study, costs which have a decreasing identifiability with the product. The highest ranking of product cost identifiability goes to the unit direct or out-of-pocket costs. But there are costs which, while not directly related to the product, do vary in some way with the volume of production.

In a broad sense and taken over the long term, fixed or constant costs, such as depreciation of equipment, can be considered variable as management adds investment from time to time. Administrative salaries, traditionally considered fixed, can also become variable as management tries to adjust its expenses to periods of business downturns.

Here, though, we are concerned with the type of cost which varies over the operating year and which, while not directly identified with specific products and therefore not varying unit by unit, does vary by changes in specific levels of operation or by activity in entire product lines. Such costs are those paid for factory supervisors, some classes of maintenance people, administrative clerical people, sales clerical staffing, and the like. It is interesting to note that, while period variable costs cannot be directly traced to product units, they often can be identified directly with entire product lines, especially since changes in total activity of product lines can result in a greater number of transactions, clerical activity, specific maintenance problems, quality control efforts, etc. Therefore, in our future discussions and examples, we shall consider that within a defined product mix there is a reasonable relationship between period variable costs and direct costs in total but not necessarily unit by unit.

PERIOD FIXED COSTS

Fixed costs are known by many other names. Interchanging these names does not change the behavior characteristics as could happen with the various classifications of variable costs. Identifying different levels of fixed costs is done for purposes of management control, even though all are usually incurred in one fixed sum for the operating year.

Specific programmed costs: These costs, while fixed in amount for the year, refer to the costs assigned by management to specific projects to fulfill company objectives. Sometimes they are called *managed costs* because they are subject to management evaluation and change. Incurred depreciation costs as the result of acquiring new equipment or adding to factory space are good examples, but there are other specific programmed period costs which are used to generate additional revenue, such as the costs of opening a district sales office or warehouse, the reduction in costs that comes from installing special quality control devices in a product line, or a special advertising program to push a particular product line. These costs are known as *separable* rather than *common* because they may be charged (without arbitrary allocation) directly to the product line or activity which is the recipient of the cost increase or decrease.

General programmed costs: While these costs are also fixed for the operating year, they are incurred for the benefit of the entire enterprise and are common rather than separable, even though they may be discontinued by management action. Typical of these costs are general and administrative salaries, research and development, selling, marketing, and promotional costs.

Constant costs: These fixed costs are neither separable nor discontinuable. They are common and *inescapable* costs as long as the enterprise is to continue in business. Among these costs are depreciation, real estate taxes, interest on mortgages, rent, etc.

In pricing, all period fixed costs are referred to as fixed costs with the understanding that all elements of these costs incurred during the operating year have been included.

COST-VOLUME-PROFIT ANALYSIS [1]

Practically every action or planned decision in a company will affect costs, prices, volume,

1 Also see Chapter 4.

and/or profits. The cost-volume-profit (cvp) analysis discloses the interplay of all these factors in a way which aids management to select the best courses of action from which to make the best price decision.

Mix of product, also known as the sales mixture, refers to the variety and quantities of products made and sold by one company during a specific period. Since it is usual for each of the products in the company's line to contribute differently to the company's profits, obviously any shift in one class of products over another will have a pronounced effect on the profit results obtained. One goal of cvp analysis is to give management accurate and objective data about the contributions made by each product so that the sales effort can then be directed accordingly.

In this respect, one of the most significant pieces of data produced by a cvp analysis is the marginal income ratio, often called the contribution ratio or profit-volume ratio (PV). This ratio is the percentage of the sales dollar available to cover fixed costs and profits after deducting direct costs. For example, in the following data:

Sales	$1,000
Direct costs	600
Fixed costs	300
Profit	$100

The contribution ratio or PV is the contribution money of $400 ($1,000–$600) divided by the sales revenue. This equals $400/$1,000 or 40 per cent and the PV is said to be .40. This means that 40 cents out of every sales dollar goes towards paying fixed expenses and providing a profit. Thus the contribution of $400 pays the $300 fixed cost and leaves a profit of $100. It should be mentioned at this point that the $300 of fixed cost referred to is not allocated but pertains to a cost specifically related to the $1,000 sales activity.

When the PV is known, it is possible to determine the effect on profits that additional business will produce. If $500 of additional business is being considered, we are able to calculate the additional profit as being $500 X .40, or $200. Under these circumstances, the $300 of fixed expenses have already been paid for by the $1,000 of sales, leaving a $100 profit. For instance, $1,200 in sales would produce $180 in profit. This simple example immediately reveals a facet of this company's profit structure, namely, that an increase of 20 per cent in sales produces an 80 per cent increase in profit. Again, this example does not mean that all businesses will respond to the same sales increase in the same way. How each company will respond is a function of its specific cvp characteristics—its profit structure. Obviously, this simple analysis could not have been made unless all costs had previously been separated into their direct and fixed elements.

HOW CVP DATA ARE USED

Cost-volume-profit analysis is vital for decision making in the areas of pricing, selective selling, volume compensation, which products to make, to buy, the effect of price on volume, effect of volume on costs, which product to add, to drop, how the product mix should be changed, etc.

For example, suppose a company makes a comparative analysis between two of its products:

Item	Product A	Product B
Selling price	$10.00	$15.00
"Full" cost	9.00	13.50
Profit	$ 1.00	$ 1.50
Return on sales, %	10	10

It finds that both products earn (ostensibly) the same profit percentage of sales and are therefore thought to be equally profitable. However, realizing the arbitrary nature of the fixed-cost allocation contained in the "full" cost figure, the company prepares cost-volume-profit data and adds the following:

Item	Product A	Product B
Direct cost	$4.00	$10.00
Contribution	6.00	5.00
PV	.60	.33

When this type of analysis is made, management realizes that both products do not contribute the same degree of economic value to its firm as was thought because of the uniform profit percentage. Nor is management deceived by the higher price of Product B. Not only does the sale of each unit of Product A produce a higher tangible cash contribution, it also generates a much higher contribution rate (PV) on its price and thus helps cover the company's *period* (not allocated) fixed costs at a faster rate.

When cvp data are available, management can take steps to direct sales emphasis towards products of greater contribution. When direct and fixed costs are not separated, but appear scrambled together into one total ("full"), management has no objective basis for evaluating one product with another or for measuring the value of one selling price over another. The only alternative is to compare the respective selling prices, which the above example shows could be quite misleading.

Another reason the contribution figure is a much more useful figure than the profit is the arbitrary nature of the fixed expenses allocated to the various products, as discussed earlier. A direct or out-of-pocket cost is directly identified with the product, but the fixed cost is incurred with time. In order to unitize the fixed expense, it is necessary to force it arithmetically into becoming a direct cost by distributing it to the various product lines (or the production centers involved in their manufacture) on the basis of some future expectation of volume or activity of each. Since the unitized fixed cost is arbitrary it makes the "full" cost as well as the unit profit arbitrary also.

This same approach is used in making the pricing decision on a "going" market price. In many instances, a market price for a product is sensible for one company to take and for another to reject if the price is below a company's out-of-pocket costs. The out-of-pocket cost should be the floor on prices, below which no businessman would want to go. Selling a product at just the out-of-pocket cost level is an exercise in evenly trading dollar bills. Without cvp data, this might very well happen. Take the following example in which two similar companies are bidding for the same order:

Item	Company A	Company B
Selling price quoted	$11	$11
"Full" cost	10	10

But, let's assume that the "going" market price is $9.00. Obviously, with only "full"-cost information available, both companies would be inclined to turn down the order. However, with cvp data, the cost ingredients might look like this:

Item	Company A	Company B
Out-of-pocket cost (direct cost)	$6.00	$8.50
Unitized fixed cost	4.00	1.50
Contribution at a $9 selling price	3.00	0.50

(Variations in out-of-pocket and fixed costs of the magnitudes shown for the same product occur because of differences in labor rates, productivities, material costs, specific fixed expenses, and volume projections.)

Obviously, Company A is in a much better position to accept the order at $9.00, whereas the contribution appears very marginal for Company B. One thing is sure: if the market price dropped below $8.50 and Company B accepted orders for that product, each increase in volume would generate specific cash losses (in addition to losing any contribution that product would make to the payment of Company B's annual period fixed expenses.) Contrary to popular notion, volume will not compensate for price in all cases. In this instance, increasing volume can only make cash losses worse for Company B.

In directing the product mix of a company, emphasis should be placed on achieving the maximum amount of contribution money for the least amount of revenue (consistent with the use of capital and the availability of facilities.). In many client engagements the question is frequently asked, "Why did we make less money this year on more sales?" Often, the answer rests with the fact that sales were being increased for the sake of generating revenue (volume) instead of contribution dollars. Naturally, in these cases, contribution information was missing because of the lack of cvp data—data in which volume and period costs are separated.

As an example of this, let's examine a simplified case in which one company earns more profit from less sales revenue on fewer items than another similar company over a period of one year. Each company produces the same product:

Item	Company X	Company Y
Unit selling price	$15	$17
Volume of units sold	100,000	130,000
Total sales revenue	$1,500,000	$1,950,000
oop cost per unit	$12	$15
Contribution per unit	$ 3	$ 2
Total contribution	$ 300,000	$ 260,000
Less: annual fixed expenses	200,000	200,000
Pretax profits	$ 100,000	$ 60,000

Company Y's out-of-pocket (oop) unit costs can be higher for various reasons: higher direct selling costs, poorer manufacturing productivity, higher cost of materials, greater waste, etc. But regardless of its higher selling price, greater number of units sold, and larger sales revenue, it makes a profit 40 per cent below Company X. Obviously, in this example, Company X used cvp data and Company Y operated on the hope that maximizing both price and volume was the pathway to higher profit. If it had separated its volume and period costs and measured contributions and had had a knowledge of the price-volume characteristics of its markets, it could have found the *combination* of price and volume which could have increased its profits.

CVP AND THE CHANGING PRODUCT MIX

In multiproduct companies, the effect of volume selling for its own sake is more critical. Exhibit 5-1 shows data for four different products made by the same company. The two mixes are presented to show the results produced by "gross dollar selling" versus a well-directed product mix. In the revised or Case B mix, more profit is earned on the same unit volume and less sales revenues. Often, when cvp data are not available, salesmen will generally push the products carrying higher prices, especially if their compensation is based on a percentage commission on booked sales dollars. The difference in results of $95,000 between the two cases is simply the result of placing emphasis on dollar contribution instead of on the revenue dollar. Besides which, the lower revenue could reduce the company's involvements in additional inventory, working space,

Cost Elements	Product I	Product II	Product III	Product IV	
O.O.P. (direct)/M	$ 11.00	$ 5.00	$ 12.00	$ 8.50	
Selling Prices/M	12.00	9.00	14.00	10.00	
Contribution/M	1.00	4.00	2.00	1.50	
Case A Mix:					Totals
Units sold	40 million	5 million	30 million	10 million	85 million
Revenue generated	$480,000	$45,000	$420,000	$100,000	$1,045,000
Contributions obtained	$ 40,000	$20,000	$ 60,000	$ 15,000	$ 135,000
Less: Fixed expenses					$ 200,000
Net Loss					($65,000)
Case B Mix:					
Units sold	5 million	40 million	10 million	30 million	85 million
Revenue generated	$60,000	$360,000	$140,000	$300,000	$ 860,000
Contributions obtained	$ 5,000	$160,000	$ 20,000	$ 45,000	$ 230,000
Less: Fixed expenses					$ 200,000
Net Profit					$ 30,000

EXHIBIT 5-1: How Product Mix Affects Profits

	Prod. A	Prod. B	Prod. C	Prod. D	TOTALS
Unit O.O.P. Cost	$ 9.00	$ 10.00	$ 11.00	$ 12.00	----
CASE I MIX:					
Unit Selling Price	15.00	16.00	17.00	18.00	----
Unit Contribution	6.00	6.00	6.00	6.00	----
Units Sold	50M	60M	40M	30M	180M
Total Revenue Generated	$750,000	$960,000	$680,000	$540,000	$2,930,000
Total Contribution Generated	300,000	360,000	240,000	180,000	1,080,000
Less: Fixed Expenses	---	---	---	---	1,000,000
Net Profit	---	---	---	---	$ 80,000
CASE II MIX:					
Unit Selling Price	$ 14.00	$ 19.00	$ 18.00	$ 20.00	----
Unit Contribution	5.00	9.00	7.00	8.00	----
Units Sold	70M	40M	40M	25M	170M
Total Revenue Generated	$980,000	$760,000	$720,000	$500,000	$2,960,000
Total Contribution Generated	350,000	360,000	280,000	200,000	1,190,000
Less: Fixed Expenses	---	---	---	---	1,000,000
Net Profit	---	---	---	---	$ 190,000

EXHIBIT 5-2: Pricing and Product Mix

and transaction costs. The selling prices shown are "going" market prices which the company has decided not to alter.

PRICING AND PRODUCT MIX

Exhibit 5-2 shows another company's experience with changing prices and the effect on product mix. In Case 1 mix, the company followed a subjective policy of pricing at some uniform contribution level. This policy, in effect, ignored the presence of market forces and especially the elasticity of demand. When the pricing gave effect to these strategic factors, the mix of Case 2 resulted. In Product A, management estimated that the drop in price would be more than offset by an increase in volume which would more than restore the previous contribution in Case 1 mix. Product B was priced below competitive levels in Case 1 mix and adjusted for this condition in the Case 2 mix. Here the increase in price of $3 increased contribution by 50 per cent, which just offset the one-third drop in volume. In Product C, management found that its demand was inelastic, i.e., a small increase in price did not affect volume with a consequent increase in contribution. In Product D also, the $2 increase in price increased contribution enough to more than offset the drop in volume. Thus, the results of Case 2 mix produced more than twice the profit at less unit sales volume and at approximately the same sales revenue.

Chapter 6

The Break-Even System

Having invalidated the "full"-cost figure as useful in profit-planning decisions, we must turn our attention to the notion of unit profit before going further.

UNIT PROFITS

If a seller has only direct, out-of-pocket costs in conducting his business, the difference between that figure and the selling price will be considered a profit on every unit sold. However, when a seller incurs a period or time cost which is fixed in amount during the operating year (does not vary with the number of units sold), then no profit develops until that fixed cost has been paid for. Since the vast majority of businesses operate with some kind of fixed cost, it can be said that there is no such thing as an order or unit profit.

By the same token, it cannot be said that a price is a profitable one if it is in excess of "full" costs, nor can we say that a price pegged below the "full"-cost level is unprofitable. If a selling price is in excess of "full" cost in which the seller obtains less activity volume than he originally projected, thus minimizing the amount of unitized fixed cost, it is possible for that price to show an eventual loss. The reverse is also true. For example, let's take a simple case of a retailer of candy bars who buys them from his supplier at 8 cents and sells them for 10 cents each. His only fixed cost is his rent of $1,000 per year. If he desires to project an estimate of "full" cost on each, he would have to forecast an expected volume level. Let's assume he projects a volume of 100,000 bars per year:

Item	One bar	100,000 bars per year
Sales revenue	$0.10	$10,000
Out-of-pocket cost	0.08	8,000
Unitized fixed cost	0.01	1,000 (annual total)
Total cost	$0.09	$ 9,000
"Profit"	$0.01	$ 1,000

Seems reasonable, doesn't it? The only trouble is it won't work in pricing. The only single condition under which profit per bar will be 1 cent is if, in fact, 100,000 bars are actually sold during the year. If fewer bars are sold, the unit profit is less; if more bars are sold, the unit profit is more. If, during the year one bar happens to sell for 15 cents, far above the "full"-cost level, that 6 cents cannot be called profit unless at least 100,000 bars wind up being sold. The trouble is that no one knows in advance whether or not this will actually be the figure sold. Should only 25,000 bars be sold in that year, all except one being sold at 15 cents, the entire operation is still a loss and that 15-cent sale cannot be considered as contributing to profits.

In the reverse case, if actual activity turns out to be 200,000 bars sold for the year, "full" cost are 8 1/2 cents each and any bars sold at anything above this level are actually profitable.

Every time the retailer sells a candy bar at 10 cents, he generates a *contribution* of 2 cents. This contribution figure is the only tangible benefit he receives from making a sale. The point is that enough of these 2-cent contribution pieces must be generated to pay the annual rent of $1,000. Obviously, this would be $1,000/$0.02, or 50,000 bars. This figure is the man's break-even point: the level of sales volume which produced pooled contributions equal to the period fixed expenses. If 50,000 candy bars is the volume break-even point, then, when the 50,001st bar is sold, the full profit on that bar is 2 cents. If only 50,001 bars are sold in the year, the total true profit for the year's operations would be just 2 cents.

The unit profit notion implies that each time the man sells a candy bar, a profit of 1 cent is earned. Obviously, this cannot be correct since below the 50,000 annual volume level, losses are being incurred and above that level, a profit of 2 cents each is being earned.

From this simple example, we can define contribution in two ways:

1. *Below the break-even point:* Contribution monies are pooled first to pay the fixed expenses, and the PV indicates the speed of contribution inflow.
2. *Above the break-even point:* Previously pooled contributions have fully paid for the fixed expenses, and contribution above the break-even point *is* profit and the rate of profit is the PV.

Obviously, the faster contribution money is generated, the sooner the break-even point will be reached and passed. But one thing should be made crystal clear at this point: assume that instead of a candy store operation, we are talking about a typical manufacturing company which operates in a competitive market in which market prices fall on either side of this manufacturer's "full" cost. How successful will he be if he pursues a policy of "full"-cost pricing until he passes his break-even point and only after that he prices competitively? Using this approach to pricing, the chances are good that he may never reach his break-even point! A seller's customers are not going to be tolerant about their supplier's need to reach his break-even point before getting competitive prices. Customers are not interested in their suppliers' costs, cost systems, pricing systems, break-even points or this book. All other things being equal, they are interested in getting the lowest price they can. In a manner of speaking, realistic, flexible, rational pricing must start on the first day of the operating year, setting acceptance or rejection levels based on the unit contribution of the transaction, the state of the accumulated contributions pooled to date and the way they stack up against fixed expenses prorated for the same period, the economical use of capital, the state of facility loading, inventory, and space commitments, etc. The inference that profit is earned only on the last sales made is fallacious, since contribution must be as vigorously pursued in January as in June or December!

THE BREAK-EVEN SYSTEM

The break-even system[1] is a simple and easily understandable method of picturing to management the effect of changes in prices and volume on profits. Detailed analysis of break-even data will reveal to management the effect of alternative decisions that convert costs from direct to

1 Spencer A. Tucker, *The Break-even System: A Tool for Profit Planning,* Prentice-Hall, Inc., Englewood Cliffs, N.J., 1963.

fixed or vice versa, the effect of decisions which reduce or increase costs and those which increase sales volume and income, and, most important, the effect of decisions to change selling prices. The break-even system is a device which portrays the effects of any type of forward planning by evaluating alternative courses of action.

The break-even *point* can be defined as that sales revenue at which losses cease and profits begin or vice versa, or it can be described as that level of sales revenue at which profits are zero. For our purposes, the break-even point is better thought of as that amount and type of sales revenue which generates contributions equal to the period fixed expenses. Thus it follows that many companies can have the same break-even point for a certain period, even though their operating characteristics are vastly different. Contributions in a period are generated through the infinite interplays of differing costs, volumes, and prices, and thus the same break-even point may be reached in myriad ways by totally different companies. This, of course, is a function of the specific cvp characteristics of each company.

Finding the break-even point itself is an operation that dwindles to insignificance once the data produced by developing it become available. Surely every company wants to do more than break even. However, it is in the analyses leading to the determination of break-even that we learn about the economic character of the company from which point management can then plan its actions. As we shall see, it is possible for many companies to have the same break-even point and yet respond to proposed changes in sharply differing ways.

Pricing decisions can be made using the break-even approach in arithmetic or formula form. But equally important for some is a graphic portrayal which pictures the effects of pricing decision.

Unlike the traditional approach to break-even, which assumes a constancy between costs, volume, revenue, and profit, the break-even system (a modified concept) is able to cope with the ever-changing facets of the business enterprise—the interplay of costs, volume, prices, and profit—all within the constantly changing product mix.

BREAK-EVEN APPLICATIONS

To build a firm foundation for using the break-even system, we shall start by being very basic, using first a small business where few variables interfere with the basic concept and gradually building the concept to the point where it can give answers to pricing and operating problems encountered in the typical multi-product business. The simple formulas will be presented as needed.

EXAMPLE: Using the small retail store operation (candy bars) mentioned earlier in this chapter, the break-even formula and the break-even point is:

$$\text{Break-even (in unit quantity)} = \frac{\text{fixed expenses}}{\text{unit contribution}} \quad (1)$$

$$= \frac{\$1{,}000}{\$.02}$$

$$= 50{,}000 \text{ bars}$$

$$\text{Break-even (in revenue)} = \frac{\text{fixed expenses}}{\text{PV}} \quad (2)$$

$$\text{PV} = \frac{\text{unit contribution}}{\text{unit price}} \quad (3)$$

or

$$\text{PV} = \frac{\text{total contribution}}{\text{sales revenue}} \quad (4)$$

Using Eq. (3)

$$PV = \frac{\$.02}{\$.10} = .20$$

and substituting in Eq. (2)

$$\text{Break-even} = \frac{\$1{,}000}{.20} = \$5{,}000$$

(Of course, the reader recalls that Unit contribution = unit price − unit out-of-pocket costs; of Total contribution = sales revenue—total out-of-pocket costs.)

PROBLEM A: If the man increases his fixed expenses to $1,500 per year, what is the effect on the break-even point? *Solution:*

$$\text{Break-even} = \frac{\$1{,}500}{.20} = \$7{,}500 \text{ (increase of } \$2{,}500) \quad (2)$$

PROBLEM B: If he raises his price per bar to 11 cents, what is the new break-even point? *Solution:* The PV is now 3 cents/11 cents or .273, and

$$\text{Break-even} = \frac{\$1{,}500}{.273} = \$5{,}500 \text{ (approx.)} \quad (2)$$

PROBLEM C: If fixed expenses remain at $1,500, but instead of raising prices, he is able to buy candy bars from his supplier for 7 cents each instead of 8 cents, what is the new break-even? *Solution:* The PV is now 3 cents/10 cents or .30, and

$$\text{Break-even} = \frac{\$1{,}500}{.30} = \$5{,}000 \text{ (the original break-even point)} \quad (2)$$

Comment: Certain guideposts emerge from even these simple problems at this point:

a. A change in just the fixed expenses changes only the break-even point.
b. A change in the price and/or the out-of-pocket cost changes both the break-even as well as the PV.
c. An increase in prices and/or a decrease in out-of-pocket costs can offset a rise in fixed expenses.

PROBLEM D: Comparing the conditions in the original example where the break-even point is $5,000 with those in Problem C where the break-even point is identical, compute profits in both cases when sales reach $8,000. *Solution:* For this problem, other formulas have to be presented:

$$\text{Profit} = (\text{sales revenue} \times PV) - \text{fixed expenses} \quad (5)$$

$$\text{or Profit} = \text{profitable range of sales} \times PV \quad (6)$$

substituting in Eq. (5) for *Original Case:* Profit = ($8,000 × .20) - $1,000
= $600

substituting in Eq. (5) for PROBLEM C: Profit = ($8,000 × .30) - $1,500
= $900

Comment: This leads to additional guideposts:

d. Two companies can have the same break-even point but will earn profits or losses at their own PV rate above and below that point.

e. Above or below the break-even point, the differences in the PV's of two different companies will be proportionate to their differences in profits or losses.

PROBLEM E: What is meant by the "profitable range of sales"? *Solution:* The range of these sales extends from the break-even level of sales up to the operating sales level. For both the Original Case as well as the case of Problem C, this range would be from \$5,000 to \$8,000, or \$3,000. Using Eq. (6) for the Original Case, Profit = \$3,000 × .20, or \$600; and for the case in Problem C, Profit = \$3,000 × .30, or \$900.
Comment: And an additional guidepost:

f. Above or below the break-even point, profits or losses are generated at the PV rate.

PROBLEM F: What must the bars be priced at to generate a profit of \$1,450 at a \$9,000 sales level if out-of-pocket costs are \$.078 each and fixed costs are \$1,700 per year? *Solution:* This calls for new formulas:

$$\text{PV} = \frac{(\text{target profit} + \text{fixed expenses})}{\text{sales revenue}} = \frac{(\$1{,}450 + \$1{,}700)}{\$9{,}000} = .35 \tag{7}$$

$$\text{Unit price} = \frac{\text{out-of-pocket costs}}{(1 - \text{PV})} = \frac{\$.078}{(1 - .35)} = \$0.12 \text{ each} \tag{8}$$

Comment: Another rule:

g. If it is desired to establish a price to produce a target PV, divide the oop costs by the complement of the PV.

CONSTRUCTING BREAK-EVEN CHARTS

Basically, there are three lines on a break-even chart. One shows the fixed expenses over the volume range, another shows the total cost lines, and the third is the revenue line. The point at which the revenue line intersects the total cost line is the break-even point. In order to draw the various lines, it is necessary to have a scale of values for each.

1. *Break-even chart for the candy store:* In the simplest form of chart, the sales revenue is shown on the x axis or horizontal scale and the expenses are plotted on the y axis or vertical scale. Both are expressed in identical dollars on the identical scale; therefore any point on the diagonal 45-degree revenue line will produce the same value when referred to either the vertical or horizontal scale. When the total cost line intersects this revenue line at any point, at that sales volume costs and revenue are equal—the break-even point.

Exhibit 6-1 shows the break-even chart for the candy store operation in the original case. The data for this chart are given as \$1,000 annual fixed expenses, unit selling price of 10 cents, and unit oop cost of 8 cents. The dollar values on both horizontal and vertical scales are identical. The dashed line parallel to the horizontal axis shows the values of the fixed expenses with changes in volume. Of course, this value remains the same over the operating year. The revenue line is drawn as a 45-degree diagonal as explained above. The total cost line starts at the fixed expense level at zero sales volume (because the total cost at zero volume are the fixed expenses) and requires another point before the line can be drawn. To find another point, simply calculate what the total cost is for a corresponding sales revenue. For example, at a volume of 80,000 bars the total cost and revenue would be:

oop cost ($0.08 x 80,000)	$6,400
Fixed cost	1,000
Total cost	$7,400
Total sales ($0.10 x 80,000)	$8,000

Therefore, the second point through which the total cost line must pass is a point on the chart where a revenue of $8,000 corresponds to a total cost of $7,400. When this total cost line is drawn, it intersects the revenue line at $5,000—the break-even point.

2. *Dynamics of cvp:* Profit and loss can be measured directly on the chart for any volume level. Since profits or losses occur between cost and revenue, the wedges enclosed by the total cost and revenue lines are the profit or loss areas or zones. The amount of profit or loss at any volume is the perpendicular distance between the cost and revenue lines.

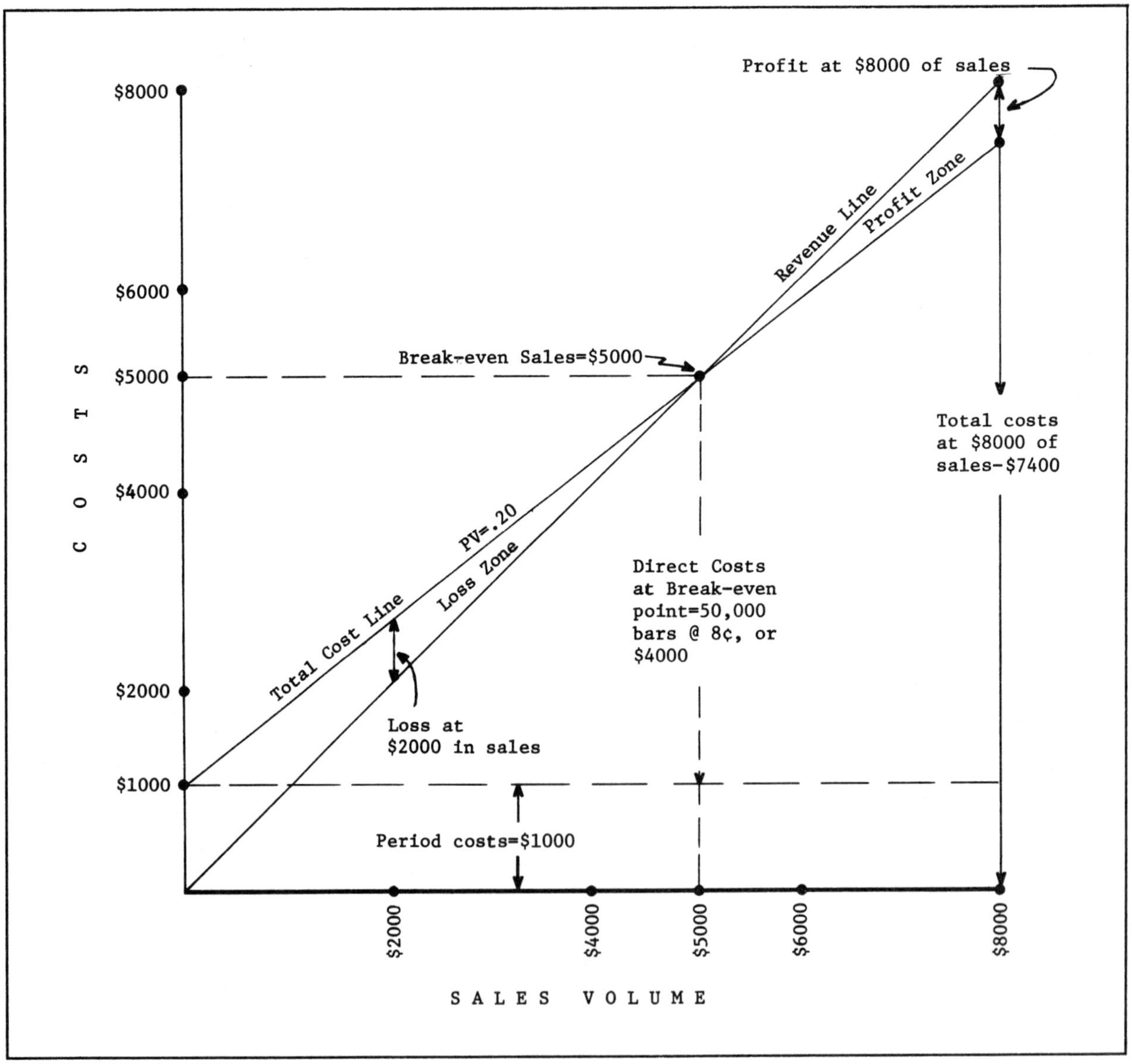

EXHIBIT 6-1: **Break-Even Chart: One-Product Candy Store**

Things are not so uniform in business. This type of chart assumes that each dollar of revenue will have the same cost, the same PV, and, ultimately, the same profit. The dynamics of practical operating would have these effects on the chart:

a. A decrease in the oop cost, with no change in the fixed expenses, would lower the slope of the total cost line, thereby reducing the break-even point and widening the profit wedge (because of the increase in PV). In this kind of situation, not only do profits start earlier (at a lower break-even) but when they do start, they are generated at a higher rate of profit (the PV rate). A reverse condition would produce opposite effects.

b. An increase in prices for the same volume, with no change in fixed expenses, would reduce the

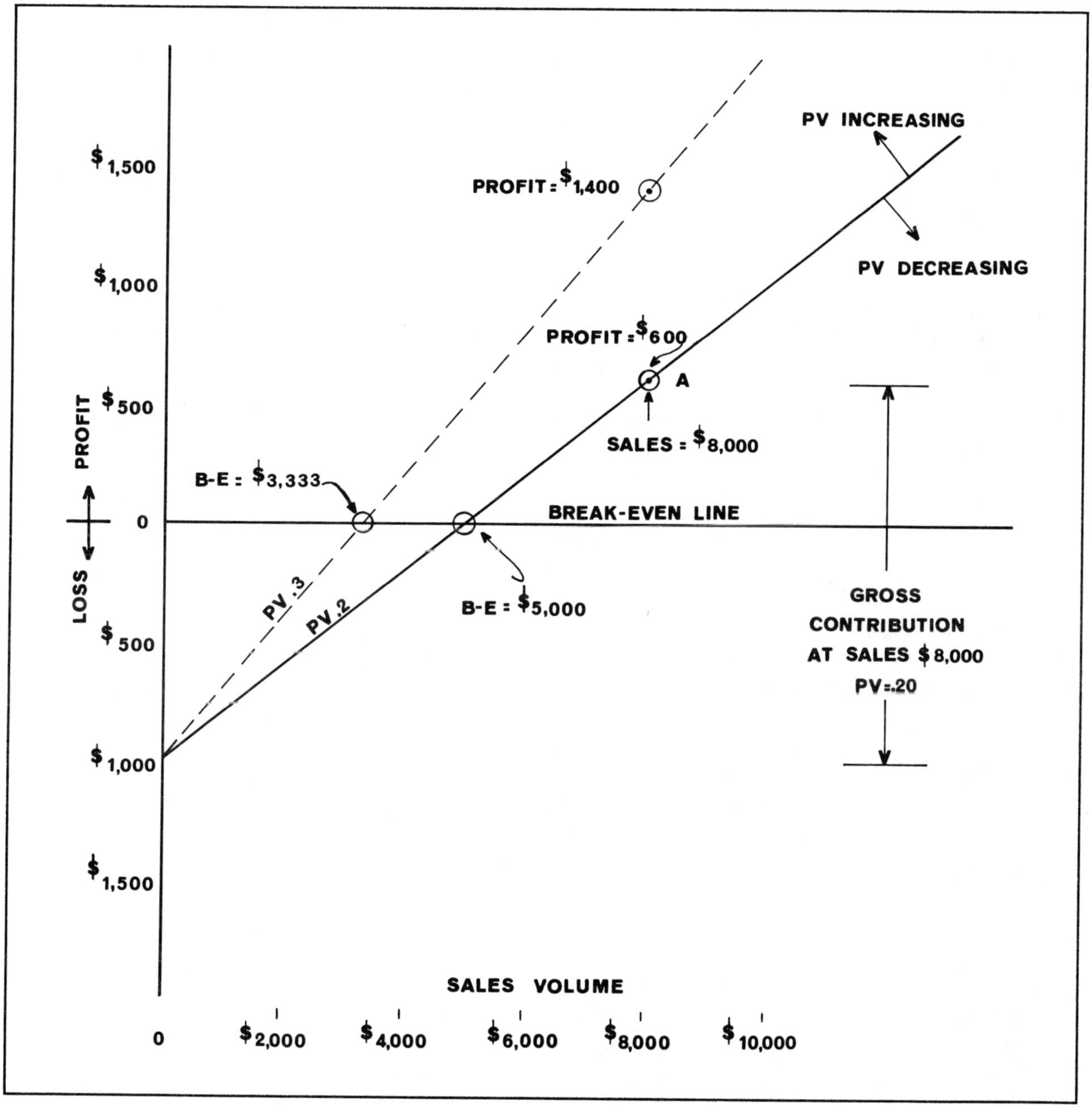

EXHIBIT 6-2: Basic PV Chart

oop content in the sales dollar (increase in contribution), which would lower the slope of the total cost line (increase in PV), causing a lower break-even and a greater angle of wedge with similar effects as above.

c. Increasing or decreasing the fixed expenses, with no other change taking place, would increase or decrease the break-even point accordingly, thereby causing profits to start earlier or later, but at the same PV rate.

As can be seen, the interplay of changes in any or all of the price, volume, cost ingredients of the profit structure can be displayed on the break-even chart or may be calculated by formula. Proposals which would affect any of these profit ingredients always should first be tested to make sure they are compatible with the goals of management.

THE BREAK-EVEN CHART IN PV FORM

As we have said earlier, not all sales dollars produce the same PV in multiproduct businesses. Even the small retail operator discussed earlier could have a product mix. Besides the candy bars which have a PV of .20, he could be selling newspapers for 10 cents at a PV of .10, cigars at a PV of .25, and toys at a PV of .40. He would have to sell twice as many newspapers as candy bars to gross the same contribution that the candy bars alone did. He would have to sell only one-half as many toys as candy bars to generate the original contribution of the bars.

Thus, it would be possible to earn a greater profit on fewer sales and a smaller profit on more sales, as the product mix swings from a more favorable to a less favorable mix.

Because the contribution rates of different products within the typical multiproduct firm are different and the amounts of volume each generates are also different, the oop costs, unit prices, and revenue figures are all different and changing. Because the cost line on a conventional break-even chart assumes no changes, it is limited for making pricing decisions. What is needed is a chart on which the effect of different PV's of products can be seen and measured simply. In the PV chart, a single line or multiple lines are drawn (each indicating a certain PV) which show directly the variation in profit with volume and a variation in prices on PV and profit. Exhibit 6-2 shows a PV chart for the candy store operation. The PV = .2 line is produced when candy bars are bought for 8 cents each and the unit contribution is 2 cents. In the dashed PV = .3 line, bars are bought for 7 cents each. The PV line can be visualized as hinged at the fixed expense point and swinging about the break-even horizontal line changing as the specific PV changes. Profit at any volume is the distance between the break-even line at the desired sales volume and the specific PV line.

1. *Price-volume sensitivity:* PV charts are convenient for observing the effect of volume and prices on contribution. As we mentioned in an earlier chapter, before the pricing decision is made, management should be in intimate touch with the reactions of the market to proposed changes in prices, particularly to evaluate how an increase or decrease in price will affect volume and gross contribution. The following is a tabulation which shows the likely effect of a decision to increase or decrease prices. Decision B is the data for normal pricing; Decision A involves a reduction in price but an increase of 30 per cent in volume; Decision C details the increase in price and a 20 per cent decrease in volume.

Item	Decision A	Decision B	Decision C
Unit selling price	$7	$8	$9
Unit oop cost	6	6	6
Unit contribution	$1	$2	$3
PV	.143	.250	.333
Volume of units sold	1,300,000	1,000,000	800,000
Revenue generated	$9,100,000	$8,000,000	$7,200,000
Fixed expenses	$1,000,000	$1,000,000	$1,000,000

Exhibit 6-3 is a PV chart which shows the profit available from the three decisions. Obviously, if the response of the market to increased prices is expected to follow this pattern, the wisest course of action would be to follow Decision C.

2. *Pretesting pricing decisions:* Often management is confronted with the question of maintaining prices, lowering them, or increasing them. Let's take a company which is presently earning a profit of $500,000 on one of its products. The market research department estimates that if prices were reduced, the company's territorial penetration would be increased and new markets generated to provide a higher sales volume. Others in management believe that prices should be raised to a point where the lower resulting volume at the higher price would still provide more contributions than the price reduction.

Obviously, the selection of either one of these alternatives will produce risks and will impose pressures on the company. Before either step is taken, the wise course would be to test their

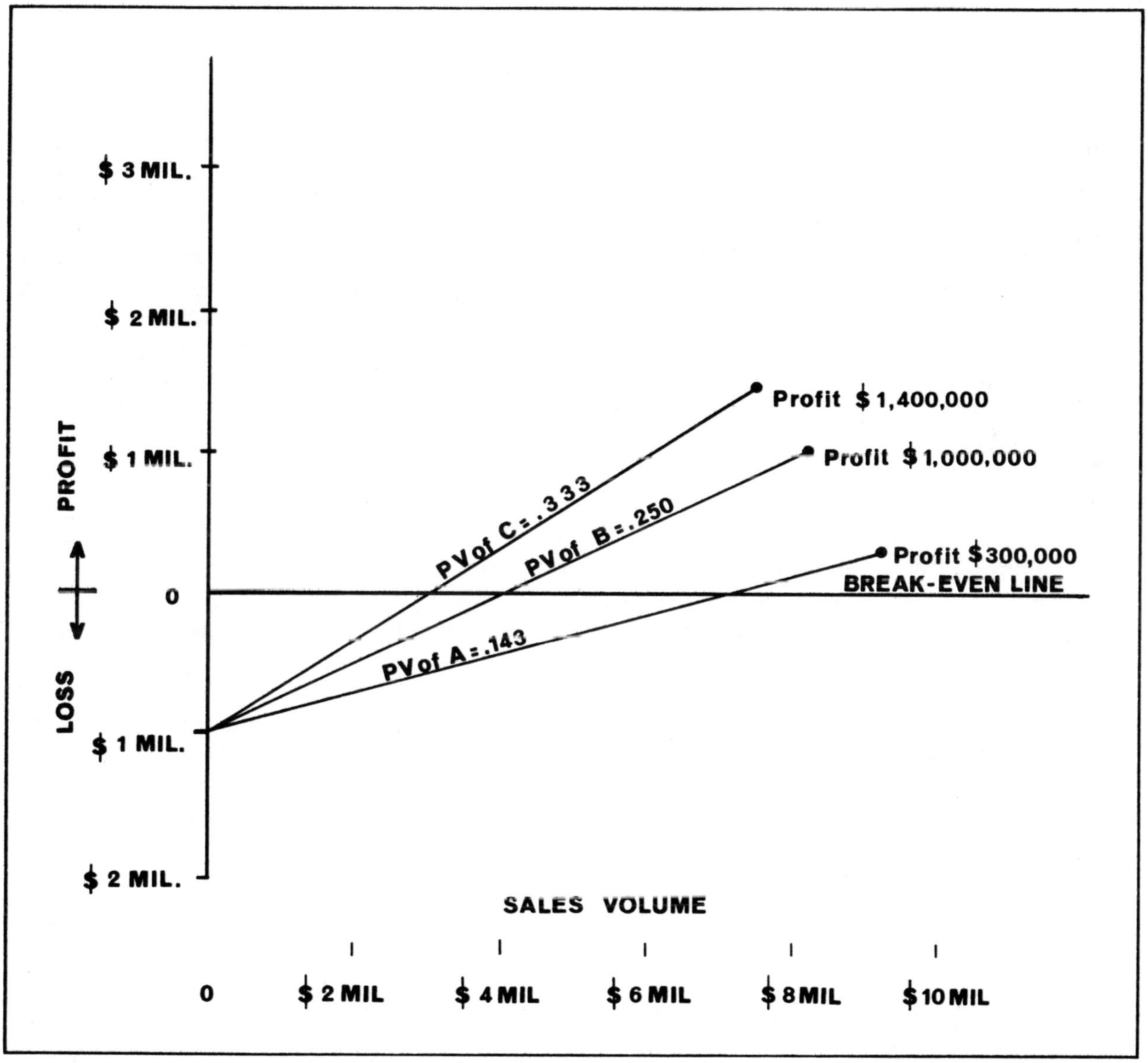

EXHIBIT 6-3: Price-Volume Combinations

respective effects on the PV chart. For purposes of illustrating the method, we shall assume the following data:

Item	No price change	Decrease prices 5%	Increase prices 5%
Unit selling price	$0.60	$0.57	$0.63
Unit oop cost	0.45	0.45	0.45
Unit contribution	$0.15	$0.12	$0.18
PV	.250	.210	.286
Fixed expenses	$750,000	$750,000	$750,000

To find the sales revenue required to attain the desired profit of $500,000, use the following formula: Sales revenue = (target profit + fixed expenses)/PV (9) and the required sales revenues and unit volumes are:

Sales revenue required to attain desired profit	$5,000,000	$5,950,000	$4,375,000
Unit volume required	8,333,333	10,438,000	6,944,000

Exhibit 6-4 shows the effect on profits of the two price changes. To accomplish the same desired profit with a price decrease of 5 per cent, the sales volume would have to increase by 19 per cent and the unit volume by 26 per cent. Had the market analysts persuaded management that a 5 per cent cut in price would boost volume 10 per cent and management believed (without testing) that the 10 per cent increase would justify the price reduction, it would have earned less than the target profit, since actually 19 per cent is the offsetting sales increase required. The actual profit earnable at a 10 per cent sales increase is shown in dotted lines on Exhibit 6-4. On the other hand, if information on the market's elasticity of demand is such that it will produce $4,375,000 of business at the higher price, this would appear to be the more favorable move. Obviously, if business in excess of this figure can be booked, the move toward higher prices is to be preferred.

While all products and markets do not have a proportionate relationship between the amount of price change and the amount of revenue change, there still are some which do, and it is possible under these circumstances to find that the same profits can be generated with different price-volume combinations. In these cases, the lower volume decision is usually to be preferred because it generally involves the seller in less working capital, space, facility loadings, transaction costs, etc.

3. *Pricing and product-mix decisions:* Even though selling prices for several products in a company's line may be equitable or at the level targeted by management, the profit results may be severely affected by an unpoliced product mix. It is desirable to use the break-even system as a detection device as well as a tool for pretesting other internal decisions. The following are the data for a multiproduct company:

Product	PV	Total planned volume, %
A	.30	50
B	.20	30
C	.10	20

Annual fixed expenses are $500,000. It is now desired to compute the break-even point and to determine profits at various sales levels. Obviously, before the break-even point can be found, the proper PV must be used, following the formula, Break-even = fixed expenses/PV. Three PV's are

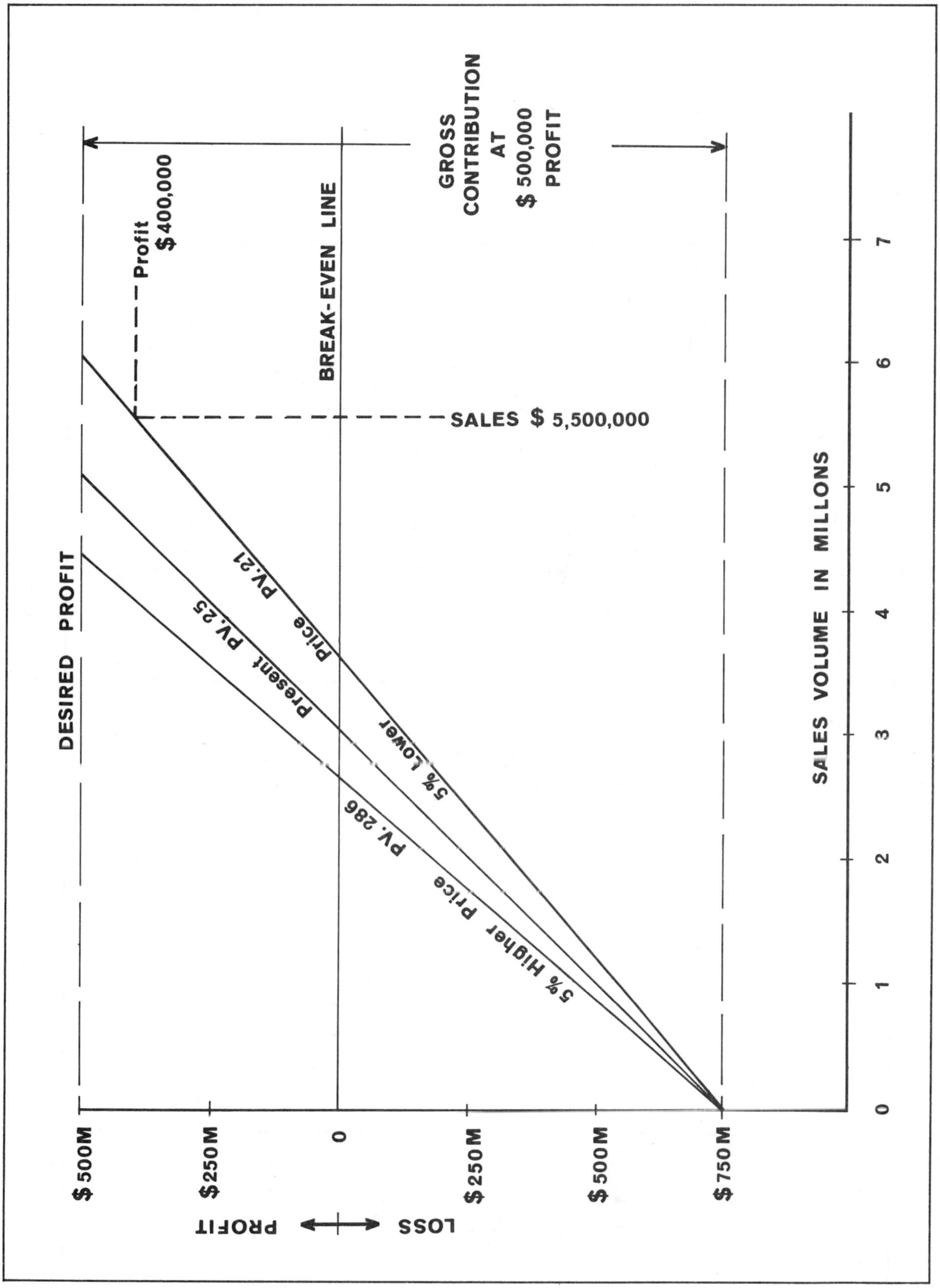

EXHIBIT 6-4: Alternative Pricing Decisions

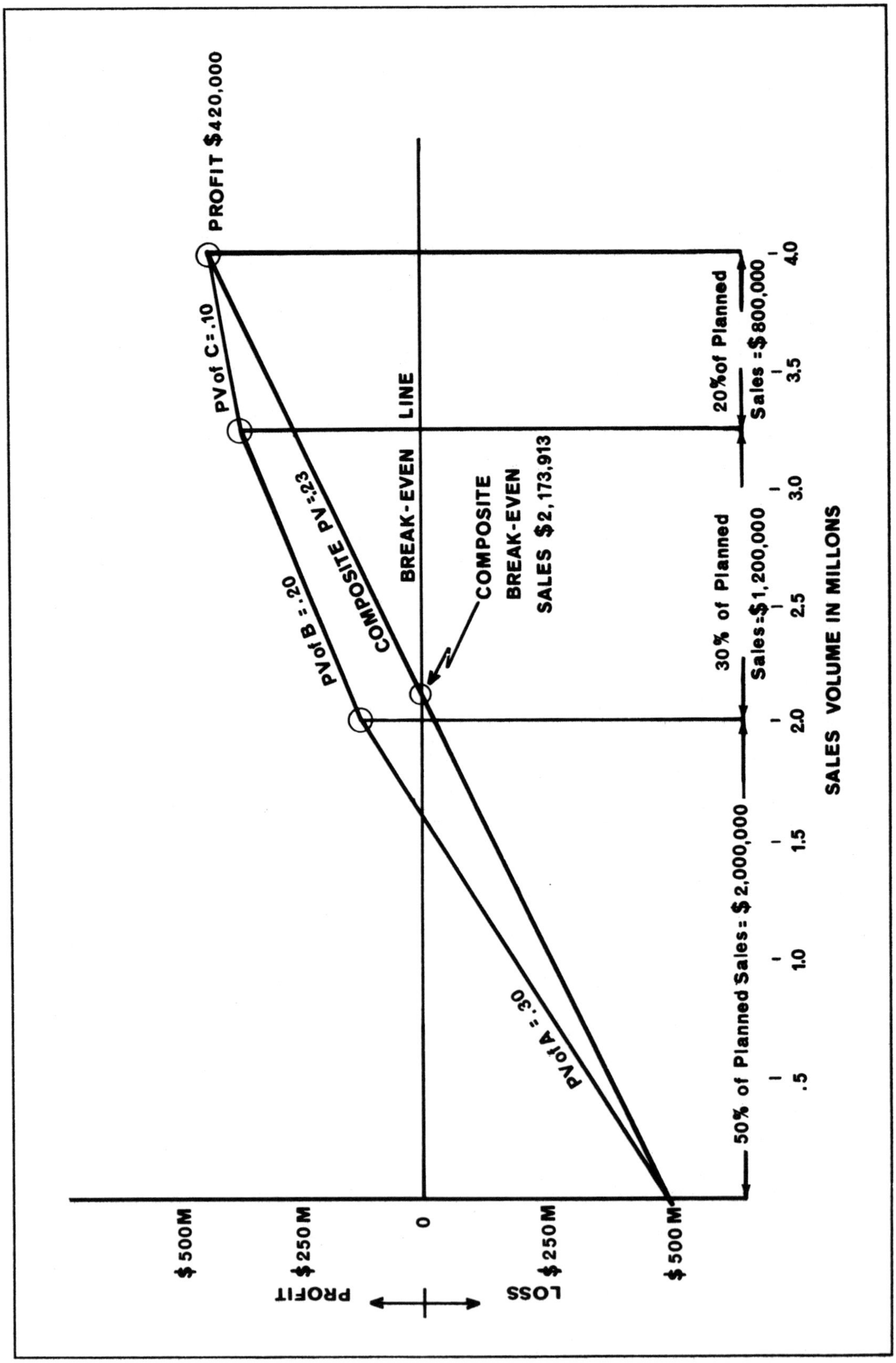

EXHIBIT 6-5: Composite PV

given in the above tabulation; which one is to be used? No one PV can be used by itself. A large PV generated at a small volume of product can have as little impact on the profit structure as a small PV produced from a large volume of product. Therefore, what must be considered in determining the PV to use is the integration between PV and volume, as this is what generates the contribution. In multiproduct companies, the PV is obtained by weighting the PV of each product by the volume each generates or by relating each product's PV to its percentage of the total volume of all products.

Finding the composite PV by weighting the product-volume mix produces:

Product	*Weighted PV for three products*
A	.30 × 50% = .15
B	.20 × 30% = .06
C	.10 × 20% = .02

Total of weights = the composite PV = .23

And the break-even point is:

$$\text{Break-even} = \frac{\text{fixed expenses}}{\text{PV}} = \frac{\$500{,}000}{.23} = \$2{,}173{,}913$$

Profit at, say, \$4,000,000 sales may be obtained from (2)

$$\begin{aligned}\text{Profit} &= (\text{sales} \times \text{PV}) - \text{fixed expenses}\\ &= (\$4{,}000{,}000 \times .23) - \$500{,}000\\ &= \$420{,}000\end{aligned}$$

Exhibit 6-5 shows the profit structure of this condition in PV chart form. The horizontal scale shows only the increase in sales volume and should not be interpreted to mean an increase in time. Product A is not necessarily being produced and sold first and Product C last. The reverse may actually occur, or all three products may be transacted simultaneously. Therefore, do not draw the inference that Product A has its own break-even point since its PV line crosses the break-even line. This would be true only if Product A did not require common fixed expenses, for, in that case, Product A would have its separate break-even or PV chart.

Now let's solve the following problems if the volume mix of the three products is allowed to change to:

Product	*Total planned volume, %*
A	20
B	30
C	50

a. Compute the break-even point.
b. Compute profit at \$4,000,000 sales point.
c. Compute the level of sales required at this volume mix to generate a profit of \$420,000, the profit available from the original mix at the same sales volume.

We can solve these problems by following the above procedure.

a. The composite PV is .17, and the break-even is:

$$\text{Break-even} = \frac{\$500{,}000}{.17} = \$2{,}941{,}176 \qquad (2)$$

b. The profit is

$$\text{Profit} = (\$4{,}000{,}000 \times .17) - \$500{,}000$$
$$= \$180{,}000 \text{ (43\% of the original profit)} \qquad (5)$$

c. To find the sales level that will restore the original profit of $420,000, it must be realized that whereas each sales dollar generated 23 cents of contribution under the original conditions of mix, the changed mix only produces 17 cents per sales dollar. The new sales level that must be found must be high enough to produce $420,000 of profit and must overcome the $500,000 of fixed expenses:

$$\text{New sales} = \frac{(\text{desired profit} + \text{fixed expenses})}{\text{PV}}$$
$$= \frac{(\$420{,}000 + \$500{,}000)}{.17}$$
$$= \$5{,}411{,}765 \qquad (7)$$

The change in the product-volume mix which dropped the composite PV from .23 to .17 had a marked effect on profits, reducing them from $420,000 to $180,000. If the company markets this mix, it will have to increase planned sales from $4,000,000 to $5,411,765 to maintain the $420,000 profit target. In other words, the drop in profit of $240,000 will have to be made up by an additional sales volume of $1,411,765 at a composite PV of .17, viz, $1,411,765 x .17 = $240,000.

In an attempt to correct for this poorer PV, management decides to raise prices 10 per cent on all three products. This change produces the following data:

Product	Original PV	New PV	New total planned volume %	Weight
A	.30	.364	10	.0364
B	.20	.273	30	.0819
C	.10	.182	60	.1092
				.2275 (Composite PV)

In summarily raising prices, management tries to force the external factors of competition and market demand to support its internal needs for profit. While the PV is substantially restored to the original .23, the effects of price-volume sensitivity caused a drop in sales to $2,500,000, thereby generating a gross contribution of $568,750 and a profit of $68,750, barely one-third of the previous condition and only 16 per cent of the original profit of $420,000.

Where there is a large difference in PV's among various products in a company's line, a favorable revision in product mix is usually more effective than an increase in price. The following example discusses a situation in a company which makes only two products. Annual fixed expenses are $100,000 and the two products are sold under three conditions of changing product mix: a 2:2 proportion, 1:3 proportion, and a 3:1 proportion—all for the same sales level of $1,000,000:

Product	Volume mix	PV	Weight
A	1/2	.70	.35
B	1/2	.10	.05
			.40 (Composite PV)
A	1/4	.70	.175
B	3/4	.10	.075

			.25 (Composite PV)
A	3/4	.70	.525
B	1/4	.10	.025
			.55 (Composite PV)

Exhibit 6-6 shows the effect that the three different mixes have on profits. It is clear to see that the slope of the PV line, which determines the profit at any sales level, is a function of pricing, volume and product mix.

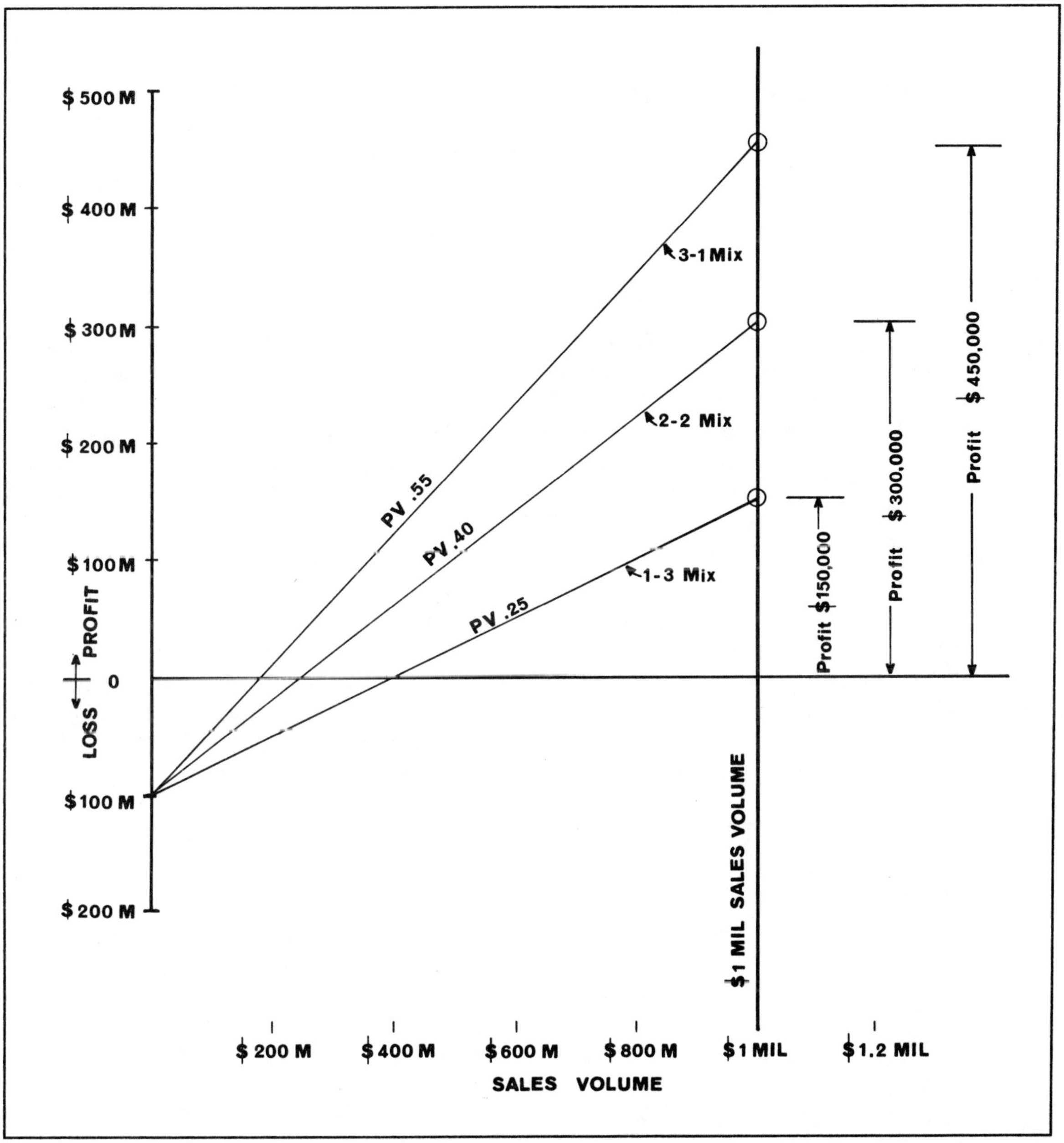

EXHIBIT 6-6: Effect of Product Mix on Profits

Chapter 7

The Break-Even System for Proposal Evaluations

OPERATING DECISIONS

The out-of-pocket cost of a product or order is one of the most important and tangible pieces of operating information that is available to management. As a single objective fact about a product or order, the oop cost can be used to measure the contribution which any given price will provide. From this contribution measurement, the contribution per facility-hour can be developed, the most profitable quantity range can be determined, a profit plan can be stated from which separate markup factors on the major elements of oop cost can be developed, and, by no means last, the seller can have a firm knowledge of his pricing floor.

In addition to its value in making these pricing decisions, the oop cost, whether by product, order, department, facility, or period, can be used to make many other operating decisions which managements frequently encounter during their daily routine. It is important to realize that it is not always necessary to have a known selling price in order to make contribution measurements. While sales revenue less oop costs equals contribution, it is also true, irrespective of whether or not a price is involved, that *a change in oop implies an equal but opposite change in contribution.* That is, if in a given activity area of a company an oop cost increases over a previous level, the contribution decreases, even though no price may be directly involved.

SELECTING MOST ECONOMICAL PRODUCTION FACILITY

The typical multiproduct company makes a variety of different items, some of which are completely different in function and application and some of which have the same function and application but vary in size, capacity, etc. Besides variety of product, there is also great variety in the kinds of equipment used for producing the product. Some equipment is used specifically for one kind of product; other machinery is used as joint facilities to produce many different products.

In the case of a given product, let's say a steel ring requiring many holes to be drilled, either a single-spindle drill may be used, or a more expensive multidrill may be set up to accomplish all the drilling in one pass. The single-spindle drill is faster (and less expensive to set up), but the drilling of the steel ring will take much longer than if it were drilled with the multidrill. But setting up the multidrill takes much longer and is much more expensive. So the question must arise, Which method shall be used to drill x quantity of steel rings? The question is better phrased, Which method will produce the lowest oop cost for x quantity?

Assuming bottlenecks do not exist, both alternate methods are available at the same time, quality factors are the same for both methods and no other strategic factors are to be considered, the sole economic criterion for setting manufacturing policy is to use that method which will produce the lower oop cost for a specific quantity.

Questions like these probably arise every day in multiproduct, multifacility companies. Unfortunately, they are usually answered by employing rule-of-thumb formulas, "full" costs, and any pet prejudice held by the local foremen or supervisors. Usually, a policy formulated under these conditions (if, in fact, one exists) is an admixture of emotion, pride, prejudice, and arbitrarily exercised autonomy.

An industry in which this question constantly arises is the printing industry. Here we have a meshing of multicolor jobs with single and multicolor presses with a wide range of makeready times and running speeds. For example, a four-color job may be run one pass through a four-color press or two passes through a two-color press. A four-color press may cost more to make ready, but it may run more impressions per hour. The two-color press may make ready faster, but two run-throughs are needed, for which the running speed could be slower. Obviously, if a very large quantity is to be printed, the higher makeready cost of the four-color press dwindles in importance compared with the lower cost of running per thousand. In effect, the higher makeready cost is spread very thinly over a large number of impressions. However, placing this large quantity on the two-color press boosts the run cost to the point where the lower makeready cost has very little effect.

The reverse is also true. If a small quantity is run on the four-color press, the higher makeready cost becomes significant because there is not enough quantity to produce enough savings to make up for the higher makeready cost. But when the small quantity is placed on the two-color press, the savings in makeready cost may offset the higher run cost for the smaller quantity.

The point is that a quantity can be found at which placing the job on either press will be the same. This point is called the quantity crossover point. For order quantities in excess of this crossover quantity, the method which has the higher makeready cost (or first cost) and the lower running cost should be used. Orders less than the crossover quantity should be run on facilities on which the first cost is less and the run cost higher.

As crossover points are established for a host of production alternatives, management can issue an objective policy for equating methods with quantities and thus reduce oop costs and increase contribution. Unlike the contribution produced from pricing, this type of contribution is internally generated irrespective of the sales effort.

As an example of how this technique works, we shall apply it to a commercial printing firm. Here are the facts concerning two of its presses:

Type of press	Speed imp./hr	Makeready time, in hr	oop MHR[1] for makeready	oop MHR for run
Two-color	1,800	4	$23	$23
Four-color	3,600	11	$51	$58

The company now receives a four-color job which can be run once through the four-color press or

1 The oop MHR is developed in later chapters.

twice through the two-color press. The problem is to find the quantity at which the costs of printing the job on both presses will be the same. Then, depending on the specific quantity of the order, the least costly method can be selected. To solve this problem, we use Eq. (1):

$$\text{Break-even quantity} = \frac{\text{fixed expenses}}{\text{unit contribution}} \tag{1}$$

In this case, the fixed expenses are those which are fixed or constant for the job to be run, namely, the first cost or makeready cost. For printing the job on the two-color press, this cost would be

Data for Alternate Methods:

Press:	Speed:	MR Time:	MR OOP MHR:	Run OOP MHR:	No. of Passes:
2-color	1800 IPH	4 hrs/pass	$23	$23	2
4-color	3600 IPH	11 hours	$51	$58	1

$$\text{Cross-Over (B-E) Quantity Point} = \frac{\text{Increase in MR Costs}}{\text{Decrease in Running Costs/M}}$$

$$= \frac{\$377}{\$9.46/M}$$

$$= 39{,}850 \text{ impressions}$$

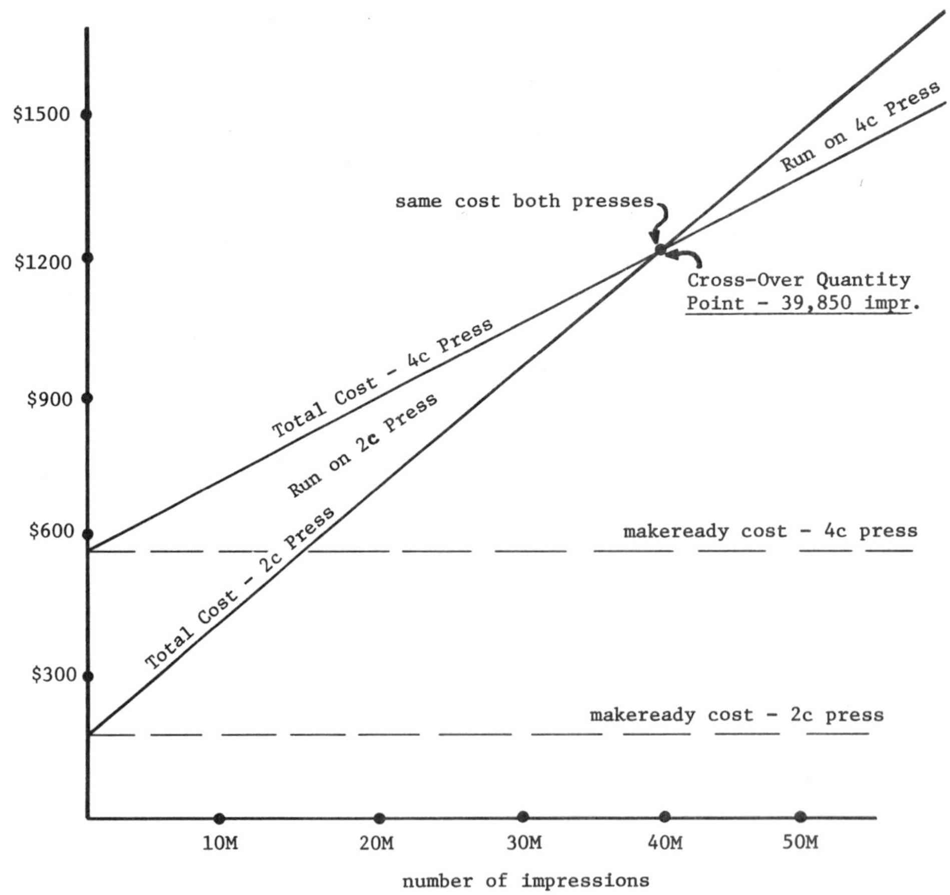

EXHIBIT 7-1: Finding the Lowest Cost Method to Run the Order

twice times 4 hours at \$23 per hour, or \$184. (Remember that the two-color press has to be made ready two times, one for each pass). The makeready cost on the four-color press would be 11 hours at \$51 per hour, or \$561. If the job is placed on the four-color press, the company will incur \$377 (\$561 – \$184) more of makeready cost. This additional cost can be justified only by the lower running cost of the four-color press. The running cost per thousand on the two-color press would be twice times \$23/1.8 per thousand (M), since the job must run through twice, or \$25.56. The running cost on the four-color press would be \$58/3.6 per thousand, or \$16.10. Thus, even though the makeready cost on the four-color press is \$377 higher, the running cost per thousand on that press is \$9.46 (\$25.56 – \$16.10) less. The problem resolves into how many thousand impressions, each of which produces an additional \$9.46 of contribution, are required to pay for the additional \$377 of makeready cost. Applying the break-even formula, we obtain

$$\text{Break-even quantity (crossover point)} = \frac{\$377}{\$9.46 \text{ per M}} = 39{,}850 \text{ impressions}$$

The formula to use in solving problems involving costs of alternative methods is

$$\text{Crossover quantity} = \frac{\text{change in constant processing costs}}{\text{change in contribution per unit}} \tag{10}$$

and substituting the above data:

$$= \frac{(\$561 - \$184)}{(\$25.56 - \$16.10)} = 39{,}850 \text{ impressions}$$

Again, the reader is reminded that a difference in oop costs constitutes a change in contribution. Exhibit 7-1 shows how the quantity crossover point is found by means of a break-even chart. Often a visual presentation is easier to understand.

The same type of problem is experienced regularly in a different segment of the converting industry. The company has a job which calls for printing cellophane film in rolls and then shipping without converting into bags. The width of the rolls to be printed is 13.5 inches, the customer's web width. The company may run the job through its slower 30-in. flexographic press "two-up" (i.e., two printed images across the web), slit the printed roll at the end of that web, and ship without rewinding. Or it may print the rolls on its faster 42-in. press, "three-up." If it uses this latter method, it will have to rewind the rolls and then send them through its slitter-rewinder. The question is, What quantity justifies which method? Here are the facts:

Item	Method 1/Method 2		
	30-in. Flexo	42-in. Flexo	Slitter-rewinder
Speed, in ft./min	300	700	300
oop MHR: Makeready	\$10.20	\$12.34	\$6.34
oop MHR: Run	\$10.20	\$12.34	\$6.34
Makeready time, in hr.	2	5	.25
Output per hour, in lb.	324	1,057	454

Using these data to compute costs, we have:

Item	30-in. Flexo	42-in. Flexo	Slitter-rewinder
Makeready cost	\$20.40	\$61.70	\$1.58
Hr/M lb.	3.08	0.946	2.2
Run cost/M lb.	\$31.50	\$11.70	\$13.90

Applying Eq. (10) gives us

$$\text{Crossover quantity} = \frac{(\$61.70 + \$1.58) - \$20.40}{\$31.50 - (\$11.70 + \$13.90) \text{ per M lb}}$$
$$= 7{,}268 \text{ lbs}$$

Thus, technically, an order exceeding 7,268 pounds should be run on Method 2, and if less, on Method 1. Again, this concept assumes equal quality from either method, the availability of all three facilities, etc. Usually a crossover quantity is more practical to specify as a range. Thus, one would allow individual supervisory latitude between, say, 7,000 and 7,500 pounds.

MAKE OR BUY?

Practically every manufacturing business operates as a result of a previous make-buy decision. The fact that a piece of equipment is operating means that the decision was to make rather than to buy work produced from that machine. These decisions are not made consciously or frequently but rather continue as "make" once the piece of equipment has been acquired. However, competitive pressures, time commitments to customers, quality requirements, production methods, available working capital, and cost of capital have been changing this picture.

Why make? One of the major reasons for making rather than for buying is that the required quality cannot be purchased from the outside. If new products are involved, this reason may be a valid one. Otherwise, the chances are good that outside suppliers will be able to deliver the desired quality. However, if the company attempts to attain a quality level that others cannot obtain, a large possibility of failure exists. Another reason for making is the assurance of controlling the flow of quantity of product and the time when it is needed. From the cost viewpoint, the most obvious reason for making rather than for buying is that the company itself can make the product for less. Of course, there are many other noncost reasons for making, such as the desire to preserve a trade secret. These reasons are strategic and beyond the area of cost analysis.

Why buy? The reasons for buying are generally the reverse of the reasons for making. The company finds it impossible to make the desired quality, use of vendors' facilities and more specialized skills would be too costly for the purchaser to acquire, the purchaser benefits from the research activity of a skilled supplier, thus allowing the purchaser to keep flexible and up with the times. If the purchaser buys from several suppliers, he has better assurance against delays than if he makes everything himself. Other reasons for buying are to meet emergencies when the purchaser lacks capacity and/or is unable to have work done on overtime or additional shifts, the purchaser has the capacity but wishes to employ it for other more profitable work, the purchaser wishes to reduce the amount of variable capital employed. Cost considerations are, obviously, a desire to buy in order to avoid paying overtime premiums as well as a desire for a lower cost of buying.

Cost evaluations: The cost of making calculated on a unit cost basis is misleading because of the intermixture of fixed costs and volume. When the make-buy decision involves a short term, and plant capacity is not altered, the incremental method is the one to use. Generally, costs which are not changed by the decision are not considered. The reason is that in casting a budget for a period alternately for the make as well as for the buy decision, the costs which remain unchanged would appear in equal amounts in both budgets. These unchanging costs are generally fixed costs. For example, in a company having a seasonal product, the company might decide to make in the slow periods certain items which are normally purchased in busy periods. Under these conditions, fixed costs remain unchanged in either period because of the period nature of the fixed expense.

A major factor in determining the make-buy decision is the change in the amounts of variable capital being carried and its effect on the working capital picture of the company. Work that is made in the plant requires a higher level of current capital because of additional payroll, raw materials, work in process, etc. Often a company will have raw materials shipped and billed to a supplier to avoid loading up the current investment levels. While this fact may or may not be considered by the supplier in arriving at a price for the purchaser, the incremental amount tends to be below the cost of carrying this additional inventory in the company's plant.

Basis of decisions: The following example is presented to illustrate the mechanics of making a short-term decision to farm out or not. A converter is considering what to do about a regular piece of business which involves 20,000 pounds per month of flexographically printed plastic film. The company can buy this printed film at 80 cents per pound, or it can make it in its plant for 92.5 cents per pound, "full" cost. In addition, if the company makes the film itself, the average variable capital employed rises by $150,000 per year. Exhibit 7-2 shows the details of the comparisons.

COST ELEMENTS	20,000 lbs./mo.			
	MAKE		BUY	
	PER LB.	TOTAL	PER LB.	TOTAL
Direct Material Cost	$.350	$ 7,000		
Conversion Cost - o.o.p.	.325	6,500		
Conversion cost - Fixed	.250	5,000		
TOTAL O.O.P.		$13,500	$.80	$16,000
"FULL" COSTS		$18,500		
Average Capital Employed:				
Cash & Accts. Receivable		$88,000		$99,000
Inventory		463,000		302,000
Total Variable Capital		$551,000		$401,000

$$\text{Return on Average Capital Employed} = \frac{\text{Increase in Annual Contribution}}{\text{Increase in Variable Capital}}$$

$$= \frac{(\$16,000 - \$13,500) \times 12}{\$150,000}$$

$$= 20\%$$

EXHIBIT 7-2: Make or Buy?

The first thing to notice is that the $0.25 per pound and $5,000 per month figures are both unitized fixed costs and are not tangibly related to this decision because the company has the press anyway but perhaps wishes to use it on more profitable work. The determining costs are the oop costs of $13,500, which are incurred directly with the make and are not incurred without the make. The use of the "full" costs would mislead the company into believing that if it farmed this work out, it would be saving 12.5 cents per pound. The allocated fixed portion of the "full" costs, is developed from an expected forecasted level of activity. If, in this example, activity was understated, the "full" costs are inflated to the point where they might deprive the company of a sizeable amount of contribution. Buying for 80 cents per pound may seem attractive if "full" costs are considered, but "full" costs are not cash outlay costs. Since the company already owns a press, the period fixed costs are unchanged and inescapable unless the machine is sold. Therefore, both situations should be analyzed by comparing cash in versus cash out versus the change in current capital.

Cash in and out versus capital change: If this company's oop costs are 67.5 cents for making and 80 cents for buying, obviously it makes a tangible cash saving of 12.5 cents per pound by making. The question to be answered is how much will current capital rise to support this internal production effort and what return on this additional capital will be provided by the cash savings (increase in contribution).

The annual increase in contribution is the monthly cash saving of ($16,000 – $13.500) × 12, or $30,000. To generate this saving, an additional $150,000 in current capital must be invested annually. The annual return on this incremental investment is therefore $30,000/$150,000, or 20 per cent. The formula for making this kind of decision to arrive at the rate of return is

$$\frac{\text{incremental contribution}}{\text{incremental investment}}$$

Summarizing:

1. Fixed costs should not be considered, since these can only be unitized or allocated costs. The facility now exists in the company and does not involve getting new equipment to support the make or disposing of equipment if the company decides to buy.
2. Make-buy decisions, when the facility exists in the manufacturer's plant, should be made only on an oop basis by comparing the comparative cash inflows and outflows.
3. Any tangible cash savings must be compared to the amount of additional current capital that is required to generate such savings. This provides the ultimate appraisal of the return on variable capital.

SECTION II

Development and Construction of The Direct-Cost Machine-Hour Rate System

INTRODUCTION

The purpose of this section is to show how to develop a set of Machine-Hour Rates which is the basis for obtaining direct conversion costs, as discussed in the previous section. Instructions are given step-by-step to enable the reader to build a set of MHR from his specific data.

Several complete sets of MHR's for different companies are presented to give a broad cross-section of the techniques employed. The various examples apply to converters where processing is done to specific customers' orders and not to stock, under competitive price-bid conditions. Typical markets served are wide in scope: the facilities are used in common with many product lines and customers; and completely in common for the different markets each converter serves. Other variables which contribute to the task of profit-planning are: the widely differing order sizes; the mixture of a variety of raw materials; broad ranges of direct conversion costs; the use of alternate facilities based on order quantity; the myriad varieties in product type, style, size, etc. In short, very little is predictable at the start of each of the converter's operating year.

Because of the prevalence of the "all-inclusive" or "full"-cost Machine-Hour Rates, the first chapter in this Section will deal with traditional MHR showing its fallacies and the dangers it creates for its users and for the industry of which it is a member.

The following chapters of this Section present all of the steps in the development of a proper MHR system. In Section III, four complete Machine-Hour Rate Systems for four other companies are presented and detailed to give a wider base for identification.

Chapter 8

Traditional Machine-Hour Rate Cost Estimating

A Machine-Hour Rate is the cost of owning and operating a machine and/or handwork facility for one hour. The traditional MHR is an all-inclusive cost (except for material cost and perhaps other order-related costs) and is developed from total costs, unseparated as to period and direct costs, and statistically allocated to the facilities. The use of these costs lead to an order or product "full" cost, from which it is impossible to measure *contribution.*

For purposes of illustration and to disprove the validity of using all-inclusive rates, we will show the mechanics of such a system, step-by-step.

Production Center	No. of Units	HP	Working Space Occupied*	Present Market Value*	Annual Assigned Hours*	Hp-Hours*
Print	1	12	800'	$20,000	1200	14,400
C & C	1	15	800'	15,000	1600	24,000
Glue	1	10	600'	30,000	1200	12,000
TOTALS			2200'	$65,000	4000	50,400

Purpose: Marshalls all mechanical and physical facts concerning production facilities which are to be used as the subject of job estimates.

*Allocation factors used on the EAW

EXHIBIT 8-1: Simple Converting Facilities Classification Sheet (CFCS) - folding carton plant

MACHINE-HOUR RATES

The Machine-Hour Rate is a *conversion cost* solely. It is a pre-determined rate of cost which is expected to be incurred in the future. The term conversion refers to all of the acts and operations that must be imposed on the raw material to convert it into a finished product according to a customer's special requirements. The term *cost* refers to those expenditures which the company must disburse in order to manufacture and sell the order, and to collect its sales revenue. The term *conversion cost,* then, includes all of the company's expenditures except materials (and perhaps other order-related costs, like freight out, commissions, etc.) and is divided into two parts. One part of conversion cost represents the cost of productive labor who operate the converting facilities; the second part is paid for overhead or burden costs representing wages and salaries of people who do not work at the converting facilities plus other expenses, such as rent, electricity, supplies, administration, etc.

TRADITIONAL MHR STRUCTURE

In the following exhibits, 8-1 through 8-5, the MHR development steps and schedules for a small folding-carton company are given. In the following chapters more detailed instructions and criteria are given together with the introduction of additional procedures. For the moment, we will examine the composition of the rates and the limitations it imposes on cost estimating and pricing.

Converting Facilities Classification Sheet (*CFCS*): Exhibit 8-1 shows how to marshall all the functional and mechanical facts for the three production centers, which have been selected as estimating centers. The four columns on the right are chosen because of their cause-and-effect relationships with expenses to be allocated in the development of the hourly rates. In this example, we are assuming that this small company uses only the three listed machines to produce its output.

Crew Composition Table (*CCT*): Exhibit 8-2 shows how manning is assigned to the production centers selected on the CFCS. Only the base hourly rates are tabulated and the extensions by the respective annual assigned hours, shown on the CFCS, develop the right column which is also used as an allocation factor.

Expense Classification Worksheet (*ECW*): Exhibit 8-3 is not a repetitive step in the development of the MHR. It is used to classify similar expenses into cause-and-effect categories as preparation for later allocation. This work has to be performed once in any company installation, assuming that this initial effort will set the pattern for expense classification on the company's chart of accounts. Once all overhead expenses have been classified (starting usually with previous expenses) then budgeting for the coming period can commence.

Allocable Budget (*AB*): Exhibit 8-4 budgets or projects overhead expenses for the coming year to support the planned operations shown on the CFCS and CCT. The condensed data for each budget category have been selected to tie in with the five allocation factors of the previous two steps.

Production Center	Std. Crew	No. Req'd	Base Hourly Rate	Extension	Unit Hourly Rate	D.L. Budget
Print					$3.90	$4,680
	Feeder	1	$1.70	$1.70		
	Pressman	½	3.00	1.50		
	Mtls Hdler	½	1.40	.70		
C & C					3.90	6,240
	Feeder	1	1.70	1.70		
	Pressman	½	3.00	1.50		
	Mtls Hdler	½	1.40	.70		
Glue					7.30	8,760
	Mechanic	1	2.80	2.80		
	Feeder	1	1.60	1.60		
	Catcher	1	1.50	1.50		
	Packer	1	1.40	1.40		
						$19,680*

Purpose: Assigns manning to the production centers on the CFCS.

*Allocation factor used on the EAW

EXHIBIT 8-2: Simple Crew Composition Table - Run (CCT) - folding carton plant

MARTIN & TUCKER, INC.
ENGINEERS

EXPENSE ACCOUNT (partial list)	TOTAL AMOUNT	Included in Overhead Portion of Machine-Hour Rate on E.A.W.									BUDGET EXCLUSIONS	DCB* DOC* P&L*
		BUDGET CATEGORIES										
		MANUFACTURING COSTS					NON-MANUFACTURING COSTS					
		Space	Power	Machinery	Indirect	F. B.	W. & D.	Selling	Admin.	F. B.		
Clerical salaries - gen'l	$ 8000								8000			
Depreciation of F & F	500								500			
Real estate taxes	1600	1600										
Holiday pay - factory	1400					1400						
Factory manager's salary	10000				10,000							
Sales commissions	7000										7000	DOC
Depreciation of building	2000	2000										
Overtime premium - factory	1200					1200						
Parts for gluer	600										600	DCB
Interest on mortgage	2000	2000										
Electricity - factory	2500		2500									
Advertising	500							500				
Building heat	400	400										
Electrotypes	6000										6000	DOC
Depreciation of truck	1000						1000					
Vacation pay - office	2000									2000		
Bleached manila board	45000										45,000	DOC
Gen'l machine-shop supplies	1200				1200							
Truck operating costs	1000						1000					
Baling expense	2500										2500	P&L
Sales clerks	6000							6000				
Depreciation - prod. eqpt.	9400			9400								
Sweeper-porter	2000				2000							
Shipping clerk	6000						6000					
Freight out - comm. carriers	4500										4500	DOC
Maint. & repair - printer	800										800	DCB
Billable art work cost	2000										2000	P&L
Factory payroll surcharges	2500					2500						
Officer's salary	15000								15,000			
Sales allowances - quality	1000				1000							
Sales allowances - price	600							600				
Material waste allowances	2800										2800	DOC
TOTALS	$149,000	6,000	2,500	9,400	14,200	5,100	8,000	7,100	23,500	2,000	71,200	
BUDGETED TOTALS	77,800											

*excluded costs: added to MHR in conversion costs (DCB); added as direct-order charges (DOC); and/or excluded from conversion and orders as separate profit-and-loss transactions (P&L)

EXHIBIT 8-3: Sample Expense Classification Worksheet (ECW)

Budget Category	Previous Expenses from Ex. 8-3 (ECW)	Budgeted Expenses (Projected)
Manufacturing Costs:		
Space	$6,000	$6,500
Power	2,500	3,000
Machinery	9,400	11,000
Indirect	14,200	16,000
Fringe Benefits	5,100	4,500
TOTAL MFG.	37,200	41,000
Non-Mfg. Costs:		
Whse. & Deliv.	8,000	10,000
Selling	7,100	9,000
Administrative	23,500	25,000
Fringe Benefits	2,000	2,000
TOTAL NON-MFG.	40,600	46,000
ANNUAL BUDGETED O.H.	$77,800	$87,000

Purpose: Provides funds for the manned production centers to support planned operations.

Budget Exclusions: Direct charges to Printer = $800
" " to Gluer = $600

EXHIBIT 8-4: Simple Allocable Budget (AB)
(folding-carton plant)

MARTIN & TUCKER, INC.
ENGINEERS

Production Center	Allocation Factors: Occupancy	Hp-Hrs. M's	PMV M's	Annual Hours	D.L.B.	Manufacturing Costs: Space	Power	Mach'y	Indir.	F.B.	Total Mfg. Costs	Non-Mfg. Costs	Annual OH Costs	M.H.R. (OH only)	Hourly: Direct Charges	D.L.	Total M.H.R.
Print	800'	14.4	$20	1200	$4680	$2364	$857	$3385	$4800	$1070	$12,476	$13,998	$26,474	$22.06	$.67	$3.90	$26.63
Cut & Crease	800'	24.0	15	1600	6240	2364	1429	2538	6400	1427	14,158	15,884	30,042	18.78	—	3.90	22.68
Glue	600'	12.0	30	1200	8760	1772	714	5077	4800	2003	14,366	16,118	30,484	25.40	.50	7.30	33.20
Totals	2200'	50.4	$65	4000	$19,680												
Totals from Allocable Budget						$6500	$3000	$11,600	$16,000	$4,500	$41,000	$46,000	$87,000				
Allocation Factors						Occupancy	Hp-Hrs.	PMV	Ann. Hrs.	DLB	X	Mfg. Costs	X				
Allocation Fractions						6500/2200	3000/50.4	11,600/65,000	16,000/4,000	4500/19,680	X	46,000/41,000	X				
Allocation Ratios						2.9545	5.9523	.1692	4.000	.2287	X	1.122	X				

From CFCS
From CST

PROCEDURE:

1. Enter cost totals from Allocable Budget
2. Select Allocation Factors, set up fractions, and develop Allocation Ratios.
3. For each cost category, multiply Allocation Ratio by respective Production Center data, viz:
   - 3.1 To get allocated SPACE COST for PRINT: 2.9545 x 800 ft. = $2364
   - 3.2 To get allocated INDIRECT COST for CUT & CREASE: 4.00 x 1600 hrs. = $6400
   - 3.3 To get allocated NON-MFG. COST for GLUE: 1.122 x $14,366 = $16,118

DIRECT CHARGES:

1. PRINTER: $800/1200 hrs. = $.67 per hour
2. GLUER: $600/1200 hrs. = $.50 per hour

EXHIBIT 8-5: Basic Expense Assignment Worksheet (EAW), with Procedural Steps (Folding-carton plant)

Expense Assignment Worksheet (*EAW*): Exhibit 8-5 shows the way each of the five allocation factors are used, on a cause-and-effect basis, to product the "full" or all-inclusive Machine-Hour Rates. Procedural steps are shown in the lower left of this exhibit.

Even though considerably simplified, these four steps show the method by which traditional MHR's are developed. The question now is how do we use these rates in cost-estimating and pricing or for any other purpose?

COST-ESTIMATING WITH "FULL" MHR

Let's try to cost estimate and price evaluate an order inquiry for 100,000 cartons. The estimate is as follows:

Production Center	Estimated Hours	"Full" M.H.R.	"Full" Conversion Cost
Print	10	$26.63	$266.30
Cut & crease	10	$22.68	$226.80
Glue	10	$33.20	$332.00
	Total conversion cost		$825.10
	Est. materials cost		$600.00
	"Full" cost		$1,425.10
	"Full" cost/M		$14.25
	Markup 10%		$ 1.43
	Target S.P.		$15.68

When the salesman quotes this target selling price to his prospect, he is told that the "going," competitive or prevalent market price is $12 per M. This is $2.25 per M below the converter's "full" cost and so the tendency would be to reject the order at the offered $12 per M price. Without having the direct costs of that inquiry, the converter has no other choice but to use other rationales for booking the order, like: "We'll take the $12 price anyway because we need the business," or "We must keep our presses busy" or "The order is so big that somehow we'll make money on it," etc., ad nauseam.

If the converter did have direct costs available, he would be able to measure the *contribution* he could get by booking the order. For example, if proper data had shown an oop cost of $9 per M, then the converter could make a rational decision on the basis of the adequacy of the $3 per M contribution. This is why all-inclusive rates have constantly led converters to inadvertently turn down good business and winding up only with orders where the price levels accidently were at or above their "full" costs. This makes the operation customer-dominated instead of converter-directed.

INDUSTRY-WIDE MHR

Industry-wide manuals of Machine-Hour Rates, "budgeted hourly cost rates," "conversion cost rates," etc., are well-intentioned attempts by trade associations to give valuable service to their members. From the member point of view, these manuals seem to provide a convenient shortcut for estimating, without the individual company having to go to the expense and effort of developing their own specific cost data.

These manuals inadvertently give the impression that the published rates are accurate and equitable to the member company providing it refers to the "right" number. Thus, rates are published by geographic area, and by common sales size. A refinement is to suggest the acceptably high, low and median rates in the aforementioned categories. A member located in Chicago, with an annual sales level in the range of $2 to $3 million, operating a specific type of production machine, is told that the acceptable hourly rates in his area range from $28, $21 down to $15. Now, which does he select in estimating his job inquiries?

It should be obvious that none of the three rates are necessarily the correct one for the member company. While, in a labor union environment hourly base rates may be similar in a close geographical area, there's no guarantee that the same degree of similarity will apply to workers' productivity, non-chargeable time, fringe benefits (above local scale), specific machine manning, machine condition and speed limitations, product mix, etc. Nor does sales size have a direct relationship to rates. This seems to be an interesting although deceptive statistic, one which has the effect of engendering a feeling of security. There is an almost universal compulsion to see "how I'm doing compared to my competitors and with the averages in my industry." This is like managing a company with someone else's costs and is tantamount to swapping medical prescriptions.

Even though the aforementioned three hourly rates are not "full" costs (which is extremely rare), and it was possible thereby to measure the estimated contribution against a proposed selling price, imagine the variance in PV and gross order contribution. Obviously, the $28 rate could price the member company out of its markets; the $15 rate could attract a large volume of profitless business; and the $21 rate could still be very wrong for that company.

Just like in the use of production standards (see Chapter 19), Machine-Hour Rates must be tailored to fit the individual company, using the company's own, very specific costs. This is the only way the company can know its own economic operating personality so that it understands objectively what work is good for it and what work should be avoided. Industry-wide manuals make companies into quotation mills instead of converters and turns them into their brothers' keeper by proxy.

SUMMARY

In the following chapters, we overcome the limitations of "all-inclusive" ("full"-cost) Machine-Hour Rates, by constructing a MHR system (actual industry case) which develops an oop cost per hour for every facility. Only in this way, can the company estimate its direct conversion cost and measure its profit contribution against a market or competitive selling price.

Chapter 9

Constructing the Machine-Hour Rate System

The model company used for illustrating the first MHR construction represents one of the most complex segments of the converting industry from the viewpoint of cost estimating, pricing and profit planning. It is a member of the flexible-packaging converting industry. Its products are printed and unprinted plastic bags used in the bakery, frozen food, hardware, garment and other industries. The company also produces a line of gravure-printed laminated pouch stock, which packages small individual portions of shaving lotion, shoe polish, scented cleaning napkins, catsup, etc. Web-fed flexographic printing presses, slitters and bag machines manufacture the bags to customers' orders. Pouch stock and extruded laminated films are made on gravure printing presses and adhesive laminators. All the equipment is used in common (joint facilities) for all customers, product lines, end-use categories, etc.

These characteristics plus those mentioned in the introduction to this Section, are typical to those of other converters, such as commercial printers, folding-carton manufacturers, machine shops, fabric converters, furniture plants, and the vast majority of U. S. industry—in terms of the numbers of enterprises.

STEP 1: CONVERTING FACILITIES CLASSIFICATION SHEET (CFCS)

The Converting Facilities Classification Sheet, abbreviated to CFCS, is the first piece of organized data required in the preparation of Machine-Hour Rates. The CFCS determines and lists the production centers in the company which should correspond to those listed on the estimating sheet. The same production centers should be used consistently for each preparatory step in the construction of the rates.

The CFCS represents an inventory and marshalling of productive work stations, regardless of whether they involve machines. A press can be a production center if its operational use is to be estimated during the coming twelve months. In a similar manner, a completely hand work station, like inspection, can be a production center. The CFCS does not include productive operations which the company plans not to use in the coming period. It also does not include non-productive equipment, such as forklift trucks, balers, etc. The cost of operating this equipment is included in the Allocable Budget (AB).

The listing of production centers shall include only that equipment used to perform only those operations which are the subject of the cost estimate. So that no equipment is omitted from the list, the preparer shall start at a designated point in the plant and proceed from there in a direct line to the end of the plant, listing equipment and work stations as they are found, without regard to operational sequence.

Exhibit 9-1 shows the CFCS for the model company. The following explains the columnar data and gives the necessary criteria:

1. Production Center

A production center consists of one or more machines or work stations at which the same operation is performed. These machines or work stations do not have to be located in the same geographic area in the plant. Sometimes they are widely separated for functional reasons; in other cases, it is due to poor plant layout. However if the machines or handwork stations meet certain criteria, they would be classed as members of the same production center.

In a screw-machine shop there are several sizes and types of automatic screw machines. These should or should not be grouped into the same center depending on the number of spindles and spindle diameters, and other factors. In a foundry, moldmaking would be grouped by hand and machine types, sizes and configurations, to name the most important criteria. In a plastic plant, injection molding would not be combined into the same production center with compression molding. Likewise, in a commercial printing operation, one would not combine letterpresses with offset facilities.

Criteria for determining machine production center content are:

1.1 *Capabilities:* Similarity of function, viz: in printing, not only the distinction between letterpress and offset, but also the number of colors printed in one "pass" by either method. In a machine shop, not only the difference between a turret lathe and engine lathe, but number of spindles and diameters of the former, and chuck capacity of the latter. Basically, if considering how to list two similar machines, one of which cannot do what the other can, two production centers having one unit each, should be established.

1.2 *Manning:* Size of the worker crew, viz: if two machines having similar capabilities have the same number of people in the crew, each of whom receive the same base pay and fringe benefits, then the two machines can be *tentatively* grouped into the same production center. If however, the composite hourly pay is different because of differences in longevity which can affect in-grade base rate, entitled vacation pay and other fringe benefits, two production centers are required. Such differences can have an appreciable effect in the final direct MHR and thus in the oop cost of the order inquiry, the measurement of contribution and PV.

1.3 *Speed.* All other factors being equal, differences in speed make the placement in the same center invalid. Besides the obvious difference in oop conversion cost per M which would affect contribution measurements, invalid grouping would deprive management of vital information regarding the economy of their facilities. Such practice would also weaken the converter's production standards, which would then require an average rather than a specific approach to the measurement of productivity.

1.4 *Production Standards:* A basic rule: if you don't have production standards for a production station or, if you don't intend to develop standards for that station, and/or, if it is clearly uneconomical to develop such standards, *do not* designate such operations

MARTIN & TUCKER, INC.
ENGINEERS

Production Center	No. of Units	Hp. per Unit	FOR PRODUCTION CENTER: Working Space Occup.	Present Market Value in M's	Annual Assigned Hours**	Shifts per Unit	Hp-Hrs* in M's
45" Dilts Extruder-Laminator	1	70	600'	$350	6000	3	321
8-color 30" Champlain Gravure pr.	2	100	2000'	650	8000	2	450
Mosstype Mounter-Proofer	1	-	350'	3	2000	1	-
Acraplate Molder	1	20	200'	10	2000	1	34
6-color 42" Hudson-Sharp Flexo	1	50	900'	150	4000	2	153
5-color 30" Kidder Flexo	1	35	600'	60	4000	2	107
Cameron Slitter-Rewinder	2	25	400'	80	8000	2	170
Stanford Slitter-Rewinder	1	10	150'	12	2000	1	17
Schjeldahl 40" side-weld bag machine	3	10	400'	60	9000	1½	76.5
42" Beck Sheeter	1	15	150'	10	2000	1	25.5
			5750'	$1385	47000	-	1354.0

Notes: Misc. non- prod. eqpt. = $115,000
1 full activity shift = 2000 hours

*For "Run" portion of chargeable time
**Makeready + Run standard hours (includes expected non-chargeable time)

EXHIBIT 9-1: Converting Facilities Classification Sheet (CFCS) (flexible packaging converter)

as production centers. Establishing production centers for operations not time-standardized, means that there is no intention to estimate work passing through those stations, thereby resulting in the understating of conversion costs.

1.5 *Output Quality:* While all other physical facts can remain the same, a substantial difference in quality would call for separate centers rather than multiple units within the same production center. Thus: one machine is able to hold its accuracy to a closer tolerance than another very similar one; one printing press, because of age and/or condition, is not capable of holding its cylinder-to-cylinder register as well as its brother press, but is the same in all other respects. This factor has a direct bearing on estimating practices mentioned later.

1.6 *Electrical Consumption:* As obvious as this sounds, similar machines can use electrical energy at different rates. Often, one machine in a homogeneous grouping has had motors and other electrical devices changed during the years. For major capital equipment, this hourly oop cost could be appreciable thereby requiring separate production center listing because of the aforementioned effect on contribution measurement.

1.7 *Estimating Practices:* Regardless of the criteria in the previous six factors, if the estimating department ignores the existence of separate centers and chooses to shortcut their work by grouping machines and centers, the careful delineation made for production centers is rendered academic and harmful. Such estimating practice obscures the inherent profitability of machines and deprives management of data by which machinery acquisition and disposal decisions can be made. Most importantly, such averaging distorts the true measurement of contribution—the primary go-no-go determinant of order acceptances and rejections.

For example, two similar machines (in separate production centers) were grouped by the estimator. Their respective speeds were 1000 and 1500 pieces per hour. Each carried an oop MHR of $20, yielding oop conversion costs of $20 and $13.33 per M respectively. A 3000-piece order was being considered (which required only the one machine for processing, with the customer supplying the materials) which had a market selling price of $16 per M, or $48 for the 3000 pieces. If the order was run on the slower machine, its oop conversion cost of $60 would yield a negative contribution of $12. If run on the faster machine, the positive contribution would be $8. However, if the estimator chose to group the machines and averaged the speeds to 1250 per hour, the calculated oop conversion cost would show $48 for the order and zero contribution. The advice given to management would be to turn down the order. Yet, if the order had been booked and happened to run on the faster machine, the contribution would have been $8, a PV of .167. The distortions are better seen if the offered selling price was $22 per M. Then if the booked order used the slower machine the contribution would be $6, a PV of .091. For the faster unit, the contribution would be $26, or a PV of .394.

Surely, if the demand for this equipment exceeded the capacity of the faster machine, management would want to duplicate it or replace the slower unit with it. The averaging of both machines into one production center would bury this profit opportunity.

1.8 *Major Criterion:* Where the expected oop conversion cost per unit of output (per C or M pieces, lbs., rolls, etc.) at a machine is different than another machine of exactly the same type, each must be in a separate center. The ultimate and overriding criterion is the closeness of the oop conversion cost and the resulting closeness of the contribution measurements. To get the correct contribution and PV, you must "tell it like it is," regardless of tempting conveniences and shortcuts.

2. Number of Units

2.1 List the total number of units of machinery or work stations included in each production center, using the aforementioned criteria.

3. Horsepower

3.1 The total of all the electrical items per unit must be computed. This includes the ratings of the inductive devices such as the prime mover motors, auxiliary motors, etc., plus non-inductive devices, such as heaters. The former are rated in horsepower while the latter are generally rated in kilowatts. To convert watts into horsepower, simply divide the watts by 746. For example, if a heater used for drying is rated at 5 KW, (5000 watts), the horsepower is 5000/746, or 6.7 HP. In other words, 1 KW = 1.34 HP. In a case where a central compressor serves a group of machines, the HP of the motor driving the compressor can be apportioned and added to the HP per unit by the portion of air capacity required at the unit. This is a relationship between pounds of pressure and cubic feet per minute which the plant engineer can calculate.

3.2 Where specific energy charges (cost per kilowatt-hour) are identified on the Direct-Charge Budget (DCB), this factor is included on the CFCS for allocating the fixed electrical demand charge for "full"-cost MHR development. Otherwise, it is omitted.

4. Net Working Space

4.1 This is an allocation factor used in the development of "full" rates and distributes the fixed costs of occupancy, viz: rent, real estate taxes, interest on the mortgage, depreciation of the building, etc. Where fuel consumption used for heating varies with the volume of activity, this factor is also used for apportioning this direct-cost increment in the construction of the oop rates. For example, the annual cost of heating fuel is $66,000 under present volume conditions with average inside temperature in the winter held to 68°. At minimum activity levels, the inside temperature is held to 60° because of the need to maintain the dimensional stability of stored raw materials, and this annual cost is $58,000. Under these circumstances, the $58,000 would be considered the fixed cost and anything above that would be the direct-cost increment.

4.2 The calculation would be for the entire production center regardless of the number of units and includes the space occupied by the machines, workers, input and output materials, skids, conveyors related to the center, etc. Aisle space, long-term storage and warehouse areas, offices, etc. are not included since occupancy cost dollars is the item to be allocated. NWS for each center acts to distribute these total costs according to the space proportions among all centers.

5. Present Market Value

5.1 This item is also used as an allocation factor in assigning fixed costs associated with the ownership of equipment. Primarily, it is used in developing all-inclusive MHR. However, in those instances where there are general direct costs generated by the maintenance of machinery, which are not identified with specific pieces of equipment (and not included on the DCB), the PMV factor is used to apportion those costs on the Allocable Budget (AB).

5.2 There are endless and often fruitless discussions about what number to use for PMV, viz: replacement value new; in kind; sound insurable value; depreciated value; etc. Since PMV is not a cost but rather an allocation factor, the criterion is the correct proportions of relative values. Experience has shown that the most equitable figure to use is value of the equipment in terms of what it would cost to replace (from say, a used machinery dealer) in its same condition, capability, etc. Residual book value would distort the proportions, as this would assign a zero factor to fully written-off equipment. In fact, such machinery may be operating and functional and would have a value to be depreciated if a competitor bought a similar machine from a used machinery dealer. Depreciation is a tax-motivated expense figure having no reference to marketplace prices for converted products.

5.3 The following three columns of values all will produce the *same allocated amounts* in the final development of the rates:

Production Center	PMV-1	PMV-2	PMV-3
A	$8,000	$15,000	$4
B	$16,000	$30,000	$8
C	$12,000	$22,500	$6
D	$24,000	$45,000	$12

6. Assigned Annual Hours

6.1 This refers to the annual *standard chargeable* hours a center is expected to operate in the coming period. It is used as an allocation factor for a small portion of the converter's expense, namely, that projected on a small portion of the direct costs listed on the Allocable Budget. The highest quality oop MHR results from being able first to identify specifically every direct cost with a production center. Inevitably, some direct costs are incurred in blanket form and can't be identified directly with a center. These are the expenses placed in the AB.

6.2 The more important uses for AAH lay in the development of workers' subsidy pay and non-chargeable time costs. These are vital excess oop costs directly affecting the oop rates and the advanced form of the two-part MHR. We will treat these items in the next chapter. Here are some do's and don'ts on projecting AAH:

6.2.1 *Estimate from production:* Getting foremen's or plant managers' estimates is a useless effort even though they might come up with a set of numbers. Typically, they'll say something like, "figure a 10% increase over last year's hours"—a socially acceptable response. Advice: don't ask them unless they are charged with generating the sales volume which will determine the activities of machines.

6.2.2 *Accountant's estimate:* Ditto

6.2.3 *Estimator's guess:* Ditto

6.2.4 *Salesmen's survey:* Better, but not coordinated and consistent.

6.2.5 *Marketing department:* If this is where an annual sales forecast is assembled, this is the place to find out about future planning. Foremen, accountants, estimators and individual salesmen are not required to know, nor to be responsible for, future activity. This entire area is volume based and not under the influence of manufacturing, accounting or the mix of customers' orders handled by an individual salesman. To be effective for AAH, the parameters of a sales forecast should be recognized:

6.2.5.1 The projection should be made by product lines and not as a composite company total.

6.2.5.2 Further separations should be made for the products within each product line.

6.2.5.3 Expected common product sales should then be converted to hours required at each production center and totalled. The manufacturing department will be involved at the point where sales dollars are converted to center hours. Production standards should be used to project this machine activity. See Exhibit 9-2 for a sample projection and conversion.

A sales forecast is obviously arbitrary unless one is blessed with

Customer	EXPECTED ANNUAL SALES		
	Product Line A	Product Line B	Product Line C
Jones	$400,000	---	$150,000

Product Line A	Product a	Product b	Product c	Product d
for Jones	$100,000	---	$300,000	---
Product Line C	**Product m**	**Product n**	**Product o**	**Product p**
for Jones	---	$50,000	---	$100,000

for Jones:

Products	ANNUAL FACILITY HOURS							
	1	2	3	4	5	6	7	8
a	50			30			10	
b								
c	5	70			45		30	
d								
•								
•								
•								
m								
n	5	30	10		10		5	
o								
p			25	10		20		10
Totals	60	100	35	40	55	20	45	10

EXHIBIT 9-2: Sample Sales Forecast & Facility Projection (for Customer Jones)

clairvoyance, ESP, and other psychic skills—and is really an exercise in foretelling the future. At the start of the projected year no one knows whether such a set of hours will come to fruition. That is, whether actually used hours will equal forecasted hours. Of course, frequent comparisons (by means of variance reporting) can be used to purify the projections and thus, the rates. But still, certain order commitments have been made prior to corrections of hours which variance reporting cannot change.

While this element of aribtrariness is still present in the most sophisticated MHR, its effects can be minimized as will be discussed later. Without this refinement, management mistakenly depends on unknown future factors to plan its profits.

6.3 Vital to the projection of future activity is an understanding of the kind of hours to use. If for example, we were to use 2000 annual hours for one-shift expected activity on a machine, we would want to know several things:

1. Are these the hours that are to be charged to customers' jobs?
2. Are these standard hours or elapsed clock hours?

6.3.1 *Non-chargeable time:* The annual hours projected should be *chargeable* hours, that is the annual hours which are expected to be directly charged to the job. Annual hours should not include non-productive or unassigned or standby time. If a worker gets paid for 2000 annual hours, and it is expected that 1600 annual hours will be charged to jobs, the 400 hours is pay for hours not worked and considered *non-chargeable* time. The cost of this worker unproductive time (if he is retained for the entire year) is calculated in the Crew Composition Table (CCT) as part of the direct labor excess. The 1600 annual chargeable hours is the first step in getting the correct Annual Assigned Hours figure. Of course, if his 400 hours are nonchargeable at a specific center but it is planned to assign him to another operation which will convert some or all of these 400 hours to a chargeable base, then the cost of his non-chargeable time will be less on the CCT at the two or more assigned centers.

6.3.2 *Subsidy cost:* The chargeable hours assigned should be those worked at a standard rate of output and not at a variety of productivities. In this latter case, it would then use elapsed or clock hours which obviously would not be uniform and consistent. Thus, if the 1600 chargeable hours at a center is expected to operate (from the viewpoint of worker effort) at 75% productivity, the *chargeable standard* hours would be 1200 annual hours. This is the purified AAH to use on the CFCS as shown in later MHR constructions. The 25% subsidy cost is the amount of money the company has to "make-up" in the computation of an earned standard hour. For example, if a standard hour's work is to produce 1000 units and only 750 are actually produced, the worker is said to be 75% productive and earns 75% of his base hourly pay rate. If the worker receives an hourly base rate of $4.00 and works at 75% productivity, he has *earned* only $3.00 or .75 hours and the company has to subsidize the difference of $1.00 per hour. This unearned pay is an excess cost and is calculated in the CCT.

6.3.3 *Annual Projected Chargeable Standard Hours:* This is the proper description of the AAH. If projected actual clock hours are used instead, the planned activity is weakened by the intermix of varying nonproductive time levels and the wide changes in day-to-day productivities.

6.4 The final question is what the content of the finally selected annual hour should be. That is, should it be purely "running" time? Or should it contain the time needed for preparation and later clean up? Preparation time, viz: setting up a machine; changing over to another size on the same machine; making ready a printing press; washing up for a color change; etc., all should be included in the activity hour. That is, the AAH should include these hours when making the projection. In the aforementioned 2000/1600/1200 annual hour example, the 1200 hours may consist of 1000 "run" hours and 200 of preparation.

In a proper standards program, both run and makeready standards are developed, and in some instances, washup and cleanup are also standardized. Where it is impractical to develop washup and cleanup standards (and thereby eliminate them from direct order estimating), their costs can be picked up in the DCB or CCT.

7. Horsepower-Hours

7.1 This is an extension of horsepower per unit multiplied by AAH and is used to allocate the electrical energy costs (oop) if not stated on the DCB. In the traditional "full"-cost MHR approach, this factor also allocates the demand (fixed) charges for electrical power.

Chapter 10

Constructing the Machine-Hour Rate System

STEP 2: CREW COMPOSITION TABLE (CCT)

The Crew Composition Table, abbreviated to CCT, is the second piece of organized data required in the preparation of Machine-Hour Rates. The CCT specifies the standard manning needed at each of the production centers listed on the CFCS. The CCT can be prepared in several different ways depending on the specific company operation.

A complete CCT shows hourly base rates for the crew, whether full or fractional people are assigned, together with the cost of non-chargeable time, subsidy pay and all fringe benefits. Exhibit 10-1 shows the CCT for the model company in condensed form:

1. Standard Crew per Unit

A standard crew is composed of one or more workers (and in some cases, only a fractional portion of one worker) normal to each production center. In some instances, one worker may operate two machines in the center; in others one worker may service more than one machine. Proper distribution is attained by fractional assignment of people.

Criteria for determining the standard crew are:

1.1 *Identifiability:* A worker who operates a machine or work station in a production center is to be a member of the standard crew. Other supporting labor such as: helpers, assistants, feeders, packers, material handlers, etc. specifically employed at that machine unit, should be assigned to a crew on a full-body or fractional basis depending on need. Care must be exercised to insure that fractional assignments to machine units are reconciled to equal full bodies. The cost of unassigned fractional labor should either be reflected in non-chargeable time on the CCT, or in excess general labor on the AB.

1.2 *Discontinuability:* This concept relates to labor which does not directly work on the machines, such as department foremen and other supervisors. In the traditional approach to MHR development, this type of labor is considered "indirect"—a most misleading term. This reference motivates placing of this cost in the period or fixed

MARTIN & TUCKER, INC.
ENGINEERS

Production Center	Std. Crew* per Unit	HOURLY Base Pay per Unit	N/C Cost per Unit	Cost of Sub-std. Product-ivity	O.T. & F.B. per Unit**	Crew Pay per Unit
Extruder-Laminator	2.2	$8.36	$1.25	$.84	$1.91	$12.36
Gravure Presses	2.2	9.02	1.36	.90	4.27	15.55
Mounter-Proofer	.6	1.80	.12	.19	.32	2.43
Molder	.6	1.80	.11	.11	.47	2.49
6c 42" Flexo	1.8	6.48	.97	.86	2.05	10.36
5c 30" Flexo	1.8	6.48	.97	.67	1.73	9.85
Cameron Sl-Rewind	1.2	3.60	.46	.31	.53	4.90
Stanford Sl-Rewind	1.2	3.60	.38	.31	.85	5.14
Bag machines	2.3	4.83	1.06	1.40	.69	7.98
Sheeter	1.1	3.30	.34	.20	.24	4.08

*Includes fractional assignment of foremen, adjusters and/or helpers.
**Includes holiday, vacation, rest periods, and cost of pay for other time not worked, except non-chargeable time.

EXHIBIT 10-1: Crew Composition Table - Run (CCT) (flexible packaging converter)

category of the AB, which in most instances is wrong because it understates oop cost and exaggerates the contribution measurement. Such distortions, as mentioned earlier, can lead to booking business which does not have as high a contribution as management believes it has and which they require for a particular class of work.

When this cost is treated as indirect, but placed in the *direct* category of the AB, all centers wind up with a piece of this oop expense even though they may not be the recipient of this service. And those centers which actually use this service carry a smaller portion of this cost than they should.

The rational method of making the determination of where to place such costs is to subject it to a test question involving discontinuability, viz: "If we discontinue the bindery department by farming out the work to a trade bindery, will we still need the bindery foreman?" Or, turning the question around, "If we decide to take our bindery work out of the trade bindery we presently use, and set up our own in-plant bindery, will we have to hire a foreman to supervise it?" If the answers to the respective questions are no and yes, then the cost of the foreman is a directly-related one in practically the same way as a helper on a machine is, and therefore should be included fractionally as a member of the standard crew. How the crew cost is calculated is shown in the following item.

2. Base Pay per Unit

This includes the base hourly pay rates of the workers in the crew, plus the anticipated increases scheduled in the coming 12-month period. Care should be taken on projected increases since this affects the cost of non-chargeable time, subsidy and most fringe benefits. A typical manning showing the composition and base rates to derive the base pay per unit follows:

Production Center	Title	Hourly Base Rate	No. per Unit	Hourly Base Pay per Unit	
6-color 61" Offset Press					
	Chief Pressman	$7.00	1	$ 7.00	
	Asst. Pressman	5.50	1	5.50	
	Asst. Pressman	4.70	2	9.40	
	Helpers	2.80	2	5.60	
	Material Handlers	2.20	1	2.20	
	Quality Inspector	4.10	.5	2.05	
	Foreman	8.00[1]	.25	2.00	
			Total Hourly Base Pay/Unit		$33.75

3. Non-Chargeable Cost per Unit

This includes the pay for hours not worked, and not assigned to other machine units or work stations. Getting this figure requires an estimate based on what work is expected in the coming period. However, a *characteristic* n/c figure based on the immediately previous experience will be helpful, if proper records are available. Basically, the records should show what portion of a worker's annual paid hours have been charged to jobs and which hours were not charged to any job. Then these figures can be modified to reflect expected future conditions.

The following example applied to the above Chief Pressman illustrates the approach to obtaining *annual* n/c cost:

Chief Pressman:	*Hourly Base Pay Rate*	= $7.00
One year		= 365 days
Less: Saturdays & Sundays		= 104 days
Less: Paid Holidays		= 10 days
Less: Entitled Vacation		= 15 days
Less: Illness & Other Time Off		= 5 days
Net Working Days Available		= 231

1 Converted from annual salary to hourly basis.

Annual Clock Hours Available @ 8 hours per day	= 1848
Annual Base Pay Cost	= $12,936
Expected N/C Time of 20%	= 369.6 hours
Annual Chargeable Clock Hours	= 1478.4
Expected Annual N/C Cost	= $2,587.20

4. Subsidy Cost per Unit

This is the cost of sub-standard productivity, and evaluates the extent to which workers at a machine unit perform below production standard levels. Where equitable, engineered production standards are in effect, the productivity % can be obtained from production records. Like non-chargeable time, productivity is generally a characteristic of a machine unit and the workers assigned to it.

In the case of the above Chief Pressman, 1478.4 chargeable clock hours are projected. The question now is at what average rate of productivity will those chargeable clock hours be worked? If 90% productivity is typical at that center, then the number of annual earned standard hours will be less than 1478.4, as shown in the following calculation:

Annual Chargeable Clock Hours	= 1478.4 hours
Annual Cost of Chargeable Clock Hours	= $10,348.80
Expected Average Annual Productivity	= 90%
Annual Chargeable Standard Hours	= 1330.56 hours
Annual Sub-standard Hours	= 147.84 hours
Expected Annual Subsidy Cost	= $1,034.88

5. Non-Chargeable and Subsidy Cost per Unit per Chargeable Standard Hour

To get these two costs to an hourly basis for rate construction, both annual costs must be divided by *chargeable standard* hours, viz:

N/C Cost per hour = $2,587.20 ÷ 1330.56 = $1.94 chargeable standard
Subsidy Cost per hour = $1,034.88 ÷ 1330.56 = .78 " "

5.1 There are certain exceptions to treating these two costs. For example, they may not be applied to all members of the standard crew where such members do not directly affect activity at a center to the point where they would get pay for hours not worked. Nor will some of them affect productivity. This is generally true for quality control people, supervisors and the like. In such instances, these excess hourly costs are to be developed only for people working directly on the machine.

5.2 In a later chapter, using a different company, we will show a different derivation of this *gross hourly cost.*

6. Overtime Premium Cost per Unit per Chargeable Standard Hour

This includes the cost of planned overtime premium and is explained by the following calculation for the aforementioned Chief Pressman:

Annual Clock Hours Available	= 1848
Planned Working Hours	= 1900
Planned Overtime Clock Hours	= 52
Overtime Premium Cost (52 x $3.50)	= $182
Overtime Premium Cost per Chargeable Standard Hour	= $.14

7. Fringe Benefit Costs

This group of costs includes all other costs that the company must pay to support the employment of its workers, besides the hourly pay rate, non-chargeable costs and subsidy pay. These costs include: hourly payroll costs, such as paid holidays; and non-hourly, non-payroll expenses such as the cost of employees' summer picnics. The following is a typical list of fringe benefits from one company, although this is not to imply it covers all of the fringe benefits paid in industry:

..Overtime premium
..Paid holidays
..Entitled vacation
..Night differential
..Entitled sick pay
..Time off: funerals
..Time off: jury duty
..Holiday gifts
..Direct payment medical
..F.I.C.A. Employer contributions
..Union medical contributions
..Disability payments
..Blue Cross, hospitalization
..Major medical
..Workmen's compensation
..Uniform cost
..Pension plan contributions
..Union welfare
..Cafeteria Contribution

7.1 *F. B. Cost per Unit per Chargeable Standard Hour:*
Making the calculation for the Chief Pressman, we might having the following:

Paid Holiday Hours	=	80	=	$ 560.00
Entitled Vacation Hours	=	120	=	840.00
Illness, etc. Hours	=	40	=	280.00
Payroll surcharges, medical, group insurance, workmen's compensation, etc.			=	1940.00
Annual Fringe Benefit Cost				$3620.00
Cost per Chargeable Standard Hour			=	$2.72

8. Gross Cost per Unit per Chargeable Standard Hour

Summarizing for the Chief Pressman:

Hourly Base Pay Rate	=	$ 7.00
N/C Hourly Cost	=	1.94
Hourly Subsidy Cost	=	.78
Hourly O.T. Premium Cost	=	.14
Hourly F. B. Cost	=	2.72
Gross Hourly Cost	=	$12.58

9. Standard Crews

The standard crews shown on Exhibit 10-1 are for manning the production centers for the condition "run." In a center where the composition of a crew changes during preparatory operations such as makeready or setup, an additional "crew pay per unit" must be developed. Often at a facility, the run crew may be four workers, but during the makeready operation, perhaps only two or three are assigned. Of course, if by labor-management agreement there are to be no crew changes regardless of the operation being performed, and/or where the surplus members of the crew during a makeready are not assigned elsewhere, then there is no need to develop separate crew rates.

Chapter 11

Constructing the Machine-Hour Rate System

STEP 3: DIRECT-CHARGE BUDGET (DCB)

The Direct-Charge Budget, abbreviated to DCB, is the third piece of organized data required in the preparation of Machine-Hour Rates. The DCB marshalls all of the specific charges which are identified directly with each machine unit and production center. These directly-attributable costs deal with maintenance and repair of machine units, power consumed, and other specific machine-related expenses. In the shortcut approach to rate development, this direct concept is not used and instead, these costs are combined with blanket (non-identifiable) costs and allocated on a statistical basis. This practice increases MHR's for centers which don't incur these specific costs and lowers the rates in those centers which do.

Getting DCB data is not simple since most expense records in industry are not structured to yield the information in the form required. For example, in only a small percentage of cases have we seen daily reports filled out by repair and maintenance people to show on which facilities they spent their time. Obviously, it is only in this way, that we can charge specific inside maintenance labor to a particular machine. Also, very few industry time and production reporting systems break down delay time to show how much unassigned time was spent waiting for a machine malfunction to be corrected. Obviously, this type of idle time should be attributed to the repair event.

Exhibit 11-1 shows the DCB for the model company. The following costs should be included:

1. Repair and Maintenance Inside Labor

These are the costs incurred by payroll people who work directly on machine units within production centers. General machine-shop labor, millwrights or others whose efforts are not specifically identified with production centers should be budgeted on the AB. Where previous records *by machine* are available, these data form an excellent base for next year's projection. Where only the annual labor costs (plus all fringe benefits, of course) are available, then estimates have to be made by which these costs are distributed to machine units. Often, this is done in the form of percentages which convert the annual labor costs to specific machine unit cost. There is no

MARTIN & TUCKER, INC.
ENGINEERS

Prod. Center	Repairs, Mainten., Supplies, Parts & Outside Service	Special Items	Direct Power			Annual Direct Ch'ges	Annual Assign Hours	Direct Charges per Hour
			Elec.	Gas	Other			
	$	$	$	$	$	$		$
Ex-Lam	4200		8300			12500	6000	2.08
Gravure	9100	Re-etch cylind. =48000	11700	1400		70200	8000	8.78
M-P						0	2000	0
Molder			900			900	2000	.45
6c-Flex	2200		4000	600		6800	4000	1.70
5c-Flex	1000		2800	400		4200	4000	1.05
Cam S-R	1900		4400			6300	8000	.79
Stn S-R	400		440			840	2000	.42
Bag	4300		2000			6300	9000	.70
Sheet	200		600			800	2000	.40
			TOTAL			$ 108,840		

EXHIBIT 11-1: Direct-Charge Budget (DCB)
(flexible packaging converter)

alternative to doing this but then the company should set up daily reporting for these workers to capture what time is being spent on the various machines. From this technique, management can then establish variance reporting by which to purify their original percentage guesses.

2. Repair and Maintenance Outside Labor

Where this type of work is farmed out either on a specific or annual contract basis, it is easier to get information by specific machine. At least, the outside people should in the first instance, be required to identify their invoice by machine. And in the second, to show how their time has been applied during each month or period in which their invoices are submitted. Naturally, some plants use both inside and outside labor to keep their equipment in good repair. For example, the company may elect to do their own mechanical repairs but farm out the rewinding of large motors.

3. Specific Supplies and Repair Parts

This should cover anything from solvents and wiping rags at printing presses to replacement of bearings or grinding shafts and journals at other machines. It should not include motor maintenance for one of their lathes in the machine shop. This latter item would be included in the AB. A distinction should also be made between a repair part and a capital alteration. Often this question revolves around whether the part is to be expensed or capitalized. Another issue is in the buying of repair parts and keeping them in inventory. Obviously, only the usage of these parts constitute the expense, not the purchased amount.

4. Unassigned Inside Standby Productive Labor

While this is a form of idle time and perhaps non-chargeable as far as any one job is concerned, it is certainly chargeable to the machine unit involved. This is the direct-productive labor which cannot be assigned elsewhere while the repair is taking place. Since it is generated by the need for repair, it should be considered a repair cost and charged directly to the machine in the DCB. Non-chargeable time in the CCT is that caused by inactivity (lower sales volume) and is a valuable managerial tool. To place this unassigned inside standby productive labor in the CCT would distort the activity measurement as well as lowering the true cost of machine maintenance. In an effective time and production reporting system, waiting times would be codified together with reasons for such delays. In that eventuality, this type of delay should be separately included for easy extraction.

5. Special Items

The costs of these items are for cost events which happen transiently and not a subject for regular reporting. This is the case with the re-etching cost for gravure cylinders shown in Exhibit 10-1. In other instances, it can cover what are really raw materials, providing such materials are being consumed at the same rate per hour regardless of product mix. An example may be the consumption of adhesive at the folding machine making a certain standard size envelope all year long.

6. Direct Power

Mostly, this category applies to energy charges for electricity as billed to the company in kilowatt-hours. Demand charges rated in kilowatts is considered a fixed charge, even though there are slight load variations, and included in the AB for "full" rate construction. As will be seen in later chapters, there is no need to develop the annual direct energy charge by production center and then divide by AAH to get its direct charge per hour.

Before giving an example of a direct calculation, it is necessary once again to bring up the question of the purity of the 60-minute hour. When electricity is being consumed by the clock hour (the basis for the charge), that hour can be an hour in which a myriad number of productivities are being attained. While a kilowatt-hour may cost two cents, and a center consuming 500 watts for 1000 hours (500 KW-HRS) would cost $10, that calculation is true only if productivity is equal to 100%. Where productivity is below that level, it means the center has to work a greater number of clock hours to attain the projected output. This is compensated for by raising the cost per kilowatt-hour by the extent of the sub-standard productivity or subsidy percentage. If at the above center the productivity is expected to be 80%, then the cost per KW-HR to use is \$.02/.80 = \$.025 and the center's electrical energy cost for the 1000 hours would be \$12.50.

An example of a sample calculation follows:

Production Center A = 20 HP = 26.81 KW; expected productivity 80%
Energy cost per KW-HR @ × level of annual usage = \$.018
Adjusted KW-HR cost = \$.018/.80 = \$.0225
Energy cost per chargeable standard hour for A = 26.81 × \$.0225 = \$.60

After reducing all other direct charges to an hourly basis, this electrical energy cost can be added to yield the total direct charges per chargeable standard hour per production center.

The same approach would be used for other power items such as: gas used on productive equipment (not for general space heating); steam used in direct processing, as for a corrugator or combiner in a kraft corrugated paper container plant. (Some of these companies consider this steam cost as part of direct materials.)

In following MHR constructions, other methods for making this electrical energy adjustment are shown.

Chapter 12

Constructing the Machine-Hour Rate System

STEP 4: ALLOCABLE BUDGET (AB)

The Allocable Budget, abbreviated to AB, is the fourth piece of organized data required in the preparation of Machine-Hour Rates. This is the schedule of expenses which are incurred in blanket form and cannot be directly identified with a production department, production center, machine unit within a center, and/or an order. (Order-related costs are added to conversion costs without allocation. Some of these, to be discussed later, are: direct materials, salesmen's commissions, etc.)

If all conversion costs could be directly identified with production centers, et al, we would have a set of MHR free from any arbitrary element. Therefore, in building rates, every attempt should be made to first tie every expense to a production center, machine unit, order, etc. Then, whatever costs are left over are placed on the AB. This involves careful study and analysis and is well worth the effort.

Exhibit 12-1 shows the AB for the model company. For allocation reasons the blanket expenses are separated into *Manufacturing* and *Non-Manufacturing* segments and then further into the categories of each. Even though we are interested only in the direct costs for purposes of constructing oop rates, the period costs are also given. There are two reasons for this:

1. Identifying the period or fixed portion of each expense gives us the basis for determining the direct portion.
2. Carrying the period segment into the rates allows us to develop "full" rates, even though we know these are useless for cost-estimating, pricing and profit planning. However, experience has taught that at the beginning of the direct-cost approach to evaluating the contribution of orders, no matter how much this rational concept is believed, there is usually a residual skepticism. Often the management feels a little more secure when it has the "full" cost of the order in front of him when making pricing decisions. It usually takes the form of, "Well, let's just for fun see what the costs look like the old way." This is perfectly understandable and as soon as he sees

the uselessness of the "full" rates (takes anywheres from a few months to a year), he drops the "full" rates, and cost and rate schedules from that point on are expressed in oop cost only.

The segments and categories shown on Exhibit 12-1 are those selected for this model company. Suggestively other appropriate categories can be used for other companies. The determinants of categories are the previously established cause-and-effect allocation factors mentioned in earlier chapters. In this instance, the categories established support the allocation factors selected on the CFCS.

MARTIN & TUCKER, INC.
ENGINEERS

Projected Expenses	Period	Direct	Total
MANUFACTURING COSTS:			
Space:			
Rent	$30,000	-	$30,000
Repairs to building	6,000	-	6,000
Heat	8,000	$2,000	10,000
	44,000	2,000	46,000
Power:			
Electricity*	5,000	4,000	9,000
Machinery:			
Depreciation	150,000	-	150,000
Price-level adj=8%	12,000	-	12,000
Insurance, equipment	3,000	-	3,000
General machine shop*	7,000	14,000	21,000
	172,000	14,000	186,000
Indirect:			
Plant manager	17,000	-	17,000
Indirect labor, not specifically identified by production center**	8,000	24,000	32,000
Timekeeper	5,000	-	5,000
Porter-sweeper	4,000	-	4,000
	34,000	24,000	58,000
TOTAL MFG. COST	$255,000	$44,000	$299,000

*costs not included on Direct-Charge Budget (DCB)
**costs not included on Crew Composition Table (CCT)

EXHIBIT 12-1: Allocable Budget (AB)
(Flexible packaging converter)

MARTIN & TUCKER, INC.
ENGINEERS

Projected Expenses	Period	Direct	Total
NON-MANUFACTURING COSTS:			
Whse & Del:			
Rent	$10,000	-	$10,000
Wages: Shpg. Clerks	-	$8,000	8,000
: Truck Drivers*	-	5,500	5,500
Insurance, inventory	500	500	1,000
Truck depreciation	1,500	-	1,500
Truck operating costs	-	5,000	5,000
	12,000	19,000	31,000
Selling:			
Sales Manager's salary	20,000	-	20,000
Sales clerks' salaries	6,000	30,000	36,000
Estimator	9,000	-	9,000
Auto expenses	-	8,000	8,000
Non-billable art work	-	15,000	15,000
	35,000	53,000	88,000
Administrative:			
General Manager's salary	25,000	-	25,000
Office expenses	2,000	-	2,000
Accounting salaries	9,000	-	9,000
Clerical salaries	10,000	45,000	55,000
Other	20,000	10,000	30,000
	66,000	55,000	121,000
Fringe Benefits:			
Payroll surcharges	12,000	17,000	29,000
Whse & del O.T. premium	-	1,000	1,000
Hospitalization insur.	2,000	-	2,000
Xmas bonuses	15,000	-	15,000
	29,000	18,000	47,000
TOTAL NON-MFG. COST	$142,000	$145,000	$287,000
from p. 1: TOTAL MFG. COST	255,000	44,000	299,000
ANNUAL BUDGETED OVERHEAD COST	$397,000	$189,000	$586,000

*costs not included in Direct-Order Charges (DOC)

EXHIBIT 12-1 (continued)

1. Allocable Budget

The purpose of the AB (or any budget for that matter) is to project financial support of future operations. The AB does *not* plan cash needs for direct materials, sales commissions, direct labor, direct machine charges, etc. Budgeting every item of expense in a company is used for other purposes, like cash flow planning and has little to do with the type of budget designed exclusively for Machine-Hour construction. The AB is a statement of what blanket, non-identifiable *overhead* expenses are required to support the planned operations expressed on the CFCS.

2. Manufacturing Costs

2.1 *Space:* Typical expense items under this category are: rent; real estate taxes; depreciation of building; maintenance of building; electrical lighting expense; insurance on building; heat; etc. The allocation factor to be used in the next step is NWS.

2.2 *Power:* This category has such costs as: electrical demand as well as non-identifiable energy (direct) costs, gas and oil, steam, etc. These costs will be allocated to centers using the CFCS HP-HRS as the factor.

2.3 *Machinery:* Included under this category are: depreciation; price-level adjustments (to compensate for the coming year's inflationary effect of the dollar); insurance on equipment; personal property taxes on equipment (in some states); maintenance and repair of productive equipment, if not included in the DCB; equipment rentals directly related to production centers; general machine-shop expenses; etc. PMV is the allocation factor.

2.4 *Indirect:* Included here are labor as well as non-labor expenses: timekeepers; factory expediters; production reporting supplies; porter-sweepers and their materials; plant manager and his assistants (not production department foremen); idle time (n/c) of production workers, if not included on the CCT; cost of sub-standard productivity, if not included on the CCT; etc. AAH is the allocation factor used in this model company.

2.5 *Fringe Benefits:* Not shown on Exhibit 12-1 but used if the CCT employed is simplified and excludes fringe benefits. This approach is not recommended because it ignores the different levels of fringes paid at different production centers. The result is a smoothing out of these costs with each center receiving the same increment over the base hourly direct labor cost, since generally, the direct labor cost would be used as the allocation factor.

3. Non-Manufacturing Costs

3.1 *Warehousing & Delivery:* This category includes such expense items as: rent and/or other related occupancy costs; wages of shipping and receiving clerks; wages of warehousemen and material handlers not assigned to production centers on the CCT; wages of the drivers of owned or leased trucks; depreciation of trucks, trailers, internal transportation equipment, such as fork lifts; operating expenses of all transportation equipment; insurance on raw and finished goods inventory; etc.

3.2 *Selling Expenses:* Grouped under this category are expenses which are not volume related. These latter costs are not included in the rates, but rather are treated as Direct-Order Charges (DOC) and added to conversion costs on the job estimate. Examples of expenses in this category are: salaries of sales managers, sales clerks; sales correspondents; customer service people; traveling and entertainment expenses not volume related; estimators; telephone expenses; office rental; advertising expenses; supplies, etc.

3.3 *Administrative Expenses:* This category has such expenses as: salaries of general manager, executives and principals (except for those executives whose time is volume related in the producing of sales revenue); salaries of office, clerical and accounting personnel; office rent; depreciation of office assets; stationery, postage, telephone; business interruption insurance; bank charges and interest expenses; charitable contributions; data processing expenses; etc.

3.4 *Fringe Benefits:* This applies to the salary/wage portion of the three previous categories: 3.1, 3.2, 3.3. The only purpose of keeping this category separate is for managerial control. In many instances, this category can be eliminated and the above salaries and wages stated inclusive of fringes.

3.5 *Allocation Method:* In the model company, categories 3.1, 3.2 and 3.3 are totalled and then allocated by means of the total Manufacturing Costs, as shown in the next chapter.

4. Separation of Costs

As discussed in Chapter 8, the "full" costs of an order estimate is no guide to pricing decisions since contribution measurement is impossible. Before we can measure contribution, all costs must be stated in direct-cost terms so that the oop cost of the job inquiry becomes available. In Exhibit 8-2, the crew costs are stated, which of course are considered as all direct cost. However, in Exhibit 8-4, the AB shows no separation of costs; all are stated in their total amounts. Obtaining oop rates from this approach is not possible. Obviously then, the AB is the place where this refinement has to be made.

In the model company of this chapter, the CCT and DCB give oop costs. The AB also shows the separation of costs to give us the oop component. Here are some guideposts for making these separations.

4.1 The first task is to design a new Chart of Accounts using the approach of the ECW of Chapter 8. This need not disturb the custodial auditing functions and can still provide the convenience of grouping or classifying costs according to the AB categories. Some approaches are shown in Exhibits 12-2 and 12-3. When the separations are completed, the Chart of Accounts can be set up to resemble Exhibit 12-4. Notice that the numbering system is of the Dewey-decimal type, a preference of the author's. However, if and when accounting and profit planning data are computerized, the numbering would have to conform with the software design and programming requirements.

4.2 When these mechanical details are completed, the major task begins: that of separating each cost according to its individual behaviors and responses to volume changes. Criteria for this effort were discussed in the chapters of Section I. However, it would be helpful to sample a few AB expenses of Exhibit 12-1:

4.2.1. *Electricity $9,000:* The $5,000 is the demand charge for the entire plant, and while the $4,000 direct is affected by volume, none of it can be attributed to the production facilities.

4.2.2 *General Machine Shop $21,000:* This department employs 3 men, one of whom the company believes it would require for minimum production volume levels, and 2 to support the present activity. Thus, the salaries of the 2 volume-related men are treated as direct or oop costs.

4.2.3 *Indirect Labor $32,000:* Here again, we're dealing with costs not directly related to production centers but yet related to the company's general volume of production activity. The approach is to determine how many bodies would be required at minimum volume and to consider those additional as direct.

4.2.4 *Clerical Salaries $55,000:* The separation of this expense deals more with the transactional effort than with production volume, but it is still related to overall company sales activity. The test approach can be used for expenses of this nature, viz: How many people do we need to support the present level of activity? If volume dropped by x%, how many people would be dismissed? If volume rose by x%, how many people would we have to add? If volume kept dropping what would be the minimum number of people required to the point where further drops in volume would not justify further dismissals of people? If answers to the earlier questions suggest that the number of people would change with volume, we know that there is a direct component of the expense. And, if the answer to the last question pegs a minimum level of people who remain unchanged with further volume drops, then we know that it has a period or fixed component. This was the basis used for the separation shown in the model AB.

Direct (OOP) Costs	Period (Fixed) Costs
CONVERSION:	CONVERSION:
Mfg:	Mfg:
Direct, productive labor Fringe benefits on d.l. Overtime premium pay Mechanics' pay and fringes Materials handlers: a portion Repair labor and fringes Repair parts and supplies Electricity: energy portion Subsidy pay for sub-standard productivity Cost of non-chargeable direct labor Blankets for offset presses Etc.	Depreciation: prod'n eqpt. Rent and/or bldg. depreciation, real estate taxes, etc. Electricity: demand portion Insurance of Eqpt. & contents Porter-sweeper Etc.
Non-Mfg:	Non-Mfg:
Warehouse & delivery labor: a portion Truck operating costs Clerical salaries: a portion Administrative: a portion Sales clerks: a portion Tel. & tel: a portion Etc.	Warehouse & delivery labor: a portion Truck depreciation Clerical salaries: a portion Administrative: a portion Sales clerks: a portion Tel. & tel: a portion Legal & audit Office rent Depreciation of F & F Etc.
ORDER ADDITIVES:	
All direct materials All preparatory materials Packing materials Freight out costs Commissions Royalties Special storage charges Small-order transaction cost Etc.	

EXHIBIT 12-2: A Partial List of Separated Direct and Period Costs

Manufacturing Overhead	Period	Direct	Non-Mfg. Overhead: Selling	Period	Direct
Machinery maintenance	x	x	Sales manager's salary	x	
Repair parts	x	x	Sales trainees	x	x
Supervision	x	x	Commissions		x
Depreciation	x		Travel expenses		x
Equipment rental		x	Advertising expenses	x	
Payroll surcharges		x	Telephone expenses	x	x
Electricity	x	x	Deprec: salesmen's cars	x	
Non-Mfg. Overhead: Delivery			**Non-Mfg. Overhead: Adminis.**		
Drivers' wages		x	Principals' salaries	x	
Warehousing labor		x	Clerical salaries	x	x
Depreciation: trucks	x		Professional fees	x	
Truck expenses		x	Office Supplies	x	x
Supervision	x		Public relations		x
Workman's compensation	x	x	Business insurance		x
Purchased delivery		x	Interest expenses	x	x

EXHIBIT 12-3: Major Budget Categories for MHR: Direct and Period (Partial List)

Acct. No.	Account Name	Period	Direct
88.	OPERATING EXPENSE CONTROL		
.01.	Printing Department		
.01	Productive labor		XX
.03	Materials handling		XX
.06	Press supplies		XX
.09	Electricity: energy		XX
.14	Outside contract maintenance		XX
.16	Supervision		XX
.20	Inside maintenance		XX
.51	Depreciation of equipment	XX	
.52	Inside maintenance	XX	
.54	Electricity: demand	XX	
.09.	Warehouse & Delivery		
.01	Truck drivers		XX
.02	Warehousemen		XX
.03	Shipping & receiving clerks		XX
.06	Truck operating expenses		XX
.52	Supervision	XX	
.56	Depreciation of delivery trucks	XX	
.57	Depreciation of material trucks	XX	
.58	Depreciation of warehouse	XX	
.11.	Selling		
.01	Salesmen's commissions		XX
.02	Brokerage		XX
.03	Traveling expenses		XX
.04	Salesmen's base salaries		XX
.05	Sales office clerks		XX
.51	Sales manager's salary	XX	
.53	Customer services	XX	
.62	Advertising	XX	
.71	Tel. & tel.	XX	
.87	Depreciation of autos	XX	
.12.	Administration		
.03	Clerical salaries		XX
.04	Fringe benefits on direct portion		XX
.50	Executive salaries	XX	
.53	Clerical salaries	XX	
.54	Fringe benefits on period portion	XX	
.58	Interest on Mortgage	XX	
.69	Protection service	XX	
.91	Dues & subscriptions	XX	

EXHIBIT 12-4: Partial Chart of Accounts (Separated for Period & Direct)

Chapter 13

Constructing the Machine-Hour Rate System

STEP 5: EXPENSE ASSIGNMENT WORKSHEET (EAW)

The Expense Assignment Worksheet, abbreviated to EAW, is the fifth and last piece of organized data required in the preparation of Machine-Hour Rates. The four previous steps organized and marshalled the mechanical, human and financial facilities of the manufacturing effort. From these four tabulations, we are now able to assign to each of the selected production centers the expenses required to build the individual MHR's.

The manning costs and the direct specific overhead charges (from the CCT and DCB), have been developed per hour for each production center and therefore require no statistical allocation. These costs are charged to each center by simple addition. However, the blanket direct overhead costs in the AB are not identified by production center until we perform statistical allocation procedures. This is the main purpose of the EAW.

The EAW shown on Exhibit 13-1 for the model company develops the unidentifiable direct overhead costs for each center (and also the fixed portion, as discussed earlier) by the use of logical and equitable relationships between the various expenses and the physical events which generated such expenses. These cause-and-effect factors for the model company are those established on the CFCS, viz:

. . Space Costs:	On the basis of Net Working Space
. . Power Costs:	" " " " HP-HRS
. . Machinery Costs:	" " " " Present Market Value
. . Indirect Costs:	" " " " Annual Assigned Hours
. . Total Non-Manufacturing Overhead Costs:	On the basis of Total Manufacturing Overhead Costs

Specific allocating instructions are:

1. Enter cost totals under Space, Power, Machinery, Indirect, Total Manufacturing Overhead and Non-Manufacturing Overhead from the Allocable Budget.

MARTIN & TUCKER, INC.
ENGINEERS

UNITS	PRODUCTION CENTER	MANUFACTURING COSTS: Space		Power		Machinery		Indirect		F. B.		TOTAL MFG. OVERHEAD		NON-MFG. OVERHEAD		TOTAL ANNUAL OVERHEAD COSTS		M.H.R. OVERHEAD ONLY		HOURLY		TOTAL M.H.R.	
		Period	Direct	Period	Direct	Period	Direct	Period	Direct	Period	Direct	Period	Direct	Period	Direct	Direct	Total	OOP	"Full"	DCB	CCT	OOP	"Full"
1	Extruder-Laminator	4591	209	1185	949	43,465	3528	4340	3064			53,581	7760	29,837	25,572	33,332	116,750	5.56	19.46	2.08	12.36	20.00	33.90
2	Gravure Creaser	15,305	695	1663	1330	30,722	6570	5787	4085			103,477	12,680	57,623	41,784	54,464	215,564	6.82	26.95	8.78	15.55	31.15	51.28
1	Mounter-Proofer	2678	122	—	—	373	30	1447	1021			4498	1173	2505	3866	5039	12,042	2.52	6.02	—	2.43	4.95	8.45
1	Molder	1530	70	125	100	1242	101	1447	1021			4344	1292	2419	4258	5550	12,313	2.78	6.16	.45	2.49	5.72	9.10
1	6c - 42" Flexo.	6887	313	565	452	18,629	1516	2894	2043			28,975	4324	16,135	14,250	18,574	63,684	4.64	15.92	1.70	10.36	16.70	27.98
1	5c - 30" Flexo.	4591	209	395	316	7451	607	2894	2043			15,331	3175	8527	10,463	13,638	37,506	3.41	9.38	1.05	9.85	14.31	20.28
2	Cameron S.-R.	3061	139	628	502	9935	809	5787	4085			19,411	5535	10,809	18,240	23,775	53,995	2.97	6.75	.79	4.90	8.66	12.44
1	Stanford S.-R.	1148	52	63	50	1490	121	1447	1021			4148	1244	2310	4100	5344	11,802	2.67	5.90	.42	5.14	8.23	11.46
3	Bag Machines	3061	139	282	226	7451	607	6510	4596			17,304	5568	9636	18,351	23,919	50,859	2.66	5.65	.70	7.98	11.34	14.33
1	Sheeter	1148	52	94	75	1242	101	1447	1021			3931	1249	2189	4,116	5365	11,485	2.68	5.74	.40	4.08	7.16	10.22
	Totals	44,000	2000	5000	4000	172,000	14,000	34,000	24,000	—	—	255,000	44,000	142,000	145,000	189,000	586,000						
	Allocation Factors	Occupancy		Hp.-hrs.		P.M.V.		ANN. HRS.		—				MFG. COSTS									
	Allocation Fractions	44000/5750	2000/5750	5000/1354M	4000/1354M	172,000/1385M	14,000/1385M	34,000/47,000	24,000/47,000	—	—			142,000/255,000	145,000/44,000								
	Allocation Ratios	7.6522	.34783	.00369	.00295	.12419	.10108	.7234	.51064	—	—			.556863	3.29545								

ALL F.B. ON C.C.T.

EXHIBIT 13-1: Expense Assignment Worksheet (EAW) (flexible packaging)

2. Select allocation factors (as previously listed), set up fractions, and calculate allocation ratios.
3. For each cost category, multiply allocation ratio by respective production center figure as per following examples:
   3.1 To get allocated Direct Space Cost for the Extruder-Laminator, multiply .34783 by 600 = $209.
   3.2 To get allocated Direct Machinery Cost for the 42" Flexographic Press, multiply .01011 by 150 = $1,516.
   3.3 To get allocated Direct Non-Manufacturing Cost for the sheeter, multiply 3.29545 by $1,249 = $4,116.
4. After the allocated amounts have been developed, crossfoot to get Total Annual Overhead Costs. Dividing by the AAH produces the allocated overhead portion of the MHR.
5. The hourly unallocated amounts from the DCB and CCT are then inserted and crossfooted with the previous hourly overhead to give the total MHR, as expressed in oop and "full."
6. The use of an electronic calculator having a constant is recommended. Allocation ratios should be carried out to several places (to insure "squaring the sheet"), after which each can be locked in with a multiplying constant to generate each allocated amount.

ALLOCATION FACTORS

Not all companies, even companies who are members of the same industry should necessarily use the same allocation factors for their AB's. Converters have individualistic ways of conducting business and have an economic personality of their own. For example, if repair and maintenance labor was not placed on a company's AB, they would not want to allocate this expense, together with others grouped under Manufacturing Costs: Machinery, if they were using Present Market Value as the factor. Obviously, this would assign to high valued machines a large portion of this expense which might not be justified in the case of a new machine requiring a small amount of this type of service.

In some instances, a factor can be a compounding of more than one of the previously-established allocation factors. For example, the Machinery category might be allocated by the compound factor: PMV-AAH. This would give weight to usage as well as values involved in facility expenses.

Where weight of product has a definite effect on an expense category, this might give rise to another type of factor. For example, in a corrugated paper container plant, warehousing and handling of large heavy kraft paper rolls is a major expense. Thus, a converter might elect to separate the warehousing expense from the Warehousing & Delivery category in the Non-Manufacturing portion of the AB and allocate its expenses using footage of finished flat corrugated board or roll tonnage expected to feed the corrugator during the year.

Again, cause-and-effect parameters should be studied closely before arriving at a decision. Most importantly, if enough effort has been applied to identify direct expenses with production centers or orders, there will be a minimum of expense remaining for statistical allocation on the AB. Under these circumstances, the varying cost effects from the use of different but logical factors will not have a great effect on the ultimate oop Machine-Hour Rates.

Chapter 14

Constructing the Machine-Hour Rate System

TECHNIQUES FOR HANDLING DIRECT-ORDER CHARGES WITH MHR

Direct-order charges, abbreviated to DOC, are those costs which are order related rather than facility related. These are costs which are incurred directly by the order. Facility-related costs ultimately find their way into the order via MHR's. Direct labor cost is directly related to a facility at a certain rate per hour. It then reaches the order by the amount of time required at each operation to produce the order.

Some people make the mistake of including DOC's in the MHR in order to simplify the estimating process. This distorts the estimated cost and leads inevitably to turning down good business and booking poor jobs. For example, some companies include "freight out" in MHR. This is like making apple sauce and then trying to convert the mixture back into whole apples, when the expense relates to common carrier charges. If an expense is incurred at a rate which is related to an order, like ton-miles, simply add it to the order in computing total oop order costs.

TYPICAL DIRECT-ORDER CHARGES

1. Direct Production Materials

This category of materials includes all raw materials which subsequently become converted into the finished order. Not only does it include the product's materials but it also includes packing materials and varying percentages of waste for each material. In an envelope converting company, DPM would cover paper, ink, adhesive, cartons, corrugated containers, tape, string, etc.

2. Direct Preparatory Materials

This type of material refers to items which have to be made especially for the job, even though it does not change with the quantity of the order.

In this sense then, preparatory materials are makeready materials. In a foundry, patterns and molds are made especially for the job and then discarded. In the envelope plant, these materials would include: rubber plates, art work, mechanicals, etc.

3. Freight Out, Common Carriers

As discussed previously.

4. Freight Out, Company Trucks

If the cost of local delivery on company-owned and operated trucks are included in the AB, limits can be set by which incremental costs are added for distant delivery.

5. Royalties

Where a company operates one or more pieces of equipment under another's license, this cost can be included in the MHR of the respective machine. However, where royalties are payable by the finished piece, then such costs are considered DOC's.

6. Direct Selling Costs

This is one of the most contentious areas in order cost estimating, even among those who use the modern contribution concepts. The logic is consistent: if these costs can be identified with orders, it will minimize the amount on the AB which becomes subject to arbitrary statistical allocation. More importantly, if these costs are identified with orders, we will have a truer measurement of contribution.

6.1 *Sales compensation:* Commission payments are clearly DOC's since most of these incentive plans are based on the sales revenue generated. (Such plans produce more profit for the company if the commissions are based on the contribution generated.[1]) However, when direct contact field salesmen are paid straight salaries, then the tendency would be to place those direct costs in the AB. This is not trying hard enough! *The method of payment does not determine the behavior of the cost!* Hopefully, straight salary carries a strong implication of volume. That is, management would not consider equitable to its company the continued payment of salary unless it was receiving a certain level of volume from the salesman. If this is the case, then where one salesman fails to give the company what it considers to be a "fair day's work," he will be replaced by another who can produce a satisfactory sales volume. Management should then equate salary against a "normal" volume level and *convert the salary into a sales commission* to get a proper oop cost and a rational contribution measurement. When such salaries are included in the AB because of the annual salary payment, each production center is loaded with a portion of these salaries, and orders passing through these centers in the estimating process wind up with too little or too much oop conversion cost depending on the nature of the order, who sold it, how it was sold, etc.

6.2 *T & E:* Travel and entertainment expenses is a group of expenses that can be directly identified with salesmen and their orders and should be converted to percentages and added to the basic compensation percentages in estimating order inquiries. It is the author's recommendation that T & E not be included as part of the sales compensation by increasing the commission rates. This does not encourage salesmen to spend the money, particularly in the entertainment area. In the proper managerial control of sales, the manager should equate sales volume generated against actual entertainment money to see whether the salesman is spending that type of money where he should. This in terms of the customer's annual volume being generated and the additional potential available from that account.[2] Again, the tendency is to place T & E in the AB. This causes similar distortions to those detailed in item 6.1.

---

1 See *Pricing for Higher Profit*, by Spencer A. Tucker, McGraw-Hill Book Co.

2 See *Successful Managerial Control by Ratio-Analysis* by Spencer A. Tucker, McGraw-Hill Book Co.

6.3 *Internal sales activity:* This is an area of cost which involves sales and/or customer service, sales correspondents, field expediters, and the like. If these are all directly related to the sales revenue, these salaries can be converted to a percentage of sales and included in the total oop cost.

6.4 *Order transactions:* Transaction cost is an item usually neglected in the cost-estimating area because it is regarded as negligible. In a recent study of a $4 million converting operation, this cost was pegged at $63 per order. Transaction cost has both constant and variable elements and starts at the cost-estimating and pricing point. Then it proceeds to encompass: credit checking, quoting, booking, acknowledging, order entry, scheduling, instructing, materials ordering, reporting, bills of lading, receipting, invoicing, collecting, etc. Several of these items are fixed in cost regardless of the size of the order, such as affixing a first-class stamp on the envelope containing the invoice to the customer. Such constant costs can be permanently added to the estimating form by pre-printing the amount. The variable portion can be added using one or more parameters in either dollar amount or percentage. In the author's experience, the dollar amount method is more equitable because of the lack of linearity between the transactional amount and the sales size of the order.

6.5 *Small order upcharges:* This is another area of indifference but this cost can be great enough to wipe out the contribution inherent in a small order. This technique is most effective when the converter is selling his services from an industry-wide price list. The approach is that it costs more per dollar of sales (or contribution) to process a small order. This is due to the various constant processing costs of makeready, setting up a machine, etc. While proper cost-estimating will show the full impact of makeready cost regardless of running time, small quantities on a pre-priced list may not for fear of having the price structure "out-of-line."

6.6 *Capital costs:* This pertains to the storing and holding of a customer's unpaid finished goods. In this instance it is the cost of short-term money financing of this inventory that's used. Strictly speaking, this would not be a DOC as far as any one customer's order is concerned, but would be charged to a customer's contribution log when measuring overall customer profitability. The cost is measured in dollar-months vs. interest rate. This technique is discussed in later chapters.

6.7 *Other items:* The following costs are not DOC's but are mentioned here for the sake of completeness:

6.7.1 *Separate P & L costs:* Often, a customer will pay separately for dies, tools, art work, etc. The revenue generated from these sales are offset by a corresponding oop cost and the contribution should be captured apart from conversion contribution.

6.7.2 *Baling waste:* The income here should also be related directly to the specific baling cost and the "profit" shown as either non-conversion income and expense or non-conversion profit.

6.7.3 *Wasted conversion:* This is the oop conversion cost which has been accrued on the raw material at the reject point. This is handled in the chapter on cost estimating.

6.7.4 *Anticipated rejects from customers:* ditto.

6.7.5 *Discount allowed:* This is an anticipated amount of revenue reduction and should enter into the basic contribution measurement. More on this later.

SECTION III

Model Machine-Hour Rate Constructions

Chapter 15

A Complete MHR System for Company A

Exhibits 15-1 through 15-5 show the basic schedules leading up to the final MHR's in the last exhibit. Company A is an envelope converter and the approach is similar to that shown on exhibits in Chapters 9 through 13.

The AB has been expanded to show examples of typical expense accounts normally handled on this budget. The format of the DCB is somewhat different to reflect Company A's specific operating characteristics.

And as in Chapter 13, the Manufacturing:Fringe Benefits column has not been used because all direct labor costs and related expenses have been handled on the CCT—a preferable procedure.

In the following chapters, the MHR treatment will be more sophisticated and will expand into new areas.

MARTIN & TUCKER, INC.
ENGINEERS

PRODUCTION CENTER	NO. OF UNITS	HP PER UNIT	FOR PRODUCTION CENTER			
			WORKING SPACE	PRESENT MACH'Y VALUE*	ANNUAL ASSIGNED HOURS	HP-HRS in M's
Maxson Sheeter	1	1.5	1200	$ 27,000	1500	2.25
Seybold Guillotine	1	5.0	300	7,000	1500	7.50
Hobbs Die-In-Head Press	1	5.0	300	7,000	2000	10.00
Automatic Die Presses	3	15.0	900	45,000	5000	75.00
W & D - 18Q Printer	2	6.5	400	26,000	6000	39.00
" - 18M "	3	6.5	600	45,000	10000	65.00
" - 31J "	1	6.0	200	15,000	4000	24.00
" - 10E "	1	8.0	100	26,000	2500	20.00
Window Cutters	2	.5	250	4,000	5000	2.50
Smithe - WR Std.	2	4.5	400	15,000	7000	27.50
" - WRW,cut,patch	2	8.5	500	40,000	7000	59.50
" - WRW, "kit"	2	14.0	500	64,000	7000	98.00
" - MO,cut,patch	1	13.5	400	47,000	4000	54.00
" - MO	1	10.0	400	33,000	4000	40.00
" - LO	1	13.5	400	38,000	3000	40.50
" - SO	1	3.0	200	20,000	2500	7.50
W & D-127GS,cut,patch	1	49.0	400	55,000	3000	147.00
" -126G	1	47.0	400	52,000	3000	141.00
TOTALS			7850	566,000	78000	860.25

* NOTE: Misc. non-prod. eqpt. = $64,000

EXHIBIT 15-1: Converting Facilities Classification Sheet (CFCS)

MARTIN & TUCKER, INC.
ENGINEERS

PRODUCTION CENTER	STD. CREW* PER UNIT	HOURLY BASE PAY PER UNIT	HOURLY N/C COST PER UNIT	HOURLY COST OF SUB-STD. PROD'Y	HOURLY O. T. & F.B.** PER UNIT	HOURLY CREW PAY PER UNIT
Maxson Sheeter	1.5	$3.47	$.09	$.35	$.87	$4.78
Seybold Guillotine	1.0	2.70	.13	.27	.68	3.78
Hobbs Die-in-Head	1.2	3.36	.17	.34	.84	4.71
Auto. Die Presses	1.2	3.36	.17	.34	.84	4.71
W & D - 18Q Printer	1.2	3.44	.35	.47	.86	5.12
" - 18M "	1.2	3.44	.35	.47	.86	5.12
" - 31J "	1.2	3.44	.35	.47	.86	5.12
" - 10E "	1.2	3.44	.35	.47	.86	5.12
Window Cutters	1.0	1.56	.08	.16	.39	2.19
Smithe-WR Std.	1.4	3.06	.16	.31	.77	4.30
" -WRW,cut,patch	1.5	3.35	.25	.34	.84	4.78
" -WRW, "kit"	1.5	3.35	.25	.34	.84	4.78
" -MO,cut,patch	1.7	4.01	.37	.60	1.00	5.98
" -MO	1.7	4.01	.37	.60	1.00	5.98
" -LO	1.7	4.01	.24	.60	1.00	5.85
" -SO	1.7	4.01	.21	.60	1.00	5.82
W &D-127GS,cut,patch	1.8	4.34	.57	.65	1.09	6.65
" -126G	1.8	4.34	.66	.65	1.09	6.74

* Includes fractional assignment of Foremen, Adjusters and/or Helpers.

**Includes holiday, vacation, rest periods, and cost of other time not worked, except non-chargeable time

EXHIBIT 15-2: Crew Composition Table (CCT)

MARTIN & TUCKER, INC.
ENGINEERS

EXPENSE CLASSIFICATION	PERIOD	DIRECT	TOTAL
MANUFACTURING COSTS:			
Space:			
Rent	30,000	---	30,000
Bldg. Maint.	5,000	---	5,000
Heat	6,000	2,000	8,000
Bldg. insur.	1,000	---	1,000
	42,000	2,000	44,000
Power:			
Electricity	5,000	30,000	35,000
Gas (on DCB)	---	---	---
	5,000	30,000	35,000
Machinery:			
Depreciation*	63,000	---	63,000
Price-level adj. (app.8%)	5,000	---	5,000
Mach'y insur.	2,000	---	2,000
General maint.	7,000	14,000	21,000
Shop supplies	---	4,000	4,000
Outside services	---	4,000	4,000
	77,000	22,000	99,000
Indirect Costs:			
Plant Manager	15,000	---	15,000
Timekeeper	5,000	---	5,000
Indirect labor (not on CCT)	6,000	18,000	24,000
Misc. supplies	1,000	---	1,000
Porter-Sweeper	4,000	---	4,000
Cost of n/c time (on CCT)	---	---	---
Subsidy cost (")	---	---	---
	31,000	18,000	49,000
TOTAL MFG. COST	$155,000	$72,000	$227,000

*on $630,000 eqpt. value

EXHIBIT 15-3: Allocable Budget (AB)

MARTIN & TUCKER, INC.
ENGINEERS

EXPENSE CLASSIFICATION	PERIOD	DIRECT	TOTAL
NON-MANUFACTURING COSTS:			
Shpg., Whse. & Del:			
Rent	15,000	---	15,000
Wages: Shpg. clerks	7,000	6,000	13,000
Truck Drivers	---	12,000	12,000
Depreciation on trucks	1,000	---	1,000
Truck Operating Costs	---	2,000	2,000
	23,000	20,000	43,000
Selling:			
Mgr's salary (no comm.)	20,000	---	20,000
Clerks' salaries	5,000	20,000	25,000
Auto expense	3,000	7,000	10,000
T & E Expense	4,000	21,000	25,000
Tel & Tel	4,000	---	4,000
Advertising	2,000	---	2,000
Salesmen's salaries (no comm.)	10,000	16,000	26,000
	48,000	64,000	112,000
Administrative:			
Officers' Salaries	70,000	---	70,000
Office expense	10,000	---	10,000
Controller's salary	15,000	---	15,000
Clerical salaries	15,000	40,000	55,000
Estimator	10,000	---	10,000
Rent (S & A)	5,000	---	5,000
Legal & audit	8,000	---	8,000
	133,000	40,000	173,000
Fringe Benefits:			
Payroll surcharges	6,000	1,000	7,000
OT PREM: S,W & D	---	2,000	2,000
Hospitalization insur.	2,000	---	2,000
Group insurance	3,000	---	3,000
Holiday & vaca. pay	2,000	3,000	5,000
Pension & Welfare	4,000	20,000	24,000
	17,000	26,000	43,000
TOTAL NON-MFG. COST	221,000	150,000	371,000
from p.1: TOTAL MFG.COST	155,000	72,000	227,000
ANN. BUDGETED OH COST	$376,000	$222,000	$598,000

EXHIBIT 15-3 (continued)

MARTIN & TUCKER, INC.
ENGINEERS

PRODUCTION CENTER	SPECIFIC REPAIRS & MAINT.	SPECIFIC SUPPLIES & GAS*	TOTAL DIRECT CHARGES	ANNUAL ASSIGNED HOURS	D.C. PER HOUR
Maxson Sheeter	$ 310	$ 80	$ 390	1500	$ .26
Seybold Guillotine	30	110	140	1500	.09
Hobbs Die-in-Head Press	110	40	150	2000	.08
Automatic Die Presses	--	--	--	5000	--
W & D - 18 Q Printer	410	170	580	6000	.10
" - 18 M "	140	120	260	10000	.03
" - 31 J "	310	160	470	4000	.12
" - 10 E "	470	240	710	2500	.28
Window-Cutters	--	--	--	5000	--
Smithe - WR - Std.	2,610	740	3,350	7000	.48
" - WRW, cut, patch	1,810	830*	2,640	7000	.38
" - WRW, "Kit"	720	1,100	1,820	7000	.26
" - MO, cut, patch	1,020	1,400	2,420	4000	.61
" - MO	960	1,160	2,120	4000	.53
" - LO	620	1,240	1,860	3000	.62
" - SO	480	480*	960	2500	.38
W & D - 127GS, cut, patch	1,780	1,440	3,220	3000	1.07
W & D - 126 G	1,320	1,300	2,620	3000	.87
		TOTAL	$23,710		

EXHIBIT 15-4: Direct-Charge Budget (DCB)

MARTIN & TUCKER, INC.
ENGINEERS

UNITS	PRODUCTION CENTER	MANUFACTURING COSTS: Space		Power		Machinery		Indirect		F. B.		TOTAL MFG. OVERHEAD		NON-MFG. OVERHEAD		TOTAL ANNUAL OVERHEAD COSTS		M.H.R. OVERHEAD ONLY		HOURLY		TOTAL M.H.R.	
		Period	Direct	Period	Direct	Period	Direct	Period	Direct	Period	Direct	Period	Direct	Period	Direct	Direct	Total	OOP	"Full"	DCB	CCT	OOP	"Full"
1	Sheeter	6420	306	13	78	3673	1049	596	346			10,702	1779	15,259	3706	5485	31,446	3.66	20.96	.26	4.78	8.70	26.00
1	Guillotine	1605	76	44	262	952	272	596	346			3197	956	4558	1992	2948	10,703	1.97	7.14	.09	3.78	5.84	11.01
1	Die-in-Head	1605	76	58	349	952	272	795	462			3410	1159	4862	2415	3574	11,846	1.79	5.92	.08	4.71	6.58	10.71
3	Auto. die presses	4818	229	436	2616	6122	1749	1987	1154			13,363	5748	19,053	11,975	17,723	50,139	3.54	10.03	—	4.71	8.25	14.74
2	18 Q	2140	102	227	1360	3537	1011	2385	1385			8,289	3858	11,818	8,037	11,895	32,002	1.98	5.33	.10	5.12	7.20	10.55
3	18 M	3210	153	378	2267	6122	1749	3974	2306			13,677	6475	19,501	13,489	19,964	53,142	2.00	5.31	.03	5.12	7.15	10.48
1	31 J	1070	51	139	837	2041	583	1590	923			4840	2394	6901	4987	7,381	19,122	1.85	4.78	.12	5.12	7.09	10.02
1	10E	535	25	116	697	3537	1011	994	577			5182	2310	7388	4812	7122	19,692	2.85	7.88	.28	5.12	8.25	13.28
2	Window cutters	1338	64	15	87	544	155	1987	1154			3884	1460	5538	3042	4502	13,924	.90	2.78	—	2.19	3.09	4.97
2	WR-STD	2140	102	160	961	2041	583	2782	1615	ALL F.B.	ON C.C.T.	7123	3261	10,156	6794	10,055	27,334	1.44	3.90	.48	4.30	6.22	8.68
2	WRW, cut + patch	2675	127	346	2075	5442	1555	2782	1615			11,245	5372	16,033	11,191	16,563	43,841	2.37	6.26	.38	4.78	7.53	11.42
2	WRW - "Kit"	2675	127	570	3420	8707	2488	2782	1615			14,734	7650	21,008	15,937	23,587	59,329	3.37	8.48	.26	4.78	8.41	13.52
1	MO, cut + patch	2140	102	314	1883	6394	1827	1590	923			10,438	4735	14,883	9864	14,599	39,920	3.65	9.98	.61	5.98	10.24	16.57
1	MO	2140	102	232	1395	4489	1283	1590	923			8451	3703	12,049	7714	11,417	31,917	2.85	7.98	.52	5.98	9.36	14.49
1	LO	2140	102	235	1412	5170	1477	1192	692			8737	3683	12,457	7673	11,356	32,550	3.79	10.85	.62	5.85	10.26	17.32
1	SO	1070	51	43	262	2721	777	994	577			4828	1667	6884	3473	5,140	16,852	2.06	6.74	.28	5.82	8.26	12.94
1	127GS, cut + patch	2140	102	854	5126	7482	2138	1192	692			11668	8058	16,636	16,787	24,845	53,149	8.28	17.72	1.07	6.65	16.00	25.42
1	126G	2140	102	819	4917	7074	2021	1192	692			11,225	7732	16,005	16,108	23,840	51,070	7.95	17.02	.87	6.74	15.56	24.63
	Totals	42,000	2,000	5,000	30,000	77,000	22,000	31,000	18,000	—	—	155,000	72,000	221,000	150,000	222,000	598,000						
	Allocation Factors	OCCUPANCY		HP-HRS		P.H.V.		ANN. HRS.		—				TOTAL MFG.									
	Allocation Fractions	42,000/7,850	2,000/7,850	5,000/860.25	30,000/860.25	77,000/566,000	22,000/566,000	31,000/78,000	18,000/78,000	—	—			221,000/155,000	150,000/72,000								
	Allocation Ratios	5.35032	.2548	5.8122	34.8735	.13604	.03887	.39743	.23077	—	—			1.4258	2.0833								

EXHIBIT 15-5: Expense Assignment Worksheet (EAW) (envelope)

Chapter 16

A Complete MHR System for Company B

Exhibits 16-1 through 16-6 comprise the MHR construction for Company B which is in the folding-carton converting business. The approach here is different from previous MHR constructions.

CFCS

Two refinements have been added to this schedule:

1. The division of annual hours between Assigned Clock and Chargeable Clock.
2. The Run Ratio, or the ratio of running time to total activity time.

For the first, the reader is referred to paragraph 6 of Chapter 9 to understand the progression from Annual Assigned Clock Hours to Annual Chargeable Clock Hours and finally to Annual Chargeable Standard Hours. In the construction of Company B's MHR, Exhibit 16-5 shows the derivation of these latter hours. However, on the CFCS, we require the chargeable clock hours to use as the basis of electrical energy consumption. Subsidy, the difference between chargeable clock and chargeable standard hours, has no effect on the electrical cost. That is, the clock hour consumes the energy regardless of the productivity level being attained.

The second addition to this sheet provides for the fact that all of the chargeable clock hours are not *run* hours, that is, a portion of those activity hours are involved in making the facility ready to run. The .75 ratio for the Harris 2-color press means that 75% of the 1,896 hours is the time the press is expected to run and consume electrical energy. Therefore, the horsepower-hours are .75 × 1,896 x 9.3 = 13.23M.

CCT

This schedule also shows a different presentation with respect to the standard crew. Whole and fractional assignment of workers are shown for each production center. And the Direct Labor Budget, for profit planning reasons (to be shown in a later chapter) uses the annual chargeable standard hours.

The gross pay rate includes all fringe benefits, non-chargeable time, subsidy costs, etc., which derives from workers' Gross Hourly Cost Sheets. This refinement is shown for Company D in Chapter 18.

DCB

On this improved schedule, all direct facility costs are expressed in annual totals and then divided by the annual chargeable standard hours to reduce them to an hourly basis for final rate construction. By the use of this technique, the adjustment for subsidy time is automatically considered. That is, since annual electrical consumption is expressed by the chargeable *clock* hour, dividing by chargeable *standard* hours adjusts the electrical cost per hour per unit to a higher level, as explained in paragraph 6 of Chapter 11. Again, the chargeable standard hours are taken from Exhibit 16-5.

AB

Similar to previous AB's.

DERIVATION OF ANNUAL CHARGEABLE STANDARD HOURS

On Exhibit 16-5, the progression from assigned clock to chargeable standard hours is given. As will be seen in the following MHR for Company D, these data are taken from workers' Gross Hourly Cost Sheets.

EAW

This worksheet has been streamlined to list the direct costs only. This can usually be accomplished after a company new to the direct-cost approach is convinced of the uselessness and dangers of "full"-cost rates.

MARTIN & TUCKER, INC.
ENGINEERS

Production Center	NO. OF UNITS	Hp. per Unit	FOR PRODUCTION CENTER					
			Working Space Occup. sq. ft.	Present Market Value in M's	ANNUAL HRS.*		RUN RATIO**	ANNUAL Hp-hrs. in M's
					ASSGN'D CLOCK	CHARG'LE CLOCK		
Die Making	1	1.0	483	6.0	2,500	2,120	1	2.12
Plate Making	1	5.5	462	3.0	500	456	1	.46
Harris 2-Color	1	9.3	625	30.0	2,120	1,896	.75	13.23
Miehle 1-Color	1	20.5	626	14.5	550	494	.75	7.60
0/2 Print/Cut	1	17.0	1,484	26.3	1,650	1,482	.70	17.64
Chandler & Price	5	1.2	1,840	5.0	8,400	6,664	.85	6.80
Harris 2-Color	2	22.9	2,592	71.0	4,240	3,822	.80	70.02
Harris 1-Color	1	7.6	419	10.3	2,120	1,956	.80	11.89
Heidelberg Cutter	1	13.0	957	40.0	2,100	1,836	.85	20.29
Miehle Cutter	1	7.6	957	12.8	2,120	1,936	.80	11.77
Miehle Cutter 5/0	1	12.3	1,534	19.5	525	469	.75	4.33
Miehle Cutter	1	10.4	1,321	18.0	1,675	1,407	.70	10.24
Bobst Cutter	1	19.6	3,034	141.4	2,240	2,056	.75	30.22
Consolidated Cutter	1	16.6	1,131	63.9	2,240	1,975	.80	26.23
Air Strip	4	3.4	1,023	1.7	4,320	3,952	1	13.44
Staude Gluer	1	15.0	1,162	65.5	2,140	1,916	.90	25.86
F/Z Right Angle Gluer	2	15.0	5,320	130.0	4,280	3,872	.90	52.72
F/G Gluer	1	16.0	1,660	50.0	2,140	1,916	.90	27.59
Hand Work (Stripping)	3	--	500	--	6,360	4,970	1	--
TOTALS	--	--	27,130	708.9	52,200	45,195	--	352.45

* See Exhibit 16-5
** Ratio of running time to total activity time.

EXHIBIT 16-1: Converting Facilities Classification Sheet (CFCS)

MARTIN & TUCKER, INC.
ENGINEERS

Production Center	No. of Units	Std. Crew Per Unit Per Shift	HOURLY Gross Pay Rate	HOURLY Gross Pay Ext'd	HOURLY Crew Pay Per Unit Per Shift*	ANNUAL CHARGEABLE STD. HOURS**	Direct Labor Budget
Die Making	1	1.00			8.92	1,590	$14,183
Operator		.8566	9.21	7.89			
Supervisor		.1434	7.18	1.03			
Plate Making	1	1.00			4.80	365	1,752
Operator		.90	4.42	3.98			
Supervisor		.10	8.24	.82			
Harris 2-Color (8-T)	1	1.25			9.52	1,517	14,442
Operator		1.00	7.14	7.14			
Supervisor		.25	8.24	2.06			
Guillotine (partial)				.32			
Miehle 1-Color	1	1.03			6.99	395	2,761
Operator		1.00	6.69	6.69			
Supervisor		.03	8.24	.25			
Guillotine (partial)				.05			
Miehle Prt/Cut	1	1.15			8.09	1,186	9,595
Operator		1.00	6.69	6.69			
Supervisor		.15	8.24	1.24			
Guillotine (partial)				.16			
Chandler & Price	5	1.01			5.16	5,998	30,950
Operator		1.00	5.08	5.08			
Supervisor		.01	8.24	.08			
Harris 2-C	2	2.70			16.23	3,058	49,631
Operator		1.00	7.17	7.17			
Helper		1.00	5.14	5.14			
Supervisor		.20	8.24	1.65			
Mtls. Hdlr.		.50	3.15	1.58			
Guillotine (partial)				.69			
Harris 1-Color	1	1.12			5.46	1,565	8,545
Operator		1.00	4.37	4.37			
Supervisor		.12	8.24	.99			
Guillotine (partial)				.10			

* from Gross Hourly Cost Sheets
** from Exhibit 16-5

EXHIBIT 16-2: Crew Composition Table (CCT)

MARTIN & TUCKER, INC.
ENGINEERS

Production Center	No. of Units	Std. Crew Per Unit Per Shift	HOURLY Gross Pay Rate	HOURLY Gross Pay Ext'd	HOURLY Crew Pay Per Unit Per Shift*	ANNUAL CHARGEABLE STD. HOURS**	Direct Labor Budget
Heidelberg Cutter	1	2.20			11.14	1,469	$16,365
Operator		1.00	5.37	5.37			
Stripper		1.00	3.59	3.59			
Supervisor		.20	7.93	1.59			
Guillotine (partial)				.59			
Miehle Cutter	1	1.35			7.93	1,549	12,284
Operator		1.00	4.88	4.88			
Supervisor		.35	7.93	2.78			
Guillotine (partial)				.27			
Miehle Cutter 5/0	1	1.10			5.90	375	2,213
Operator		1.00	5.06	5.06			
Supervisor		.10	7.93	.79			
Guillotine (partial)				.05			
Miehle Cutter	1	1.35			8.00	1,126	9,008
Operator		1.00	5.06	5.06			
Supervisor		.35	7.93	2.78			
Guillotine (partial)				.16			
Bobst Cutter	1	2.25			15.95	1,645	26,238
Operator		1.00	7.07	7.07			
Helper		1.00	5.29	5.29			
Supervisor		.25	8.19	2.05			
Guillotine (partial)				1.54			
Consol. Cutter	1	1.25			8.91	1,580	14,078
Operator		1.00	6.17	6.17			
Supervisor		.25	8.19	2.05			
Guillotine (partial				.69			
Air Stripping	4	1.30			6.27	3,162	19,826
Operator		1.00	3.81	3.81			
Supervisor		.30	8.19	2.46			
Handwork	3	1.20			5.84	4,970	29,025
Operator		1.00	4.20	4.20			
Supervisor		.20	8.19	1.64			

* from Gross Hourly Cost Sheets

** from Exhibit 16-5

EXHIBIT 16-2 (continued)

MARTIN & TUCKER, INC.
ENGINEERS

Production Center	No. of Units	Std. Crew Per Unit Per Shift	HOURLY Gross Pay Rate	HOURLY Gross Pay Ext'd	HOURLY Crew Pay Per Unit Per Shift*	ANNUAL CHARGEABLE STD. HOURS**	Direct Labor Budget
Staude Gluer	1	3.75			18.91	1,533	$28,989
Operator		1.00	6.61	6.61			
Helper		2.00	4.35	8.70			
Supervisor		.15	8.10	1.22			
Mtls. Hdlr.		.60	3.95	2.38			
FZ Right Angle	2	3.85			18.09	3,098	56,043
Operator		1.00	4.72	4.72			
Helper		2.00	4.20	8.40			
Supervisor		.35	8.10	2.84			
Mtls. Hdlr.		.50	4.26	2.13			
FG Gluer	1	3.75			18.29	1,533	28,039
Operator		1.00	6.53	6.53			
Helper		2.00	4.08	8.16			
Supervisor		.15	8.10	1.22			
Mtls. Hdlr.		.60	3.95	2.38			

TOTAL $373,967

* from Gross Hourly Cost Sheets
** from Exhibit 16-5

EXHIBIT 16-2 (continued)

MARTIN & TUCKER, INC.
ENGINEERS

Production Center	ANNUAL SPECIFIC Supplies, Parts & Outside Service (1)	ANNUAL SPECIFIC Inside Repairs & Mainte-nance (2)	ANNUAL ELEC. ENERGY* Hp-Hrs in M's	ANNUAL ELEC. ENERGY* KW-Hrs in M's	ANNUAL ELEC. ENERGY* Ann. Cost (3)	Annual Direct Ch'ges (1)+(2) + (3)	Annual Charg'le Std. Hours**	Direct Charges per Charg'le Std. Hour
Die Making	$ 400	$100	2.12	1.57	$ 47	$ 547	$1,590	$ .34
Plate Making	800	100	.46	.34	10	910	365	2.49
Harris 2-C	1,500	300	13.23	9.79	294	2,094	1,517	1.38
Miehle 1-C	300	200	7.60	5.62	169	669	395	1.69
0/2 Print/Cut	900	400	17.64	13.05	392	1,692	1,186	1.43
Chandler & Price	600	200	6.80	5.03	151	951	5,998	.16
Harris 2-C	8,000	600	70.02	51.81	1,554	10,154	3,058	3.32
Harris 1-C	400	200	11.89	8.80	264	864	1,565	.55
Heidelb'g Cut.	400	300	20.29	15.01	450	1,150	1,469	.78
Miehle Cut.	800	200	11.77	8.71	261	1,261	1,549	.81
Miehle 5/0 Cut	300	100	4.33	3.20	96	496	375	1.32
Miehle Cut.	600	200	10.24	7.57	227	1,027	1,126	.91
Bobst Cutter	3,000	800	30.22	22.36	671	4,471	1,645	2.72
Consol. Cutter	1,300	500	26.23	19.41	582	2,382	1,580	1.51
Air Strip	150	150	13.44	9.94	298	598	3,162	.19
Staude Gluer	1,200	500	25.86	19.14	574	2,274	1,533	1.48
FZ R/A Gluers	700	500	52.72	39.01	1,170	2,370	3,098	.77
FZ Gluer	150	50	27.59	20.42	613	813	1,533	.53
Hand Work	--	--	--	--	--	--	4,970	--
TOTALS	21,500.	5,400	352.45	260.78	7,823	34,723	37,714	

* at the rate of $.025 per KW-Hr.
** from Exhibit 16-5

EXHIBIT 16-3: Direct-Charge Budget (DCB)

MARTIN & TUCKER, INC.
ENGINEERS

Projected Annual Overhead Expenses	Period	Direct	Total
MANUFACTURING COSTS:			
Space:			
Rent	$ 31,440		$ 31,440
Amortization	3,960		3,960
Water, Fuel	1,908	3,480	5,388
Bldg. Maintenance	1,008	960	1,968
Real Estate Taxes & Insurance	7,500		7,500
SUB.	45,816	4,440	50,256
Power:			
Electricity	2,160	-0-	2,160
SUB.	2,160	-0-	2,160
Machinery:			
Depreciation	48,240		48,240
Rent-Mach. & Equip.	45,480		45,480
Gen'l. Maintenance	5,520	5,520	11,040
Personal Property Taxes	2,400	4,440	6,840
Insurance	1,740		1,740
Price Level Adj.	5,796		5,796
SUB.	109,176	9,960	119,136
Indirect:			
Plant Manager	22,200		22,200
Assist. Plant Manager	7,860	7,860	15,720
Maintenance Sup.	3,000		3,000
Salvage & Repair		3,636	3,636
Janitorial	5,676	5,664	11,340
Factory Clerical		13,224	13,224
Other, Incl. Facil. Variance & OSHA	2,520	28,680	31,200
Personnel, not incl. on C.C.T.	3,132	32,820	35,952
SUB.	44,388	91,884	136,272
TOTAL MFG. COST	$201,540	$106,284	$307,824

EXHIBIT 16-4: Allocable Budget (AB)

MARTIN & TUCKER, INC.
ENGINEERS

Projected Annual Overhead Expenses	Period	Direct	Total
NON-MANUFACTURING COSTS:			
Whse. & Del:			
Ship., Supplies, etc.		6,912	6,912
Maint. Bldg. & Equip.	7,920		7,920
Receiving & Whse. Labor	9,944	12,256	22,200
Depreciation Equip. & Insur.	3,600		3,600
Rent Bldg. & Equip.	57,624		57,624
Light,Power,Water,&Fuel (not on DCB)	156	4,704	4,860
Property Taxes & R.E. Taxes	13,800	6,240	20,040
Shipping Labor	13,150	28,200	41,400
SUB.	106,194	58,362	164,556
Selling:			
Repairs & Depreciation (Plane&Cars)	5,124	11,796	16,920
Insurance	1,200	1,800	3,000
Sales Manager (25%)	5,556		5,556
President (40%)	38,208		38,208
Estimators (2)	16,500	8,520	25,020
Tel. & Tel.	1,632	6,528	8,160
General Mgr. (50%)	39,600		39,600
Professional Services	7,500		7,500
Gas, Oil, Tires, & Misc.	3,600		3,600
Sample Making		12,096	12,096
SUB.	118,920	40,740	159,660
Administrative:			
Misc. Direct		17,028	17,028
Property & R.E. Taxes	5,760		5,760
Depreciation & Rent	28,596		28,596
Interest, Life Ins., Donations	46,440	1,440	47,880
Light, Power, & Fuel		2,412	2,412
Repair, Maintenance & Janit.	9,432	924	10,356
Office, Salaries	64,800	39,540	104,340
President (20%)	19,104		19,104
Gen'l Mgr. (50%)	39,600		39,600
SUB.	213,732	61,344	275,076
Fringe Benefits:			
Whse, & Del.	8,052	13,692	21,744
Selling	3,900	7,416	11,316
G & A	18,648	7,056	25,704
TOTAL NON-MFG. COST	$469,446	$188,610	$657,456
from p. 1: TOTAL MFG. COST	201,540	106,284	307,824
ANNUAL BUDGETED OVERHEAD COST	$670,986	$294,894	$965,880

EXHIBIT 16-4 (continued)

MARTIN & TUCKER, INC.
ENGINEERS

PRODUCTION CENTER	NO. OF UNITS	ANNUAL CLOCK		% STD. SUBS'DY*	ANNUAL CHARGEABLE STD. HOURS
		ASSGN'D CLOCK HOURS	CHARGEABLE HOURS		
Die Making	1	2,500	2,120	25	1,590
Plate Making	1	500	456	20	365
Harris 2-Color	1	2,120	1,896	20	1,517
Miehle 1-Color	1	550	494	20	395
0/2 Miehle Cut/Crease	1	1,650	1,482	20	1,186
Chandler & Price	5	8,400	6,664	10	5,998
Harris 2-Color	2	4,240	3,822	20	3,058
Harris 1-Color	1	2,120	1,956	20	1,565
Heidelberg Cutter	1	2,100	1,836	20	1,469
Miehle Cutter	1	2,120	1,936	20	1,549
Miehle Cutter 5/0	1	525	469	20	375
Miehle Cutter	1	1,675	1,407	20	1,126
Bobst Cutter	1	2,240	2,056	20	1,645
Consolidated Cutter	1	2,240	1,975	20	1,580
Air Strip	4	4,320	3,952	20	3,162
Staude Gluer	1	2,140	1,916	20	1,533
F/Z Right Angle Gluers	2	4,280	3,872	20	3,098
F/G Gluer	1	2,140	1,916	20	1,533
Handwork (Stripping)	3	6,360	4,970	0	4,970
TOTALS	--	52,220	45,195	--	37,714

* from Gross Hourly Cost Sheets

EXHIBIT 16-5: Derivation of Annual CHARGEABLE STANDARD Hours

MARTIN & TUCKER, INC.
ENGINEERS

UNITS	Production Center	DIRECT MFG OVERHEAD COST				DIRECT NON-MFG. O.H.	TOTAL DIRECT O.H. COST	Ann. Chgbl STD. Hrs.	Machine-Hour Rate			
		Space	Machy	Indir	Total				OOP O.H.	DCB	CCT	TOTAL OOP
1	Die Making	79	84	3874	4037	7164	11,201	1,590	7.04	.34	8.92	16.30
1	Plate Making	76	42	889	1007	1787	2794	365	7.65	2.49	4.80	14.94
1	Harris 7/c	102	421	3695	4218	7485	11,703	1517	7.71	1.38	9.52	18.61
1	Miehle 7/c	102	204	962	1268	2250	3518	395	8.91	1.69	6.99	17.59
1	O/2 Prt/Cut	243	370	2889	3502	6215	9717	1186	8.19	1.43	8.09	17.71
5	Chandler & Price	301	70	14,613	14,984	26,590	41,574	5998	6.93	.16	5.16	12.25
2	Harris 2/c	424	997	7,450	8871	15,742	24,613	3058	8.05	3.32	16.23	27.60
1	Harris 1/c	69	145	3813	4027	7146	11,173	1565	7.14	.55	5.46	13.15
1	Heidelberg C.	157	562	3579	4298	7627	11,925	1469	8.12	.78	11.14	20.04
1	Miehle C.	157	180	3774	4111	7295	11,406	1549	7.36	.81	7.93	16.10
1	Miehle C. 5/0	251	274	914	1439	2554	3993	375	10.65	1.32	5.90	17.87
1	Miehle C.	216	253	2743	3212	5700	8912	1126	7.91	.91	8.00	16.82
1	Babat C.	497	1987	4008	6492	11,520	18,012	1645	10.95	2.72	15.95	29.62
1	Consol. C.	185	898	3849	4932	8,752	13,684	1580	8.66	1.51	8.91	19.08
4	Air Strip	167	24	7704	7895	14,010	21,905	3162	6.93	.19	6.27	13.39
1	Staude Gluer	190	920	3735	4845	8,598	13,443	1533	8.77	1.48	18.91	29.16
2	F2 Rt L Gl.	871	1826	7548	10,245	18,180	28,425	3,098	9.18	.77	18.09	28.04
1	FG. Gluer	272	702	3735	4709	8356	13,065	1533	8.52	.53	18.29	27.34
3	Handwork	82	0	12109	12,191	21,634	33,825	4970	6.81	—	5.84	12.65

Space	Machy	Indir	Total	Direct Non-Mfg. O.H.	Total Direct O.H. Cost	
4440	9960	91,884	106,284	188,610	294,894	AB Totals
OCCUP.	PMV	STD CH. HRS	—	MFG.	—	Allocation Factors
4440 / 27,130	9960 / 708.9	91884 / 37714	— / —	188610 / 106284	— / —	Allocation Fractions
.16366	14.04994	2.43634	—	1.77458	—	Allocation Ratios

EXHIBIT 16-6: Expense Assignment Worksheet (EAW) (folding carton)

Chapter 17

A Complete MHR System for Company C

Company C is a converter which produces labels from a web-fed operation. The variety of paper types, adhesives, coatings, label designs, colors, printing processes et al is broad. The effect of the interrelationships of these variables present to the profit planner an almost infinite number of differences. These manifest themselves in a wide range of speeds, ink coverages, product sizes, etc. Add to that a range of order sizes from the very small to enormous, and a selling price level starting at around $2.50 per M, and it will impress on the reader the need for a high degree of accuracy and the absolute necessity of capturing every cost no matter how seemingly small.

Exhibits 17-1 through 17-7 follow the formats of the previous Company B. An exception is Exhibit 17-5 which explains some of the allocations between those listed on the AB and those charged elsewhere.

However, Exhibits 17-8 through 17-14 are concerned solely with Direct-Order Charges (DOC's), which are vital elements in obtaining proper gross oop order costs. The reader is referred to Chapter 14 to review the concepts which support this approach. No estimating of order inquiries can take place before developing this crucial information.

PREPARING FOR ESTIMATING

Once the EAW is complete and MHR's available, another review of the AB should be made to insure that every expense which can be identified with an order or a producing facility has been excluded. These budget exclusions are included in:

1. The Crew Composition Table—facility related.
2. The Direct-Charge Budget—facility related.
3. The Direct-Order Charges—order related.
4. Non-conversion Expenses—related to the overall results.

The last two have been covered in Chapter 14, but now it is necessary to show how some of the

DOC's are developed so that these cost factors can be attributed and charged directly to the order being estimated. The poorer alternative is to include them as some sort of markup on materials, or worse yet, include them in the AB. Either of these alternatives will obscure the true measurement of gross oop order cost and subsequent measurements of contribution, et al.

DIRECT PREPARATORY MATERIALS (DOC)

1. *Printing Plates:* Exhibit 17-8 shows how the data are developed. The costs to be charged to the order for this work is shown under paragraph 11. For example, in estimating metal plate cost for an order for labels to be run 12 up, one color, size 1.875" × 3.5", would require the following calculation: cost of plate per square inch × number of square inches of label × the number of plates to be used per impression (number up) × the number of colors. This would be equal to $.1592 (from para. 11) × 6.56 × 12 × 1 = $12.54.

2. *Sales Commissions & Expenses:* Exhibit 17-9 shows how these costs are developed. Paragraph 4 gives the 5 different markups to reflect the specific sales costs of the transaction. Using some average percentage markup as a convenience will distort measurement of expected order contribution.

3. *Art Department Costs:* Exhibit 17-10 develops the DOC additives for the various operations performed in the Art Department. As can be seen in paragraph 9, the costs vary by a low-to-high multiple of 4. This would invalidate the use of any flat dollar amount for this preparatory effort.

DIRECT PRODUCTION MATERIALS (DOC)

1. *Imprint Ink:* This cost is established to transfer to the customer ink costs which he will use in the client's imprinting machines. Exhibit 17-11 shows how the dilution calculation is made.

2. *Printing Ink:* Exhibit 17-12 shows how to calculate costs of production inks consumed during the running of the job. In the absence of a mileage chart, which is the most accurate method of estimating the ink cost, this exhibit establishes that the consumption of ink is largely a function of running time. Thus, on an order to be printed on a flexographic press requiring 10 running hours, the ink cost on the order is 10 × $4.87 or $48.70.

3. *Delivery Charges:* Exhibit 17-13 shows the method of charging customers for delivery and shipping containers. The fact that these are separately billed items does not preclude their quantification.

SUMMARY

Exhibit 17-14 summarizes the six categories of DOC's and is made available to the estimator in chart form. It is presented here to allow the reader to trace the basic data.

MARTIN & TUCKER, INC.
ENGINEERS

Production Center	NO. OF UNITS	Hp. per Unit	FOR PRODUCTION CENTER					
			Working Space Occup. sq. ft.	Present Market Value in M's	ANNUAL HRS.***		RUN RATIO**	ANNUAL Hp-hrs. in M's *
					ASSGN'D CLOCK	CHARG'LE CLOCK		
New Era 9x12 L.P. 3-C	5	13.79	2,475	140.0	20,000	17,600	.75	182
New Era 9x12 L.P. 3-C	2	12.96	960	66.0	8,000	7,040	.75	68
New Era 9x12 L.P. 3-C	1	13.79	480	28.0	4,000	3,520	.65	32
New Era 9x12 L.P. 3-C	1	14.66	480	33.0	4,000	3,520	.75	39
New Era 9x12 L.P. 4-C	2	14.92	1,030	66.0	8,000	7,040	.80	84
New Era 9x12 L.P. 5-C	1	14.17	520	38.0	4,000	3,520	.75	37
New Era 9x12 L.P. 5-C	1	14.05	520	38.0	4,000	3,520	.70	35
New Era 9x12 L.P. 5-C	1	15.14	530	38.0	4,000	3,520	.80	43
Nilsaton Flexo 22",4-C	2	31.40	1,800	100.0	2,800	2,240	.70	49
Int'l Flexo 9",5-C	2	17.90	1,800	140.0	5,200	4,420	.80	63
Roto Gravure 14",5-C	1	71.70	1,300	70.0	3,400	2,686	.80	154
Roto Gravure 20",7-C	1	144.00	2,000	100.0	600	438	.70	44
Coater/Slit. 21"/26"	1	145.05	1,050	63.0	4,000	3,600	.80	420
Coater 14½"	1	57.75	550	40.0	2,000	1,800	.85	88
Coater 21"	1	64.15	670	50.0	4,000	3,600	.70	162
Coater 27"	1	57.43	880	60.0	4,000	3,600	.80	165
Arrow Slitter 36"	1	12.25	150	15.0	4,000	3,440	.70	29
Arrow Slitter 18 3/4"	1	8.47	100	10.0	1,500	1,290	.90	10
Champl. Punch 15"	1	29.14	450	40.0	2,000	1,780	.90	47
Champl. Punch 21"	3	23.87	1,650	150.0	8,000	7,120	.80	136
Wadson Punch 27 3/4"	1	14.78	300	25.0	500	445	.90	6
Beck Sheeter	1	6.82	315	10.0	800	640	.70	3
Lawson Cutter	1	3.50	200	12.0	1,200	1,080	.90	3
Rewinders	4	.63	240	7.0	3,400	2,890	1	2
Cut & Stack	3	.33	150	3.0	600	510	1	.2
TOTALS			20,600	1,342.0	104,000	90,859		1,901.2

* This column represents the Hp-Hours (electricity consumption) during the chargeable hours.
** Ratio of running time to total activity time.
*** See Exhibit 17-6

EXHIBIT 17-1: Converting Facilities Classification Sheet (CFCS)

MARTIN & TUCKER, INC.
ENGINEERS

Production Center	No. of Units	Std. Crew Per Unit Per Shift	HOURLY Gross Pay Rate	HOURLY Gross Pay Ext'd	HOURLY Crew Pay Per Unit Per Shift	ANNUAL CHARGEABLE STD. HOURS	Direct Labor Budget
New Era, Press 3-C	5			9.28	9.28	14,080	$130,662
Operator		1.00	8.33	8.33			
Leadman		.07	6.27	.45			
Foreman		.07	7.06	.50			
New Era, Press 3-C	2			9.47	9.47	5,632	53,335
Operator		1.00	8.52	8.52			
Leadman		.07	6.27	.45			
Foreman		.07	7.06	.50			
New Era, Press 3-C	1			9.47	9.47	2,816	26,668
Operator		1.00	8.52	8.52			
Leadman		.07	6.27	.45			
Foreman		.07	7.06	.50			
New Era, Press 3-C	1			9.42	9.42	2,816	26,527
Operator		1.00	8.47	8.47			
Leadman		.07	6.27	.45			
Foreman		.07	7.06	.50			
New Era, Press 4-C	2			9.29	9.29	5,632	52,321
Operator		1.00	8.34	8.34			
Leadman		.07	6.27	.45			
Foreman		.07	7.06	.50			
New Era, Press 5-C	1			8.47	8.47	2,816	23,852
Operator		1.00	7.52	7.52			
Leadman		.07	6.27	.45			
Foreman		.07	7.06	.50			
New Era, Press 5-C	1			9.46	9.46	2,816	26,639
Operator		1.00	8.51	8.51			
Leadman		.07	6.27	.45			
Foreman		.07	7.06	.50			
New Era, Press 5-C	1			8.73	8.73	2,816	24,584
Operator		1.00	7.78	7.78			
Leadman		.07	6.27	.45			
Foreman		.07	7.06	.50			

EXHIBIT 17-2: Crew Composition Table (CCT)

MARTIN & TUCKER, INC.
ENGINEERS

Production Center	No. of Units	Std. Crew Per Unit Per Shift	HOURLY Gross Pay Rate	HOURLY Gross Pay Ext'd	HOURLY Crew Pay Per Unit Per Shift	ANNUAL CHARGEABLE STD. HOURS	Direct Labor Budget
4C Nilsaton Flexo 22"	2			13.96	13.96	1,680	$ 23,453
Operator		1.00	9.74	9.74			
Helper		.50	8.43	4.22			
5C Internt'l Flexo 9"	2			12.05	12.05	3,682	44,368
Operator		1.00	7.83	7.83			
Helper		.50	8.43	4.22			
Roto-Gravure 14" 5C	1			17.88	17.88	2,229	39,855
Operator		1.00	9.35	9.35			
Helper		1.00	8.53	8.53			
Roto-Gravure 20" 7C	1			17.88	17.88	364	6,508
Operator		1.00	9.35	9.35			
Helper		1.00	8.53	8.53			
Coater & Dusen. Slit	1			17.96	17.96	2,970	53,341
Operator, coat.		1.00	6.82	6.82			
Operator, slit.		1.00	8.36	8.36			
Leadman		.28	6.61	1.85			
Adh. prep.		.14	6.62	.93			
Coater #42	1			11.24	11.24	1,350	15,174
Operator		1.00	8.46	8.46			
Leadman		.28	6.61	1.85			
Adh. prep.		.14	6.62	.93			
Coater #43	1			10.12	10.12	2,970	30,056
Operator		1.00	7.34	7.34			
Leadman		.28	6.61	1.85			
Adh. prep.		.14	6.62	.93			
Coater #44	1			10.51	10.51	2,700	28,377
Operator		1.00	7.73	7.73			
Leadman		.28	6.61	1.85			
Adh. prep.		.14	6.62	.93			

EXHIBIT 17-2 (continued)

MARTIN & TUCKER, INC.
ENGINEERS

Production Center	No. of Units	Std. Crew Per Unit Per Shift	HOURLY Gross Pay Rate	HOURLY Gross Pay Ext'd	HOURLY Crew Pay Per Unit Per Shift	ANNUAL CHARGEABLE STD. HOURS	Direct Labor Budget
Arrow, slit. #52,36"	1			9.38	9.38	2,494	$ 23,394
Operator		1.00	8.64	8.64			
Leadman		.11	6.69	.74			
Arrow, slit #53,18 3/4	1			8.93	8.93	968	8,644
Operator		1.00	8.19	8.19			
Leadman		.11	6.69	.74			
Champ. Roto Punch #61	1			9.16	9.16	1,335	12,229
Operator		1.00	8.42	8.42			
Leadman		.11	6.69	.74			
Champ. Roto Punch #62 #63 #64	3			8.54	8.54	5,874	50,164
Operator		1.00	7.80	7.80			
Leadman		.11	6.69	.74			
Wadson Punch	1			8.93	8.93	334	2,983
Operator		1.00	8.19	8.19			
Leadman		.11	6.69	.74			
Beck Sheeter	1			7.52	7.52	512	3,850
Operator		1.00	6.78	6.78			
Leadman		.11	6.69	.74			
Lawson Cutter	1			7.52	7.52	864	6,497
Operator		1.00	6.78	6.78			
Leadman		.11	.74	.74			
Rewinders	4			6.45	6.45	2,601	16,776
Operator		1.00	6.45	6.45			
Cut & Stack	3			6.78	6.78	459	3,112
Operator		1.00	6.78	6.78			

EXHIBIT 17-2 (continued)

MARTIN & TUCKER, INC.
ENGINEERS

	ANNUAL ALLOCT'D			ANNUAL SPECIFIC		ANNUAL ELEC. ENERGY*					
	Gas (1) $	Water (2) $	Heat Oil (3) $	Supplies, Parts & Outside Service (4) $	Inside Repairs & Maintenance (5) $	Hp-Hrs. in M's	KW-Hrs. in M's	Annual Cost (6) $	Annual Direct Ch'ges (1) thru (6)	Annual Chgble Std.Hrs **	Direct Charges per Chgble Std.Hr
	--	--	425	17,600	6,125	182	135	1,820	25,970	14,080	$ 1.84
	--	--	160	7,040	2,450	68	50	680	10,330	5,632	1.83
	--	--	80	3,520	1,225	32	24	320	5,145	2,816	1.83
	--	--	80	3,520	1,225	39	29	390	5,215	2,816	1.85
	--	--	180	7,040	2,450	84	62	840	10,510	5,632	1.87
	--	--	90	3,520	1,225	37	27	370	5,205	2,816	1.85
	--	--	90	3,520	1,225	35	26	350	5,185	2,816	1.84
	--	--	95	3,520	1,225	43	32	430	5,270	2,816	1.87
	792	--	300	8,288	1,800	49	36	490	11,670	1,680	6.95
	1,188	--	300	16,354	3,600	63	47	630	22,072	3,682	5.99
	2,967	--	220	12,893	3,000	154	114	1,540	20,620	2,229	9.25
	495	388	340	2,102	600	44	33	440	4,365	364	11.99
	--	1,385	180	6,720	3,000	420	311	4,200	15,485	2,970	5.21
	742	693	100	1,680	1,050	88	65	880	5,145	1,350	3.81
	1,484	970	120	3,360	2,700	162	120	1,620	10,254	2,970	3.45
	2,225	1,109	150	3,360	2,700	165	122	1,650	11,194	2,700	4.15
	--	--	30	860	400	29	21	290	1,580	2,494	.63
	--	--	20	323	200	10	7.4	100	643	968	.66
	--	249	80	445	400	47	35	470	1,644	1,335	1.23
	--	750	300	1,780	1,200	136	101	1,360	5,390	5,874	.92
	--	--	60	111	100	6	4.4	60	331	334	.99
	--	--	60	160	100	3	2	30	350	512	.68
	--	--	40	270	100	3	2	30	440	864	.51
	--	--	80	723	100	2	1.5	20	923	2,601	.35
	--	--	30	128	100	.2	.2	2	260	459	.57
TOTALS	9,893	5,544	3,610	108,837	38,300	--	--	19,012	185,196	--	--

* at the rate of $.0135 per KW-Hr.
** from Exhibit 17-6

EXHIBIT 17-3: Direct-Charge Budget (DCB)

MARTIN & TUCKER, INC.
ENGINEERS

Projected Annual Overhead Expenses	Period	Direct	Total
MANUFACTURING COSTS:			
Space:			
Gas (Heat)	3,200		3,200
Bldg. Maint. Service, Note 1	7,656		7,656
Real Estate Taxes	9,621		9,621
Depreciation of Bldg. & Improv.	8,500		8,500
SUB.	28,977	-0-	28,977
Power:			
Electric (Demand Charges)	12,497		12,497
BT Electric Services		6,000	6,000
SUB.	12,497	6,000	18,497
Machinery:			
Gen'l Factory Maint.Service, Note 2	3,828		3,828
Gen'l Mach. Shop Maint. (44%)	6,000		6,000
Depreciation of Machinery	51,500		51,500
Property Taxes (Machinery), Note 14	11,600		11,600
SUB.	72,928	-0-	72,928
Indirect:			
Janitorial Maint.Service, Note 3	7,656		7,656
Plant Supt.	18,948		18,948
Asst. Supt.		14,935	14,935
Nite Supt.		13,460	13,460
Technical Director (50%)	8,004		8,004
Industrial Engr.	18,462		18,462
Production Control, Note 4	19,828	23,574	43,402
Bailer/Janitor (2 days & 1 nite)	17,924	9,577	27,501
SUB.	90,822	61,546	152,368
TOTAL MFG. COST	205,224	67,546	272,770

EXHIBIT 17-4: Allocable Budget (AB)

MARTIN & TUCKER, INC.
ENGINEERS

Projected Annual Overhead Expenses	Period	Direct	Total
NON-MANUFACTURING COSTS:			
Whse. & Del:			
Shipping Supplies (excl. ctns.)		10,000	10,000
Stock Hander (1 day, 1 nite)		18,506	18,506
Ship. Suprv. (50%)	5,976		5,976
Ship. Clerk	11,664		11,664
Other Ship. Wages, Note 5		44,469	44,469
Property Tax (Inventory) Note 14		8,000	8,000
(Janitors, office supplies, postage, subsc., travel exp., etc., Note 11)		22,110	22,110
SUB.	17,640	103,085	120,725
Selling:			
Estimating (50% of Div. Mgr.)	13,840		13,840
Technical Director 25% Sales	4,002		4,002
25% R & D	4,002		4,002
Sales Services, Note 6	7,760	25,429	33,189
Order Entry, Note 7	13,124	18,324	31,448
Sales Mgr. (50%)	6,662	6,663	13,325
Secretary (50%)	4,180		4,180
Export (2%)	500		500
Unrecovered Art Work		14,400	14,400
Telephone & Telegraph	6,600	6,930	13,530
Branches', "fixed" Sell.Exp.,Note 8	8,500		8,500
Bonuses (based on volume)		45,862	45,862
SUB.	69,170	117,608	186,778
Administrative:			
Div. Mgr. (50%)	13,840		13,840
Accounting (Corp. Charges)	6,600	25,200	31,800
Purchasing (Corp. Charges)	2,000	2,000	4,000
Data Processing (Corp. Charges)	10,000	6,600	16,600
Personnel Advisor (Corp. Charges)	8,000	14,700	22,700
Director (5%)	2,768		2,768
Misc. Taxes,Fire&Gen'l Ins.Office Equip. Maint. Depreciation, Note 9	32,340		32,340
Misc., Note 10	16,380		16,380
Short-term Interest Charges		12,000	12,000
Prof. Services	46,000		46,000
SUB.	137,928	60,500	198,428
Fringe Benefits: Notes			
Period Fringes(Re:Corp.Chrgs.) 12	37,800		37,800
Variable Fringes(Re:Corp.Chrgs.) 13		3,360	3,360
SUB.	37,800	3,360	41,160
TOTAL NON-MFG. COST	262,538	284,553	547,091
from p. 1: TOTAL MFG. COST	205,224	67,546	272,770
ANNUAL BUDGETED OVERHEAD COST	467,762	352,099	819,861

EXHIBIT 17-4 (continued)

MARTIN & TUCKER, INC.
ENGINEERS

1. 40% of $19,400, a previously allocated expense.

2. 20% of $19,400, a previously allocated expense.

3. 40% of $19,400, a previously allocated expense.

4. Includes salaries & fringe benefits as follows:

	Period		Direct		
George	14,090				
Elwood	5,738		5,739		
Ben			10,876		
Doris			6,959		
TOTAL	19,828	+	23,574	=	$43,402

5. Includes salaries & fringe benefits of 4 ship. packers.

6. Includes salaries & fringe benefits of Paul, Frank, and Joanne.

7. Includes salaries & fringe benefits of Millie, Rona, Litlin and Kim.

8. Includes SF and Chicago offices as pro-rated for Label activity. All other selling expenses not on AB are accounted for as DOC's.

9. 42% of $77,000, a previously allocated expense.

10. 42% of $39,000, a previously allocated expense.

11. 33% of $67,000, a previously allocated expense.

12. 42% of $90,000, a previously allocated expense.

13. 42% of $8,000, a previously allocated expense.

14. Property taxes on machinery and inventory are based on a different calculation than the composite corporate allocation to Label Division.

EXHIBIT 17-5: Notes to Allocable Budget (AB)

MARTIN & TUCKER, INC.
ENGINEERS

Production Center	NO. OF UNITS	ANNUAL CLOCK ASSGN'D CLOCK HRS.	ANNUAL CLOCK CHARGEABLE HOURS	% STD. SUBS'DY	ANNUAL CHARGEABLE STD. HOURS
New Era Press 3-C	5	20,000	17,600	20	14,080
New Era Press 3-C	2	8,000	7,040	20	5,632
New Era Press 3-C	1	4,000	3,520	20	2,816
New Era Press 3-C	1	4,000	3,520	20	2,816
New Era Press 4-C	2	8,000	7,040	20	5,632
New Era Press 5-C	1	4,000	3,520	20	2,816
New Era Press 5-C	1	4,000	3,520	20	2,816
New Era Press 5-C	1	4,000	3,520	20	2,816
Nilsaton Flexo 22"	2	2,800	2,240	25	1,680
International Flexo 9"	2	5,200	4,420	16.7	3,682
Roto Gravure 14",5-C	1	3,400	2,686	17	2,229
Roto Gravure 20",7-C	1	600	438	17	364
Coater & Slitter 21"/26"	1	4,000	3,600	17.5	2,970
Coater 14½"	1	2,000	1,800	25	1,350
Coater 21"	1	4,000	3,600	17.5	2,970
Coater 27"	1	4,000	3,600	25	2,700
Arrow Slitter 36"	1	4,000	3,440	27.5	2,494
Arrow Slitter 18 3/4"	1	1,500	1,290	25	968
Champlain Punch 15"	1	2,000	1,780	25	1,335
Champlain Punch 21"	3	8,000	7,120	17.5	5,874
Wadson Punch 27 3/4"	1	500	445	25	334
Beck Sheeter	1	800	640	20	512
Lawson Cutter	1	1,200	1,080	20	864
Rewinder (Horiz. & Vert.)	4	3,400	2,890	10	2,601
Cut & Stack	3	600	510	10	459
TOTAL HOURS	—	104,000	90,859	—	72,810

EXHIBIT 17-6: Derivation of Annual CHARGEABLE STANDARD Hours

MARTIN & TUCKER, INC.
ENGINEERS

UNITS	Production Center	Direct Mfg. Costs			DIRECT NON-MFG. O.H.	TOTAL DIRECT O.H. COSTS	Ann. Chgble STD. Hrs.	Machine-Hour Rate			
		Power	Indir	Total				OOP O.H.	DCB	CCT	TOTAL OOP
5	New Era Press - 3c	574	11,909	12,483	52,581	65,064	14,080	4.62	1.84	9.28	15.74
2	" " " - "	215	4,760	4,975	20,950	25,925	5,632	4.60	1.83	9.47	15.90
1	" " " - "	101	2,380	2,481	10,452	12,933	2,816	4.59	1.83	9.47	15.89
1	" " " - "	123	2,380	2,503	10,545	13,048	2,816	4.63	1.85	9.42	15.90
2	" " " - 4c	265	4,760	5,025	21,160	26,185	5,632	4.65	1.87	9.29	15.81
1	" " " - 5c	117	2,380	2,497	10,520	13,107	2,816	4.65	1.85	8.47	14.97
1	" " " - "	110	2,380	2,490	10,490	12,980	2,816	4.61	1.84	9.46	15.91
1	" " " - "	136	2,380	2,516	10,600	13,116	2,816	4.66	1.87	8.73	15.26
2	Nilsaton Flexo - 22"	155	1,430	1,585	6,678	8,263	1,680	4.92	6.95	13.96	25.83
2	Int'l Flexo - 9"	199	3,112	3,311	13,939	17,250	3,682	4.68	5.99	12.05	22.72
1	Gravure, 14" - 5c	486	1,884	2,370	9,985	12,355	2,229	5.54	9.25	17.88	32.67
1	" , 20" - 7c	139	308	447	1,883	2,330	364	6.40	11.99	17.88	36.27
1	Coater & Slit 21"/26"	1,324	2,510	3,834	16,143	19,977	2,970	6.73	5.21	17.96	29.90
1	Coater, 14½"	278	1,141	1,419	5,978	7,397	1,350	5.48	3.81	11.24	20.53
1	" , 21"	511	2,510	3,021	12,727	15,748	2,970	5.30	3.45	10.12	18.87
1	" , 27"	521	2,282	2,803	11,809	14,612	2,700	5.41	4.15	10.51	20.07
1	Arrow Slitter 36"	92	2,108	2,200	9,269	11,469	2,494	4.60	.63	9.38	14.61
1	" " 18¾"	32	818	850	3,581	4,431	968	4.58	.66	8.93	14.17
1	Champion Punch 15"	148	1,128	1,276	5,376	6,652	1,335	4.98	1.23	9.16	15.37
3	" " 21"	429	4,965	5,394	22,715	28,109	5,874	4.79	.92	8.54	14.25
1	Walson, 27¾"	19	282	301	1,268	1,569	334	4.70	.99	8.93	14.62
1	Beck Sheeter	10	433	443	1,866	2,309	512	4.51	.68	7.52	12.71
1	Lawson Cutter	10	730	740	3,118	3,858	864	4.47	.51	7.52	12.50
4	Rewinders	6	2,198	2,204	9,285	11,489	2,601	4.42	.35	6.45	11.22
3	Cut & Stack	–	388	388	1,635	2,023	459	4.41	.57	6.78	11.76

	Power	Indir	Total	DIRECT NON-MFG. O.H.	TOTAL DIRECT O.H. COSTS	Ann. Chgble STD. Hrs.	
Totals	6,000	61,546	67,546	284,553	352,099	72,810	AB Totals
Allocation Factors	M HP-HRS	STD CH. HRS	—	MFG.	—	—	Allocation Factors
Allocation Fractions	6,000 / 1,901.2	61,546 / 72,810	— / —	284,553 / 67,546	— / —	— / —	Allocation Fractions
Allocation Ratios	3.156	.8453	—	4.213	—	—	Allocation Ratios

EXHIBIT 17-7: Expense Assignment Worksheet (EAW) (label)

MARTIN & TUCKER, INC.
ENGINEERS

PAGE 1 OF 5

ANALYSIS & SUMMARY OF DIRECT ORDER CHARGES (DOC)

Chart No. 1

MATERIAL: PRINTING PLATES: RUBBER + COPPER AND NICKEL ELECTROS

0. This chart covers the plates used in the Letterpress and Flexo production departments as well as the rubber logos, metal name plates and inter-company plate work.

0.1 All of the plates in this chart require metal flats. Therefore, all unit charges are based upon square inches.

1. SUMMARY FOR BUDGETING AND PROFIT PLANNING:

1.1	Letterpress (para 11) \$.1592 x annual sq. in. (para 2.7) 498M	=	\$ 79281.60
1.2	Rubber Flexo and letterpress (para 11) \$.2275 x annual sq. in. (para 2.8 - 2.9) 124M	=	28210.00
1.3	Logo (para 11) \$.5931 x annual sq. in. (para 2.9) 33M	=	19572.30
1.4	Nameplate (para 11) \$.062 x annual sq. in. (para 2.5) 25M	=	1550.00
1.5	TOTAL Plate Cost		\$128613.90
1.6	Transferred to Art DOC (para 15.1 + 15.2) = \$1181		
1.7	Transferred to Bottled Ink DOC (para 15.3 + 15.4) = \$1118		

2. METAL SHEET SPECIFICATIONS, USAGE, TRIM, COST, & ANNUALIZED SQUARE INCHES:

DEPT	FLAT SPECS Ga. x W x L	Sq. In. AREA	c/o TRIM	NET AREA	FLATS /YR.	UNIT COST /FLAT	UNIT COST \$/YR.	SQ. IN. /YEAR
2.1 Letterpress	.153" x 20" x 25½"	510	13	393	1224	\$10.84	13268	481M
2.2 Letterpress	.153" x 18" x 24"	432	10	389	44	8.70	383	17M
2.3 Flex-logo L.P.	.064" x 20" x 24"	480	09	437	226	4.50	1017	98M
2.4 Flex-logo L.P.	.064" x 22" x 28"	616	27	450	132	6.43	849	59M
2.5 Name Plate	.032" x 18" x 24"	432	15	367	70	4.85	340	25M
2.6 TOTALS							15,857	680M

2.7 481M + 17M = 498M Sq In of LETTERPRESS
2.8 98M + 59M = 157M Sq In of Flexo + Logo + Letterpress
2.9 (680M - 25M) x 5% = 33M Sq In of LOGO PLATES
2.10 LETTERPRESS - (\$13268 + 383) ÷ 498M Sq In = \$.0274/sq in
2.11 RUBBER (\$1017 + 849) ÷ 157M Sq In = \$.0119/sq in
2.12 NAMEPLATE (\$340) ÷ 25M Sq In = \$.0136/sq in

CLIENT COMPANY: ______ DATE ISSUED: ______ REVISION DATES: ______
DIVISION/PLANT: ______ M. & T. ENGINEER: ______
SUPERVISORY ACCEPTANCE: ______ M. & T. APPROVAL BY: ______

#411

EXHIBIT 17-8: Direct-Order Charges; Printing Plates: Company C

MARTIN & TUCKER, INC.
ENGINEERS

ANALYSIS & SUMMARY OF DIRECT ORDER CHARGES (DOC)

PAGE 2 OF 5

Chart No. 1

MATERIAL: PRINTING PLATES: RUBBER + COPPER AND NICKEL ELECTROS

3. MAJOR CHEMICAL COST FOR METAL PLATES:

	CHEMICAL	CONTAINERS	UNITS/ CONT	UNIT COST	$ /YEAR
3.1	Oil-Metal Etch	59/Year	5 gal	6.25/gal	$1844
3.2	P.V. Top Coater	24/Year	1 gal	6.25/gal	150
3.3	Nitric Acid	100/Year	175 pounds	9.50/cwt	1800
3.4	TOTAL				$3794
3.5	Metal plates chemicals ($3794) ÷ (680M sq in)				= $.0056/Sq In

4. FILM AND DEVELOPING CHEMICALS:

4.1	Step and repeat	34/year	50 Shts/box	$102.50/bx	$3485
4.2	8 x 10	2/year	300 Shts/box	91.00/bx	188
4.3	11 x 14	2/year	50 Shts/box	29.00/bx	58
4.4	Misc + chemical developer				4726
4.5	TOTAL				$8457
4.6	$8457 ÷ 680M Sq In				= $.0124

5. MISCELLANEOUS SUPPLIES (est $388/mo) or
5.1 $4655 - 680M Sq In = $.0068/Sq In

6. RUBBER PLATE MATERIAL:

			UNITS/YR	UNIT COST	
6.1	Flexo Impi	.060 NAT RUBBER	400 lbs	$2.04	$ 816
6.2	Flexo Nilsaton	.090 NAT RUBBER	300 lbs	2.04	612
6.3	Flexo Nilsaton	.110 NAT RUBBER	200 lbs	1.77	354
6.4	Letterpress & logo	.060 BUNA N	200 lbs	2.03	406
6.5	TOTAL				$2188
6.6	$2188 ÷ 157M Sq In				= $.0139/Sq In

7. RUBBER PLATE SUPPLIES:

7.1	.015 x 18" x 25 yds	Flexstick Sticky Back	2 Rolls	$55.50/roll	$111
7.2	.015 x 18" x 36 yds	3M Sticky Back	2 Rolls	76.50/roll	153
7.3	25½" x 51"	Mat Board	60 Shts	9.95/sht	597
7.4	25 yds	Friction Cloth	25 Yards	2.02/yd	51
7.5	TOTAL				$912
7.6	$912 - 157M Sq In			= $.0058/Sq In	

CLIENT COMPANY: ______ DATE ISSUED: ______ REVISION DATES: ______
DIVISION/PLANT: ______ M. & T. ENGINEER: ______
SUPERVISORY ACCEPTANCE: ______ M. & T. APPROVAL BY: ______

#411

EXHIBIT 17-8 (continued)

MARTIN & TUCKER, INC.
ENGINEERS

ANALYSIS & SUMMARY OF DIRECT ORDER CHARGES (DOC)

PAGE 3 OF 5

Chart No. 1

MATERIAL: PRINTING PLATES: RUBBER + COPPER AND NICKEL ELECTROS

8. METAL LABOR COST:

	NAME & ANNUAL PAY + FRINGES		LETTERPRESS %	LETTERPRESS $	FLEXO %	FLEXO $	LOGO %	LOGO $	INTER PLANT %	INTER PLANT $	NAMEPLATE %	NAMEPLATE $
8.1	Durrant	$13549	50	6775	40	5420	5	677	4	542	1	135
8.2	Sod	11566	80	9253	10	1157	5	578	4	463	1	116
8.3	Smith	11187	80	8950	10	1119	5	559	4	447	1	112
8.4	Gregson	11187	90	10068	10	1119		0		0		0
8.5	Brown	11187	80	8950	10	1119	5	559	4	447	1	112
8.6	Khouri	11432	75	8574	15	1715	5	572	4	457	1	115
8.7	TOTAL			52570		11649		2945		2356		590

8.8 LETTERPRESS + FLEXO + INTERPLANT $/SQ. IN:
($52570 + 11649 + 2356) ÷ [498M + (157M − 33M Sq In)] = $.1070/Sq In

8.9 LOGO − $2945 ÷ 33M = $.0892/Sq In

8.10 NAMEPLATES $/Sq In:
$590 ÷ 25M = $.0236/Sq In

9. LOGO METAL $/SQ IN + LOGO LABOR/SQ IN:

9.1 Metal .003 x 6" = $.003/Sq In

9.2 Metal .015 x 5" = $.004/Sq In

9.3 Labor for .003 & .015 = (.055 Hrs/plate x 9.00/Hr)

10. RUBBER LABOR COST:

	NAME & ANNUAL PAY + FRINGES		LETTERPRESS %	LETTERPRESS $	FLEXO %	FLEXO $	LOGO %	LOGO $	INTER PLANT %	INTER PLANT $	NAMEPLATE %	NAMEPLATE $
10.1	Wallace	$11187	10	1119	80	8950	5	560		0		0
10.2	Klyde	$11187		0		0	95	10628				
10.3	TOTAL			1119		8950		11188				

10.4 Letterpress + Flexo − ($1119 + $8950) ÷ 157M Sq In = $.0641/Sq In

10.5 Logos = ($11188) ÷ 25M = $.4475/Sq In

11. TOTAL PLATE COST BY KIND OF PLATE/SQ IN:

ELEMENT	LETTERPRESS $ Metal	LETTERPRESS $ Rubber	FLEXO $	LOGO $ (A)	NAMEPLATES $	$ INTERPLANT
Metal	.0274	.0119	.0119	.0119	.0136	.0274
Rubber	0	.0131	.0139	.0139	0	0
Chemicals, etc.	.0056	.0056	.0056	.0056	.0056	.0056
Film & developer	.0124	.0124	.0124	.0124	.0124	.0124
Miscellaneous	.0068	.0068	.0068	.0068	.0068	.0068
Rubber supplies	0	.0058	.0058	.0058	0	0
Metal labor	.1070	.1070	.1070	.0892	.0236	.1070
Rubber labor	0	.0641	.0641	.4475	0	0
TOTAL	.1592	.2275	.2275	.5931	.0620	.1592

CLIENT COMPANY: DATE ISSUED: REVISION DATES:
DIVISION/PLANT: M. & T. ENGINEER:
SUPERVISORY ACCEPTANCE: M. & T. APPROVAL BY:

#411

EXHIBIT 17-8 (continued)

MARTIN & TUCKER, INC.
ENGINEERS

ANALYSIS & SUMMARY OF DIRECT ORDER CHARGES (DOC)

PAGE 4 OF 5

Chart No. 1

MATERIAL: PRINTING PLATES: RUBBER + COPPER AND NICKEL ELECTROS

11. (A) Logo .003 x 6" = $.003 +$.5931 +$.0892 = $.6853/Sq In
Logo .004 x 6" = $.004 +$.5931 +$.0892 = $.6863/Sq In
Add this charge to Art Department DOC charge par. 8.3

12. Annual Square Inches of Rubber Plate Material Consumed + Waste + Remakes
12.1 Natural Rubber .060 - 400 lbs - .00357 lbs/Sq In = 112044 Sq In
12.2 Natural Rubber .090 - 300 lbs - .00505 lbs/Sq In = 59405 Sq In
12.3 Natural Rubber .110 - 200 lbs - .00357 lbs/Sq In = 56022 Sq In
12.4 Buna A .060 - 200 lbs - .00306 lbs/Sq In = 65359 Sq In
12.5 TOTAL SQUARE INCHES 293830
12.6 (293830 - 157000) ÷ 157M Sq In = 87% trim, waste, remakes etc.

13. NOTES:
13.1 THESE COSTS INCLUDE TRIM WASTE AS INDICATED IN PARA 1.
13.2 Labor costs include mounting rubber plates to metal bases in letterpress and logos.
13.3 These costs do not include Flexo Plate mounting on cylinders.
13.3.1 These costs do include the remake of flexo plates which are mounted improperly.
13.4 Labor costs include plate routing, sawing and trimming done by plate department personnel.
13.4.1 These costs do not include routing and trimming by press personnel.
13.5 Remaking defective metal plates is included in these costs.
13.6 Remaking worn plates is included in these costs.
13.6.1 Added contribution can be made by using attached chart to charge for worn plates.

14. ESTIMATED IMPRESSIONS/PLATE BY TYPE OF PLATE:

	LETTERPRESS TYPE OF COPY	RUBBER	IMPRESSIONS COPPER	NICKEL
14.1	Minute copy (to 3/16" x 3/4") spread	0	35M to 70M	65M to 90M
14.2	Over minute (to 50% of copy design)	35M to 60M	70M to 140M	90M to 180M
14.3	Over 50% of copy design	50M to 85M	85M to 175M	175M to 250M

14.4 Note: The selection of type of material is not restricted to number of impressions. Certain ink types and specific presses require rubber plates.

CLIENT COMPANY: DATE ISSUED: REVISION DATES:
DIVISION/PLANT: M. & T. ENGINEER:
SUPERVISORY ACCEPTANCE: M. & T. APPROVAL BY:

#411

EXHIBIT 17-8 (continued)

MARTIN & TUCKER, INC.
ENGINEERS

ANALYSIS & SUMMARY OF DIRECT ORDER CHARGES (DOC)

PAGE 5 OF 5

Chart No. 1

MATERIAL: PRINTING PLATES: RUBBER + COPPER AND NICKEL ELECTROS

15. TRANSFERS TO OTHER CHARTS:

15.1	Film used by art department	= $812
15.2	Print paper	369
15.3	Ink bottling 5% ($11187)	559
15.4	Ink bottling 5% ($11187)	559
15.5	Ink bottling material	

- 15.5.1 Black ($36.40) + ink conditioner ($4.88)/gal = $44.76/gal
- 15.5.2 Red ($22.25) + ink conditioner ($4.88)/gal = $30.61/gal
- 15.5.3 Brown ($26.80) + ink conditioner ($4.88)/gal = $35.16/gal
- 15.5.4 Bottle + caps + freight $.735/gal
- 15.5.5 Solvent ($.61/gal x 9165/gal) ÷ 2 = 2.745/gal

CLIENT COMPANY: ______ DATE ISSUED: ______ REVISION DATES: ______
DIVISION/PLANT: ______ M. & T. ENGINEER: ______
SUPERVISORY ACCEPTANCE: ______ M. & T. APPROVAL BY: ______

#411

EXHIBIT 17-8 (continued)

MARTIN & TUCKER, INC.
ENGINEERS

ANALYSIS & SUMMARY OF DIRECT ORDER CHARGES (DOC)

PAGE 1 OF 2

Chart No. 2

DOC Sales Commissions & Expenses

		Where Recovered	
1. Expense Distribution: (Allocated to Label Division)		MHR-AB	DOC
1.1	San Francisco Office (Western):		
1.1.1	George Ferne Salary (6%)	$ 1,500	
1.1.2	Sec'ty Salary (3%)	200	
1.1.3	Depreciation (8%)	300	
1.1.4	Commissions		2,541
1.1.5	Auto Lease		3,700
1.1.6	Travel, Ent., T. & T., Etc.		10,384
1.1.7	Total	$ 2,000	$16,625
1.2	Chicago Office (Midwestern):		
1.2.1	Henry Butterfly Salary (20%)	$ 5,000	
1.2.2	Rent (46%)	1,500	
1.2.3	Commissions		23,123
1.2.4	Auto Lease		7,900
1.2.5	Travel, Ent., T. & T., Etc.		29,473
1.2.6	Total	$ 6,500	$60,496
1.3	Independents (12 salesmen)		
1.3.1	4 Salesmen "Fixed Cost" (40%)		11,520
1.3.2	8 Salesmen "Fixed Cost" (58%)		38,100
1.3.3	Commissions for 1.3.1 & 1.3.2		60,466
1.3.4	Travel, Ent., T & T., Etc for 1.3.1 and 1.3.2		28,056
1.3.5	Total	$ 0	$138,142
1.4	Home Office:		
1.4.1	Sales Mgr. (A. Basse) (50%)	$13,325	
1.4.2	Sec'ty (50%)	4,180	
1.4.3	Total	$17,505	$ 0
1.5	Export Dept.:		
1.5.1	R. Sod (2%)	$ 336	
1.5.2	Mary Patterson (2%)	164	
1.5.3	Travel, Ent., T. & T., Etc.		1,000
1.5.4	Total	$ 500	$ 1,000
1.6	Annual Total Selling expenses for profit plan =	$26,505	$216,263

CLIENT COMPANY: ______ DATE ISSUED: ______ REVISION DATES: ______
DIVISION/PLANT: ______ M. & T. ENGINEER: ______
SUPERVISORY ACCEPTANCE: ______ M. & T. APPROVAL BY: ______

#411

EXHIBIT 17-9: Direct-Order Charges; Sales Expenses: Company C

MARTIN & TUCKER, INC.
ENGINEERS

ANALYSIS & SUMMARY OF DIRECT ORDER CHARGES (DOC)

PAGE 2 OF 2

Chart No. 2

DOC Sales Commissions & Expenses

2. Sales Distribution:

		Year	% of Total
2.1	San Francisco	$ 105 M	2.9
2.2	Chicago	962.4M	26.7
2.3	Independents	2,498 M	69.3
2.4	Exports	38 M	1.1
2.5	Total	$3,604.4M	100.0%

3. Selling Expenses % to Sales Volume (DOC $ ÷ Sales $)

3.1	San Francisco	$16,625 ÷ $150M = 15.8%
3.2	Chicago	$60,496 ÷ $962.4M = 6.30%
3.3	Independents	$138,142 ÷ $2,498M = 5.53%
3.4	Exports	$1,000 ÷ $38M = 2.63%

4. Selling Price Markup to Recover Sales Expenses:

4.1 To obtain gross selling price which will recover sales expenses, multiply target selling price by following factors:

- 4.1.1 San Francisco Factor 1.188
- 4.1.2 Chicago Factor 1.068
- 4.1.3 Independent Factor 1.059
- 4.1.4 Export Factor 1.027
- 4.1.5 Example:
  - 4.1.5.1 Target Selling Price before sales expense (to obtain a desired P.V.) = $1.20/M
  - 4.1.5.2 $1.20/M x 1.188 = $1.43/M Selling price for San Francisco.

5. Alternative method of recovery:

Subsidize the Western office to reduce selling expenses to 7.9%. Required subsidy = $8,312. Redistribute above amount as follows:
$3,312 to 3.2 for a total of $63,808
$5,000 to 3.3 for a total of $143,142

	New % Expense/Sales $		TSP MARKUP FACTOR
5.1	San Francisco	7.90%	1.086
5.2	Chicago	6.63%	1.071
5.3	Independents	5.73%	1.061
5.4	Exports	2.63%	1.027

CLIENT COMPANY: DATE ISSUED: REVISION DATES:
DIVISION/PLANT: M. & T. ENGINEER:
SUPERVISORY ACCEPTANCE: M. & T. APPROVAL BY:

#411

EXHIBIT 17-9 (continued)

MARTIN & TUCKER, INC.
ENGINEERS

ANALYSIS & SUMMARY OF DIRECT ORDER CHARGES (DOC)

PAGE 1 OF 4

Chart No. 3

DOC Art Department Charges

1. Summary for Profit Planning:

		Total $
1.1	L.P. (par. 9.1.2) $.427 x Annual Sq. In. (par. 9.1.1) 168M	$ 71736
1.2	Rubber Flexo & L.P. (par. 9.2.1) $.108 x Annual Sq. In. (par. 9.2.1) 124M	$ 13392
		$ 85128
1.3	Logo (par. 9.3.1) $.490 x Annual Sq. In. (par. 9.3.1) 33M	$ 16170
1.4	Interplant (par. 9.4.2) $.332 x Annual Sq. In. (35639) =	$ 11952
1.5	Total Art DOC	$113250
1.6	Transferred to AB as "Unrecovered Art Work"	14440
		$127690

2. Letterpress: (L.P.)

2.1 Sketches		Pay + Fringes	X	% Time	=	Dept. $
2.1.1	T. Pierre	$ 12256		92		$ 11276
2.1.2	L. Thompson	11855		70		8299
2.1.3	S. Suzanne	11855		66½		7884
2.1.4	Total	$ 35966		x		27459
2.1.5	Supvn.	-0-		-0-		7219
2.1.6	Total + Supvn.	-0-		-0-		$ 34678
2.1.7	AB Nonrecovered = (34678) x .415 =					$ 14391
2.1.8	Total + Supvn. (34678) -			(14391)	=	(20287) chgs. in Dept.

2.2 Paste Up		Pay + Fringes	X	% Time	=	Dept. $
2.2.1	H. Greene	$ 9741		98		$ 9546
2.2.2	Supvn.	-0-		-0-		2507
2.2.3	Total + Supvn.	-0-		-0-		12053

2.3 Drawings: (Drwg.)		Pay + Fringes	X	% Time	=	Dept. $
2.3.1	F. Butler	$ 8784		93.3		$ 8195
2.3.2	S. Licker	8828		88		7769
2.3.3	M. Harris	11276		69½		7836
2.3.4	Total	$ 28888		-0-		23800
2.3.5	Supvn.	-0-		-0-		6245
2.3.6	Total + Supvn.	-0-		-0-		$ 30345

2.4 Supervision: (Supvn.)		Pay + Fringes	X	% Time	=	Dept. $
2.4.1	G. Kern	$ 15322		30		$ 4597
2.4.2	P. Fellows	12723		89.4		11374
2.4.3	Total	$ 28045		-0-		$ 15971

CLIENT COMPANY: DATE ISSUED: REVISION DATES:
DIVISION/PLANT: M. & T. ENGINEER:
SUPERVISORY ACCEPTANCE: M. & T. APPROVAL BY:

#411

EXHIBIT 17-10: Direct-Order Charges; Artwork: Company C

MARTIN & TUCKER, INC.
ENGINEERS

ANALYSIS & SUMMARY OF DIRECT ORDER CHARGES (DOC)

PAGE 2 OF 4

Chart No. 3

DOC Art Department Charges

2.5 Assignment of Supervision $ to Letterpress Art Departments:

2.5.1 Supvn. $/Dept. = (A L.P. Dept. $ Pay + Fringes) / (Total L.P. Dept. $ Pay + Fringes) X (L.P. Supvn.) (Dept. $)

2.5.2 Example:

$$\text{L.P. Sketches Supvn. \$ (7884)} = \frac{\$27459}{(27459+9546+23800)} \times (\$15971)$$

2.6 Art Department Total Labor L.P. $ (1.1.8+1.2.3+1.3.6) = $76776.

3. Flexo Nilsaton:

3.1 Sketches		Pay + Fringes	X	% Time	=	Dept. $
3.1.1	T. Pierre	$ 11855		15%		$ 1778
3.1.2	L. Thompson	11855		15%		1778
3.1.3	Total					$ 3556
3.2 Paste Up & Drawings + Supervision:						
3.2.1	F. Butler	$ 8784		1.7%		149
3.2.2	S. Licker	8828		8.0%		706
3.2.3	M. Harris	11276		9.5%		1072
3.2.4	P. Fellows	12723		4.0%		509
3.2.5	G. Kern	15322		14.0%		2145
3.2.6	Total					$ 4581

3.3 Total Flexo Nilsaton Labor $ (3.1.3 + 3.2.6) = $8137

4. Flexo Impi:

4.1 Drawings, Paste Up & Supervision:				
4.1.1	F. Butler	$ 8784	5%	$ 440
4.1.2	S. Licker	8828	4%	353
4.1.3	M. Harris	11276	21%	2368
4.1.4	G. Kern	15322	14%	2145
4.1.5	P. Fellows	12723	6.6%	840
4.1.6	Total			$ 6146

5. Logo:

5.1 Logo Copy + Varitype + Supervision:				
5.1.1	N. Lancer	$ 5534	50%	$ 2767
5.1.2	S. Harvey	7738	100%	7738
5.1.3	G. Kern	15322	4%	613
5.1.4	V. Ancin	7315	50%	3658
5.1.5	Total			$ 14776

CLIENT COMPANY: ______ DATE ISSUED: ______ REVISION DATES: ______
DIVISION/PLANT: ______ M. & T. ENGINEER: ______
SUPERVISORY ACCEPTANCE: ______ M. & T. APPROVAL BY: ______

#411

EXHIBIT 17-10 (continued)

MARTIN & TUCKER, INC.
ENGINEERS

ANALYSIS & SUMMARY OF DIRECT ORDER CHARGES (DOC)

PAGE 3 OF 4

Chart No. 3

DOC Art Department Charges

6. Interplant:

6.1 Paste Up, Sketches, & Supervision:

		Pay + Fringes	X	% Time	=	Dept. $
6.1.1	H. Greene	9741		2%		195
6.1.2	T. Pierre	12256		8%		980
6.1.3	L. Thompson	11855		15%		1778
6.1.4	S. Suzanne	11855		18.5%		2193
6.1.5	G. Kern	15322		37%		5669
6.1.6	Total					$ 10815

7. Supplies + Roto:

7.1	Purchases for Dept. by Dept. =	$ 9600
7.2	Purchases for Dept. made by Plate Dept.	
7.2.1	Film	812
7.2.2	Print Paper	369
7.2.3	G. Kern, 1%	153
7.3	Total	$10934

7.4 Allocate on Basis of Labor Dollars/Dept.

7.4.1 $10934 Supplies + Roto ÷ $116660 = .094 of Supplies per Dept. Labor $.

7.4.2 Letterpress $76776 x .094 = $7216 Supplies

7.4.3 Flexo Nilsaton $8137 x .094 = $765 Supplies

7.4.4 Flexo Impi. $6146 x .094 = $578 Supplies

7.4.5 Logo $14776 x .094 = $1389 Supplies

7.4.6 Interplant $10815 x .094 = $1017 Supplies

8. Art Charges/Department:

8.1	Letter Press = ($76776 + $7216) $83992	83992	
8.2	Flexo Nilsaton = ($3556 + $4581 + $765) $8902	8902	
8.3	Flexo Impi. = ($6146 + $578) $6724	6724	$99618
8.4	Logo = ($14776 + $1389) $16165	16165	
8.5	Interplant = ($10815 + $1017) $11832	11832	
8.6	Total	$127615	

8.7 Transfer to AB Construction as "Non Billable Art Work" = $14400

8.7.1 $14400 ÷ 99618 = 14.5%

8.7.2 Deduct 14.5% from Flexo & L.P. Department costs when calculating Unit Cost for Art Work.

CLIENT COMPANY: ______ DATE ISSUED: ______ REVISION DATES: ______

DIVISION/PLANT: ______ M. & T. ENGINEER: ______

SUPERVISORY ACCEPTANCE: ______ M. & T. APPROVAL BY: ______

#411

EXHIBIT 17-10 (continued)

MARTIN & TUCKER, INC.
ENGINEERS

ANALYSIS & SUMMARY OF DIRECT ORDER CHARGES (DOC)

PAGE 4 OF 4

Chart No. 3

DOC Art Department Charges

9. Art Department Unit Charge/Department Serviced:
9.1 Letterpress:
9.1.1 498M sq. in. per plate DOC x 33 1/3% (A) = 168M sq. in. New Plates
9.1.2 ($83992 x .855) ÷ 168M sq. in. = $.427/sq. in. of plates (B)
9.2 Flexo Impi., Flexo Nilsaton & Letterpress Rubber:
9.2.1 ($8902 + 6724) x (.855) ÷ 124M sq. in. = $.108/sq. in. of plates (C)
9.3 Logo:
9.3.1 ($16165 ÷ 33M sq. in. = $.490/sq. in./plate (D)
9.4 Interplant:
9.4.1 Square Inches = L.P. sq. in.+Flexo-Logo=292M sq. in. (E)
9.4.2 ($83992+8902+6724)+($11835)x(.855) ÷ 292M sq. in. = $.332/sq. in. Art Work

Note (A): No data is available on how many plate square inches are New Plates requiring Art Work. A conference resulted in the conclusion that 33 1/3% of L.P. Plates are new plates requiring Art Work.

Note (B): This charge/sq. in. of plate will have to be applied to the (Die-Design dimensions x No. Up) x No. colors/copy-design.
Example: Die-Design xxx=2½"x1¼"= 3 1/8 sq. in./die-design x 20 up = 62½ sq. in./plate/color. $Cost/Color = $ .427/sq. in.x 62½ sq. in. = $26.69/plate color. $ cost/copy design = $26.69/plate x 2 colors = $53.38/copy-design on die-design xxx.

Note (C): Use same procedure for calculating die-design & copy design cost as used in Letterpress.

Note (D): Multiply Logo Imprint area by unit cost ($.490/sq. in.) & add to Logo Plate cost in Plate DOC par. 1A

Note (E): Multiply Interplant copy area by unit cost ($.332/sq. in.) to determine Interplant charge.

10. The Industrial Engineer can use the work areas used in this chart to verify necessary adjustments in Art Dept. time to assure full recovery of Flexo Art Work $.

11. The Industrial Engineer can use the plate product classifications & obtain the separation of Flexo Impi., Flexo Nilsaton & Letterpress flats for measurement of New Plate & Art Work Costs.

CLIENT COMPANY: DATE ISSUED: REVISION DATES:
DIVISION PLANT: M. & T. ENGINEER:
SUPERVISORY ACCEPTANCE: M. & T. APPROVAL BY:

#411

EXHIBIT 17-10 (continued)

MARTIN & TUCKER, INC.
ENGINEERS

ANALYSIS & SUMMARY OF DIRECT ORDER CHARGES (DOC)

PAGE 1 OF 1

Chart No. 4

MATERIAL: Imprint Ink Rebottled & Sold - OOP Cost

0. These inks are sold to customers for use in the client's Imprinting Machines. Basically, there are two types which provide the major $'s. These are diluted and undiluted inks.

0.1 Diluted inks are 11 parts ink to 5 parts solvent.

0.2 Undiluted inks are sold on the basis of rebottling only.

1. The following can be used to determine OOP cost/gallon.

	Rebottle Cost Element	Diluted	Undiluted
1.1	(A) Ink Base, Black	$36.40	$36.40
1.2	Bottle + Caps + Freight $	.74	.74
1.3	(B) Solvents (.455 Gal. x $5.50 /Gal.)	2.50	.00
1.4	Mixing & rebottling labor (Currently, 5% of two men in Plate Dept. @ $559 each including fringes) ÷ 170 gallons sold/year = ($1,118 ÷ 170 = $ 6.58/gal.)	6.58	.00
1.5	Total OOP Cost/Gal. =	$46.22	$37.14

2. Notes:

(A) This unit price changes with color of Ink Base. For example: Red Ink Base cost = $22.25/Gal.

(B) Special Solvents are used for dilution; these are bought in small quantities.

CLIENT COMPANY: DATE ISSUED: REVISION DATES:
DIVISION/PLANT: M. & T. ENGINEER:
SUPERVISORY ACCEPTANCE: M. & T. APPROVAL BY:

#411

EXHIBIT 17-11: Direct-Order Charges; Imprint Ink: Company C

MARTIN & TUCKER, INC.
ENGINEERS

ANALYSIS & SUMMARY OF DIRECT ORDER CHARGES (DOC)

PAGE 1 OF 2

Chart No. 5

MATERIAL: Printing Inks: Flexo, Gravure and Letterpress

1. Projected ink $'s for Gravure and Flexo printing:
   - 1.1 Gravure $35,380
   - 1.2 Flexo $26,140
   - 1.3 Solvent is a common factor in 1.1 and 1.2 (not included in above projection). Solvent $ have been captured in DCB, under supplies.
   - 1.4 Per Gravure Std. No. 132, Chart 7, "All Gravure Inks" are special formulations in accordance with customer requirements.
     - 1.4.1 The minimum purchases for these ingredients can be charged to the order for which purchased.
   - 1.5 Per Flexo Std. No. 2-21/24, Chart 2, there are standard inks in this department; however, without mileage charts, it is difficult to make a charge to an order.
     - 1.5.1 Non-standard Flexo inks can be handled in the same manner as Gravure inks in par. 1.4.1.
   - 1.6 Temporarily, it would be possible to recover these $ for Gravure and Flexo inks in estimating.
     - 1.6.1 Gravure $ (35,380) ÷ Annual Std. Chargeable Hours (2,593) = $13.64/Std. Hour.
     - 1.6.2 Flexo $ (26,140) ÷ Annual Std. Chargeable Hours (5,362) = $4.87/Std. Hour.
   - 1.7 Note: NONE OF THE ABOVE INCLUDE ANY LABOR ALLOWANCE FOR MIXING INKS.

2. Letterpress projected $ for ink = $54,329.
   - 2.1 Per letterpress, Std. No. 1-01/14, Chart 2, there are standard inks in this department.
   - 2.2 Temporarily, it would be possible in estimating to recover these $.
     - 2.2.1 Letterpress $ (54,224) ÷ Annual Std. Chargeable Hours (39,424) = $1.38/Std. Hour.
   - 2.3 A mileage chart in this area can be developed by Industrial Engineering without too much difficulty.
     - 2.3.1 All printing = over 50% coverage + less than 50% coverage down to minute copy + minute copy.
     - 2.3.2 Any 3 plus color jobs could provide copy for testing.
     - 2.3.3 For each of the standard ink types (oil and moisture set) start with controller quantities for each print type.
     - 2.3.4 Accurately, measure impressions and quantity of ink consumed for each print style. The die-design

CLIENT COMPANY: DATE ISSUED: REVISION DATES:
DIVISION PLANT: M. & T. ENGINEER:
SUPERVISORY ACCEPTANCE: M. & T. APPROVAL BY:

#411

EXHIBIT 17-12: Direct-Order Charges; Printing Ink: Company C

Martin & Tucker, Inc.
Engineers

ANALYSIS & SUMMARY OF DIRECT ORDER CHARGES (DOC)

PAGE 2 OF 2

Chart No. 5

MATERIAL: Printing Inks: Flexo, Gravure and Letterpress

number and number up will provide the relationship to area for factoring.

2.3.4.1 Small, intermediate and/or very large orders should be observed for balanced consumption.

3. Summary

3.1 Ink, DOC Annual projection:

3.1.1	Gravure	$ 35,380
3.1.2	Flexo	26,140
3.1.3	Letterpress	54,329
3.1.4	Total for Profit Plan	$115,849

3.2 Method of recovery when estimating ink $

3.2.1	Gravure	$ 13.64/Std. Hr.
3.2.2	Flexo	4.87/Std. Hr.
3.2.3	Letterpress	1.38/Std. Hr.

CLIENT COMPANY: DATE ISSUED: REVISION DATES:
DIVISION/PLANT: M. & T. ENGINEER:
SUPERVISORY ACCEPTANCE: M. & T. APPROVAL BY:

#411

EXHIBIT 17-12 (continued)

MARTIN & TUCKER, INC.
ENGINEERS

ANALYSIS & SUMMARY OF DIRECT ORDER CHARGES (DOC)

PAGE 1 OF 1

Chart No. 6

DOC: Delivery Charges (freight out) and Shipping Containers (ctns)

1. Delivery Charges:

   1.1 Delivery charge is handled as a separate billable item. It is excluded from the order revenue as well as from the order cost, thereby not distorting the P.V. measurement (even though the order contribution remains the same).

   1.2 All orders are sold FOB the client's plant. The cost-revenue transactions (on an even exchange) between the client and customer and between the client and carrier are handled in a separate account.

   1.3 Method of recovery is based on actual freight rates per cwt.

2. Shipping Containers

   2.1 Average cost per shipping container = $285/M ctns.

   2.2 Such a container varies in size and can hold anywhere from 2 to 20 rolls, depending on width of label.

   2.3 Ctns cost per order = $ .285 x No. of rolls/order ÷ No. of rolls/ctn.

   2.4 Projected annual carton $ = $12,500 for the profit plan.

CLIENT COMPANY: ____ DATE ISSUED: ____ REVISION DATES: ____
DIVISION PLANT: ____ M. & T. ENGINEER: ____
SUPERVISORY ACCEPTANCE: ____ M. & T. APPROVAL BY: ____

#411

EXHIBIT 17-13: Direct-Order Charges; Delivery Expenses: Company C

MARTIN & TUCKER, INC.
ENGINEERS

ANALYSIS & SUMMARY OF DIRECT ORDER CHARGES (DOC)

PAGE 1 OF 2

Chart No. 1 Thru 6

Summary of all DOC charts for estimating

1. PLATE CHARGES CHART 1:
   1.1 Letterpress metal = $.1592/sq. in.
   1.2 Letterpress rubber = $.2275/sq. in.
   1.3 FLEXO - IMPI = $.2275/sq. in.
   1.4 Flexo - Nilsaton = $.2275/sq. in.
   1.5 Logo = $.6853/sq. in. (metal plate included)
   1.6 Nameplates = $.0620/sq. in.
   1.7 Interplant = $.1592/sq. in.
   1.8 NEW ORDER
   Estimating formula = (Die-design length x width) x (No. up) x (sq. in. $) x (NO. COLORS)
   1.9 REPEAT or LARGE ORDERS - (NO. ORDER IMP ÷ IMP/PLATE x (NEW ORDER FORMULA).
      1.9.1 IMP/PLATE. Use this on all orders of 35M or More Impressions.
      1.9.2 PURPOSE:
         1.9.2.1 Determine quantity of plates to run large orders.
         1.9.2.2 Determine number repeat orders that can be run before replacement plates required.
      1.9.3 Guidelines for Additional Plate DOC Charges to be added to Estimates and/or Orders

	IMPRESSIONS/PLATE		
	RUBBER	COPPER	NICKEL
A. MINUTE COPY (up to 3/16" x 3/4") Spread	0	35M to 70M	65M to 90M
B. OVER MINUTE UP TO 50% of DIE-DESIGN AREA	35M to 60M	70M to 140M	90M to 180M
C. OVER 50% of DIE-DESIGN AREA	50M to 85M	85M to 175M	175M to 250M

      1.9.4 Certain inks require rubber, but this refinement will be deferred until a later date since no orders designate type of ink and ink color.

2. ART WORK CHART 3:
   2.1 Letterpress = $.427/sq. in.
   2.2 Flexo = $.108/sq. in.
   2.3 Logo = $.490/sq. in.
   2.4 Interplant = $.332/sq. in.
   2.5 New Order Estimating Formula = Same as Plate New Order Estimating Formula
   2.6 Repeat order/plate copy-design change = Same as 2.5 with No. Colors = to No. plate copy-design changes

CLIENT COMPANY: ____ DATE ISSUED: ____ REVISION DATES: ____
DIVISION/PLANT: ____ M. & T. ENGINEER: ____
SUPERVISORY ACCEPTANCE: ____ M. & T. APPROVAL BY: ____

#411

EXHIBIT 17-14: Direct-Order Charges; Summary: Company C

MARTIN & TUCKER, INC.
ENGINEERS

ANALYSIS & SUMMARY OF DIRECT ORDER CHARGES (DOC)

PAGE 2 OF 2

Chart No. 1 Thru 6

Summary of all DOC charts for estimating

3. INK CHART 5:
   - 3.1 Letterpress = \$1.38/std. hr./ORDER
   - 3.2 Flexo = \$4.87/std. hr./ORDER
   - 3.3 Gravure = \$13.64/std. hr./ORDER

4. SALES COMMISSION CHART 2:
   - 4.1 San Francisco = Selling Price x 1.188 for 15.8% net
   - 4.2 Chicago = Selling Price x 1.068 for 6.3% net
   - 4.3 Independents = Selling Price x 1.059 for 5.53% net
   - 4.4 Exports = Selling Price x 1.027 for 2.63% net
   - 4.5 Alternate to provide subsidy for San Francisco office
     - 4.5.1 San Francisco = Selling Price x 1.086 for 7.90% net
     - 4.5.2 Chicago = Selling Price x 1.071 for 6.63% net
     - 4.5.3 Independents = Selling Price x 1.061 for 5.73% net
     - 4.5.4 Exports = Selling Price x 1.027 for 2.63% net

5. DELIVERY CHARGES CHART 6:
   - 5.1 Shipping Containers = (\$.285 x No. of ROLLS/ORDER) ÷ NO. ROLLS/CARTON
   - 5.2 Shipping freight charges = (Shipping Wt.) x (Commercial freight rate)

6. IMPRINT INK CHART 4:
   - 6.1 Diluted Ink = \$46.22/gallon
   - 6.2 Undiluted Ink = \$37.14/gallon

CLIENT COMPANY: ______ DATE ISSUED: ______ REVISION DATES: ______
DIVISION PLANT: ______ M. & T. ENGINEER: ______
SUPERVISORY ACCEPTANCE: ______ M. & T. APPROVAL BY: ______

#411

EXHIBIT 17-14 (continued)

Chapter 18

A Complete MHR System for Company D

Exhibits 18-1 through 18-6 derive the final oop MHR's as in the previous two chapters. However, additional exhibits are introduced to show the derivative data for a production center as well as the derivation of the workers' Gross Hourly Cost.

PRODUCTION CENTER DERIVATIVE DATA

Exhibit 18-7 shows the form used for deriving the basic data for one production center before entry on the CFCS. The data are straightforward and require no involved explanation, except for the fact that in this case, there are two sizes of equipment merged into the same center, i.e., 56" and 41". This decision is the result of how the estimating department uses the MHR's. In this example, it was decided that the planned product mix would rarely, if ever, make use of webs exceeding the limits of the 41" bag machine. In effect then, the company runs nine 41" machines.

The preferred method is to divide the nine units into two centers: one for the 56" and one for the 41" machines, if the product mix indicates this type of usage. Often, even under this circumstance, the estimators may claim that it is easier for them to use one center. This practice deprives management of variances which, if large enough, may motivate the disposal or acquisition of units to maximize their contribution by reducing unfavorable oop variances. While it is rare to achieve a perfect alignment between the estimated and ultimately run machine, effort should be made to select the most appropriate center. Then, if unfavorable *facility change* variances build up high enough, it may call for the aforementioned changing of equipment.

GROSS HOURLY COST

Even if the hourly base rate paid to certain workers is exactly the same, there are enough differences to warrant the development of separate *gross* hourly pay rates because:

1. Not all of these workers are expected to work the same amount of overtime.
2. Not all have the same longevity and therefore, the same number of entitled vacation days.

3. Not all are assigned to production centers which have the same amount of non-chargeable time.
4. Not all have the same rate of productivity, which affects the amount of subsidy cost.
5. Not all participate to the same extent in group life insurance plans, profit sharing, etc.

Exhibit 18-8 shows how to assemble and use the wage data to arrive at line u, the gross wage cost per *chargeable standard* hour. The information developed in this example is for the supervisor in the printing department. His gross hourly cost of $7.38 is then fractionalized in various centers in accordance with his efforts applied.

CONFUSION ABOUT HOURS

There are clock hours, actual hours, elapsed hours, subsidy hours, non-chargeable hours, productive and non-productive hours, chargeable clock hours, chargeable standard hours, etc. To help unravel the confusion, we present Exhibits 18-9, a generalized case of Gross Hourly Cost, and 18-10 that reduces these data to bar chart form for better visualizing.

MARTIN & TUCKER, INC.
ENGINEERS

Production Center	No. of Units	Hp. per Unit	FOR PRODUCTION CENTER				
			Working Space Occup. sq. ft.	Present Market Value in M's	Annual Assigned Hours	Run Ratio	Hp-hrs. in M's *
Plate Mounting	4	2.1	1886	13.5	12000	.80	20.0
Laminator/Coater	1	119.0	2941	125.0	2650	.55	173.5
Print - 36" 4C	1	53.0	1764	96.8	3250	.65	112.2
Print - 45" 6C	1	72.8	2242	116.6	5000	.65	236.6
Print - 45" 6C	1	72.8	1829	116.6	6000	.65	283.9
Slitter - 50"	1	29.6	900	25.7	6300	.80	149.3
Slitter - 54"	1	12.5	462	16.5	6000	.85	63.7
Slitter - 32"	1	12.5	269	10.5	6000	.90	67.5
Bag-Side Seal	9	10.1	7337	96.0	36000	.95	345.4
Bag-End Seal	2	.9	682	3.0	2800	.95	2.4
TOTALS			20312	619.2	86000		1454.5

* For "Run" portion only.

EXHIBIT 18-1: Converting Facilities Classification Sheet (CFCS)

MARTIN & TUCKER, INC.
ENGINEERS

Production Center	No. of Units	Std. Crew Per Unit Per Shift	HOURLY Gross Pay Rate	Gross Pay Ext'd	Crew Pay Per Unit Per Shift	ANNUAL CHARGEABLE STD. HOURS	Direct Labor Budget
Plate Mtg.	4	1.25			7.30	9,690	$ 70,737
Operator		1.00	5.87	5.87			
Helper		.17	4.95	.83			
Supervisor		.08	7.40	.60			
Laminate/Coat	1	3.78			27.23	1,749	47,625
Operator		1.00	8.50	8.50			
Helper		2.00	6.38	12.76			
Supervisor		.78	7.65	5.97			
Print - Kidder 4C	1	2.64			16.22	2,677	43,421
Operator		1.00	7.03	7.03			
Helper		1.00	5.34	5.34			
Trainee		.43	5.34	2.30			
Supervisor		.21	7.38	1.55			
Print - Kidder 6C	1	2.64			16.28	3,937	64,094
Operator		1.00	7.09	7.09			
Helper		1.00	5.34	5.34			
Trainee		.43	5.34	2.30			
Supervisor		.21	7.38	1.55			
Print - Kidder 6C	1	2.64			16.29	4,860	79,169
Operator		1.00	7.10	7.10			
Helper		1.00	5.34	5.34			
Trainee		.43	5.34	2.30			
Supervisor		.21	7.38	1.55			
Slitting - 50"	1	1.05			6.83	4,738	32,360
Operator		1.00	6.44	6.44			
Supervisor		.05	7.51	.39			

EXHIBIT 18-2: Crew Composition Table (CCT)

MARTIN & TUCKER, INC.
ENGINEERS

Production Center	No. of Units	Std. Crew Per Unit Per Shift	HOURLY Gross Pay Rate	HOURLY Gross Pay Ext'd	HOURLY Crew Pay Per Unit Per Shift	ANNUAL CHARGEABLE STD. HOURS	Direct Labor Budget
Slitting - 54"	1	1.05			6.57	4,512	$ 29,644
Operator		1.00	6.18	6.18			
Supervisor		.05	7.51	.39			
Slitting - 32"	1	1.05			5.94	4,512	26,801
Operator		1.00	5.55	5.55			
Supervisor		.05	7.51	.39			
Bag-Side Seal	9	1.59			9.04	26,928	243,429
Operator		1.00	5.45	5.45			
Setup Man		.33	5.74	1.92			
Box Maker		.11	5.38	.59			
Supervisor		.15	7.20	1.08			
Bag-End Seal	2	1.025			5.64	2,190	12,352
Operator		1.00	5.45	5.45			
Supervisor		.025	7.56	.19			

Page 1 TOTAL: $337,406
Page 2 TOTAL: $312,226
GRAND TOTAL: $649,632

EXHIBIT 18-2 (continued)

MARTIN & TUCKER, INC.
ENGINEERS

Production Center	ANNUAL SPECIFIC		ANNUAL ELEC. ENERGY*			Annual Direct Ch'ges (1)+(2) + (3)	Annual Charg'le Std. Hours	Direct Charges per Charg'le Std. Hour
	Supplies, Parts & Outside Service (1)	Inside Repairs & Mainte-nance (2)	Hp-Hrs in M's	KW-Hrs in M's	Ann. Cost (3)			
Plate Making	$14,274	$ 2,579	20.0	14.7	$ 368	$ 17221	$9,690	$ 1.78
Lamin/Coat	9,804	6,448	173.5	127.7	3193	19445	1,749	11.12
Print - 36"	5,358	1,934	112.2	82.6	2065	9357	2,677	3.50
Print - 45"	5,358	1,934	236.6	174.1	4353	11645	3,937	2.96
Print - 45"	5,358	1,934	283.9	209.0	5225	12517	4,860	2.58
Slitter - 50"	804	645	149.3	109.9	2748	4197	4,738	.89
Slitter - 54"	804	645	63.7	49.7	1243	2692	4,512	.60
Slitter - 32"	804	645	67.5	46.9	1173	2622	4,512	.58
Bag-Side Seal	13,716	14,508	345.4	254.2	6355	34579	26,928	1.28
Bag-End Seal	720	967	2.4	1.8	45	1732	2,190	.79
TOTALS	57,000	32,239	1454.5	1070.5	26768	116007		

* at the rate of $.025 per KW-Hr.

EXHIBIT 18-3: Direct-Charge Budget (DCB)

MARTIN & TUCKER, INC.
ENGINEERS

Projected Annual Overhead Expenses	Period	Direct	Total
MANUFACTURING COSTS:			
Space:			
Maintenance & Bldg. Repair	$ 3,389		$ 3,389
Gas (Heat)	12,000	$ 6,000	18,000
Water	600	1,400	2,000
SUB	15,989	7,400	23,389
Power:			
Electric (Demand)	3,375		3,375
Electric (Fuel oil adjustment)	2,496		2,496
SUB	5,871		5,871
Machinery:			
Depreciation	120,000		120,000
Property Tax	34,720		34,720
SUB	154,720		154,720
Indirect:			
Mfg. Mgr.	12,769		12,769
Personnel Clerk	2,266		2,266
Plant Mgr.		16,651	16,651
Janitorial	9,897		9,897
Prod. Scheduling	12,966		12,966
General Help		22,248	22,248
Production Clerk	7,338		7,338
SUB	45,236	38,899	84,135
TOTAL MFG. COST	$221,816	$46,299	$268,115

EXHIBIT 18-4: Allocable Budget (AB)

MARTIN & TUCKER, INC.
ENGINEERS

Projected Annual Overhead Expenses	Period	Direct	Total
NON-MANUFACTURING COSTS:			
Whse. & Del:			
Supervision	$ 12,330		$ 12,330
Receiving Clerk		$ 10,674	10,674
Shipping Clerk		10,722	10,722
SUB	12,330	21,396	33,726
Selling:			
Correspondents		26,318	26,318
Estimator	7,992		7,992
Customer Service	12,861		12,861
Technical Director	16,380		16,380
Research & Development	4,736		4,736
Admn.-Sales/Customer Service	12,768		12,768
Nonbillable Art Work		12,000	12,000
Plan/Layout/Service	7,080		7,080
SUB	61,817	38,318	100,135
Administrative:			
General Manager	30,350		30,350
Secretarial	9,064		9,064
Purchasing	4,140		4,140
Receptionist	6,251		6,251
Plant Accountant	11,764		11,764
Acctg. Clerks		19,197	19,197
Plant Cost Accountant	2,483		2,483
Division Charges from Corporate	64,000		64,000
SUB	128,052	19,197	147,249
TOTAL NON-MFG. COST	$202,199	$ 78,911	$281,110
from p. 1: TOTAL MFG. COST	221,816	46,299	268,115
ANNUAL BUDGETED OVERHEAD COST	$424,015	$125,210	$549,225

EXHIBIT 18-4 (continued)

MARTIN & TUCKER, INC.
ENGINEERS

Production Center	ANNUAL CLOCK Assd. Clock Hours	ANNUAL CLOCK Chargeable Hours	% Std. Subsy.	ANNUAL CHARGEABLE STD. HOURS
Plate Mounting	12000	11400	15	9690
Laminate/Coat	2650	2186	20	1749
PRINT Kidder 4C	3250	2974	10	2677
PRINT Kidder 6C	5000	4500	12½	3937
PRINT Kidder 6C	6000	5400	10	4860
SLITTER 50"	6300	5922	20	4738
SLITTER 54"	6000	5640	20	4512
SLITTER 32"	6000	5640	20	4512
SCHJELDAHL Bag Side Seal	36000	31680	15	26928
Simplex Bag End Seal	2800	2576	15	2190
Total Hours	86000	77918		65793

EXHIBIT 18-5: Derivation of Annual CHARGEABLE STANDARD HOURS

MARTIN & TUCKER, INC.
ENGINEERS

UNITS	Production Center	Direct Mfg. Costs			DIRECT NON-MFG. O.H.	TOTAL DIRECT O.H. COSTS	Machine-Hour Rate			
		Space	Indir	Total			OOP O.H.	DCB	CCT	TOTAL OOP
4	Plate Mounting	687	5,729	6,416	10,936	17,352	1.79	1.78	7.30	10.87
1	Laminator-Coater	1,072	1,034	2,106	3,589	5,695	3.26	11.12	27.23	41.61
1	4c Print - 36"	642	1,583	2,225	3,792	6,017	2.25	3.50	16.12	21.97
1	6c Print - 45"	817	2,329	3,146	5,362	8,508	2.16	2.96	16.28	21.40
1	6c Print - 45"	666	2,873	3,539	6,033	9,572	1.97	2.58	16.29	20.84
1	Slitter - 50"	328	2,801	3,129	5,333	8,462	1.79	.89	6.83	9.51
1	Slitter - 54"	168	2,667	2,835	4,832	7,667	1.70	.60	6.57	8.87
1	Slitter - 32"	98	2,667	2,765	4,712	7,477	1.66	.58	5.94	8.18
9	SideSeal Bag Mach.	2,674	15,921	18,595	31,692	50,287	1.87	1.28	9.04	12.19
2	EndSeal Bag Mach.	248	1,295	1,543	2,630	4,173	1.91	.79	5.64	8.34
	Totals	7,400	38,899	46,299	78,911	125,210	AB Totals			
	Allocation Factors	OCCUP.	STD. CH. HRS.	—	MFG.	—	Allocation Factors			
	Allocation Fractions	7,400 / 20,312	38,899 / 65,793	— / —	78,911 / 46,299	— / —	Allocation Fractions			
	Allocation Ratios	.3643	.5912	—	1.70438	—	Allocation Ratios			

EXHIBIT 18-6: Expense Assignment Worksheet (EAW) (laminator/bag)

P.C. No.___________

MARTIN & TUCKER, INC.
ENGINEERS

Operation	UNITS	HP Per Unit	Total HP	Space Occupied Per Unit	Total Space Occupied	Present Market Value	Annual Assigned Hours	Run Ratio
Side sealing bags. Schjeldahl, split roll side weld machines:								
No. Size:								
017 56"	1	9.67	9.67	637	637	$ 9,000	4200	.95
021 56"	1	9.67	9.67	728	728	10,000	4400	.95
022 56"	1	9.67	9.67	546	546	9,000	3800	.95
016 56"	1	9.67	9.67	588	588	9,000	3600	.95
014 41"	1	8.67	8.67	614	614	8,000	3200	.95
015 41"	1	8.67	8.67	462	462	7,000	4800	.95
026 41"	1	8.67	8.67	504	504	7,000	4400	.95
020 41"	1	8.67	8.67	546	546	7,000	4600	.95
019 41"	1	8.67	8.67	483	483	7,000	3000	.95
Auxiliary eqpt:								
..overhead cranes	9	.67	6.00		incl	18,500		
..drill press	1		.25		48	500		
..guillotine	1		2.75		132	3,500		
..hand truck	1					500		
Other areas:								
staging					2049			
TOTALS	9	10.1	91.00	--	7,337	$96,000	36,000	

EXHIBIT 18-7: Production Center Derivation

MARTIN & TUCKER, INC.
ENGINEERS

DERIVATION OF EMPLOYEE GROSS HOURLY COST

CLIENT: ____________________

Annual Salary: Date __________, 19 __

Position: ______________ By ______________

NAME ______________ DEPT. __________ PROD. CENT. ______________

CLOCK #________ SCHED. DAILY HRS._____ SHIFT_____ MACHINE #(s) ______________

DATE HIRED ______________ VACATION DAYS __________ PRODUCTIVITY ____________ &

CURRENT HRLY. RATE $______ PROJECTED INCR.-YEAR______% PROJECTED HRLY.RATE $______

NON-CHARGEABLE TIME ______%

HRS. (FRACTIONALIZED) IN PROD. CENT. #________HRS, #________HRS, #________HRS

ITEM	ANNUAL HOURS	ANNUAL COST	ANNUAL EXCESS COST
a. Regular annual paid hours	2,000	9,160.00	
b. Planned overtime clock hours	500	2,290.00	
c. Gross annual paid hours	2,500	11,450.00	
d. Overtime premium cost			1,145.00
e. Paid holiday hours (currently 11)	88	403.04	
f. Entitled vacation hours (2%/weekx5daysx8 hours)	64	293.12	
g. Other paid time off, hours (3 days or 24 hours)	24	109.92	
h. Expected non-chargeable hours (1) (% of c)	250	1,145.00	
i. Sub-total of: e + f + g + h	426	1,951.08	1,951.08
j. ANNUAL CHARGEABLE CLOCK HOURS (c - i)	2,074	9,498.92	
k. Expected performance subsidy ______ (% of j)	207	949.89	949.89
l. ANNUAL CHARGEABLE STANDARD HOURS (j - k)	1,867	8,549.03	
m. Group life, Hospital & Surgical			340.00
n. Workmen's compensation			70.00
o. Payroll taxes, FICA, etc.			631.20
p. FUT, State UT			137.76
q. Annual cost saving plan			--
r. TOTAL EXCESS cost=(d + i + k + m + n + o + p + q)			5,224.93
s. EXCESS hourly rate ($ r/l hrs)	$ 2.80		$ 2.80
t. Projected hourly rate	4.58		
u. Effective Gross hourly rate (s + l)	7.38		
v. % increase in base hourly rate (s/t) 2.80/4.58			61%

FOOTNOTES:

(1) Include only those elements not included in OOP MHR, or in Production Standard

NOTE: Incentive premiums, or bonuses paid should not be included in (s).

EXHIBIT 18-8: DERIVATION OF EMPLOYEE GROSS HOURLY COST

MARTIN & TUCKER, INC.
ENGINEERS

DERIVATION OF EMPLOYEE GROSS HOURLY COST

CLIENT: ABC Printing Co. DIVISION: — LOCATION: — DATE: 4/7x

Name: MARY JONES Dept: BINDERY Clk #: 131 Prod Ctr: 74

Job Title: Operator Mach.# 74C Shift: 1 Shift Hrs: 8 Est. Prod'y: 90 %

Subsidy: 10 % Entitled Vaca. Days: 10 Holidays: 8

Hrly. Base Rate: Current $ 2.39 ; Projected $ 2.53

Annual Item	Annual Hours	Annual Cost	Annual Excess Cost
1. Regular paid clock hours	2000	$ 5,060.00	$
2. Planned overtime clock hours	50	126.50	
3. Gross paid clock hours	2050	5,186.50	
4. Overtime premium cost	—	63.25	63.25
5. Paid holiday hours	64	161.92	
6. Entitled vacation hours	80	202.40	
7. Other paid time off, in hours	24	60.72	
8. Expected non-chargeable hours*	125	316.25	
9. Sub-total: (5+6+7+8)	293	741.29	741.29
10. CHARGEABLE CLOCK hours (3-9)	1757	4445.21	
11. Expected performance subsidy (10 % x 10)	175.7	444.52	444.52
12. CHARGEABLE STANDARD hours (10-11)	1581.3	4000.69	
13. Non-hourly costs:			
13.1 Fed. payroll taxes, FICA, etc.		296.00	
13.2 State, city, etc. taxes			
13.3 Workmen's compensation			
13.4 Group, accident, sickness insur.			
13.5 Hospital'n, major medical plans, etc.			
13.6 Pension, union welfare, etc.		100.00	
13.7 Bonus, gifts, C.O.L. adj.		78.00	
13.8 Uniforms, special benefits		12.00	
13.9 Profit-sharing costs		104.00	
13.10 Other			
14. Sub-total: (13.1 thru 13.10)		590.00	590.00
15. Excess costs (4+9+11+14)			1839.06

16. EXCESS hourly rate (15/12)	$ 1.163
17. Projected hourly base rate	$ 2.530
18. Effective GROSS HOURLY COST (16+17)	$ 3.693
19. Increase in hourly base rate (16/18)	46 %

* Include only those hours (washups, etc.) which are not part of any other MHR schedule or not included in production standards.

NOTE: Do not include incentive premium costs on this sheet.

EXHIBIT 18-9: DERIVATION OF EMPLOYEE GROSS HOURLY COST

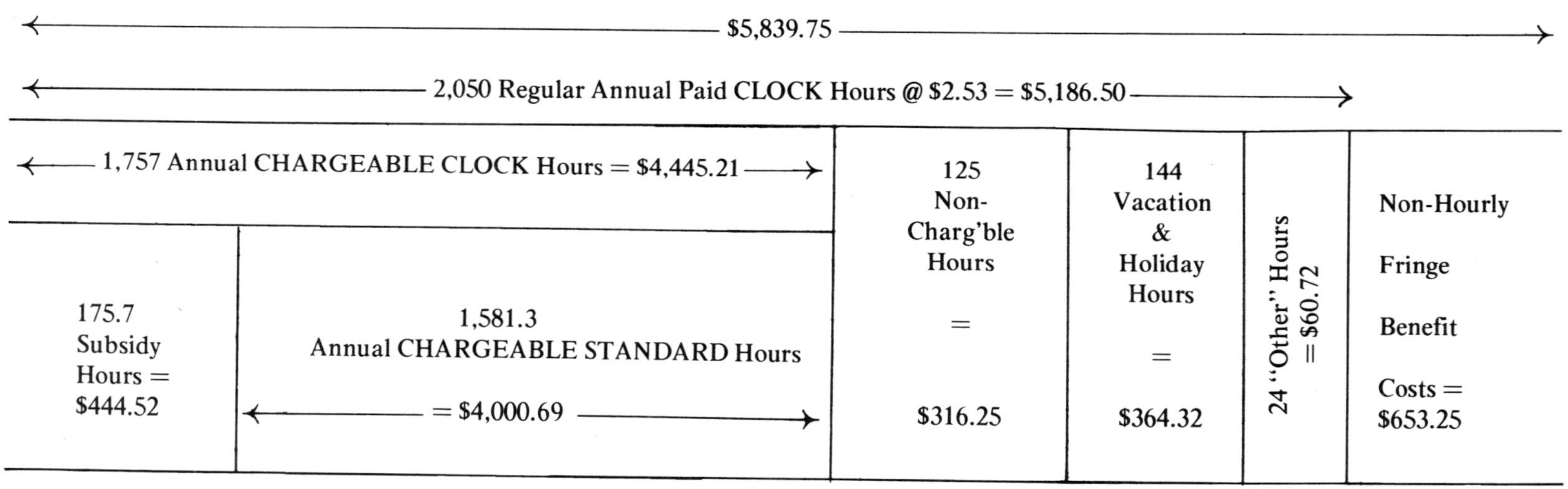

Costs per CHARGEABLE STANDARD Hour

Base hourly rate	$2.5300
Subsidy pay	.2811
Non-chargeable time	.2000
Vaca., Holiday & Other	.2688
Non-hourly fringes	.4131
TOTAL	$3.693

EXHIBIT 18-10: Bar Chart: Gross Hourly Cost and Chargeable Standard Hours (not to scale)

SECTION IV

Applying Direct-Cost Machine-Hour Rates In Cost-Estimating Jobs and Products

Chapter 19

The Role of Production Standards in Cost Estimating

Once we have developed the conversion cost rates (MHR) to express order conversion in out-of-pocket costs, we are ready with one-half of the cost estimating equation. The Machine-Hour Rate gives the rate of direct-cost at each facility which the company uses to process its output. Before these rates can be applied to cost-estimate a specific order, it is first necessary to determine the number of hours which is expected to be used by each facility or production center. To do this, estimated or standard production time must be determined. In effect, the company must be prepared to measure the work speed at each facility. These statistics are generally compiled into what are known as *production standards,* and the calculated standard hours are then used to convert a conversion *cost rate* into a conversion *cost.*

PRODUCTION STANDARDS

For a proper discussion of production standards, we should understand the meaning of the word "standard." A standard, used in the generic sense, represents a universally accepted unit of measurement of some physical characteristic. Thus, when 12 inches is used to define a foot, that measurement of length is a standard. The same is true of a unit of weight, such as the pound.

A production standard is a measurement of work. To develop this unit of work measurement, industrial engineers, motion study researchers, and industrial psychologists performed experiments over several generations. Their studies took them into areas of endurance, effort, fatigue, monotony, boredom, specific working conditions, various delays, and the physical factors constituting any given job. The result is the notion of a fair day's work pace. As labor unions became vitally interested in the application of production standards, there was insistence that the fair day's work pace be equated to a fair day's pay. The concept of a normal or fair rate of work is now defined as that rate of speed at which the worker fully earns his hourly pay rate, the pace at which he is delivering a fair day's work for a fair day's pay. At that pace, he is said to be performing at standard, or 100 per cent productivity. While there are many variations of this standard-hour plan in various forms of measured daywork and wage incentives in companies, the basic principles remain the same.

To develop a production standard for the large number of variables which generally are present at any facility, the industrial engineer or timestudy man will time the operation, breaking it down into certain specific motions which he can then analyze. He will next select the valid motions constituting the operation and choose which of the cycle times best fit the elements and methods being used. He then will take his observed stopwatch readings and will normalize them (also called speed rating or leveling) to indicate the extent his observed readings deviate from what he believes to be the normal, or 100 per cent, work pace. Having computed the standard times for each element of the operation, he will add time allowances for unavoidable delays, personal needs, and expected fatigue in order to arrive at the standard time for the job. Standard time for an operation may be presented in terms of standard hours per unit of quantity or in standard unit of quantity per hour.

Thus, a standard for an operation may be expressed in terms of 800 pieces per hour, or 1.25 standard hours per thousand (M). If an order of 10,000 pieces is being processed through a facility whose Machine-Hour Rate is \$23, the conversion time and cost through that facility is

$$10{,}000 \times 1.25\ \text{hr/M} = 12.50\ \text{standard hours}$$
$$\text{Conversion cost} = 12.50 \times \$23,\ \text{or}\ \$287.50$$

Unlike the unvarying measure of a standard unit of length or weight, the production standard is qualified by the geographic area in which it is being developed. In some areas, the 100 per cent speed rating requires a higher rate of effort to attain; in other areas, the effort required is lower. These variances are a function of the historical work tempi of the specific area coupled with the local philosophy towards work. In small rural manufacturing communities down South, the 100 per cent concept is "tighter" than it would be in a large Northern city. Much of this difference is the result of union education of the rank and file membership and generally the degree of militance which unions bring to bear on wages and jobs. In addition, when jobs are scarce and workers plentiful, the 100 per cent rating tends to be pegged to a higher level of effort. In any event, production standards covering specific operations are usually valid neither country-wide nor industry-wide but generally are applicable only to the specific plant for which they are developed. Industry-wide standards do not account for individual differences in working conditions, machinery conditions, specific methods, skill levels, nor in the concept of the normal speed level.

It is up to management to recognize these differences and to have available proper production standards which reflect its expected output from each facility. Sloppy production standards cannot be compensated for by accurate Machine-Hour Rates and vice versa. Obviously, since processing hours are multipled by the Machine-Hour Rate, errors in *either* factor will cause an error of the *same* magnitude in calculating conversion costs.

PARAMETERS OF PRODUCTION STANDARDS

When many products pass through one given processing facility, it may be inequitable to have only one speed figure for that facility. Generally, a converting facility is the place where many different orders are processed on their way to the next facility. Each of these orders may not be run through at the same speed because of its individual characteristics. Often then, a group of production standards has to be developed for each facility to reflect the various classes of work expected to pass through the facility.

When production standards are developed, therefore, the variables of the operation which cause the basic time to change must be recognized and tabulated. This procedure sets the stage for the correct format of standards.

Exhibits 19-1 through 19-29 are examples of production standards which are developed and formatted with parameters to show that a production standard for a facility in the converting industry is *rarely one number.* A discussion of some of the standards will aid the reader in the approach to proper parameter recognition.

EXAMPLES OF PRODUCTION STANDARDS

Exhibits 19-1 and 19-2 show the "run" standards for a flexographic printing press. Exhibit 19-1 expresses the standards in "standard impressions per hour" and Exhibit 19-2 in "standard hours per thousand impressions." One is the reciprocal of the other, i.e., the standard of 10,925 per hour is the same as .092 hours per thousand. The latter of course, is used on the estimate sheet. The parameters, or the factors which make the time vary at the facility are:

1. *The size of the order (feet on order)*: This is essential for showing that running time is not linear at all times. For a very small order, like 20M feet, getting the press up to "cruising" speed is recognized and will reduce the average running speed during the processing of that order. Perhaps during such a small run, the press is taken up to cruising speed for the last 5M feet of the order; the first 15M feet being the period where the press speed is being inched up.

2. *Number of colors (color combination)*: In this example, the number of colors are not recognized on small orders. But starting with 25M, the effect of the number of colors to be printed comes into play. Here, the parameter accounts for the drying time of the various ink colors, i.e., greater care (and slower speed) must be used when printing 3 or 4 colors, in addition to other technical processing reasons.

3. *Allowances:* Technical factors which can be applied regardless of the size of the order or number of colors (in this inştance) are treated as overall allowances added to standard time. These generally refer to variations in quality or the nature of the material being processed.

Exhibit 19-3 is a computation sheet to demonstrate to the estimator how the standards are to be used in pre-determining the standard direct cost of a job inquiry to be estimated and priced.

Exhibit 19-4 uses the parameters of feet per minute, number of cuts to be made, and the form of material, viz: whether supplied in sheeting or tubing.

Exhibit 19-5 is a standard which explains the physical factors of the operation and suggests, using a nomogram, how to extract standard times within the practical range of operation. Exhibit 19-6 tabulates these data according to two parameters:

1. Bag length.
2. Gauge of the material.

The size of the order in this standard is handled more equitably as an allowance, listed under Quantity Variation.

Exhibit 19-7 shows the parameters of bag width and gauge. The allowances provide for the small order, extra-heavy gauge, and special items different from the major product mix.

Exhibits 19-8 through 19-10 deal with the standardization of a facility which can handle a variety of materials in different ways. Exhibit 19-8 shows the variations in the materials, viz: type, gauge, adhesives, coatings and the mechanical specifications of the process. Exhibit 19-9 shows for one type of generic product, i.e., "2-ply laminations," the practical combinations of material-to-material-to-adhesive-to-coating. Thus, there are 15 parameters for this product. In Exhibit 19-10 for 3-ply laminations, the number of parameters are 7.

Exhibit 19-11 is a "makeready" or setup standard. The work involved in this preparatory operation is identified with a job and is considered chargeable time. This makeready operation is broken down into three steps: basic makeready, press washup, and remove makeready. Not all makereadies require the same degree of preparation, and these variations are reflected in the parameters under the heading "number of colors."

STD. NO. IV (a)
CHART NO. 7

PRODUCTION STANDARD

MARTIN & TUCKER, INC.
ENGINEERS

PAGE 2 OF 4

MACHINE NO. 2 DESCRIPTION: HUDSON SHARPE 4 - C PRINTING PRESS; PROD. CTR. # 13

OPERATION: PRINT FLEXO - ANILINE ELEMENT: RUN

STD. IMPRESSIONS PER HOUR

(5) FEET ON ORDER	12M - 25M	25,000 - 60,000		60,000 - 160,000		160,000 - over	
COLOR COMBINATION	1,2,3, or 4 Colors	3 or 4 Colors	1 or 2 Colors	3 or 4 Colors	1 or 2 Colors	3 or 4 Colors	1 or 2 Colors
	#2 Press Output, for 1 out, Impressions/Hr or Bags/Hr Foot per Minute Settings						
Circumference of Ptg. Cyl.	250	300	350	400	450	500	550
12 1/2"	10,925	13,100	15,275	17,475	19,650	21,825	24,025
13 1/2"	10,100	12,125	14,150	16,175	18,200	20,225	22,225
14 1/2"	9,400	11,300	13,175	15,050	16,950	18,825	20,700
15 3/4"	8,650	10,400	12,125	13,850	15,600	17,325	19,050
16 "	8,525	10,225	11,950	13,650	15,350	17,050	18,750
16 1/4"	8,400	10,075	11,750	13,425	15,125	16,800	18,475
16 3/4"	8,150	9,775	11,400	13,025	14,650	16,300	17,925
17 1/2"	7,800	9,350	10,925	12,475	14,025	15,600	17,150
18 1/4"	7,475	8,975	10,475	11,950	13,450	14,950	16,450
18 1/2"	7,375	8,850	10,325	11,800	13,275	14,750	16,225
19 1/4"	7,075	8,500	9,925	11,350	12,750	14,175	15,600
20 3/4"	6,575	7,900	9,200	10,525	11,825	13,150	14,475
21 1/4"	6,425	7,700	9,000	10,275	11,550	12,850	14,125
22 1/4"	6,125	7,350	8,575	9,800	11,025	12,275	13,500
23 1/4"	5,875	7,050	8,225	9,400	10,575	11,725	12,900
24 1/4"	5,625	6,750	7,875	9,000	10,125	11,250	12,375

ALLOWANCES:

1. For close register printing: decrease Std. IPH 10%.
2. For tone and process printing: decrease Std. IPH 10%.
3. For tubing over 2.5 mil up to 3.5 mil: decrease Std. IPH 20%.
4. For tubing over 3.5 mil up to maximum: decrease Std. IPH 30%.
5. See Page 4 of 4, Standard No. IV for determining lineal feet on order.

To determine pounds per hour use formula (3). See also Extrusion Standard, Page 2 Footnote 4.

(3) Lbs./Hr. = Roll Width x Gauge x .800 x F.P.M. x 60 (Tubing)
Lbs./Hr. = 48 x Roll Width x Gauge* x F.P.M.

* in inches

CLIENT COMPANY: DATE ISSUED: REVISION DATES:
DIVISION/PLANT: M. & T. ENGINEER:
SUPERVISORY ACCEPTANCE: M. & T. APPROVAL BY:

THE STANDARDS CONTAINED HEREIN ARE APPLICABLE TO THE MACHINE OR OPERATION AND METHODS EMPLOYED AS OF AND ARE SUBJECT TO REVISION PENDING ANY ALTERATION OR CHANGE IN METHODS OR EQUIPMENT.

EXHIBIT 19-1

STD. NO. IV (a)
CHART NO. 7

PRODUCTION STANDARD

MARTIN & TUCKER, INC.
ENGINEERS

PAGE 3 OF 4

MACHINE NO. 2 DESCRIPTION: HUDSON SHARPE 4 - C PRESS; PROD. CTR. # 13

OPERATION: PRINT FLEXO - ANILINE ELEMENT: RUN

STD. HOURS PER M IMPRESSIONS

(5) LINEAL FEET ON ORDER	12,000 - 25,000	25,000 - 60,000		60,000 - 160,000		160,00 - over	
COLOR COMBINATION	1,2,3, or 4 Colors	3 or 4 Colors	1 or 2 Colors	3 or 4 Colors	1 or 2 Colors	3 or 4 Colors	1 or 2 Colors
	#2 Press Standard Time, for 1 out, Hours/M Impressions or, Hours/M Bags — Foot per Minute Setting						
Circumference of Ptg. Cyl.	250	300	350	400	450	500	550
12 1/2"	.092	.076	.065	.057	.051	.046	.042
13 1/2"	.099	.082	.071	.062	.055	.049	.045
14 1/2"	.106	.088	.076	.066	.059	.053	.048
15 3/4"	.116	.096	.082	.072	.064	.058	.052
16 "	.117	.098	.084	.073	.065	.059	.053
16 1/4"	.119	.099	.085	.074	.066	.060	.054
16 3/4"	.123	.102	.088	.077	.068	.061	.056
17 1/2"	.128	.107	.092	.080	.071	.064	.058
18 1/4"	.134	.111	.095	.084	.074	.067	.061
18 1/2"	.136	.113	.097	.085	.075	.068	.062
19 1/4"	.141	.118	.101	.088	.078	.071	.064
20 3/4"	.152	.127	.109	.095	.085	.076	.069
21 1/4"	.156	.130	.111	.097	.087	.078	.071
22 1/4"	.163	.136	.117	.102	.091	.081	.074
23 1/4"	.170	.142	.122	.106	.095	.085	.078
24 1/4"	.178	.148	.127	.111	.099	.089	.081

ALLOWANCES:

1. For close register printing: increase Std. Hours 10%.
2. For tone and process printing: increase Std. Hours 10%.
3. For tubing over 2.5 mil up 3.5 mil: increase Std. Hours 20%.
4. For tubing over 3.5 mil up to maximum: increase Std. Hours 30%.
5. See Page 4 of 4, Standard No. IV for determining lineal feet on order.

To determine pounds per hour use formula (3). See also Extrusion Standard, Page 2, Footnote 4.

(3) Lbs./Hr. = Roll Width x Gauge x .800 x F.P.M. x 60

Lbs./Hr. = 48 x Roll Width x Gauge* x F.P.M. (Tubing)

* (in inches)

CLIENT COMPANY: ______ DATE ISSUED: ______ REVISION DATES: ______
DIVISION/PLANT: ______ M. & T. ENGINEER: ______
SUPERVISORY ACCEPTANCE: ______ M. & T. APPROVAL BY: ______

THE STANDARDS CONTAINED HEREIN ARE APPLICABLE TO THE MACHINE OR OPERATION AND METHODS EMPLOYED AS OF ______ AND ARE SUBJECT TO REVISION PENDING ANY ALTERATION OR CHANGE IN METHODS OR EQUIPMENT.

EXHIBIT 19-2

STD. NO. IV (a) & (b)

CHART NO. 7

PRODUCTION STANDARD

MARTIN & TUCKER, INC.
ENGINEERS

PAGE 4 OF 4

MACHINE NO. 1, 2 DESCRIPTION: HUDSON SHARPE OR KIDDER PRESS; PROD. CTR. # 13, # 14

OPERATION: ELEMENT:

COMPUTATION SHEET

To compute "Lineal Feet on order" follow this example:

1.	Quantity of bags	20,000
2.	% overage	7%
3.	Bag style, B.S. or S.W.	S.W.
4.	Bag size, width first	9½ x 12 x 3" BG & ½" lip
5.	No. of colors (parameter)	3
6.	Which press?	H/S
7.	Mil thickness (for allowances)	1.25
8.	Sheeting or tubing (for allowances)	Tubing, "J" Film
9.	Circ. of Printing cylinder (parameter)	19 ¼"
10.	Number up (= number around x number across)	2

a. Feet length = 20,000 x 1.07 x 9.5 ÷ 12 = 17,000 feet. This information indicates the length of press run. At 250 feet per minute, it will take 68 minutes plus standard allowances of 24.2% = 84 minutes.

b. To determine HRS/M impressions use Chart No. 7: at 250 feet per minute and circ. of ptg. cyl. 19 1/4"

with 1 up = .141 hours/M

with 2 up = .0705 hours/M

for 20,000 bags = .0705 hours/M x 20,000 = 1.41 hours = 84 min.

c. To get pounds and pounds per hour:

lbs. = .8 x roll width x gauge x feet length (tubing)
lbs. = .4 x roll width x gauge x feet length (sheeting)

lbs./hour = 48 x roll width x gauge x FPM (tubing)
from chart
lbs./hour = 24 x roll width x gauge x FPM (sheeting)

In the above example:

lbs. = .8 x 13 3/4" x .00125" x 17,000 (tubing) = 233 lbs.
lbs./hour = 48 x 13 3/4" x .00125" x 250 (tubing) = 207 lbs./hour

less 24.2% standard allowance = 158 lbs/hour

Standard hours = 233 ÷ 158 = 1.47 hours - same as method (b).

CLIENT COMPANY: DATE ISSUED: REVISION DATES:

DIVISION/PLANT: M. & T. ENGINEER:

SUPERVISORY ACCEPTANCE: M. & T. APPROVAL BY:

THE STANDARDS CONTAINED HEREIN ARE APPLICABLE TO THE MACHINE OR OPERATION AND METHODS EMPLOYED AS OF _____ AND ARE SUBJECT TO REVISION PENDING ANY ALTERATION OR CHANGE IN METHODS OR EQUIPMENT.

EXHIBIT 19-3

STD. NO. V
CHART NO. 1

PRODUCTION STANDARD

MARTIN & TUCKER, INC.
ENGINEERS

PAGE 1 OF 1

MACHINE NO. 1 DESCRIPTION: SLITTER - DUSENBERRY; PROD. CTR. # 16

OPERATION: SLITTING AND REWINDING ELEMENT: RUN STD. OUTPUT FT/HR
STD. TIME HRS/M FEET

POLY (1)

REWIND ONLY	SHEETING	550 FPM	= .031 HRS M/FT	PLUS ADDITIONAL 3 MINUTES or .050 HOURS PER ROLL CHANGE (2)
	TUBING	500 FPM	= .033 HRS M/FT	

SLITTING PLAIN (4)	FT/MIN (3)	450	350	250	175	100
	No. of Cuts	1	3	5	7	15
	or No. Out	2	4	6	8	16
	FT/HR	27,000	21,000	15,000	10,500	6,000
	HRS/M FT	.037	.048	.067	.095	.167
PLUS ADDITIONAL TIME TO LOAD ORIGINAL ROLL AND REMOVE SLIT ROLLS		EA. 3 min. .050 HR	8 min. .134 HR	12 min. .200 HR	15 min. .250 HR	20 min. .330 HR
		YOU MUST DETERMINE NUMBER OF ROLLS TO BE SLIT				

To determine the roll length in feet use formula (a):

lbs. = .4 x roll width x gauge x feet length (Sheeting)

(a) 1 Feet length = $2.5\left(\frac{\text{pounds}}{\text{roll width x gauge}}\right)$ (Sheeting)

(a) 2 Feet length = $1.25\left(\frac{\text{pounds}}{\text{roll width x gauge}}\right)$ (Tubing)

FOOTNOTES & EXPLANATION:

(1.) For CELLO, Rewind run: 650 FPM = .025 HRS/M FT.
Slitting run: 20% faster than poly (roll change - same)

(2.) For example to rewind 10 sheeted rolls, each 3,300 feet, standard hours = 3.3 x 10 x .031 + 10 x .050 = 1.05 + .5 = 1.55 Hrs. That is 93 min. or about 9 min/roll.

(3.) When slitting printed poly: reduce run speed by 10%.

CLIENT COMPANY: ____ DATE ISSUED: ____ REVISION DATES: ____
DIVISION/PLANT: ____ M. & T. ENGINEER: ____
SUPERVISORY ACCEPTANCE: ____ M. & T. APPROVAL BY: ____

THE STANDARDS CONTAINED HEREIN ARE APPLICABLE TO THE MACHINE OR OPERATION AND METHODS EMPLOYED AS OF ____ AND ARE SUBJECT TO REVISION PENDING ANY ALTERATION OR CHANGE IN METHODS OR EQUIPMENT.

EXHIBIT 19-4

STD. NO. I. A.
CHART NO. 1

PRODUCTION STANDARD

MARTIN & TUCKER, INC.
ENGINEERS

PAGE 1 OF 2

MACHINE NO. P1,2,6,5 DESCRIPTION: BAG MAKING - POLY; PROD. CTRS. #1, #1A, #6

OPERATION: BOTTOM SEAL MACHINES ELEMENT: STD. OUTPUT M/HR
STD. TIME HRS/M

		GAUGE	CODE
Practical Range of Bag Dimension:	2" - 20" Width *	.5 MIL - 1.99 MIL	L
	2" - 24" Length *	2.0 MIL - 2.99 MIL	M
	On P5 only: to 37½ width to 60" length	3.0 MIL - 5.00 MIL	H

STEP 1: Determine No. of Lanes (No. Up) to be used.

Bag Width*	No. Up
2" - 4½"	4
4½" - 6½"	3
6½" - 9½"	2
Over 10" -	1

Note: Since the standards are issued on a per lane basis, multiply the M/HR by the No. Up.

* Except P-5

STEP 2: Select Bag Length and Gauge Code and read off the Nomogram or, chart the standard in M/HR or HRS/M.

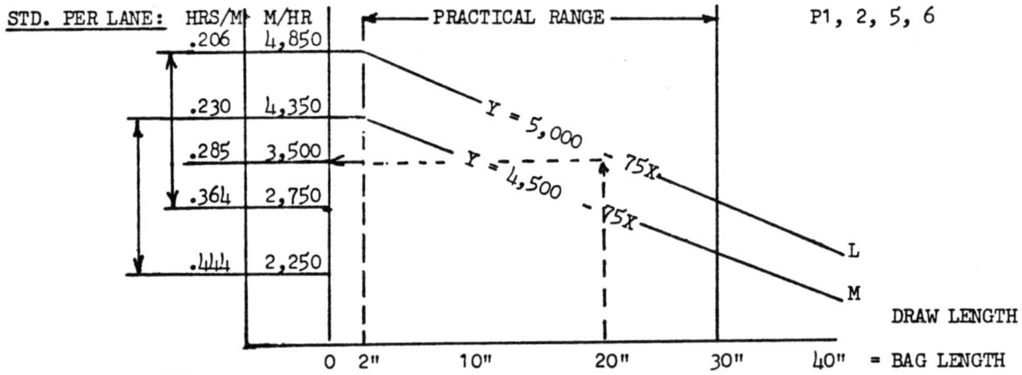

EXAMPLE:

Bag is 8" wide x 20" long x 1.5 mil (code L) No. Up = 2
Draw Length = 20"
Per Lane Standard M/HR = 3,500 bags / HR, use 2 up - standard output = 7,000 bags / HR.
or Standard HRS/M = .286 HRS/100, use 2 up - standard time = .143 HRS / M

CLIENT COMPANY: ____ DATE ISSUED: ____ REVISION DATES: ____
DIVISION/PLANT: ____ M. & T. ENGINEER: ____
SUPERVISORY ACCEPTANCE: ____ M. & T. APPROVAL BY: ____

THE STANDARDS CONTAINED HEREIN ARE APPLICABLE TO THE MACHINE OR OPERATION AND METHODS EMPLOYED AS OF ____ AND ARE SUBJECT TO REVISION PENDING ANY ALTERATION OR CHANGE IN METHODS OR EQUIPMENT.

EXHIBIT 19-5

STD. NO. I. A.
CHART NO. 1

PRODUCTION STANDARD

MARTIN & TUCKER, INC.
ENGINEERS

PAGE 2 OF 2

MACHINE NO. P1,2,6,5 DESCRIPTION: BAG MAKING - POLY; PROD. CTRS. #1, #1A, #6

OPERATION: BOTTOM SEAL MACHINES ELEMENT: STD. OUTPUT M/HR - RUN

The following table represents the standard output and standard time for each size bag (length) in increments of 2".

Select bag length, gauge code, and number of lanes.

x Bag Length	CODE L Gauge = 1 - 2 mil Y= 5,000 - 75X M/HR	HRS/M	CODE M Gauge = 2 - 3 mil Y= 4,500 - 75X M/HR	HRS/M
2"	4,850	.206	4,350	.230
4"	4,700	.213	4,200	.238
6"	4,550	.220	4,050	.247
8"	4,400	.227	3,900	.256
10"	4,250	.235	3,750	.267
12"	4,100	.244	3,600	.278
14"	3,950	.253	3,450	.290
16"	3,800	.263	3,300	.303
18"	3,650	.274	3,150	.317
20"	3,500	.286	3,000	.333
22"	3,350	.299	2,850	.351
24"	3,200	.313	2,700	.370
26"	3,050	.328	2,550	.392
28"	2,900	.345	2,400	.417
30"	2,750	.364	2,250	.444
32"	2,600	.385	2,100	.476
34"	2,450	.408	1,950	.513
36"	2,300	.435	1,800	.556
38"	2,150	.465	1,650	.606
40"	2,000	.500	1,500	.667

NOTES:

1. Quantity Variation:

Subtract: 15% for orders under 10M
10% for orders from 10M - 25M
5% for orders from 25M - 50M

CLIENT COMPANY: ________ DATE ISSUED: ________ REVISION DATES: ________
DIVISION/PLANT: ________ M. & T. ENGINEER: ________
SUPERVISORY ACCEPTANCE: ________ M. & T. APPROVAL BY: ________

THE STANDARDS CONTAINED HEREIN ARE APPLICABLE TO THE MACHINE OR OPERATION AND METHODS EMPLOYED AS OF ________ AND ARE SUBJECT TO REVISION PENDING ANY ALTERATION OR CHANGE IN METHODS OR EQUIPMENT.

EXHIBIT 19-6

STD. NO. 1
CHART NO. 2

PRODUCTION STANDARD

MARTIN & TUCKER, INC.
ENGINEERS

PAGE 2 OF 2

MACHINE NO. 9 MACHINES DESCRIPTION: SCHJELDAHL, G. T. 208 or 201; PROD. CTR. # 9

OPERATION: BAG MAKING - SIDE WELD ELEMENT: RUN

STD. CREW = 1 OPERATOR UNIT OF OUTPUT = BAGS

Order Quantity equal or over 25 M
Sheet Stock: Flat Bottoms, or Gussetted (5)

BAG WIDTH (= Draw Length)	GAUGE Code L 1.25 to 1.75 Mil		GAUGE Code M 2.00 to 3.00 Mil		GAUGE Code H 3.25 to 5.0 Mil	
	M/HR	HRS/M	M/HR	HRS/M	M/HR	HRS/M
3" to 6"	11,500	.087	8,640	.116	6,000	.167
6+ to 9"	10,560	.095	8,000	.125	5,600	.178
9+ to 12"	9,600	.104	7,420	.135	5,280	.189
12+ to 16"	8,640	.116	7,000	.143	5,000	.200
16+ to 20"	7,680	.130	6,200	.161	4,800	.208
20+ to 24"	6,720	.149	5,500	.182	4,320	.231

SCHEDULE OF ALLOWANCES

No.	Type of Allowance	Change in Std. HRS/M
1.	Order quantity under 25 M	Add 50% to Std. HRS/M
2.	Solid roll run (1 up)	Add 45% to Std. HRS/M
3.	Gauge .75 to 1.0 Mil	Add 15% to Std. HRS/M
4.	Gauge over 5.0 Mil	Add 20% to Std. HRS/M
5.	Gussetted bags, Gauge Code H only	Add 40% to Std. HRS/M
6.	"Square" bags	Add 20% to Std. HRS/M
7.	Specialty bags:	Add to Std. HRS/M:
	7.1 Header	20%
	7.2 Reinforced header	30%
	7.3 Serration (across the web)	40%
	7.4 Wicket, or other small quantity pack	20% to 40%, depending on quantity of bags/wicket
8.	Duplex bags (2 ply)	Add 35% to Std. HRS/M

DEFINITIONS:

(1) "Ideal" bag is a bag in which the ratio of width to length is under .85.

(2) "Square" bag is a bag in which the ratio of width to length is over .85.

CLIENT COMPANY: DATE ISSUED: REVISION DATES:
DIVISION/PLANT: M. & T. ENGINEER:
SUPERVISORY ACCEPTANCE: M. & T. APPROVAL BY:

THE STANDARDS CONTAINED HEREIN ARE APPLICABLE TO THE MACHINE OR OPERATION AND METHODS EMPLOYED AS OF ____ AND ARE SUBJECT TO REVISION PENDING ANY ALTERATION OR CHANGE IN METHODS OR EQUIPMENT.

EXHIBIT 19-7

STD. NO. 3 CHART NO. 1

PRODUCTION STANDARD

MARTIN & TUCKER, INC. ENGINEERS

PAGE 1 OF 3

MACHINE NO. 60 DESCRIPTION: INTA ROTO, 3 PLY, 44", 2 STATION APPLICATOR

OPERATION: LAMINATE / COAT PROD. CTR. # 2 ELEMENT: DERIVATIVE DATA

STD. CREW = 3 = 1 OPERATOR + 2 HELPERS

UNIT OF OUTPUT = M Ft.
MM Sq. In.
Lbs.
M Imp.

Machine Specifications:

Max. Web Width 44"
Min. Web Width 22"
Max. No. of Plies 3 (2 unwind stations w/ flying splicers)
Max. O.D. Unwind Roll 28" + (1 portable foil unwind station, 12" O.D. Limit, 18" O.D. other materials)
Max. O.D. Rewind Roll 28" (or 1000 lbs.)
Core I.D. (Rewind) 6"
Cylinders: Impression; (rubber, edge -trimmed) Coating; (Gravure engraved) Combining. (chrome plated steel)

Laminating or Coating standards are issued for running 1 up (= 1 web across).

Material : Polyethylene (Lam. Grade) with either one, or two of the following: Mylar, Cello, Foil, Polypropylene, Polyethylene, Nylon, and Paper.

Gauge:	FILM	FOIL	PAPER
Max.	.005	.00200	.0200 (Soft)
Min.	.001	.00035	.0025

Adhesive Material: Solvent diluted adhesives, and some water-based adhesives.

Coating Material: Solvent based coatings.

For the purpose of Lamination Production Standards the following are categorized:

FILM includes: Polyethylene, Mylar, Cello, Polypropylene, Polystyrene, and Nylon.

PAPER includes: Glassine, Pouch paper, and other papers.

FOIL includes: Aluminum only.

CLIENT COMPANY: DATE ISSUED: REVISION DATES:
DIVISION PLANT: M. & T. ENGINEER:
SUPERVISORY ACCEPTANCE: M. & T. APPROVAL BY:

THE STANDARDS CONTAINED HEREIN ARE APPLICABLE TO THE MACHINE OR OPERATION AND METHODS EMPLOYED AS OF ______ AND ARE SUBJECT TO REVISION PENDING ANY ALTERATION OR CHANGE IN METHODS OR EQUIPMENT.

EXHIBIT 19-8

STD. NO. 3
CHART NO. 2

PRODUCTION STANDARD

MARTIN & TUCKER, INC.
ENGINEERS

PAGE 2 OF 3

MACHINE NO. 60 DESCRIPTION: INTA ROTO, 3 PLY, 44", 2 STATION APPLICATOR

OPERATION: LAMINATE / COAT PROD. CTR. # 2 ELEMENT: RUN

STD. CREW = 3 = 1 OPERATOR + 2 HELPERS

UNIT OF OUTPUT = M Ft.
MM Sq. In.
Lbs.
M Imp.

Order quantity equal or over 30M Ft. (3)
2 - Ply Lamination

	Lamination Components	Std. Ft./Min.	Std. Ft./Hr.	Std. Hrs./M Ft.
1.	FILM to FILM (1)			
	1.1 Cello/Cello	440	26,400	.0379
	1.2 Cello/OPP	420	25,200	.0397
	1.3 Cello/PE	400	24,000	.0417
	1.4 Mylar/PE	360	21,600	.0463
	1.5 OPP/OPP	320	19,200	.0521
	1.6 Nylon/PE (4)	260	15,600	.0641
	1.7 PE/PE (4)	240	14,400	.0694
2.	FILM to FOIL			
	2.1 Cello/AL	400	24,000	.0417
	2.2 OPP/AL	400	24,000	.0417
	2.3 Mylar/AL	340	20,400	.0490
	2.4 PE/AL	280	16,800	.0595
3.	FILM to PAPER	360	21,600	.0463
4.	FOIL to PAPER	360	21,600	.0463
5.	FOIL to FOIL (2)			
6.	PAPER to PAPER (2)			

ABBREVIATIONS: PE = Polyethelene
AL = Aluminum
OPP = Oriented Polypropylene

FOOTNOTES:
(1) This group represents 80% of existing lamination possibilities/orders.

(2) These combinations are rarely applied.

(3) 30M Ft. = app. 550 Lbs./Ply in 1.25 Mil, P.E., 36" web.

(4) These standards represent the average condition of roll formation, the extra care required in laminating printed to plain film, etc.

CLIENT COMPANY: ______ DATE ISSUED: ______ REVISION DATES: ______
DIVISION/PLANT: ______ M. & T. ENGINEER: ______
SUPERVISORY ACCEPTANCE: ______ M. & T. APPROVAL BY: ______

THE STANDARDS CONTAINED HEREIN ARE APPLICABLE TO THE MACHINE OR OPERATION AND METHODS EMPLOYED AS OF ______ AND ARE SUBJECT TO REVISION PENDING ANY ALTERATION OR CHANGE IN METHODS OR EQUIPMENT.

EXHIBIT 19-9

STD. NO. 3
CHART NO. 3

PRODUCTION STANDARD

MARTIN & TUCKER, INC.
ENGINEERS

PAGE 3 OF 3

MACHINE NO. 60 DESCRIPTION: INTA ROTO, 3 PLY, 44", 2 STATION APPLICATOR

OPERATION: LAMINATE / COAT; PROD. CTR. # 2 ELEMENT: RUN

STD. CREW = 3 = 1 OPERATOR + 2 HELPERS

UNIT OF OUTPUT = M Ft.
MM Sq. In.
Lbs.
M Imp.

Order quantity equal or over 22M Ft. (3)
3 - Ply Lamination

	Req'd. No. of Passes	Std. Ft./Min.	Std. Ft./Hr.	Std.Hrs/M Ft.
1. FILM/FOIL/Dble. H.S. Ctg. (1)	3	240	14,400	.0694
2. PAPER/FOIL/FILM	1	320	19,200	.0521
3. FILM/FOIL/FILM	2	260	15,600	.0641
4. FILM/FILM/FILM	2	240	14,400	.0694
5. FOIL/FILM/FILM or, H.S. Ctg.	2	240	14,400	.0694
6. FILM or H.S. Ctg./ PAPER/ FILM or H.S. Ctg.	1 or 2	280	16,800	.0595
7. FILM/FOIL/PAPER (2)				

FOOTNOTES:

(1) This type of lamination "considered" as 3 ply even though it consists of 2 plies only.

(2) This and other 3 ply combinations are rarely applied, at present.

(3) 22M Ft. = app. 400 lbs./Ply in 1.25 Mil, P.E., 36" web.

CLIENT COMPANY: ______ DATE ISSUED: ______ REVISION DATES: ______
DIVISION/PLANT: ______ M. & T. ENGINEER: ______
SUPERVISORY ACCEPTANCE: ______ M. & T. APPROVAL BY: ______

THE STANDARDS CONTAINED HEREIN ARE APPLICABLE TO THE MACHINE OR OPERATION AND METHODS EMPLOYED AS OF ______ AND ARE SUBJECT TO REVISION PENDING ANY ALTERATION OR CHANGE IN METHODS OR EQUIPMENT.

EXHIBIT 19-10

STD. NO. 4
CHART NO. 3

PRODUCTION STANDARD

MARTIN & TUCKER, INC.
ENGINEERS

PAGE 1 OF 1

MACHINE NO. 179 DESCRIPTION: 2-C HARRIS OFFSET: PROD. CTR. # 20

OPERATION: PRINT 2- COLORS, OR COAT VARNISH ELEMENT: MAKEREADY

STANDARD HOURS *

NO. OF COLORS	BASIC MR	PWU	RMR	TOTAL MR
1st 2-C's	3.50	.70	.30	4.50
3rd Color, Same set up	1.75	.50	.15	2.40
1-C Complete set up	2.75	.50	.30	3.55
Varnish Coat	.30	.25	.15	.70
3rd & 4th Color Same set up	2.55	.70	.30	3.55

NOTES:

1. For a Separate Varnish Plate: Add .70 Std. Hrs.
2. For Running Against Grain : Add .50 Std. Hrs.
3. For Heavy Solids : Add 1.00 Std. Hrs.

* Std. Allowance for P, F, & D included: 10%

CLIENT COMPANY: DATE ISSUED: REVISION DATES:
DIVISION/PLANT: M. & T. ENGINEER:
SUPERVISORY ACCEPTANCE: M. & T. APPROVAL BY:

THE STANDARDS CONTAINED HEREIN ARE APPLICABLE TO THE MACHINE OR OPERATION AND METHODS EMPLOYED AS OF ____ AND ARE SUBJECT TO REVISION PENDING ANY ALTERATION OR CHANGE IN METHODS OR EQUIPMENT.

EXHIBIT 19-11

Exhibit 19-12 is a run standard for a given set of styles of folding cartons, namely: seal end, reverse tuck end and straight tuck end (SE, RTE, STE). For other styles, other standards would be used. The parameters affecting running speed are: inches of feed length, size of the order, and the thickness or caliper of the paperboard being used. Typical allowances that would be used are: heavier board, narrow width cartons, shallow depth cartons, and the use of different devices on the gluing machine.

Exhibit 19-13 is a bindery operation which combines both setup as well as run. Notice that both have their own specific parameters.

Exhibit 19-14 is a run standard for an operation in the printing and folding carton industry. The two major parameters are obvious.

Exhibits 19-15 and 19-16 show production standards for *one element* of a makeready on a web-fed printing press in the label industry, involving the changing of copy-design plates. The standard hours apply to 8 presses which are grouped into 3 production centers. The time values developed account for the fact that the changes can apply to the same number of colors, as shown on Exhibit 19-15. And it can be for jobs which pertain to variations in color combinations as it affects the number of plates, as shown in Exhibit 19-16.

Exhibit 19-17 shows the standards for another element in the makeready of the same type of press, i.e., changing the ink colors. In this standard, we are allowing for time differences when going from one kind of ink to another. Within the general categories of "standard mixed inks," "process inks," "mixed inks," and "overprint varnish inks," we show the variations in going from light and dark oil-based inks to light and dark moisture-set (MS) inks and vice versa.

Exhibit 19-18 shows the run standards for one type of product on the same press, namely: pressure-sensitive matrix removed labels. Here, the parameters are: the number of colors from 0 to 5, and the specific die to be used in running the order.

Exhibit 19-19 is the standard for the element of "change print cylinder" as part of the makeready in a gravure printing press. In order to qualify the three standard hour figures given under the 3 parameters (line 12), the methods and steps of accomplishing this operation are listed.

Exhibit 19-20 is not a production standard but requires standardization in cost for estimating purposes. This Material Standard is created to recognize that a waste allowance cannot be handled as a flat percentage added to raw material cost. Basically, there are two kinds of waste in converting:

1. That caused by unacceptable quality in the various stages of conversion, operation-to-operation. This element of waste and rejects is generally a function of the customer's order and can be recognized on the job estimate as a characteristic customer/job percentage.

2. That caused by some or all elements of a makeready or setup, i.e., waste which unavoidably occurs during the makeready up to the point where the makeready is completed and the operator starts his "run." This excess cost (in this instance) is a function of the color-to-color change, the type of material, the length of the stroke, the standard speed of the press and roll width. These latter factors are the parameters of this material standard.

Exhibit 19-21 is a standard which combines all elements of the makeready of a small printer in an envelope converting plant. The type of makeready has been broken down into classes and the sub-divisions under each. All are parameters. The additives not only provide for variations in quality required, but also give standard times for one-a-day operations, such as: morning startup.

Exhibit 19-22 shows a chart of *washup* production standards on an envelope printer. If a washup can be identified with a specific job, setting a standard is one way of handling and estimating its time. If the washup is not identifiable with any specific job, it should be included in the development of the Machine-Hour Rate for the particular facility. In some printing facilities, the washup time range can be appreciable. In this standard, the washup cycle time is from a low of .177 to 1.5 standard hours, a multiple of almost 8.5 times.

STD. NO. 1

CHART NO. 1

PRODUCTION STANDARD

MARTIN & TUCKER, INC.
ENGINEERS

PAGE 1 OF 2

MACHINE NO. 122 DESCRIPTION: SPEEDKING GLUER; PROD. CTR. # 16

OPERATION: FOLD, GLUE & PACK ELEMENT: RUN

STYLES: SE, RTE, STE, SLEEVES

STD. BLANKS PER HOUR AND STD. HOURS PER M BLANKS

INCHES OF FEED LENGTH	SIZE OF ORDER 10M - 50M, BOARD CALIPER .014" - .025"	SIZE OF ORDER 10M - 50M, BOARD CALIPER .026" - .040"	SIZE OF ORDER 50M - OVER, BOARD CALIPER .014" - .025"	SIZE OF ORDER 50M - OVER, BOARD CALIPER .026" - .040"
4"	27,000 / .037	23,000 / .044	30,000 / .034	25,000 / .040
5"	27,000 / .037	23,000 / .044	30,000 / .034	25,000 / .040
6"	27,000 / .037	23,000 / .044	30,000 / .034	25,000 / .040
7"	27,000 / .037	23,000 / .044	30,000 / .034	25,000 / .040
8"	26,000 / .038	22,500 / .045	28,500 / .035	24,500 / .041
9"	25,000 / .040	21,000 / .048	28,000 / .036	23,500 / .043
10"	24,000 / .042	20,000 / .050	26,500 / .038	22,000 / .046
11"	22,000 / .046	18,000 / .055	25,500 / .041	20,500 / .049
12"	20,000 / .050	16,700 / .060	22,000 / .045	18,500 / .054
13"	18,500 / .054	15,500 / .065	20,500 / .049	17,000 / .059
14"	17,300 / .058	14,300 / .070	19,500 / .052	16,000 / .062
15"	16,000 / .062	13,500 / .074	18,000 / .056	15,000 / .067
16"	15,000 / .066	12,500 / .079	17,000 / .059	14,000 / .071
17"	14,300 / .070	12,000 / .084	16,000 / .063	13,000 / .076
18"	13,500 / .074	11,500 / .089	15,000 / .067	12,500 / .080
19"	12,500 / .079	10,500 / .095	14,000 / .071	12,000 / .085
20"	12,000 / .084	10,000 / .100	13,300 / .075	11,000 / .090
21"	11,000 / .090	9,500 / .108	12,500 / .081	10,500 / .097

PRACTICAL RANGE

AREA OF STRAIGHT LINEAR RELATION OF OUTPUT TO FEED LENGTH

CLIENT COMPANY: DATE ISSUED: REVISION DATES:

DIVISION/PLANT: M. & T. ENGINEER:

SUPERVISORY ACCEPTANCE: M. & T. APPROVAL BY:

THE STANDARDS CONTAINED HEREIN ARE APPLICABLE TO THE MACHINE OR OPERATION AND METHODS EMPLOYED AS OF ______ AND ARE SUBJECT TO REVISION PENDING ANY ALTERATION OR CHANGE IN METHODS OR EQUIPMENT.

EXHIBIT 19-12

MARTIN & TUCKER, INC.
ENGINEERS

STD. NO. 117
CHART NO. 1

PRODUCTION STANDARD

PAGE 1 OF 1

MACHINE NO. 1042 DESCRIPTION: Baum Folder 31 x 46 (contin. air wheel)
OPERATION: Fold ELEMENT: Setup and Run

Setup Time in Each Column is Total Time For No. of Folds Indicated

Setup Operation	Setup Time – Each Folding Section: Parallel	8 Page (1st Ra)	16 Page (2nd Ra)	32 Page (3rd Ra)	
One Fold	.33	.16	.16	.16	
Two Folds	.45	.29	.29	.29	
Three Folds	.57	.41	.41		
Four Folds	.69	.53	.53		
Five Folds					
First Score, Slit, or Perf.	.09	.09	.09		
Each Add'l Score, Slit, or Perf.	.06	.06	.06		

RUNNING

Folding Factor:
Parallel Only – Use Sheet Travel Length.
Right Angle – Use ¾ Width Plus Parallel Folded Length.
Or Sheet Travel Length Whichever is Greater.

Folding Factor	Production Per Hour	Time Per M.	Folding Factor	Production Per Hour	Time Per M.	Folding Factor	Production Per Hour	Time Per M.
3			16	10225	.098	36	4690	.213
3½			17	9650	.104	37	4570	.219
4			18	9150	.109	38	4460	.224
4½			19	8690	.115	39	4345	.231
5			20	8280	.121	40	4275	.234
5½			21	7900	.127	42	4040	.248
6			22	7550	.133	44	3860	.259
6½			23	7250	.138	46	3700	.271
7	21700	.046	24	6950	.144	48	3545	.282
7½	20420	.049	25	6690	.149	50	3410	.293
8	19300	.052	26	6445	.155	52	3275	.305
8½	18300	.055	27	6210	.161	54	3160	.316
9	17380	.058	28	5990	.167	56	3045	.329
9½	16525	.061	29	5795	.173	58	2945	.340
10	15790	.064	30	5600	.179	60	2860	.351
11	14480	.069	31	5430	.184	63		
12	13375	.075	32	5260	.190	66		
13	12410	.081	33	5110	.196	69		
14	11575	.086	34	4965	.202	72		
15	10850	.092	35	4820	.208	75		

CLIENT COMPANY: DATE ISSUED: REVISION DATES:
DIVISION/PLANT: M. & T. ENGINEER:
SUPERVISORY ACCEPTANCE: M. & T. APPROVAL BY:

THE STANDARDS CONTAINED HEREIN ARE APPLICABLE TO THE MACHINE OR OPERATION AND METHODS EMPLOYED AS OF ___ AND ARE SUBJECT TO REVISION PENDING ANY ALTERATION OR CHANGE IN METHODS OR EQUIPMENT.

EXHIBIT 19-13

STD. NO. 201
CHART NO. 1

PRODUCTION STANDARD

MARTIN & TUCKER, INC.
ENGINEERS

PAGE 1 OF 1

MACHINE NO. 14A DESCRIPTION: Rutherford RMT 12499 Step & Repeat

OPERATION: Platemaking - Photocomposing ELEMENT: RUN

STANDARD HOURS

STEPS	FILM 1	2	3	4	5	6	7	8	9	10
1	.37									
2	.42	.57								
3	.47	.62	.78							
4	.52	.67	.83	.98						
5	.57	.72	.88	1.03	1.20					
6	.62	.77	.93	1.08	1.25	1.40				
7	.67	.82	.98	1.13	1.30	1.45	1.62			
8	.72	.87	1.03	1.18	1.35	1.50	1.67	1.83		
9	.77	.92	1.08	1.23	1.40	1.55	1.72	1.88	2.04	
10	.82	1.07	1.13	1.28	1.45	1.60	1.77	1.93	2.09	2.25
11	.88	1.12	1.18	1.33	1.50	1.65	1.82	1.98	2.14	2.30
12	.94	1.18	1.23	1.38	1.55	1.70	1.87	2.03	2.19	2.35
13	1.00	1.24	1.29	1.43	1.60	1.75	1.92	2.08	2.24	2.40
14	1.06	1.30	1.35	1.50	1.65	1.80	1.97	2.13	2.29	2.45
15	1.12	1.36	1.41	1.56	1.71	1.85	2.02	2.18	2.34	2.50
16	1.18	1.42	1.47	1.62	1.77	1.91	2.07	2.23	2.39	2.55
17	1.24	1.48	1.53	1.68	1.83	1.97	2.13	2.28	2.44	2.60
18	1.30	1.54	1.59	1.74	1.90	2.03	2.19	2.34	2.49	2.65
19	1.36	1.60	1.65	1.80	1.96	2.09	2.25	2.40	2.55	2.70
20	1.42	1.66	1.71	1.86	2.02	2.15	2.31	2.46	2.61	2.75
21	1.48	1.72	1.77	1.92	2.08	2.20	2.36	2.51	2.66	2.80

CLIENT COMPANY: ______ DATE ISSUED: ______ REVISION DATES: ______
DIVISION/PLANT: ______ M. & T. ENGINEER: ______
SUPERVISORY ACCEPTANCE: ______ M. & T. APPROVAL BY: ______

THE STANDARDS CONTAINED HEREIN ARE APPLICABLE TO THE MACHINE OR OPERATION AND METHODS EMPLOYED AS OF ______ AND ARE SUBJECT TO REVISION PENDING ANY ALTERATION OR CHANGE IN METHODS OR EQUIPMENT.

EXHIBIT 19-14

STD. NO. 1-01/14
CHART NO 38E

PRODUCTION STANDARD

MARTIN & TUCKER, INC.
ENGINEERS

PAGE 1 OF 2

MACHINE NO. All L.P. DESCRIPTION: New Era 9 x 12 Presses
OPERATION: Change - Copy-Design Plates ELEMENT: Makeready

FULL COPY = COMPLETE DESIGN CHANGE FOR EACH COLOR IN DESIGN.

PARTIAL COPY = DESIGN CHANGE FOR ONE COLOR IN MULTI COLOR DESIGN AFTER ORIGINAL FULL COPY DESIGN OR SINGLE LINE OR ONE WORD CHANGE (IN SAME POSITION ALL COPIES) ON ONE COLOR COPY DESIGN.

	FULL COPY STANDARD HOURS					STD. HRS.
PRODUCTION CENTERS	1 COLOR to 1 COLOR	2 COLOR to 2 COLOR	3 COLOR to 3 COLOR	4 COLOR to 4 COLOR	5 COLOR to 5 COLOR	PARTIAL (1) COPY / PLATE
1,2,3,4	.1547	.3250	.5480	X	X	.1071
5	.1547	.3250	.5480	.7058	X	.1071
6,7,8	.1547	.3250	.5480	.7058	.9862	.1071
X	X	X	X	X	X	X

NOTES:
(1) USE WHEN ESTIMATING AN ORDER WITH MULTIPLE COPY CHANGES ON ONE COPY DESIGN COLOR. (MULTIPLY NO. OF PARTIAL COPY CHANGES) X(PARTIAL COPY/PLATE STD HR.) FOR TOTAL STD. HRS. FOR PARTIAL COPY CHANGE. ADD PARTIAL COPY STD. HR. TOTAL TO ORIGINAL COPY CHANGE STD. HRS. FOR TOTAL "ALL PLATE CHANGES"/ORDER.

CLIENT COMPANY: ______ DATE ISSUED: ______ REVISION DATES: ______
DIVISION PLANT: ______ M. & T. ENGINEER: ______
SUPERVISORY ACCEPTANCE: ______ M. & T. APPROVAL BY: ______

THE STANDARDS CONTAINED HEREIN ARE APPLICABLE TO THE MACHINE OR OPERATION AND METHODS EMPLOYED AS OF ______ AND ARE SUBJECT TO REVISION PENDING ANY ALTERATION OR CHANGE IN METHODS OR EQUIPMENT.

EXHIBIT 19-15

STD. NO. 1-01/14
CHART NO. 38E

PRODUCTION STANDARD

MARTIN & TUCKER, INC.
ENGINEERS

PAGE 2 OF 2

MACHINE NO. All L. P. DESCRIPTION: New Era 9 x 12 Presses

OPERATION: Change - Copy-Design Plates ELEMENT: Makeready

FULL COPY STANDARD HOURS

PRODUCTION CENTERS	1 COL to 2 COL OR 2 COL to 1 COL	2 COL to 3 COL OR 3 COL to 2 COL	3 COL to 4 COL OR 4 COL to 3 COL	4 COL to 5 COL OR 5 COL to 4 COL	(1) 1 COLOR to NO COLOR	X X
1,2,3,4	.2985	.5215	X	X	.0265	X
5	.2985	.5215	.6793	X	.0265	X
6,7,8	.2985	.5215	.6793	.9597	.0265	X
X	X	X	X	X	X	X

NOTES:

(1) FOR IN-BETWEEN CHANGES MORE DRASTIC THAN THOSE SHOWN ABOVE USE THIS STD. HR. EXAMPLE: 5 COLOR COPY-DESIGN TO 1 COLOR COPY-DESIGN FULL CHANGE = (5 COLOR TO 5 COLOR STD. HR. PG 1) — [(1 COLOR TO NONE STD. HR.) X (4)].

CLIENT COMPANY: DATE ISSUED: REVISION DATES:
DIVISION/PLANT: M. & T. ENGINEER:
SUPERVISORY ACCEPTANCE: M. & T. APPROVAL BY:

THE STANDARDS CONTAINED HEREIN ARE APPLICABLE TO THE MACHINE OR OPERATION AND METHODS EMPLOYED AS OF AND ARE SUBJECT TO REVISION PENDING ANY ALTERATION OR CHANGE IN METHODS OR EQUIPMENT.

EXHIBIT 19-16

STD. NO. 1-01/14
CHART NO. 39E

PRODUCTION STANDARD

MARTIN & TUCKER, INC.
ENGINEERS

PAGE 1 OF 1

MACHINE NO. All L.P. DESCRIPTION: New Era 9 x 12 Presses

OPERATION: Change: Ink Color (std. mixed, process inks and varnish) ELEMENT: Makeready

NO ALLOWANCE IN THESE STANDARDS FOR INK ROLLER CHANGES ON PRINT HEADS.

"STANDARD INKS" STD. HRS./CHGE

FROM	TO	P.C. 1,5	PC2,3,4 6,7,8
NONE	DK Oil or DK MS	.0354	.0354
Lt. OIL Lt. MS	NONE NONE	.1085	.1085
Lt. OIL DK.OIL DK MS NONE	Lt. OIL DK·OIL,DK.MS &NONE NONE Lt. MS	.1592	.1592
Lt.OIL Lt.MS DK.OIL DK.MS	DK.OIL OR DK.MS Lt.OIL OR Lt.MS DK.OIL OR DK.MS Lt.OIL OR Lt.MS Lt.OIL DK·OIL OR DK·MS	.2411	.2250
Lt·OIL DK.MS	Lt.MS Lt.MS	.2880	.2660

"PROCESS INK" STD. HRS./CHGE (1)

FROM	TO	P.C. 1,5	PC2,3,4 6,7,8
DK.MS DK·OIL	NONE DK.MS	.3013	.2867
Lt.OIL DK.OIL Lt.MS DK.MS	DK.MS Lt.MS Lt·MS DK MS DK.MS	3611	.3370
Lt.OIL DK.MS	Lt.MS Lt.MS	4269	.3941
(1) FOR EACH FULL DAY OF RUN TIME ADD FOR WASH UP REQUIRED		.1090	.1090

"MIXED INKS" STD. HRS./CHGE

FROM	TO	P.C. 1,5	PC2,3,4 6,7,8
Lt. OIL Lt. MS NONE DK·OIL DK.MS.	NONE NONE DK.MS. NONE NONE	.1387	.1387
NONE Lt.OIL DK·OIL	Lt.OIL Lt.OIL Lt.OIL DK·MS	.2544	.2793
Lt.OIL DK.OIL Lt.MS DK.MS	DK.OIL OR DK.MS Lt.OIL OR Lt.MS Lt.OIL OR Lt.MS DK.OIL OR DK.MS Lt.OIL DK.OIL OR DK MS	.3510	.2958
Lt.OIL DK·OIL DK.MS	Lt.MS Lt.MS Lt.MS	.4049	.3572

"OVERPRINT VARNISH" STD. HRS/CHGE (A)

FROM	TO	P.C. 1,5	PC2,3,4 6,7,8
Lt.OIL	VARNISH #1159	.6627	.6307
Lt.MS	VARNISH #1159	.7652	.7168

NOTES:
(A) NEVER GO FROM DK.INK TO OVERPRINT VARNISH

CLIENT COMPANY: ______ DATE ISSUED: ______ REVISION DATES: ______
DIVISION/PLANT: ______ M. & T. ENGINEER: ______
SUPERVISORY ACCEPTANCE: ______ M. & T. APPROVAL BY: ______

THE STANDARDS CONTAINED HEREIN ARE APPLICABLE TO THE MACHINE OR OPERATION AND METHODS EMPLOYED AS OF ______ AND ARE SUBJECT TO REVISION PENDING ANY ALTERATION OR CHANGE IN METHODS OR EQUIPMENT.

EXHIBIT 19-17

STD. NO. 1-01/14
CHART NO. 55E

PRODUCTION STANDARD

MARTIN & TUCKER, INC.
ENGINEERS
PAGE 1 OF 1

MACHINE NO. P.C.7 DESCRIPTION: New Era 9 x 12 L.P.
OPERATION: P.S. Matrix (waste) Removed Labels ELEMENT: RUN

INK: OIL, MOISTURE SET & ALL COMBINATIONS

DIE - DESIGN GROUP	DIE DESIGN NO. UP	STD. IMP.R./HR. / STD. HRS./M IMPR.				
		BLANK OR 1 COLOR	TWO COLOR	THREE COLOR	FOUR COLOR	FIVE COLOR
Standard Dies	3-15	4745	4396	3962	3557	3192
Special Dies		.2107	.2275	.2524	.2811	.3133
1/16" Stroke	3-15	4458	4112	3718	3352	2957
Premium (X)		.2243	.2432	.2690	.2983	.3382
Standard Dies	16-28	4026	3687	3336	3010	2688
Special Dies		.2484	.2712	.2998	.3322	.3720
1/16" Stroke	16-28	3811	3403	3058	2736	2352
Premium (X)		.2624	.2939	.3270	.3655	.4252

CLIENT COMPANY: DATE ISSUED: REVISION DATES:
DIVISION/PLANT: M. & T. ENGINEER:
SUPERVISORY ACCEPTANCE: M. & T. APPROVAL BY:

THE STANDARDS CONTAINED HEREIN ARE APPLICABLE TO THE MACHINE OR OPERATION AND METHODS EMPLOYED AS OF ______ AND ARE SUBJECT TO REVISION PENDING ANY ALTERATION OR CHANGE IN METHODS OR EQUIPMENT.

EXHIBIT 19-18

STD. NO.______
CHART NO.______

PRODUCTION STANDARD

MARTIN & TUCKER, INC.
ENGINEERS

PAGE 1 OF 1

MACHINE NO. 75 DESCRIPTION: CHAMPLAIN 5 COLOR GRAVURE PRESS

OPERATION: CHANGE PRINT CYLINDER ELEMENT: MAKEREADY

NO.	ELEMENT CHANGE	FIRST COLOR Min. Occ.	FIRST COLOR Accum.	COLOR 2 & 3 ea. Min. Occ.	COLOR 2 & 3 ea. Accum.	COLOR 4 & 5 ea. Min. Occ.	COLOR 4 & 5 ea. Accum.
1.0	Remove doctor blade	2.80	2.80	2.30	2.30	1.60	1.60
1.1	Raise applicator	.20	3.00	.20		.30	1.90
2.0	Unlock chase	.45	3.45	.45	2.95	.45	2.35
3.0	Disconnect ink pump, put up cradle & remove chase from head	2.25	5.70	1.10	4.05	1.10	3.45
3.1	Wash cylinder = (get solvent, rags, wash, pumis cylinder & load cylinder onto truck)	5.60	11.30	-0-	-0-	-0-	-0-
3.2	Wash cylinder = (wash, pumis cylinder & load cylinder onto truck)	-0-	-0-	3.20	7.25	3.20	6.65
4.0	Remove cylinder from chase						
4.1	Remove collars, wash shafts, remove sling rings, scrape chase, wrap cylinder & put into storage rack	16.10	27.40	12.35	19.60	13.70	20.35
5.0	Get cylinder for next order	2.03	29.43	2.03	21.63	2.03	22.38
6.0	Reassemble chase & print cylinder						
6.1	Attach bearings, sling rings, collars, etc.	11.11	40.54	10.96	32.59	10.96	33.34
7.0	Put chase into print head (Raise applicator as necessary)	5.05	45.59	2.35	34.94	1.60	34.94
8.0	Copy register for 1st off O.K.	5.00	50.59	5.90	40.84	7.78	42.72
9.0	Observed time		50.59		40.84		42.72
10.0	Levelled time (observed x 1.10)		55.65		44.92		46.92
11.0	Allowed (Standard time) time = (Levelled time x 1.238)		68.89		55.61		58.18
12.0	Standard Hours (Std. Min. ÷ 60 min.)		1.15		.93		.97

NOTE:

Element 4.1 can vary with inks that have run several days and have hardened on sling rings. This variance has been included in ink allowance. Poorly stepped copy can cause variance in element 8. This variance is in MHR.

CLIENT COMPANY:______ DATE ISSUED:______ REVISION DATES:______
DIVISION/PLANT:______ M. & T. ENGINEER:______
SUPERVISORY ACCEPTANCE:______ M. & T. APPROVAL BY:______

THE STANDARDS CONTAINED HEREIN ARE APPLICABLE TO THE MACHINE OR OPERATION AND METHODS EMPLOYED AS OF______ AND ARE SUBJECT TO REVISION PENDING ANY ALTERATION OR CHANGE IN METHODS OR EQUIPMENT.

EXHIBIT 19-19

STD. NO. 1-01/14
CHART NO. 38WM

MATERIAL STANDARD

MARTIN & TUCKER, INC.
ENGINEERS

PAGE 1 OF 1

MACHINE NO: PC 1 thru 8 DESCRIPTION: LETTERPRESS/NEW ERA 9 x 12 PRESSES
OPERATION: CHANGE - COPY-DESIGN PLATES ELEMENT: WASTE (MAKEREADY)

MATERIAL: HEAT SEAL WKK & GEMKOTE		WASTE MATERIAL			$ COST/CHANGE
STROKE: 4½" thru 7½"		1C TO 2C	2C TO 3C	3C TO 4C	4C TO 5C
RUN STD. IMPR./HR.	ROLL WIDTH	PC 1 - 8	PC 1 - 8	PC 5,6,7,8	PC 6,7,8
6000 TO 6499	10" & 10-3/4"	3.43	5.99	7.81	11.03
	11½"	3.67	6.41	8.35	11.79
	12½"	3.99	6.97	9.08	12.83
5500 TO 5999	10" & 10-3/4"	3.16	5.52	7.19	10.15
	11½"	3.37	5.89	7.68	10.85
	12½"	3.67	6.41	8.36	11.80
5000 TO 5499	10" & 10-3/4"	2.88	5.04	6.56	9.27
	11½"	3.08	5.39	7.01	9.91
	12½"	3.35	5.85	7.63	10.77
4500 TO 4999	10" & 10-3/4"	2.61	4.56	5.93	8.39
	11½"	2.79	4.87	6.35	8.96
	12½"	3.03	5.29	6.91	9.75
4000 TO 4499	10" & 10-3/4"	2.33	4.08	5.31	27.49
	11½"	2.49	4.36	5.68	8.03
	12½"	2.71	4.73	6.17	8.72
3500 TO 3999	10" & 10-3/4"	2.05	3.60	4.68	6.61
	11½"	2.20	3.84	5.01	7.08
	12½"	2.40	4.19	5.45	7.69
STROKE: 7-9/16" thru 9"					
6000 TO 6499	10" & 10-3/4"	4.08	7.13	9.29	13.13
	11½"	4.37	7.63	9.93	14.04
	12½"	4.75	8.29	11.56	15.27
5500 TO 5999	10" & 10-3/4"	3.76	6.56	8.55	12.08
	11½"	4.01	7.01	9.15	12.92
	12½"	4.37	7.64	9.95	14.05
5000 TO 5499	10" & 10-3/4"	3.43	5.99	7.81	11.03
	11½"	3.67	6.41	8.35	11.80
	12½"	3.99	6.97	9.08	12.83
4500 TO 4999	10" & 10-3/4"	3.11	5.43	7.07	9.97
	11½"	3.32	6.41	7.56	10.67
	12½"	3.61	6.97	8.21	11.60
4000 TO 4499	10" & 10-3/4"	2.77	4.85	6.32	8.93
	11½"	2.97	5.19	6.76	9.55
	12½"	3.23	5.64	7.35	10.37
3500 TO 3999	10" & 10-3/4"	2.45	4.28	5.57	7.88
	11½"	2.63	4.57	5.96	8.43
	12½"	2.85	4.97	6.48	9.16

EXHIBIT 19-20

STD. NO. ______
CHART NO. ______

PRODUCTION STANDARD

MARTIN & TUCKER
ENGINEERS

PAGE ______ OF ______

MACHINE NO. 77,78,79 DESCRIPTION: Winkler Rotary Printer

OPERATION: Makeready Press ELEMENT: ALL

Work Class & Area	Makeready Element	Standard Hours
Class 1:		
3 sq.in.	Address change only	.1152
5 "	+ Form	.1403
Class 2:		
3-14 sq.in.	One side, one color, one plate	.2572
15-35 "	" " " " " "	.2772
76-95 "	" " " " " "	.5172
Class 5:		
5-14 sq.in.	One side, two colors, two plates	.2792
36-55 "	" " " " " "	.4242

ADDITIVES:

a. Close or hairline register, per side	.0443
b. Setup pot and fountain, aniline ink	.0535
c. Makeready perforating complete	.2100
d. Washup for ink change, per color - Machine no. 77	.0967
" " " " " " - Machine no. 77, 78	.1500
e. Replace Cylinder Jacket: remove jacket, cut new one, repack and install on cylinder, complete	.1630
f. Morning startup: remove ink covering, install and adjust rubber rolls, ink for running	.1048
g. Remove worn, cut new and replace tail	.0196
h. Clean cylinders and rolls to remove ink build up after running bleeding solids	.2140

EN

CLIENT COMPANY: ______ DATE ISSUED: ______ REVISION DATES: ______
DIVISION/PLANT: ______ M. & T. ENGINEER: ______
SUPERVISORY ACCEPTANCE: ______ M. & T. APPROVAL BY: ______

THE STANDARDS CONTAINED HEREIN ARE APPLICABLE TO THE MACHINE OR OPERATION AND METHODS EMPLOYED AS OF ______ AND ARE SUBJECT TO REVISION PENDING ANY ALTERATION OR CHANGE IN METHODS OR EQUIPMENT.

EXHIBIT 19-21

STD. NO. ____

CHART NO. ____

PRODUCTION STANDARD

MARTIN & TUCKER
ENGINEERS

PAGE ____ OF ____

MACHINE NO. All described DESCRIPTION: W & D 18Q and 20F Printers

OPERATION: Washup ELEMENT: ALL-Top & Bottom Oil Units; Flexo Unit

Element No.	Description of Washup	Std Min. per W.U.	Std Hrs. per W.U.
1	Complete 2-colors to 2 light colors	49.310	.821
2	Complete 2-colors to 2 dark colors	30.143	.502
3	Complete 2-colors to 1 light & 1 dark color	35.698	.595
4	Complete 1-color to 1 light color & 1 general W.U.	28.890	.481
5	Complete 1-color to 1 dark color & 1 general W.U.	18.992	.317
6	Complete 1-color to dark color	17.080	.285
7	Complete 1-color to light color	27.222	.453
8	General 2-color W.U.	17.008	.283
9	General 1-color W.U.	10.594	.177
10	Complete washup of Flexo unit	90.00	1.500
A	Morning preparation	18.204	.303
B	Clean up top <u>and</u> bottom drip pan	9.457	.159
C	Clean up top <u>or</u> bottom drip pan	4.677	.078

EN

CLIENT COMPANY: ____ DATE ISSUED: ____ REVISION DATES: ____

DIVISION/PLANT: ____ M. & T. ENGINEER: ____

SUPERVISORY ACCEPTANCE: ____ M. & T. APPROVAL BY: ____

THE STANDARDS CONTAINED HEREIN ARE APPLICABLE TO THE MACHINE OR OPERATION AND METHODS EMPLOYED AS OF ____ AND ARE SUBJECT TO REVISION PENDING ANY ALTERATION OR CHANGE IN METHODS OR EQUIPMENT.

EXHIBIT 19-22

Exhibit 19-23 is one sheet of a multi-sheet set of production standards for an envelope folding machine. There are two product parameters shown out of many involved in that industry. Then there are the size parameters under each product type. Again, a major parameter is the size of the order (lot), followed by the weight of the paper used, and whether the blank is plain or printed. Referring to printed line of 40M lot and over, 20#, the range in time is from .1015 to .1608 standard hours per thousand, or an increase in time of 58%. When management capriciously elects to use averages, one can understand the great effect on the estimate of oop conversion cost and its ultimate influence on the pricing decision.

Exhibit 19-24 is an interesting aspect of standards-setting on the same machine as in the previous exhibit. This sheet deals with the development of standard delay allowances, which relate to the machine changes, waiting times, and policy delays. Such an approach forms the backup data for the delay allowances included in the standards and is recommended documentation.

Exhibit 19-25 is a set of run standards for an operation in the corrugated container industry. The major parameters within the type of corrugated board furnished are the length x width of the box and the width of the blank.

Exhibit 19-26 is another standard from the same industry, using 3 parameters: area, number cutout, and the length of the cutout.

Exhibit 19-27 is a setup standard developed in the automatic screw machine industry. Here the parameters are the diameter of machine capacity and the steps to be performed in accomplishing the setup operation.

Exhibit 19-28 is a machine-shop standard for a boring mill giving a formula for arriving at the standard time. The parameters are the diameter of the mill, surface speed, feed, and depth of cut. Note that the standards are qualified by the type of material being milled and the type of tooling used.

Exhibit 19-29 is a production standard of a hand operation in the electrical wiring industry for soldering terminals. The parameters are (for one type of solder) wire gauge and the area of the terminal cross-section. Note the methods notation, i.e., the wattage of the soldering iron to use. An additive is given where soldering required all around the terminal, or on both sides of the wire.

STD. NO. ____
CHART NO. ____

PRODUCTION STANDARD

MARTIN & TUCKER ENGINEERS

PAGE ____ OF ____

MACHINE NO. 21,22,23,24,25 DESCRIPTION: Wide Range Window (WRW)

OPERATION: Open Side Folding ELEMENT: RUN

STANDARD PIECES PER HOUR and STANDARD HOURS PER M*

Run Size — Paper Weight — Printing	Commercials, Pennysavers & Bankers Flap			Glassine Windows	
Paper Weight	3½ x 6 thru 4½ x 9	4 3/4 x 11	6 x 12	4½ x 10 3/8	5 x 11½
Printing	#6 1/4-10½	#12	#16	#11	#14
40M lot & over					
20#-24#-28#:					
Plain	9,950 .1005	8,300 .1205	7,300 .1370	6,780 .1475	6,330 .1580
Printed	9,850 .1015	8,200 .1220	6,570 .1522	6,670 .1499	6,220 .1608
13#:					
Plain	7,950 .1258	7,160 .1397	5,975 .1674		
Printed	7,890 .1267	7,040 .1420	5,930 .1696		
under 40M lot					
32#:					
Plain	8,300 .1205	7,300 .1370	6,180 .1618		
Printed	8,200 .1220	7,225 .1384	6,120 .1634		
16#:					
Plain	7,625 .1311	6,950 .1439	5,975 .1674		
Printed	7,550 .1325	6,900 .1449	5,930 .1686		

*includes a 30% incentive factor in addition to standard delay allowances.

EN

CLIENT COMPANY: ____ DATE ISSUED: ____ REVISION DATES: ____
DIVISION/PLANT: ____ M. & T. ENGINEER: ____
SUPERVISORY ACCEPTANCE: ____ M. & T. APPROVAL BY: ____

THE STANDARDS CONTAINED HEREIN ARE APPLICABLE TO THE MACHINE OR OPERATION AND METHODS EMPLOYED AS OF ____ AND ARE SUBJECT TO REVISION PENDING ANY ALTERATION OR CHANGE IN METHODS OR EQUIPMENT.

EXHIBIT 19-23

STD. NO.

CHART NO.

PRODUCTION STANDARD

MARTIN & TUCKER
ENGINEERS

PAGE ____ OF ____

MACHINE NO. 21 thru 25 DESCRIPTION: WRW

OPERATION: Standard Delay Allowances ELEMENT: All

Delay Elements	Non-Window Commercials; Baronials; Booklets				Cellophane Window			
	Min. Each	Occurence Hr.	Occurence Day	Chargeable min/day	Min. Each	Occurrence Hr.	Occurrence Day	Chargeable min/day
Paper jams	.61	2.6	20.8	12.69	.77	7.00	56	43.10
Minor machine adjusting	2.88	1.2	9.6	27.65	2.88	1.20	9.6	27.65
Waiting for adjuster	1.51	.167	1.25	1.89	1.51	.167	1.25	1.89
Wash and/or scrape rollers or mach.parts	1.67	.50	4	6.68	1.67	1.00	4	6.68
Reload machine	2.25	.25	2	4.50	2.25	.25	2	4.50
Change glassine or cello roll	-	-	-	-	.90	.25	2	1.80
Washup before lunch	10.00	.125	1	10.00	10.00	.125	1	10.00
Washup at end of shift	10.00	.125	1	10.00	15.00	.125	1	15.00
TOTAL DELAY TIME				73.41 min				100.72 min

Allowances:*

	Non-Window Commercials; Baronials; Booklets	Cellophane Window
Unavoidable delay	16.8%	20.9%
Personal (relief girls; machine not idle)	-	-
Fatigue	4 %	4 %
Total	20.8%	24.9%

*not including incentive factor

EN

CLIENT COMPANY: ____ DATE ISSUED: ____ REVISION DATES: ____

DIVISION/PLANT: ____ M. & T. ENGINEER: ____

SUPERVISORY ACCEPTANCE: ____ M. & T. APPROVAL BY: ____

THE STANDARDS CONTAINED HEREIN ARE APPLICABLE TO THE MACHINE OR OPERATION AND METHODS EMPLOYED AS OF ____ AND ARE SUBJECT TO REVISION PENDING ANY ALTERATION OR CHANGE IN METHODS OR EQUIPMENT.

EXHIBIT 19-24

STD. NO. 14
CHART NO. 2

PRODUCTION STANDARD

MARTIN & TUCKER, INC.
ENGINEERS

PAGE 1 OF 1

MACHINE NO. 417 DESCRIPTION: SEMI - AUTOMATIC TAPER

OPERATION: TAPE CONTAINERS ELEMENT: RUN

350 Test Double Wall - 600# Test Double Wall
Crew Size - 1 Feeder, 1 Bundler
Standard Machine Hours Per 1000 Boxes Run

BOX				BLANK WIDTH						
Length		Width		0	10	20	30	40	50	60
Over	Incl.	Over	Incl.	10	20	30	40	50	60	
0	4	0	4	0.57	0.62	1.55	1.69	1.80	1.93	
4	8	0	4	0.75	0.83	0.92	1.79	1.89	2.08	2.62
4	8	4	8	0.70	0.73	0.79	0.91	1.90	2.11	2.41
8	12	0	4	0.95	1.06	1.19	1.23	2.03	2.18	2.78
8	12	4	12	0.87	0.90	0.98	1.07	1.26	2.27	2.56
12	16	0	4	1.03	1.14	1.28	1.38	2.13	2.34	2.91
12	16	4	16	0.93	0.97	1.10	1.20	1.32	1.90	2.00
16	20	0	4	1.09	1.22	1.41	1.47	1.54	2.45	3.08
16	20	4	20	1.01	1.05	1.20	1.30	1.45	1.70	1.97
20	24	0	4	1.15	1.28	1.49	1.58	1.61	2.57	3.25
20	24	4	20	1.05	1.13	1.28	1.37	1.50	1.81	2.04
20	24	20	24	1.11	1.15	1.31	1.52	1.67	1.88	2.11
28	32	0	4	1.23	1.41	1.62	2.44	2.48	2.64	3.20
28	32	4	24	1.37	1.47	1.63	1.81	1.93	2.10	2.25
28	32	24	32	1.99	2.11	2.38	2.62	2.81	3.17	3.42
36	40	0	4	1.55	1.79	2.06	2.70	2.82	3.01	3.59
36	40	4	8	1.68	1.76	1.96	2.61	2.84	3.04	3.10
36	40	12	24	1.89	2.01	2.22	2.47	2.62	3.48	3.23
36	40	24	36	2.14	2.27	2.58	2.85	3.04	3.44	3.59
36	40	36	40	2.39	2.47	2.80	3.04	3.42	3.59	3.71
44	48	0	4	1.81	2.01	2.32	3.14	3.21	3.38	4.14
44	48	4	8	1.85	1.99	2.19	2.99	3.18	3.37	3.85
44	48	8	20	2.03	2.17	2.39	2.69	2.80	3.20	3.48
44	48	20	28	2.18	2.32	2.64	2.97	3.23	3.54	3.69
44	48	28	36	2.41	2.52	2.90	3.07	3.55	3.69	3.84

CLIENT COMPANY: ______ DATE ISSUED: ______ REVISION DATES: ______
DIVISION/PLANT: ______ M. & T. ENGINEER: ______
SUPERVISORY ACCEPTANCE: ______ M. & T. APPROVAL BY: ______

THE STANDARDS CONTAINED HEREIN ARE APPLICABLE TO THE MACHINE OR OPERATION AND METHODS EMPLOYED AS OF ______ AND ARE SUBJECT TO REVISION PENDING ANY ALTERATION OR CHANGE IN METHODS OR EQUIPMENT.

EXHIBIT 19-25

STD. NO. 33A
CHART NO. 4

PRODUCTION STANDARD

MARTIN & TUCKER, INC.
ENGINEERS

PAGE ____ OF ____

MACHINE NO. 17 DESCRIPTION: Band & Gang Saws

OPERATION: Cut Pads ELEMENT: Run (lift = 20 pcs.)

STANDARD MAN-MINUTES PER 1000 SHEETS

Square foot area per M	Length of out in. inches								
	0 to 5	5.01 to 10	10.01 to 15	15.01 to 20	20.01 to 25	25.01 to 30	30.01 to 35	35.01 to 40	40.01 to 45
ONE OUT:									
0 - 400	12.53	13.06	13.38	13.75	14.13	14.50	15.00	15.50	16.00
400.01 - 800	13.03	13.56	13.88	14.25	14.63	15.00	15.50	16.00	16.50
800.01 -1200	13.28	13.81	14.00	14.50	14.88	15.25	15.75	16.25	16.75
1200.01 -1600	13.75	14.31	14.63	15.00	15.38	15.75	16.25	16.75	17.25
1600.01 -2000	14.28	14.81	15.13	15.50	15.88	16.25	16.75	17.25	17.75
FOUR OUT:									
0 - 400	5.90	6.44	6.75	7.13	7.50	7.89	8.38	8.88	9.38
400.01 - 800	6.19	6.73	7.04	7.41	7.79	8.16	8.66	9.16	9.66
800.01 -1200	6.46	7.00	7.31	7.69	8.06	8.44	8.94	9.44	9.94
1200.01 -1600	6.84	7.38	7.69	8.06	8.44	8.81	9.31	9.81	10.31
1600.01 -2000	7.13	7.66	7.98	8.35	8.73	9.10	9.60	10.10	10.60
SEVEN OUT:									
0 - 400	4.95	5.49	5.80	6.18	6.55	6.93	7.43	7.93	8.43
400.01 - 800	5.28	5.81	6.13	6.50	6.88	7.25	7.75	8.25	8.75
800.01 -1200	5.60	6.14	6.45	6.83	7.20	7.58	8.08	8.58	9.08
1200.01 -1600	6.03	6.56	6.88	7.25	7.63	8.00	8.50	9.00	9.50
1600.01 -2000	6.35	6.89	7.20	7.58	7.95	8.33	8.83	9.33	9.83

CLIENT COMPANY: ____ DATE ISSUED: ____ REVISION DATES: ____
DIVISION/PLANT: ____ M. & T. ENGINEER: ____
SUPERVISORY ACCEPTANCE: ____ M. & T. APPROVAL BY: ____

THE STANDARDS CONTAINED HEREIN ARE APPLICABLE TO THE MACHINE OR OPERATION AND METHODS EMPLOYED AS OF ____ AND ARE SUBJECT TO REVISION PENDING ANY ALTERATION OR CHANGE IN METHODS OR EQUIPMENT

EXHIBIT 19-26

STD. NO. 118
CHART NO. 4

PRODUCTION STANDARD

MARTIN & TUCKER, INC.
ENGINEERS

PAGE ___ OF ___

MACHINE NO. 51 ML DESCRIPTION: Single Spindle, B & S Automatic

OPERATION: Setup Screw Machine ELEMENT: All

TOOL or OPERATION	MINUTES PER SETUP		
	Machine Capacity		
	1/2"	3/4"	1 1/4"
Remove, replace and time cams, change holders, gears, collet and finger	65	65	65
Box tools (single blade)	22	22	33
Box tools (double blade)	32	42	54
Cut off tools	17	17	21
Centering and facing tools	32	32	36
Drills	22	22	32
Form tools	16	16	22
Knurls, top or bottom	32	32	42
Reamers	33	33	36
Stock stop	5	5	5
Swing tools, turning	32	32	44
Spinning operations	42	42	53
Taps	21	21	26
Thread rolling	42	42	53

CLIENT COMPANY: ___ DATE ISSUED: ___ REVISION DATES: ___
DIVISION/PLANT: ___ M. & T. ENGINEER: ___
SUPERVISORY ACCEPTANCE: ___ M. & T. APPROVAL BY: ___

THE STANDARDS CONTAINED HEREIN ARE APPLICABLE TO THE MACHINE OR OPERATION AND METHODS EMPLOYED AS OF ___ AND ARE SUBJECT TO REVISION PENDING ANY ALTERATION OR CHANGE IN METHODS OR EQUIPMENT.

EXHIBIT 19-27

STD. NO. 7C
CHART NO. 2

PRODUCTION STANDARD

MARTIN & TUCKER, INC.
ENGINEERS

PAGE ____ OF ____

MACHINE NO. 334 DESCRIPTION: 36" to 120" Boring Mill

OPERATION: Bore Cast Iron ELEMENT: Run

TOOLING: High-Speed Steel

Depth of cut in inches	SIZE OF BORING MILL								
	36- to 42-inch mill			54- to 60-inch mill			72- to 120-inch mill		
	S	F	C	S	F	C	S	F	C
1/8"	47.5	.080	.00135	47.5	.109	.00099	42.5	.25	.00049
1/4"	45.0	.080	.00143	47.5	.083	.00122	45.0	.125	.00091
3/8"	45.0	.062	.00182	47.5	.068	.00159	47.5	.094	.00115
1/2"	42.5	.062	.00192	45.0	.068	.00167	45.0	.094	.00121
5/8"	40.0	.062	.00204	42.5	.068	.00177	42.5	.094	.00128

NOTES:
1. S = Surface speed in feet per minute
2. F = Feed per revolution in inches
3. C = Time factor

TO GET HOURS REQUIRED TO COMPLETE ONE CUT:

multiply C (the time factor) by outside diameter of chip circle and length of cut.

Time factor C includes delay allowances.

CLIENT COMPANY: ____ DATE ISSUED: ____ REVISION DATES: ____
DIVISION/PLANT: ____ M. & T. ENGINEER: ____
SUPERVISORY ACCEPTANCE: ____ M. & T. APPROVAL BY: ____

THE STANDARDS CONTAINED HEREIN ARE APPLICABLE TO THE MACHINE OR OPERATION AND METHODS EMPLOYED AS OF ____ AND ARE SUBJECT TO REVISION PENDING ANY ALTERATION OR CHANGE IN METHODS OR EQUIPMENT.

EXHIBIT 19-28

STD. NO. 44
CHART NO. 1

PRODUCTION STANDARD

MARTIN & TUCKER, INC.
ENGINEERS

PAGE ____ OF ____

MACHINE NO. ____ DESCRIPTION: Handwork

OPERATION: Solder Terminals (30/70) ELEMENT: 12 to 26 ga. wire

Soldering Iron Wattage	Terminal Cross-Section in Sq. In.	TIME IN MINUTES TO SOLDER ONE SIDE ONLY — Gauge of Wire Soldered to Terminal							Add for Solder All Around Terminal
		12	14	16	18	19	20	22 to 26	
95 to 200	.0000 to .0070	.041	.038	.036	.034	.033	.032	.030	.004
150 to 200	.0070 to .0115	.047	.043	.038	.034	.033	.032	.030	.004
120	.0070 to .0115	.047	.043	.038	.034	.033	.032	.030	.009
95	.0070 to .0115	.062	.056	.049	.043	.041	.038	.034	.012
62 to 75	.0000 to .0030	.047	.043	.038	.034	.033	.032	.030	.004
62 to 75	.0030 to .0050	.051	.047	.043	.038	.036	.034	.030	.007
62 to 75	.0050 to .0070	.087	.071	.056	.041	.039	.037	.033	.010
62	.0070 to .0115	.089	.080	.070	.060	.057	.055	.049	.041
75	.0070 to .0115	.060	.056	.051	.047	.045	.043	.038	.022

CLIENT COMPANY: ____ DATE ISSUED: ____ REVISION DATES: ____
DIVISION, PLANT: ____ M. & T. ENGINEER: ____
SUPERVISORY ACCEPTANCE: ____ M. & T. APPROVAL BY: ____

THE STANDARDS CONTAINED HEREIN ARE APPLICABLE TO THE MACHINE OR OPERATION AND METHODS EMPLOYED AS OF ____ AND ARE SUBJECT TO REVISION PENDING ANY ALTERATION OR CHANGE IN METHODS OR EQUIPMENT.

EXHIBIT 19-29

Chapter 20

Cost-Estimating Exercises for Specific Order Inquiries

Direct-cost Machine-Hour Rates and engineered production standards are essential for predetermining the expected cost of a job or product. The multiplication of these two factors for each production center, summed up for all production centers needed to produce the order, gives the oop conversion cost. When materials and other direct-order charges (DOC's) are added, the result is the total oop order cost.

This is the starting point in the go-no-go pricing decision! When competitive price levels are known (and they should be with proper marketing information), the expected gross order contribution can be calculated together with the gross PV. When the characteristic PV level representing a specific class of work is available, this figure can be used with the total oop order cost to produce a target selling price which will have a high degree of market intelligence. While the total oop order cost is the *economic* floor of price, the PV-oriented target selling price gives the *practical* price floor.

The exhibits in this chapter exemplify how MHR's and production standards are used in various job estimates. Included with some estimates are the typical problems and questions which arise in the process of booking orders together with rational solutions. Most of these deal with go or no-go concessions to buyers on price, volume, throwing in "extras," quantity differentials, absorbing "first" costs, delivery and warehousing abuses, etc.

Before presenting actual estimates, some of the input data should be explained:

1. The quantity shown on each estimate is the *ordered* quantity. In practice, where the company has an overrun policy, known as a planned overrun, the quantity estimated would exceed the ordered quantity to the extent of this policy. This means that if the planned overrun is 5%, the seller knows that the buyer would be willing to pay for this additional quantity. Under this policy, it would make good economic sense to always plan to overrun the job because of the more contributing use of the preparatory costs.

2. To carry the difference between the ordered and estimated quantity further, the maker-seller should raise the estimated quantity by another percentage to provide for waste i.e., unusable, discarded product. Wasted products which are generated still require some conversion cost depending on where in the sequence of operations the product is rejected and discarded. In other words, time must be allowed to manufacture this waste, otherwise, the maker-seller will wind up with an understated oop conversion cost. Demonstrating this principle without including overrun:

A. *Ordered Quantity: 100,000* Estimated Quantity: *100,000* (no waste)

Operation	*Production Std.*	*Std. Hours*	*OOP MHR*	*OOP Conversion Cost*
Print	.20 hours/M	20	$25	$500.00
			per M	$ 5.00

B. *Ordered Quantity: 100,000* Estimated Quantity: *110,000* (10% waste)

Operation	*Production Std.*	*Std. Hours*	*OOP MHR*	*OOP Conversion Cost*
Print	.20 hours/M	22	$25	$550.00
			per M	$ 5.50

Allowing for waste by boosting the ordered quantity identified waste experience by the job and customer. In effect, it recognizes waste as a characteristic of the product and customers' specific quality requirements, rather than as a function of the facility characteristic. If waste is facility-related, it is handled by building into the MHR's excesses created by the individual facilities, viz:

C. *Ordered & Estimated Quantity: 100,000*

Operation	*Prod. Std.*	*Std. Hours*	*Charac. Waste %*	*OOP MHR*	*OOP Conversion Cost*
Print	.2 hrs/M	20	10	$27.50	$550.00
				per M	$ 5.50

The techniques shown in B and C provide for wasted oop conversion only and has nothing to do with raw material waste. This latter item is handled by a percentage markup of estimated raw material cost.

The effect of wasted oop conversion cost can have an appreciable effect on the measurement of contribution and PV. Where the ratio between conversion and material costs is high, failure to allow time to make waste in the estimate can motivate an *incorrect* decision to book what looks like a beneficial order.

3. To enable more effective estimating for quantity variations, operations are separated into preparatory (makeready, setup) and run. In many cases in the converting and other industries, there are differences in a makeready and a run MHR in a particular production center. This is caused principally by differences in the composition of the crew during these two stages of activity. In other cases, additional differences are caused by the changes in consumption of electrical energy per hour during the setup and run phases. There is usually some hourly consumption of electrical energy during a makeready but this is typically minimal compared to the hourly usage during the running. The contrast is large however, where the production machine has a high horsepower rating, and in this instance, two rates should be developed irrespective of changes in the crew.

4. As will be noted in the following exhibits, the MHR's and conversion costs are expressed in oop as well as "full" values. Even though "full" conversion costs (and therefore "full" order cost) are useless for pricing, or any other decision for that matter, the "full" values are given here to enable the reader to convince himself of that fact. Another reason for giving these figures is to anticipate what experience has taught for many years, namely, that management is usually compelled (at the beginning of the new system) to ask, "What did the cost figure out to be the old way?" Usually, the old way gives way to the new in a short time.

The following estimating exhibits are presented for review and discussion. Direct materials costs are stated but not derived.

ESTIMATE EXHIBIT 20-1

This is a simple job from the corrugated container industry involving two operations in a "sheet plant." Note that the ratio between conversion and materials cost is low which becomes significant in making price concessions on order quantity. The questions are:

1. Find the PV of this order if it is sold at its "full" cost.

Solution

If the selling price is \$20.68/C, the contribution/C is \$20.68 – \$19.91 = \$.77; PV = \$.77/\$20.68 = .037

2. If the customer agreed to double the quantity ordered, what is the selling price at the same PV?

Quantity 5,000 Box No. ABC Salesman Jones

Box Style RSC Size 18 1/8 x 14 1/2 x 20 5/8

Test 275 # Panels Printed 4 No. of Dies 4

Flute B Tape 2 1/2 Stitch — No. in Bundle 12

Blank Size 65 1/4 x 35 1/8 Sq. Ft. 79,580

C O N V E R S I O N

Production Center	Est. Hrs.	Machine-Hour Rate		Conversion Cost	
		OOP	"Full"	OOP	"Full"
Preparation:					
MR: Printer-Slotter	.40	\$12.60	\$24.10	\$ 5.04	\$ 9.64
: Semi-Auto Taper	.10	11.80	16.40	1.18	1.64
Run:					
Printer-Slotter	.90	12.60	24.10	11.34	21.69
Semi-Auto Taper	5.10	11.80	16.40	60.18	83.64
Extra Dies				2:40	2.40
		Total Conversion Cost		80.14	119.01
		Direct Materials Cost		915.10	915.10
		TOTAL ORDER COST		\$995.24	\$1034.11
		Cost per C Containers		19.91	20.68

EXHIBIT 20-1: Sample Estimate (corrugated)

Comment: This is a typical ploy of some buyers in the hope that they will get an appreciable reduction in selling price because of higher volume. In this instance, if the seller is willing to accept a PV of .037 for the original quantity, his only savings at twice the quantity is getting double the mileage from his preparatory costs. These costs are only \$6.22.

Solution

Total order oop costs will be \$6.22 + 2(\$11.34 + \$60.18 + \$2.40) + 2(\$915.10) = \$1984.26. This = \$19.84/C. To find the selling price of this oop cost to provide a PV of .037:

S.P. = oop cost/ (1 − PV)
= \$19.84/.963
= \$20.60

The customer may be expecting a large reduction in price in return for his offer to double his order. As you see though, the only reduction which can be passed on is from \$20.68 down to \$20.60, or \$.08/C.

Comment: This exercise is essential since it teaches not to make concessions blindly or emotionally because of the ever-present conflicts on the value of volume. Also, if "full" costs were used to make this decision, the doubling of volume would have the effect (ultimately) of increasing projected hours and proportionately reducing the MHR's to the point where a more substantial reduction in selling price might be offered.

3. A special die costing \$75 is not included in the estimate and the customer wanted the seller to supply it free of charge at the original selling price of \$20.68/C. What is the minimum order quantity required just to pay for the die?

Solution

This is a break-even problem, for obviously, the order quantity must provide enough contribution to pay for the additional oop cost. Therefore: Minimum quantity required = Add'l oop/contribution = \$75/\$.77 per C = 9,740 pieces.
Comment: Again, if the seller agreed to absorb this extra die cost at the original 5,000-piece quantity and selling price, the transaction would have generated a cash loss (negative contribution) since it takes 9,740 pieces to create a condition of zero contribution—nothing negative or positive. This means that positive contribution can only commence if the order *exceeds* 9,740 pieces. If the order subsequently is placed for 15,000 pieces, with the seller absorbing the \$75, the order contribution is:

(Order quantity − break-even quantity) × Unit contribution (15,000 − 9,740) × \$.0077 = \$40.50

OR:

(Order quantity × Unit contribution) − Additional oop costs = (15,000 × \$.0077) − \$75 = \$40.50

ESTIMATE EXHIBIT 20-2

This is an estimate for a folding carton inquiry which differs in several ways from the previous estimate. Here, conversion cost is a substantial portion of total order cost, and preparatory costs a much larger segment of conversion costs. Let's solve a few problems:

1. Find the gross order contribution, the contribution per M, and the PV at a selling price of \$10.01 per M.

Quantity: 1,000,000 blanks, 10 up

CONVERSION						
Production Center	Prod. Std. Hrs/M	Est. Hrs.	Machine-Hour Rate		Conversion Cost	
			OOP	"Full"	OOP	"Full"
Preparation:						
Die making	7	7	$ 7.00	$ 9.00	$ 49.00	$ 63.00
MR: Print	8	8	26.00	43.00	208.00	344.00
: C & C	6	6	15.00	28.00	90.00	168.00
: Gluer	½	½	8.00	10.00	4.00	5.00
Run:						
Print: Harris 69	.4	40	26.00	43.00	1040.00	1720.00
C & C Bobst	.3	33	18.00	31.00	594.00	1023.00
Glue 6F	.1	100	14.00	18.00	1400.00	1800.00
		Total Conversion Cost			$3385.00	$5123.00
		Direct Materials Cost			4120.00	4120.00
		TOTAL ORDER COST			7505.00	9243.00
				Cost/M	$7.51	$9.24

EXHIBIT 20-2: Sample Estimate (folding carton)

Solution

Gross order contribution = Gross revenue − Total oop cost
= \$10,010 − \$7,505
= \$2,505
per M = \$2.505
PV = \$2.505/\$10.01 *or* \$2,505/10,010
= .25

2. Find the selling price per M to generate a PV of .32.

Solution

Target Selling Price (TSP) [based on a desired PV]

= oop cost/(1 - desired PV)
= \$7.51/.68
= \$11.04 per M

3. Find the selling price per M to generate a PV of .32 at twice the estimated quantity.
Comment: Here again, we depend on the amount and spread of the preparatory costs to provide the concession, if any.

Solution

2 (Total order oop cost)—1 preparatory cost
= Total oop cost for 2 million pieces
= (2 × $7505) – $351
= $14,659
then, $14,659/2 mil. = $7.33 per M
and, TSP = $7.33/.68
= $10.77, a drop of only $.27 per M at the double quantity.

Moral? Watch price differentials for larger volume! Test first with the proper tools!

ESTIMATE EXHIBIT 20-3

This is a job from the flexible packaging industry in which two expensive facilities are used, viz: an extruder-laminator and an 8-color gravure printing press.

1. Find the PV of this order at a selling price of $.152 per M square inches.

Solution

PV = $.045/$.152
= .296

2. The customer has decided to take his business away from one of your competitors and give you a chance to book it. He has already paid your competitor once for etching gravure cylinders (etching carries the image the customer wishes to have printed on his product), and doesn't want to pay you a second time for the same work. He is willing to give you the order providing you are willing to pay this etching cost of $3,000 out of your own pocket. What contribution will you have remaining on this order if you agree to his terms?

Solution

Gross order contribution = Gross revenue – all oop costs
= ($.152/M × 60 mil.) – ($6,436 + $3,000)
= $9,120 — $9,436
= ($316)

Comment: Obviously, the 60 million order will produce a cash loss of $316 if you are required to absorb the $3,000. Good thing you tested the effects of his proposal first and were not carried away with the size of the order as a rationale for your paying for the etching. This means if you cannot increase the price and must still absorb the $3,000, your only hope of generating contribution is to get him to raise the ordered quantity.

3. Find the minimum order quantity you require under these conditions to at least break-even on the $3,000.
Comment: This is the first protective step you must take on the way to specifying the size of order you'd like to have.

Solution

Break-even quantity point = One-time oop cost/Unit contribution per M

Product: PE-Coated, adhesive-laminated foil & paper, 8 colors

Quantity: 60 mil. sq. in. = 4 mil. pkgs 2½" x 3" (pouch stock)

C O N V E R S I O N						
Production Center	Prod. Std. Hrs/M	Est. Hrs.	Machine-Hour Rate		Conversion Cost	
			OOP	"Full"	OOP	"Full"
Makeready:						
Extruder-Laminator	3	3	$16.62	$32.23	$ 49.86	$ 96.69
8c Gravure Press	6	6	26.15	48.85	156.90	293.10
Run:						
Extruder-Laminator	250fpm	14	16.62	32.23	232.68	451.22
8c Gravure Press	500fpm	7	26.15	48.85	183.05	341.95
Slitter-Rewinder	150fpm	23.3	7.15	11.24	166.60	261.89
Wrap & Palletize		16	2.30	2.50	36.80	40.00
Total Conversion Cost					825.89	1484.85
Direct Materials Cost					5610.10	5610.10
TOTAL ORDER COST					$6435.99	$7094.95
Cost per M sq. in.					.107	.118

EXHIBIT 20-3: Sample Estimate (flexible packaging)

$$= \$3{,}000/\$.045 \text{ per M}$$
$$= 66{,}666{,}666 \text{ pieces}$$

4. At this higher ordered quantity, what is the gross order contribution?

Solution

Gross order contribution = Piece quantity × Unit contribution per M − etching cost
= 66.666 mil. × \$.045 − \$3,000
= 0

Comment: Now you have the basis of requesting a higher quantity knowing that you must not go below 66.667 million.

5. You request twice the original quantity. What is the gross order contribution (GOC) and the PV of the transaction?

Solution

GOC = Gross revenue - gross oop costs

= \$18,240 – (1 prep. cost + 2 run costs + 2 materials cost + \$3,000)
= \$18,240 – (\$206.76 + \$1,238.26 + \$11,220.20 + \$3,000)
= \$18,240 – \$15,665.22
= \$2,574.78
PV = \$2,574.78/\$18,240
= .141

6. Under these circumstances, what would the GOC and PV be at this quantity if you didn't have to pay for the etching?

Solution

GOC = \$2,574.78 + \$3,000
= \$5,574.78
PV = \$5,574.78/\$18,240
= .306

Comment: Thus, even at twice the quantity, the required absorption of the \$3,000 robs the seller of 54% of the PV.

7. In problem 1, the PV was .296 and there was no question at that time of the seller paying for the \$3,000. Now let's say that the buyer is willing to grant you a higher price in return for your absorbing the \$3,000 at the original quantity of 60 million. You would like to maintain the PV at the same level of .296. What would the new selling price per M have to be?

Solution

TSP [desired PV] = Gross order oop cost/ (1 – desired PV)
= (\$6,436 + \$3,000)/(1 – .296)
= \$9,436/.704
= \$13,403.41 *or* \$.2234 per M

ESTIMATE EXHIBIT 20-4

Here is an envelope estimate with a small preparatory cost and a total oop conversion cost about one-third of the total order oop cost.

1. The market selling price of this envelope is \$11/M. The cost of a specially-shaped cutting die is \$150. Find the PV's of this transaction with and without your absorbing this die cost.

Solution

PV = \$2/\$11
= .182
PV = (\$1,540 – [\$1,260.40 + \$150])/\$1,540
= .084

2. How would the PV change at double the ordered quantity with you paying for the die?

Solution

PV = (\$3,080 – [\$20.50 + 2 × \$293.50 + 2 × 946.40 + \$150])/\$3,080
= \$429.70/\$3,080
= .14

3. Find the minimum order quantity required to avoid a below-oop selling price, if you had to pay for the special die and meet a competitive selling price of \$9.50/M.

Description: 140M, 10 x 13 OE, center seam, 2 7/16 flap, plain

C O N V E R S I O N						
Production Center	Prod. Std.	Order Hours	M. H. R. OOP	M. H. R. "Full"	Conversion Cost OOP	Conversion Cost "Full"
Prep:						
Folding Change	2	2	$10.25	$17.31	$ 20.50	$ 34.62
Run:						
Die Cut	.05	7	8.25	14.73	57.75	103.11
LO-Fold	.164	23	10.25	17.31	235.75	398.13
		Total Conversion Cost			$ 314.00	$ 535.86
		Direct Material Cost*			946.40	946.40
		Total Order Cost**			$1,260.40	$1,482.26
		Cost/M			$ 9.00	$ 10.59

*Includes cost of waste

**Normally should include all other D.O.C's viz: freight out, commissions, storage charges, small order transaction costs, split delivery upcharges, etc.

EXHIBIT 20-4: Sample Estimate (envelope)

Solution

Contribution = \$.50/M
Minimum quantity required = \$150/\$.50 per M
= 300,000 pieces

4. The customer is discussing the idea of placing with you his annual volume requirements. He says this would amount to 5 million pieces. In return for this guarantee of volume, which he reminds you "will keep your facilities busy" (but profitable?), he wants to buy them from you at \$9.25/M plus your paying for the special die. You know that you will not plan to run this entire quantity at one time; there are other customers to be serviced. Therefore, you plan to run the 5 million pieces in lot sizes of 500,000 each. What will your overall contribution and PV be on the total transaction?

Solution

Total Revenue = 5,000,000 × \$9.25 per M
= \$46,250

Total OOP Preparatory Cost = 10 × \$20.50 + \$150
= \$355.00
Total OOP Run Cost = (\$293.50/140M) × 5,000M
= \$10,482
Total Material Cost = (\$946.40/140M) × 5,000M
= \$33,800
Gross Order Contribution = \$46,250 - (\$355 + \$10,482 + \$33,800)
= \$1,613
PV = \$1,613/\$46,250
= .035

5. Ignoring the relatively low value of the die cutter and concentrating on the Model LO Folding machine, how many hours will the folder have to operate to produce the 5 million pieces of the previous problem?

Solution

Facility hours required = (10 × 2 hours) + 820 hours
= 840 hours (almost one-half shift)

6. Referring the gross order contribution of \$1,613 to this facility usage, what contribution return per hour (CPH) would you be receiving for the use of this machine?

Solution

CPH = \$1,613/840
= \$1.92

7. What is the CPH of problem 1 at the 140M original quantity with you paying for the die?

Solution

CPH = \$129.60/25
= \$5.18

Comment: A job shop or converter is in the business of selling only one commodity: the use of his facility time, profitably! Profits are made in this type of enterprise by maximizing the inflow of contribution dollars per unit of time. Marginally contributing business, as in problem 4, uses up lots of hours (sometimes interpreted by management as the path to higher profits) but provides minimal inflow of CPH. This practice uses up critical facility time and robs the company of the opportunity to use that time on other work to earn sufficient contribution to provide adequate return on their total capital employed. It does this in part by displacing more profitable (contributing) work which could have run in those hours.

8. Suppose that you are able to negotiate a slightly higher price under the conditions of problem 4, inching it up by 7%, or to \$9.90. What is the new GOC, PV and CPH?

Solution

GOC = \$49,500 – \$44,637
= \$4,863 (an increase of 301%!)

Comment: Not all orders, companies, divisions have the same economic personality and therefore do not respond in the same way to the same change. In this instance, a 7% increase in price produces a 201% increase in contribution.

PV = \$4,863/\$49,500
= .098 (a 181% increase in the rate of profit above the company's break-even point!)
CPH = \$4,863/840
= \$5.79 (directly related to GOC, the same 201% increase)

9. Suppose you had been getting a CPH of \$16 on this facility from current work and booked work to be run in the future, and you would be willing to take this 5 million-piece commitment, what would the selling price per M have to be to maintain the \$16 CPH?

Solution

TSP [desired CPH] = (CPH × Hours) + Total order oop costs
= (\$16 × 840) + \$44,637
= \$13,440 + \$44,637
Gross Revenue = \$58,077
S. P./M = = \$11.62

ESTIMATE EXHIBIT 20-5

Another envelope job, but one in which the oop conversion is greater than the material cost.

1. Find the S. P./M if we target the .182 of the previous estimate.

Solution

TSP [PV .182] = \$3.67/.818
= \$4.87

2. Find the PV of the order at a market price of \$4.70/M.

Solution

PV = \$1.03/\$4.70
= .219

3. While \$4.70 is the going market price, we wish to generate at least a PV of .25 which cannot be accomplished at the ordered quantity of 200M. The problem is to find a high enough quantity at that competitive price which will provide the desired PV.

Solution

This solution calls for some simple algebra. The way to approach the problem is to recognize that: Sales Revenue = oop costs/(1 - PV). Then because we are solving for an unknown volume, the run costs must be separated from the preparatory cost:

Preparatory costs = \$24.75 + \$24.88
= \$49.63
oop run costs/M = (\$353.50 + \$330)/200
= \$3.4175

Expanding the first equation, and letting x = unknown quantity, we have:

(S.P./M) x = [(oop run costs/M) x + Preparatory costs]/(1 – .25). and

(\$4.70) x = [(\$3.4175) x + \$49.63]/.75

and with a little transposing, we have:

Description: 200M, No. 6 3/4 window, 1 flap, diagonal seams, 1 1/8 x 4 3/4 face glassine, black c/c (letterset)

C O N V E R S I O N

Production Center	Prod. Std.	Order Hours	M. H. R. OOP	M. H. R. "Full"	Conversion Cost OOP	Conversion Cost "Full"
Prep:						
MR - 10E	3	3	$8.25	$13.28	$ 24.75	$ 39.84
Folding change	4	4	6.22	8.68	24.88	34.72
Run:						
Die cut	.02	4	8.25	14.73	33.00	58.92
10E	.10	20	8.25	13.28	165.00	265.60
WR + p.c.	.125	25	6.22	8.68	155.50	217.00
			Total Conversion Cost		$403.13	$616.08
			Direct Material Cost		330.00	330.00
			Total Order Cost		$733.13	$946.08
			Cost/M		$ 3.67	$ 4.73

EXHIBIT 20-5: Sample Estimate (envelope)

$$.75 \times \$4.70 = \$3.4175x + \$49.63$$
$$3.525x = \$3.4175x + \$49.63$$
$$.1075x = \$49.63$$
$$x = 461.67\text{M}$$

Comment: That means that in order to increase the PV from .219 to .25 at the same selling price, an increase in PV of only .031, we have to generate 2.31 times the original quantity, i.e., from 200M to 461.67M. Think how much easier it would be to improve the PV by inching the price.

4. By what percentage would the $4.70 price have to be increased to provide the .25 PV?

Solution

TSP [PV.25] = $3.67/.75
= $4.89

Increase in S. P. = $.19/$4.70
= .04 or 4%

Comment: The effort to obtain this 4% increase at the 200M quantity is worth doing in comparison to using up almost 3 times more valuable facility time, spending almost 3 times the direct labor and other oop conversion cost, and financing almost 3 times the amount of raw material—to say nothing of the additional transaction, storage costs, etc., in an attempt to get the same increase in PV.

ESTIMATE EXHIBIT 20-6

Here is another job for which only one expensive facility is employed.

1. You have been getting an average of $22 as the CPH on the expensive 129G folding machine and you see no reason to lower it in terms of the business you can expect in the future. Find the S.P./M of this estimate to provide you with this goal.

Solution

Simply expand the basic formula:
Sales revenue = Contribution + Total oop costs, into:
Sales revenue = (CPH desired × Facility hours) + Total oop costs
= ($22 × 134) + $6,801.38
= $9,749.38
S.P./M = $4.87

2. A customer wishes to purchase the same item from you at a S.P. of $3.60/M. While he knows this price is below the market, he tries to tempt you with a proposal to place his entire annual

Description: 2MM, 3½ x 8 OS, 2 flaps, diagonal seams, glassine window, blue c/c + tint

CONVERSION

Production Center	Prod. Std.	Order Hours	M. H. R. OOP	M. H. R. "Full"	Conversion Cost OOP	Conversion Cost "Full"
Prep:						
Composition	3	3	$ 4.10	$ 5.20	$ 12.30	$ 15.60
Folding change	8	8	15.56	24.62	124.48	196.96
Run:						
Die cut	.02	40	8.25	14.73	330.00	589.20
129G	.063	126	17.10	26.30	2,154.60	3,313.80
		Total Conversion Cost			$2,621.38	$4,114.56
		Direct Material Cost			4,180.00	4,180.00
		Total Order Cost			$6,801.38	$8,294.56
		Cost/M			$ 3.40	$ 4.15

EXHIBIT 20-6: Sample Estimate (envelope)

business with you, which amounts to 200 million pieces. He wants you to produce all of this volume at one time and then ship to his various branch warehouses three months later (ignore delivery costs). After this is done, you are permitted to invoice him for the full amount. Use 10% as the cost of financing the short-term capital (all oop costs) and find: the gross contribution of the contract, the PV and the CPH.

Solution

The first thing to realize is that 200 million pieces will require 12,600 hours on the folding machine. Assuming a one-shift operation at 2,000 hours per shift, you will require 6 machines with overtime premiums to pay, or 7 machines. We shall assume the latter.
The first step is to get the total oop costs of the contract:

C O N V E R S I O N

Production Center	Hours Req'd	MACHINE-HOUR RATE		CONVERSION COSTS	
		O.O.P.	"Full"	O.O.P.	"Full"
Prep:					
Linotype	1.0	$ 7.30	$14.85	$ 7.30	$ 14.85
Make up forms	4.5	6.90	12.20	31.05	54.90
Lock-up	2.5	6.90	12.20	17.25	30.50
Set hole punches and patch heads on bar	2.0	6.90	11.30	13.80	22.60
Press: (N.E. 12 x 18)					
Makeready	10.0	10.40	24.20	104.00	242.00
Run and Pack	32.0	10.70	24.20	342.40	774.40
Seal and mark cartons	10.0	4.80	9.10	48.00	91.00
	Total Conversion Costs			$ 563.80	$1,230.25
	Total Materials Costs			975.00	975.00
			Totals	$1,538.80	$2,205.25
			per M	$ 15.39	$ 22.05

EXHIBIT 20-7: Estimate Sheet
(Application of two-part Machine-Hour Rates to production tag job; 100M)

Contract oop cost = 7 preparatory costs + (100 × oop run cost) + (100 × material costs) + the cost of capital

Total oop costs = ([7 × \$136.78] + [100 × \$2,484.60] + [100 × \$4,180])1.025

= (\$667,417.46)1.025
= \$684,102.89

GOC = (200,000M × \$3.60/M)– \$684,102.89
= \$720,00 - \$684,102.89
= \$35,897.11

PV = \$35,897.11/\$720,000
= .05

CPH = \$35,897.11/12,656 hours
= \$2.84

Item: 300,000 booklets

C O N V E R S I O N

Production Center	Est. Hrs.	Machine-Hour Rate OOP	Machine-Hour Rate "Full"	Conversion Cost OOP	Conversion Cost "Full"
Preparation:					
Lino's	37.4	\$ 6.71	\$ 8.60	\$ 250.95	\$ 321.64
Hand Comp.	5.5	8.12	10.02	44.66	55.11
Lock up	11.2	7.58	8.71	84.90	97.55
MR: Miehle 76	12.0	15.11	38.81	181.32	465.72
MR: Miller TY	4.0	8.37	12.72	33.48	50.88
Run:					
Miehle 76	85.7	15.11	38.81	1294.93	3326.02
Miller TY	17.3	8.37	12.72	144.80	220.06
Baum 00	24.6	5.18	6.56	127.43	161.38
Dexter 189	111.8	7.43	8.62	830.47	963.72
Guillotines	14.1	7.76	9.36	109.42	131.98
Lawson Trimmer	12.5	17.85	20.44	223.12	255.50
McCain	44.0	11.80	14.65	519.20	644.60
Pack	64.0	4.28	5.08	273.92	325.12
Band	160.0	4.28	5.08	684.80	812.80
			Total Conversion Costs	\$4803.40	\$7832.08
			Direct Materials Cost	7987.45	7987.45
			Other Direct-Order Charges	948.00	948.00
			TOTAL ORDER COST	\$13738.85	\$16767.53
			Cost/M	45.80	55.89

EXHIBIT 20-8: Sample Estimate (publications printing)

Quantity: 1,000,000 pcs - (10 up)

C O N V E R S I O N						
Production Center	Prod. Std. Hrs/M	Est. Hrs.	Machine-Hour Rate		Conversion Cost	
			OOP	"Full"	OOP	"Full"
Preparation:						
Step & Repeat	1.5	1.5	$ 4.40	$14.70	$ 6.80	$ 22.05
Strip & Opaque	2.5	2.5	4.50	6.30	11.25	15.75
Plate Making	.5	.5	7.20	11.50	3.60	5.75
MR:Harris	4.0	4.0	9.20	29.20	38.60	116.80
Run:						
Harris Offset	.25	25.0	14.60	34.60	365.00	865.00
Guillot	.05	50.0	3.90	8.40	195.00	420.00
Fold	.033	33.3	5.60	9.00	186.48	299.70
Collate & Stitch	.067	66.7	4.40	8.10	293.48	540.27
Pack	.01	10.0	3.40	5.10	34.00	51.00
				Total Conversion Cost	$1134.21	$2336.32
				Direct Materials Cost	462.70	462.70
				Other Direct-Order Charges	187.00	187.00
				TOTAL ORDER COST	$1783.91	$2986.02
				Cost/M	1.78	2.99

EXHIBIT 20-9: Sample Estimate (commercial printing)

ESTIMATE EXHIBIT 20-7

This is a job from the label industry produced on web-fed equipment.

1. By mistake, the salesman takes the "full" cost per M figure and quotes it to his customer. The customer balks claiming that he will only pay the "going" price of $21/M. The salesman turns down the order in the belief that a price "below cost" cannot make any money for his company. If his company regularly accepts work of this type at a PV of .20, would this have been a good order for his company?

Solution

Had the salesman known the contribution concept, he would have known that at a $21 price, the contribution is $21 – $15.39, or $5.61/M, and the

PV = $5.61/$21
  = .267 (definitely, a good order)

Comment: Remove "full" costs from any estimate.

ESTIMATES EXHIBITS 20-8 AND 20-9

These are the final two estimates given in this chapter and the reader is urged to experiment with the variables previously discussed in order to make rational pricing or quantity decisions. The overriding need for all estimates is the availability of sound oop Machine-Hour Rates and a set of competently engineered production standards.

OTHER ESTIMATING DECISIONS

The reader is referred to Chapter 7 under the heading, "Selecting Most Economical Production Facility" for a discussion of estimating policies which can be established with proper standards and MHR's.

SECTION V

Applying Direct-Cost Machine-Hour Rates In Pricing

Chapter 21

The Anatomy of Price

Prices are a basic and critical factor in determining profits and, ultimately, the success or failure of a business enterprise. There are many ways for money to flow out of a firm in the form of costs. But there is only one way to bring money in. That way is by the mechanics of pricing. Pricing is not only the sole revenue generator in a company, it is also the only profit contributor—assuming, of course, that the items sold cost a company less than the prices at which they are sold.

If prices are too low in comparison with costs, volume may be great but profitless. If prices are higher than competitors', volume and profit are reduced and invested capital and facilities are rendered idle. Between these two poles, the optimum profit to the company comes from sets of prices which make contributions to profits and are acceptable in the marketplace.

WHAT PRICING DOES

Pricing determines significantly the bottom-line figure on the operating statement. Pricing determines what products will and will not be sold, in what volumes, and with what profit. In more detailed terms, pricing specifies which equipment will be operated, what inventory commitments are to be made, what cash flow can be expected, where sales efforts should be applied, which markets should be approached and penetrated, and ultimately, what return can be expected on the firm's invested capital. Therefore, pricing should not be given short shrift as an annoying but somehow necessary detail and relegated to an office clerk or estimator, unless management is quite prepared to assign to that individual full responsibility for the effective employment of the company's capital and resources.

The most modern, streamlined company—with the most productive workers, highest-speed equipment, highest quality of product, highest level of sales, and preeminent product acceptance in its markets—will lose money if the revenue produced from prices does not cover costs. While no one will disagree with this clearcut truism, the point needs strengthening since the *medieval cost-price practices* in many otherwise well-managed companies produce prices inadvertently pegged below costs. Even if prices are set with reference to costs, frequently the economic and strategic factors of market demand, competition, and product mix are ignored, thereby producing a lower return on the firm's invested capital than could otherwise be attained.

Pricing, and pricing alone, more than any other single decision-making activity, is responsible for most of the profit differences among similar firms.

How the order or product is priced will in itself determine the product mix that will be produced. The pricing action will make the product more or less attractive to the buyer; the major factor which determines the buyer's response. To the extent that costs of the mix produce both profit contributions and favorable responses from buyers, the volume sold will be profitable. The sales revenue then, is a mixture of the various prices of the different products or orders, and the resultant period profit is a mixture of their profit contributions.

BALANCING OF VARIABLES

Profits depend on a proper selection and balancing of prices against the variables of costs, volume, and product mix. Typically, orders and products differ widely in cost, volume, price, profit, and the use of facilities and capital. Orders also differ in terms of the specific product made, the markets sold to, the customer classes involved, the sales territories covered, and the channels of distribution used. Thus, *profit is not a single-valued function of time or quantity, but is rather composed of a number of pooled segments from which a net profit ultimately develops.* These sources or segments of profit are important from the viewpoint of evaluating strengths or weaknesses.

In pricing though, management must know the relative contribution which each segment makes to the profit structure in order to strike a proper balance among prices, product mix, volume, and cost. Pricing therefore, is a profit-planning problem in which management analyzes the various economic and strategic alternatives and compares them with each other to select the one which appears to be the most advantageous in each pricing situation.

The pricing method cannot be formula-ized because many factors cannot be measured objectively. Pricing is influenced greatly by, and must be related to, market conditions, competition, financial liquidity of the firm, inventory pressures, available productive capacity, investments in product line, etc.

Profits which result from the operation of a business as a whole cannot be greater than the net sum of the profits (or losses) contained in all its individual parts. These profit segments are sources for period profits and relate to individual orders at various prices, various costs, and various profit contributions. In multiproduct firms, orders have profit characteristics which go beyond the mere identification of order sizes or revenues. Orders go to different markets, geographic areas, and customers and customer classes; they are produced on different facilities and are parts of various product lines. Once these data have been sorted and analyzed by any desired segment, management has an objective guide to its sources of profits and can emphasize, eliminate, strengthen, and direct as required to enable the pricing program to attain the profit objective.

PRICING ART AND SCIENCE

Pricing is at once a science and an art. It involves more than setting, meeting, raising, or lowering prices. Pricing goals involve more than keeping facilities active, workers busy, material consumption high, or revenue generated at peak levels. Maximization in any one or all of these areas is no guarantee of profit. Then again, neither is slavishly following the pricing vagaries of market demand nor agreeing simply to follow competitive prices. Internally generated information about profit sources can be quite scientific, as later chapters will demonstrate. But, on the other hand, the pricer must be strategically artful in the way he handles this information and meshes it into the external, unpredictable, uncertain events of the marketplace.

Pricing is not a job like production scheduling or invoicing, to be decided and disposed of mechanically. Neither is pricing to be handled capriciously, arrived at by guesswork, or done in sheer desperation.

Scientific, artful pricing can provide the firm with the maximum profits obtainable during any specific state of economic weather. Otherwise, the company can be victimized by the vagaries of the market, its profit structure steered by customers and competition, and resultant profits produced by accident instead of by plan.

Objective cost data are essential in deciding whether to meet or withdraw from competitive prices. Only by showing the spread between oop costs and a price under consideration and then by balancing that contribution against the use of facilities, the capital return goals, etc., is the seller able to decide how much value the order will contribute to his company's profit and therefore, whether he should accept or reject the price. These are the scientific, internal effects of the price proposal. However, the artful, strategic factors which must be considered simultaneously are reaction from competitors, effect of the price level in the marketplace, effect on other phases of the seller's business, creating or relieving bottlenecks, displacement of more profitable work later if the order is large and competes for the use of the same facilities, etc.

Pricing requires a combination of calculation and judgment. A price must be validated by immediate market conditions and modified by management, up, down, or out, as the need would indicate.

MANAGEMENT'S ATTITUDE TOWARD PRICING

Managements tend to look for short cuts. Expenditure of time and involvement in "paperwork" are regarded as inefficient and something to be held to a minimum. The average executive is attracted by formulas and guideposts because these hold out the promise of expedient solutions to problems. This attraction is understandable in view of the maze of matters which compete daily for the executive's attention. However, some managers almost completely reject the notion that some of these guideposts may be arbitrary, indefensible, and therefore possibly misleading. "After all," they claim, "didn't we make money last year using these formulas?"

A formula gives the manager both needed security and needed timesavings but ignores the threatening analysis into which he would have to delve. He has a decision to make; he applies a formula, gets the answer and then moves on to the next task. The trouble is that the traditional, arbitrary, shallow pricing guidepost may be twisted which, in turn, leads to poor decisions and wrong actions, as we have seen demonstrated in previous chapters.

Some executives make extravagant claims to being "practical." Much of this attitude is the result of being exposed to the threats of the "numbers game" and failing to understand its workings. Being practical then, sometimes becomes a rejection of systems, procedures, and most formal, calculated data presentations. In some cases also, an executive who has been "burned" by complex, illogical systems becomes "twice shy." This is especially true if he had used a "standard" pricing system which was administered by the accounting division without any reference to product mix, market demand, and competition. In one pricing conference at which the author was present, the president was handed data concerning a certain pricing decision. He commented, "Let's forget about all these numbers and really price this thing. What do you think gentlemen? Can we get x amount for this deal?" The "go-no-go" decision was reached purely by the votes of the head shakers and the head nodders.

Our experience indicates that many client executives do not ordinarily concern themselves with pricing details; there even being many instances in which executives were not intimately aware of how their products were priced. Even among officers who were familiar with overall company pricing policy, there were those who were not able to show how the policy was applied in any specific pricing decision. In other cases, we have witnessed an indifferent attitude toward the pricing of products. Even though subordinates were familiar with the basis of pricing, management did not have a formal review policy by which it could evaluate the results of both successful and rejected pricing proposals.

Pricing a product, an order, a contract, is one of the most critical decisions management is called upon to make. Pricing decisions, which integrate the firm's costs with market strategy, business conditions, intensity of competition, customer demand, production alternatives, product variables, channels of distribution, and financial characteristics, will determine the success or failure of a business. This coordination is management's job.

PRICE DETERMINANTS

Major determinants of price are the seller's costs, competitive prices, and market demand. Prices cannot always be based successfully on individual costs, but objective, traceable cost information must be available to measure how much an order will contribute to profits when meeting a "going" price. The seller's costs are specific and identified only with him. Prices, on the other hand, represent the community of competition in the seller's markets. For the seller arbitrarily to mark up his cost to arrive at a selling price, is tantamount to *denying the existence of this competition* and market demand. Costs should not be the sole determinant of prices, but they can be used to determine whether to withdraw from a price proposal or to continue to explore the alternatives.

Regardless of any other consideration, the price determines the spread between the seller's cost and the outside market and acts as a measure of value to the seller. The crucial point is *what kind of cost* the seller must use to make this evaluation and how he develops it. This question is one of the most contentious in the entire costs-for-pricing area around which much mystery, magic formula, and just plain nonsense still persist.

When cost-plus methods of pricing are used, and the "cost" portion of the formula is arbitrarily determined, the resultant price represents a compounding of errors: the indefensible cost allocation acts as a base upon which an illusionary price structure is erected that makes no allowance for competition and demand. A profit structure results from sales bookings by accident when the seller happens to have prices lower than his competitors. These types of repetitive accidents must produce enough profit and must happen frequently enough to keep the seller in business. Obviously, if competitors using similar cost-plus formulas have substantially lower costs than the seller, the latter's days in business are numbered.

Pricing decisions involve more than *setting* prices for products offered to customers. More often than not, a pricing decision must be made about whether or not to meet a competitor's price. Thus, in many industries, price-*setting* has given way to measuring just what the taking of competitively-priced business is likely to contribute to the seller's profit structure. If information on the various profit segments is available, the seller has the opportunity of profit-*ranking* his products, orders, customers, and markets—and balancing this information against the profitable time allocation of his facilities and employment of capital.

Obviously, an inefficient high-cost manufacturer cannot successfully price higher than his efficient competitor simply because he wishes to earn the same rate of return. The chances are good that if any manufacturer sought to earn the same return on all his products, orders, or product lines, he would price some of his output out of his markets.

COST-PLUS PRICING

Cost-plus pricing methods take a number of forms. All these methods proceed by formula and make no concessions to external influences. Underlying all the methods is the assumption that prices based on an individual seller's costs will be acceptable and attractive to buyers. Even though some managements say that they use formula prices as an approximation, they admit that their prices must be manipulated in the marketplace because of buyer resistance, cost advantages or disadvantages over competitors, desire to expand market share in a given product line, segmenting the market to reach different layers of demand, etc.

Because of such price adjustments, economists are discounting the importance of formula pricing in favor of a reasoned or flexible approach to pricing. If formula prices are computed only to be abandoned in the face of market forces, why use them?

Product-order pricing is probably the most difficult as well as the most critical decision-making area in which to develop general principles or formulas. Pricing is at once an art as well as a science, combining internal cost and capital data, external market information, and the judgment of management regarding effects, both economic and strategic. Pricing is influenced by a host of factors, some objective as relating to internal information, the uncertain externals regarding market factors, and behavior and types of competition. It is not difficult to understand, therefore, why management people are unable to describe their pricing policy in definite terms. Not that a rigid pricing formula is desirable; quite the reverse. Instead, pricing should be a continuous process of scrutiny, test of alternatives, and balanced decisions that mesh the variables of internal and external factors.

COST-PRICE DISTORTION

Managements who use formula-based costs and formula-type pricing are engaging in exercises which do not strengthen either their knowledge or profit. In the first instance, "full" or total costs are computed using various methods which are all equally defensible but not objective or traceable to the specific product being manufactured and sold. Therefore, each different method produces a different cost result. Then regardless of the specific markup applied, management gets the notion of a unit profit developing if he sells his product at the formula price. This notion is highly illusionary in view of the arbitrary allocation of common or joint costs associated with a multiproduct company. The markup on a seller's costs denies the existence of competition and market forces. It fails to take into account the buyer's needs and willingness to pay and what prices competitors are offering.

For a business to grow and prosper, its management must not blindly follow competitors' prices, nor slavishly follow rigid cost methods or inflexible pricing formulas. There is no single cost figure for any one product upon which management can erect its selling price. Even if one were found, management could have no assurance that the markup to the selling price figure would be acceptable. First must come the realization that cost is only one factor to consider. Second must be the understanding that it is not the average cost figure which is important, but rather the composition of costs and the behavior of each type that are vital. Thus, management should be able to distinguish between direct and fixed costs, between traceable and blanket or common costs, between avoidable and unavoidable costs. The cost to be used for pricing decisions is one which is objective, free from arbitrary allocation or apportionment, tangibly, traceably, and identifiably related to the product, and discontinuable if the product is not manufactured. In this sense, such costs can be called marginal or incremental costs. In contrast to these costs are the blanket, period, or fixed costs which proceed unchanged with or without the product and which have been incurred to provide capacity. The scrambling together of all costs regardless of their individual behaviors produces misleading costs and illusionary prices.

SUMMARY OF COST-PRICE RELATIONSHIP

The relationship between costs and prices is varied:

1. Accounting cost may sometimes be used in pricing, or it may be used after an adjustment reflecting future conditions. In some cases, accounting cost is never a short-term determinant of price.
2. Total unit cost may be considered to be the minimum below which prices may not go in

the *long* run. In this sense only, normal total unit cost may be indicative of the normal selling price.

3. Out-of-pocket unit costs fixes the minimum price over the short run.
4. In prices fixed by policy, unit out-of-pocket costs determine the amount contributed by product unit to common costs and profit.
5. Even when prices cannot be based directly on cost, it is a basis for measuring profitability and for order acceptance or rejection. Costs, separated into fixed and variable elements, can be directly assigned to individual product, product lines, customers, sales territories, orders, etc. In this way, the cost-revenue-contribution relationships by these aggregates may be used to direct the selling and production efforts of the company.
6. Pricing decisions deal with the future; therefore, expected costs are more important than historical costs or current costs unless the latter are adjusted to provide for future changes.
7. In multiproduct manufacture, it is essential to show that each product line and product is recovering its own direct (out-of-pocket) costs and contributing something toward meeting the general (period, fixed) expenses of the business common to all products.

WHO GETS THE ORDER?

Application of a uniform markup to all of a seller's products discounts completely that various products may have to face different kinds of pressures from different markets. Competition and demand can be different for each of his products and may each face different demand elasticities. The same holds true for attempting to obtain the same return on capital for each of the seller's products. This practice can frequently cut off profit at the top of the line by pricing the prestige item below what buyers would be willing to pay, and it could reduce sales volume at the bottom of the line by overpricing items that are exposed to intense competition. Both can lead to profitless operations.

But who gets the order? What action should be taken?

1. If competitors' "full" product costs are the same as the seller's, the order is generally placed with the company having the smallest markup. (At what profit?)
2. If competitors' "full" product costs are different from the seller's (either below or above), the order usually goes to the firm whose combination of cost and markup results in the lowest price. (At what profit?)
3. If competitors' costs are not known to the seller, the seller will only get orders under those unpredictable and accidental situations in which he unknowingly has the lowest price. (At what profit?)
4. If competitors use modern cost-estimating and pricing methods against the cost-plus pricing method of the seller, the seller will price himself out of his markets in poor economic times and will underprice in boom times. (Low-volume inadequate recovery of costs versus high-volume profit-draining operations.)
5. If competitors' prices are below the seller's "full" costs, the seller rejects work, perhaps at a time when he needs it most.
6. The almost infinite interplay among the variables of costing and pricing methods between the seller and his competitors and the fact that business conditions compound the problem even further, the pricing problem cannot be solved in any other way than by guesswork.
7. Under these conditions, if the seller is a multiproduct company with a constantly changing product mix made on common facilities, all that will help is prayer.

RATIONALES FOR COST-PLUS PRICING

Many managements say they use cost-plus pricing. They say that they add a "fair" markup to average unit costs to provide a "reasonable" return on their invested capital—*even though neither they nor anyone else seems to know how much a fair markup should be.* This "plus" in cost-plus pricing is rarely a plus because it is affected by the specific nature of the cost computation as well as by the behavior of competition and market forces.

When questioned, managements give various reasons for using cost-plus pricing:

1. Instinct tells them that their method produces the "right" price.
2. Some claim loyalty to their trade assocation as they believe that any price below "full" cost would be price-cutting and anything higher than their standard markup would be price-gouging.
3. Some say that they have been making a profit using the cost-plus method and see no reason to change.
4. Some believe that prices above their standard markup would invite competitive invasion; others think that if they raised their prices other competitors would not follow suit and they would be out in left field.
5. Some believe that buyers are aware of costs and would be suspicious of prices above or below their regular prices.
6. Others think that a large turnover of products is the pathway to profits and would be difficult to achieve with higher prices.
7. Some believe it is morally wrong to earn too much profit.
8. Some managements think that if they priced below "full" cost to take advantage of an immediate opportunity, their competitors would follow suit to spoil the market.
9. Others believe that decreasing prices will not affect demand and volume.
10. Some believe it is improper to sell below "full" costs.
11. Others believe that once prices are lowered they are difficult to raise.
12. Some object to the fact that their price cuts will not be passed on by their customers.
13. Others believe that prices are implanted in the minds of their buyers and that buyers dislike price changes.
14. Some think that the market stability of prices should not be changed.
15. Others believe that it is the logical way to maximize profits in the long run.
16. Some managements realize that while it is not the most profitable way of pricing, it is the safest way.
17. Some say that cost-plus pricing is really not strictly adhered to; that most managements only say they do to impress investigators by their "respectable" approach.
18. Others say that since short-run profit maximization is really not the company's goal, cost-plus pricing is not illogical after all.
19. Some managements prefer to maximize volume rather than to raise prices because in this way they project their image of a just price and a fair margin.
20. Other businessmen believe that a cost-plus price sets a floor on their prices, refusing to commit their facilities to work which would yield substandard profits.
21. Cost-plus pricing keeps the company from losing money by getting orders. (But not from losing money by *not* getting orders. It sets a ceiling on profits but sets no floors!)
22. Some public corporations use cost-plus pricing as a device to smooth out profit peaks which would otherwise be available by more modern pricing methods. This attitude is prevalent among corporations who receive critical attention from union officials, and whose position in an inflation economy makes their prices pivotal.

23. A large portion of industry uses formula pricing as a desperation measure in the face of no other acceptable substitute.

SUMMARY OF DEFICIENCIES IN COST-PLUS PRICING

1. It completely ignores market demand and does not consider the buyer's needs, ability, and/or willingness to pay. Market demand is the major volume-generating factor with volume levels differing for each different set of prices. While the elasticity of demand is not an accurate nor an absolutely reliable indicator of price-volume sensitivity, some consideration must be given to it in pricing, otherwise the adding up of anyone's cost plus a markup would yield an attractive price and a profitable volume. What buyers are willing to pay for an item has no relation necessarily to what it costs any specific seller to produce. The seller cannot aim a gun at a buyer's head and force him to buy at the seller's price. The buyer will turn elsewhere: perhaps to a competitor, perhaps to another industry for a substitute of similar function; or perhaps he will switch to a different product.

2. In effect, it denies the existence of competition. A price erected on a seller's "full" cost can compete with a competitor's price only if the competitor's combination of cost and markup produces the same price. If both use the same cost-plus method of pricing and each seller's costs and markups are computed differently, the order generally will go to the seller with the lowest price. Competitors' behavior must be a factor to be reckoned with in pricing.

3. It assumes absolute accuracy and logic in the allocation of common costs irrespective of the fact that various sets of allocation factors may be equally defended by sets of cause-and-effect rationales. Different allocation methods will produce significantly different costs, especially in multiproduct firms where common facilities are employed and product mix does not stand still. The figures used for "full" costs are usually less objective and tangible than their use in pricing warrants. When a product is priced below market prices because of increasing volume, the Machine-Hour Rates become reduced and prices continue to drop until orders exceed manufacturing capacity. Annual profits decrease because the increase in volume does not produce enough revenue to offset the dropping of prices. Conversely, when a product is priced above market prices because of decreasing volume, the costing rates become increased to compensate for the loss in volume. The higher the prices, the lower the volume, and this vicious circle theoretically drives the costing rates and prices to even higher levels with the ultimate point being infinite cost, infinite price, and zero volume.

4. Whatever the extent of the markup, it ignores the need for different products to earn different rates of return on capital because of the typical varying proportions of materials and conversion costs. Similarly, it ignores the opportunity that each product has to earn different rates of return in terms of the marketplace. Thus, the extremes are between products which earn too little compared to their heavier capital investment and those which require little return but are overpriced.

5. Most importantly, cost-plus methods fail to distinguish between fixed and direct costs—between those costs which are directly traceable to and identifiable with a specific product and those costs which provide the capacity and readiness to do business and are incurred with the passage of time. Thus, orders which do not cover "full" costs, but which can make a contribution to profits, are rejected. Orders which are priced above "full" costs, regardless of the effect of arbitrary allocation method used, are considered real profit-makers. Thus, management operates between low volume on unrealistically high prices and low-profit high-volume work, booking orders through the accident of being the lowest bidder—and earning profits by the uncontrollable combining of whatever accidental profit occurs frequently enough in its bookings.

Obviously, there are times when market and competitive price conditions may not permit the seller to recover his "full" product costs. Therefore, before the seller can agree to meet "going" prices, he must have a knowledge of his absolute price floor. Then he can begin to determine the minimum margin above this cost at which to enter the market if he so desires. The seller's price floor is his cash outlay or out-of-pocket costs.

In a multiproduct company, the "full" cost of a single product can be determined only by the arbitrary allocation of certain kinds of cost. The vital decision on price is that the selling price of a single product or order cover at least its out-of-pocket cost and then provide an amount above that level to *contribute* toward paying some of the common or joint costs associated with all the products made to the extent of what the market will permit. In making the price decision, management must accept or reject the proposed contribution, based on the use of the facilities and employed capital it would have to use for the order, against the alternative use of the same resources for competing work on which a greater return may be earned.

To get this *single most vital piece of pricing and profit-planning information,* the seller must separate out-of-pocket costs from all his other costs in his company. Only in this way is the seller able to measure the contribution available from any price.

PRICING POLICY AND PLAN

The ultimate goal of a pricing policy is to formulate a program so that over the range of economic conditions the owners will obtain a satisfactory return on their invested capital in keeping with expected results. A proper and effective pricing policy is the result of coordination by management on costs, volume, prices, profit, competition, and market demand.

Many management people are now living through their first experiences in a tough, competitive environment and are finding it harder than ever to cope with competition to meet their profit objectives. How well they succeed will depend largely on how well they know and direct their profit structure, how well they can uncover strengths and weaknesses in the various profit segments of their operations, how well they get and use market and competitive information, and how well they make decisions on these data to implement an organized profit plan. The implication here is that executives must be responsive to a planning-oriented profit discipline.

Planning in this framework must be tied into a target return on the capital employed in each of the company's segments of profit generation. Moreover, such objective planning must be dovetailed with market-competition variables to optimize the product mix.

In most cases, factors governing prices are complex as well as dynamic. These factors cannot be waived aside by treating pricing as a hodgepodge of subjective decisions. A pricing policy and a set of objectives are vital for profit planning. These should be interwoven with prices which are to be used as part of the company's strategy in obtaining the profit objective. Then a knowledge of markets and competition will help marshal a series of pricing tactics to be used.

Pricing policy must be related to a base upon which results are expected to occur. Some firms use as an objective a target rate of return on total invested capital. Others express this goal as a return on sales. Because of the external variables of competition and market demand, a major portion of which deals with the uncertain future and the unpredictable actions of others, management is expected to have some latitude in manipulating its internal factors with these nonpricing externals to achieve its goal.

Usually there is enough room for seasoned judgment in pricing so that management is not expected to use a rigid price policy against the market forces. Rather, any price policy or method of attack should serve as a guide to pricing decisions after the appraisal of all factors and forces at work.

Of importance is a well-formulated statement of objectives, clear cut enough so key executives can communicate by means of a common language. From a statement of goals the company can then structure a formal policy. Typical statements of pricing policy include: prices that maximize profits for the entire product line, prices that are flexibly geared to the market and to competitive reactions, prices that discourage new competitors from entering the market; prices that earn a given return on capital per product line; prices that generate a maximum profit contribution per machine hour; prices that increase the longevity and growth of the company; prices for new products to be developed after a thorough market research program; etc.

INFORMATION FLOW

One of the essentials for intelligent pricing is a constant flow of reliable information from all activity areas within the company. This information should be in the form of a common language so that the different levels can establish effective communication with respect to costs, products, equipment, investment segments, markets, and competition. Price decisions must be coordinated with production, marketing, new-product and new-equipment investments, and other related decisions.

A sound program of management information should be used to coordinate these decisions so that management can be guided to act on the sum total of overall company effects instead of in the transient areas that are informally brought to its attention.

THE RATIONAL APPROACH

The rational approach to pricing adopts no specific rules because once rules are set up, they tend to remain in effect when they no longer apply. A rigid pricing method is usually based on a company's own costs and thus makes no allowance for the external factors we have discussed. The rational approach adjusts to differing or changing circumstances, irrespective of the particular pricing method employed, without ever losing sight of the interplay of all the variables discussed in this chapter.

What this chapter attempts to do so far is to explain the various factors and forces which enter into the pricing decision, to indicate what information and systems will be required for a sound pricing program, and to criticize existing methods, attitudes, and certain information gaps. Basically though, the author hopes that this chapter will place the pricing function in clearer perspective so that its value in the organizational spectrum will have a higher rank than heretofore.

EXTERNAL FACTORS IN PRICING

Sales are the result of many forces in addition to price. These forces are called external factors. Among them are market demand, competitive behavior, and alternative cost-price-quantity schedules, which are forecast to test the expected results of future demand and competition. Although basic economic theory is beyond the scope of this book, the fundamental mechanics are presented as minimum practical orientation to pricing management.

ELASTICITY OF DEMAND

One of the most influential factors affecting the pricing decision is the *elasticity of demand* for the company's various products in its various markets. Elasticity of demand is a basic device for measuring the sensitivity of sales volume to a change in one of several internal operating factors. For example, how much will volume increase with a drop in prices of 2, 5, or 12 per cent for Product A in City Y? If the advertising budget is increased by 50 per cent, how much will sales rise? The response to these changes as measured in sales volume provides the company with a barometer of market characteristics which it can use in planning pricing and profit from operations.

It is important to realize that in forecasting profits from pricing, the price-quantity schedule is not the controlling factor, but rather the relation between sales and measurable demand. A firm cannot set prices in a vacuum; information must be available by which price elasticity and competitive reactions can be predicted within reasonable limits. This fact calls for some kind of empirical analysis.

Typically, sales forecasting is concerned with short-run decisions for existing products. Long-range forecasts are infrequently made, except for the new-product forecast which deals with the question of making a large initial investment. Demand projections for existing products can be done in a routine procedure by tabulating data from existing markets and past behavior of volume, sales, and costs. Since most of the demand factors are expected to change only slightly during the short-run period, the analysis can be performed simply by concentrating on the most vital factors. Among these are survey of customers' intentions; survey of the sales and marketing divisions; survey of industry-connected people, such as jobbers or distributors; survey of trade association data; survey of industry trend data; etc.

MEASURE OF ELASTICITY

Elasticity of demand refers to how volume-sensitive a product is to change in price. If the percentage change in quantity sold is greater than the percentage change in price, the demand for that product is considered *elastic*. If it is less, it is *inelastic*. For example, if a 4 per cent decrease in price results in an 8 per cent increase in quantity sold, then the demand for that product is said to be elastic, with an *elasticity factor* of 8/4 or 2. If a 10 per cent decrease in price causes a 5 per cent increase in quantity sold, the elasticity factor is 5/10 or 1/2. In formal economic practice, an elasticity factor of less than 1 represents inelastic demand.

Price-volume sensitivity or elasticity of demand is a valuable, strategic tool of pricing. Astute managers are aware of the demand elasticities of their various products and take advantage of this factor in their pricing policies. Demand information requires a constant policing of markets and ultimate consumers. Tricky markets are customers who use the sellers' products as their raw material. In many cases, the sellers' outputs are only a portion of the customers' products and involve a mixture of demand factors; for example, paper mills which sell to converters and printers; paperboard mills which sell to folding carton plants which in turn sell to manufacturers of frozen food, cosmetics, pharmaceuticals, toys, records; steel mills which sell to distributors who sell to job machine shops.

The following tabulation demonstrates arithmetically the classic approach to measuring elasticity of demand. The product costs $6 each with an unadjusted annual volume of 100,000 units and a selling price of $10. Total profit is $400,000:

1. Elastic demand (elasticity factor = 3)

(a) Price decrease:

Price	Volume	Profit/Unit	Total Profit
$9	130,000	$3	$390,000

(b) Price increase:

Price	Volume	Profit/Unit	Total Profit
$11	70,000	$5	$350,000

2. Inelastic demand (elasticity factor = .5)

(a) Price decrease:

Price	Volume	Profit/Unit	Total Profit
$9	105,000	$3	$315,000

(b) Price increase:

Price	Volume	Profit/Unit	Total Profit
$11	95,000	$5	$475,000

If the price-volume sensitivity of products would behave predictably and consistently, lending itself to the type of arithmetic measurement shown above, it would provide a definite factor in a pricing formula. However, the marketplace (in the broadest sense) is filled with people: people who buy, people who sell, people who compete, people who react to price change, to styles and taste, to their own personal needs. People determine the changes in volume by their reactions to changes in prices, economic theory notwithstanding. That's why in some cases a price increase of 5 per cent can cut volume 30 per cent, a 5 per cent price decrease for the same product may raise volume only 8 per cent and a price decrease of 10 per cent may only raise volume to 14 per cent. Unfortunately, the elasticity factor is not linear in any amount nor in any direction. Information can be tabulated if properly developed:

Selling price	Contribution	Estimated sales volume of units*	Total contribution
$5	$1	250,000	$250,000
6	2	230,000	460,000
7	3	200,000	600,000
8	4	160,000	640,000
9	5	110,000	550,000

*Volume for which there is existing capacity.

Obviously, the company selling this product would want to peg its price level somewhere between $7 and $8.

DEMAND AND THE SPECIFIC PROFIT STRUCTURE

As will be discussed later, the profit-making characteristics of the firm are determined largely by its profit structure, which refers to the proportion of fixed costs present in total cost—the relationship between a company's fixed and direct costs.

Generally, where the demand for a product is elastic, higher profits can be made with lower prices, lower unit profit margins, and higher volume. Where the demand is inelastic, higher profits can be made with higher prices, larger unit profit margins, and lower volume. A company with a higher proportion of fixed costs would benefit from the former situation, i.e., higher volume at lower unit profit margins. This basic point is demonstrated in Exhibit 21-1.

The exhibit shows two different companies and their profit structures, both selling the same product at a unit selling price of $10. Both earn the same profit at 100,000 annual unit volume. The bottom of the exhibit shows how each company would react to changing selling prices under two elasticity factors. Obviously, Company B can not only produce profits in spite of the drop in selling prices, it can also produce greater profits as the elasticity factor rises. Company A, with a lower level of fixed expenses, shows a loss under both conditions.

One point should be made clear: a major factor for the changes in profits of both companies is the respective levels of direct expenses per unit which affect the amount of contribution. In the case of Company A, the drop in prices eliminates half of this contribution. In Company B, the reduction is only 19 per cent. Thus, it is the *rate* of increased contribution with greater volume that is controlling. With reduced prices, Company A has a contribution of $1.50 per unit; Company B, $6.50 per unit, or over four times as fast. These are evaluated by the respective PV's.

This is one reason, when considering both the elasticity of demand and the different fixed cost proportions as well as the different changes in PV's, that a price which is as high as the "market can bear" is *not necessarily* the most profitable price.

PRICING STRATEGY

Since every business is confronted by certain rates of demand for its products and since the

	Company A Low Proportion of Fixed Cost	Company B High Proportion of Fixed Cost
Annual Fixed Cost	$ 200,000	$ 700,000
Annual Direct Cost	700,000	200,000
Total Cost	900,000	900,000
Profit	100,000	100,000
Annual Sales Revenue	$1,000,000	$1,000,000
Unit Volume	100,000 pcs.	100,000 pcs.
"Normal" Unit S.P.	$10	$10
Unit "Profit"	$ 1	$ 1
Unit Contribution	$ 3	$ 8
Annual Contribution	$ 300,000	$ 800,000
Drop Price 15% to:	$ 8.50	$ 8.50
a) Elasticity Factor of 1:		
New Volume	115,000	115,000
New Sales Revenue	$ 977,500	$ 977,500
Annual Total Cost	$1,005,000	$ 930,000
Profit or (Loss)	($27,500)	$ 47,500
Unit Contribution	$ 1.50	$ 6.50
Annual Contribution	$ 172,500	$ 747,500
b) Elasticity Factor of 2:		
New Volume	130,000	130,000
New Sales Revenue	$1,105,000	$1,105,000
Annual Total Cost	$1,110,000	$ 960,000
Profit or (Loss)	($5,000)	$ 145,000
Unit Contribution	$ 1.50	$ 6.50
Annual Contribution	$ 195,000	$ 845,000

EXHIBIT 21-1: "Effect of Demand Elasticity"

quantity changes will affect the firm's cost-volume-price relationship, management must have at least a general knowledge of the elasticity of demand for its products in its various markets. Otherwise, management should consider engaging in some controlled experiments to be able to evaluate the elasticity factors.

After these data are available, the profit-planning division can prepare cost-profit schedules showing alternate projections of profit-structure data at different prices and volume levels. In other words, before the pricing program is set, it is necessary for management to select factors of demand, competition, and cost that are relevant to each pricing problem. At the same time, formal research effort must be made to get quantitative estimates for each of these elements.

Surprising results are produced from even the first attempts at price-demand experimentation. One major meat-packing firm discovered that a relatively inelastic demand existed within a given price range for a group of its products. As soon as it discovered this fact, it raised prices somewhat without any noticeable drop-off in volume and enjoyed an appreciable increase in profits.

But regardless of the specific elasticity of demand existing in an industry, if the company is operating in a highly competitive market, the seller's firm is constantly faced with an elastic demand schedule. If the seller's prices are reduced, the competitor's customers will be attracted and vice versa if prices are increased. This condition limits the pricing independence of the individual company, and thereby costs are not too controlling. As we said, costs under these circumstances are more important for determining which items to make, which to drop, and which are more profitable, than for basing prices.

MARKET SEGMENTATION

Another nonprice tool which can be used to advantage is the segmentation of the company's market to expose different layers of customer demand. Existing or potential customers will buy a range of similar products at varying prices and in different volumes. Higher-priced items will yield lower sales at greater profit margins; lower-priced items will produce greater sales volume but with lower unit profits. If customers are separated into classes, the seller can take advantage of the differences in the demand elasticities.

Frequently, it is necessary to differentiate the product to justify the different prices offered to the various layers of customer demand. This differentiation may result in offering the basic product in both standard and deluxe models or offering the product under advertised brand names and under unadvertised private labels. Often this technique is used to occupy some capacity of facilities which are also used to produce the company's regular line.

However, when market segmentation is used as one of management's tools, care must be exercised to avoid actions which may make it difficult to maintain the company's prices in its more profitable market segments. Thus a company should not sell the lower-priced items to a class of customers which competes with the company's regular customers.

MARKET FORCE

Management frequently asks, "What does a product cost?" The accountant may give an answer that includes all direct costs plus other period costs developed per unit at a volume rate which is expected to recover these expenses. This "standard" cost may not be tolerable in price competition. In many cases, the volume rate selected upon which to unitize the period costs may produce a cost that is too "big" when compared with present market or competitive prices. The test of the cost is not the addition of a markup for pricing but rather the comparison with the market which will show the return to the company if it meets the competitive price.

The concept of formula pricing e.g., Price = cost + profit, is totally unrealistic because it ignores the nonprice factors. Instead, the basis for successful pricing is Profits = market price − your cost. Regardless of the costing concept employed in the company, costs must be compared to the external bench mark of the competitive market price. From this simple comparison, management can be directed to lower or to increase its target return on invested capital; to shift sales emphasis on its various products to its various customers, end markets, etc.; to add or drop a product or customers, etc.

BASIC REQUIREMENTS FOR PRICING

In the multiproduct business enterprise of today, maximizing output and/or sales revenue does not necessarily guarantee maximum profits. These actions may in fact reduce profits. Profits depend on the proper selection and balancing of the variables of prices, product mix, volume, and costs. Every business consists of a number of segments: divisions, product lines, territories, products, facilities, end markets, classes of customers, channels of distribution. Proper pricing depends on knowing the relative contributions which each segment makes to the overall profit and then striking the proper balance. Pricing, therefore, is a profit-planning problem in which management analyzes and compares the various alternatives in order to select the one which promises to be the most advantageous.

A rational approach to pricing adopts no specific rules because once rules are set up, they tend to remain in effect when they no longer apply. The rational approach adjusts to differing or changing circumstances, irrespective of the particular pricing method employed. But regardless of which pricing method is used, it must be recognized that the major determinants of prices are market demand, competition, and cost.

Pricing decisions involve more than setting prices for products offered to customers. More often than not, a pricing decision must be made whether or not to meet a competitive or market price. Thus, price-*setting* has given way to measuring the economic benefits (contributions) to the seller of meeting a competitive price.

For sound pricing, product costs must be stated in terms of their out-of-pocket costs. Whether or not a unitized fixed cost is shown, the product cost must be separated so that the out-of-pocket level stands out and can be used for contribution measurements. Pricing based on costs which have not been so separated is usually accompanied by feelings of uncertainty. If a seller's price is rejected, has the cost been estimated as too high? Are the allocation methods correct? If the seller's price is readily accepted, was the price too low? If the price quoted was too high, should it be shaved? By how much? How low is safe?

In any estimate prepared for bid on which all costs are shown, there are both the known, tangible elements of cost and those which are arbitrary. The known elements are, of course, directly identified with the order; the arbitrary component is statistically allocated with any of several methods—all of which may be defended by rationalizing in one way or another. The sole tangible piece of cost information is the direct or out-of-pocket cost, the costs that are incurred specifically for the order and wouldn't be incurred without the order. Out-of-pocket costs consist of direct labor, direct materials, and direct overhead cost, at both the manufacturing or non-manufacturing levels and in total constitute the economic floor on price.

PRICE FLOOR

It follows then that the price floor of any order is its direct or out-of-pocket costs. Of course, if all orders throughout the operating year are sold at just the oop level, the company will incur a loss to the extent of its period or fixed expenses. That is, when all output is sold at oop cost, the annual contribution is zero. No businessman would want to continue this practice for very long, and surely he would not want to sell below his oop cost level.

Of course, there are several rationales for selling at the oop level or below. In periods of business downturn, a manufacturer may sell at just his oop cost level if it allows him to keep his doors open by which he can maintain a skeleton force of highly skilled labor. The critical shortage of such labor in normal business times and the high cost of training workers to the manufacturer's specific methods may justify such floor selling prices. In normal times, a seller may sell at his oop level or even below it if the work is part of an otherwise profitable package of orders to a customer. In this case, if the loss work is a small portion of what the customer buys in the year and does not seriously dilute the yearly contribution amount from the customer, then this pricing action is more strategic than economic and may be considered sound business. Of course, this action assumes that the seller does not have the option of dropping the loss work from the customer's entire purchasing package.

Regardless of these strategic reasons, taking an order priced below the out-of-pocket cost is like receiving $1,000 from a customer's order and then paying out $1,100 in direct labor, direct materials, and direct overhead costs to produce it. Therefore, in attempting to meet competitive prices, shouldn't a knowledge of oop costs be known in advance? The following example will demonstrate the point. In this example, the identical product is being estimated by four hypothetical companies having identical facilities:

Unit Costs	Company A	Company B	Company C	Company D
oop (known).	$ 9.20	$ 7.80	$10.60	$ 8.80
Unitized fixed (arbitrary)	3.10	6.40	3.60	5.20
"Full" (partially arbitrary)	$12.30	$14.20	$14.20	$14.00

The first question to clear up is why the oop and fixed costs are so different for the same product made on similar facilities. Since the oop cost is a cost directly identified with the product, differences among the four companies can be explained by the fact that there are differences in hourly wages paid to workers, productivity, quality, material costs, delivery effectiveness, etc. Fixed costs differences can result from differences in administrative salaries, depreciation practices, rent costs, etc. But these costs are not identifiable with a product or order since they are incurred by time and not be volume. Therefore, they are unitized to the product as a function of expected sales activity, which no one knows will come to fruition. The optimism or pessimism felt by the individual company about its future expectations reflects itself in this unitizing and generally constitutes the major reason for the unit fixed cost differences. That is, the effect of higher annual fixed costs can be reversed at the unit cost level by the projection of an optimistically high activity projection.

In the above tabulation, if both Companies B and C based their selling prices on their "full" costs and were rejected because a competitive price of $12 existed, neither company could decide objectively whether it was safe to meet it, unless it first knew its oop costs. At the "going" selling price of $12, contributions would be $2.80, $4.20, $1.40, and $3.20. Obviously, the order brings more benefit to Company B than to Company C. However, if the "going" market price were $10, the contributions would be $0.80, $2.20, ($0.60), and $1.20; Company C could not take the order. Increasing volume for Company C in this instance cannot compensate for price; it can only make losses worse. However, the other companies can be receiving contributions in the amounts shown regardless of Company C's actions.

CONTRIBUTION POOL

Just as the same product produced by different companies can yield different contribution rates (PV's), neither will each sales dollar per product in a multiproduct firm carry the same PV. Without a knowledge of its price floor, management may pursue a policy of selling for the sake of booking revenue dollars instead of for generating contribution money. Sometimes this practice takes the form of desperation pricing to keep facilities busy in the mistaken notion that the more the capacity booked, the more profits will be. Again profits, if any, are made by accident and not by plan; the ironic result is to credit any profits to the high activity of facilities, which often prompts management to acquire additional facilities which it might attempt to keep just as busy. This, in turn, because of the pricing-for-volume yardstick, can provoke competitive retaliation, driving market prices down to where *an industry cannot show an adequate return on invested capital.*

As a company books orders at given prices, the combined contributions thus generated during the operating year must exceed the annual fixed expenses if an annual profit is to be earned. Exhibit 21-2 shows graphically how contributions from each of four products of a manufacturing company are pooled. By thus exposing the tangible economic value of each of the four product types, management is in a better position to know which products to push and which to discourage, which are the real contributors and which simply have a high price but do little more than swap dollar bills between the supplier and the seller.

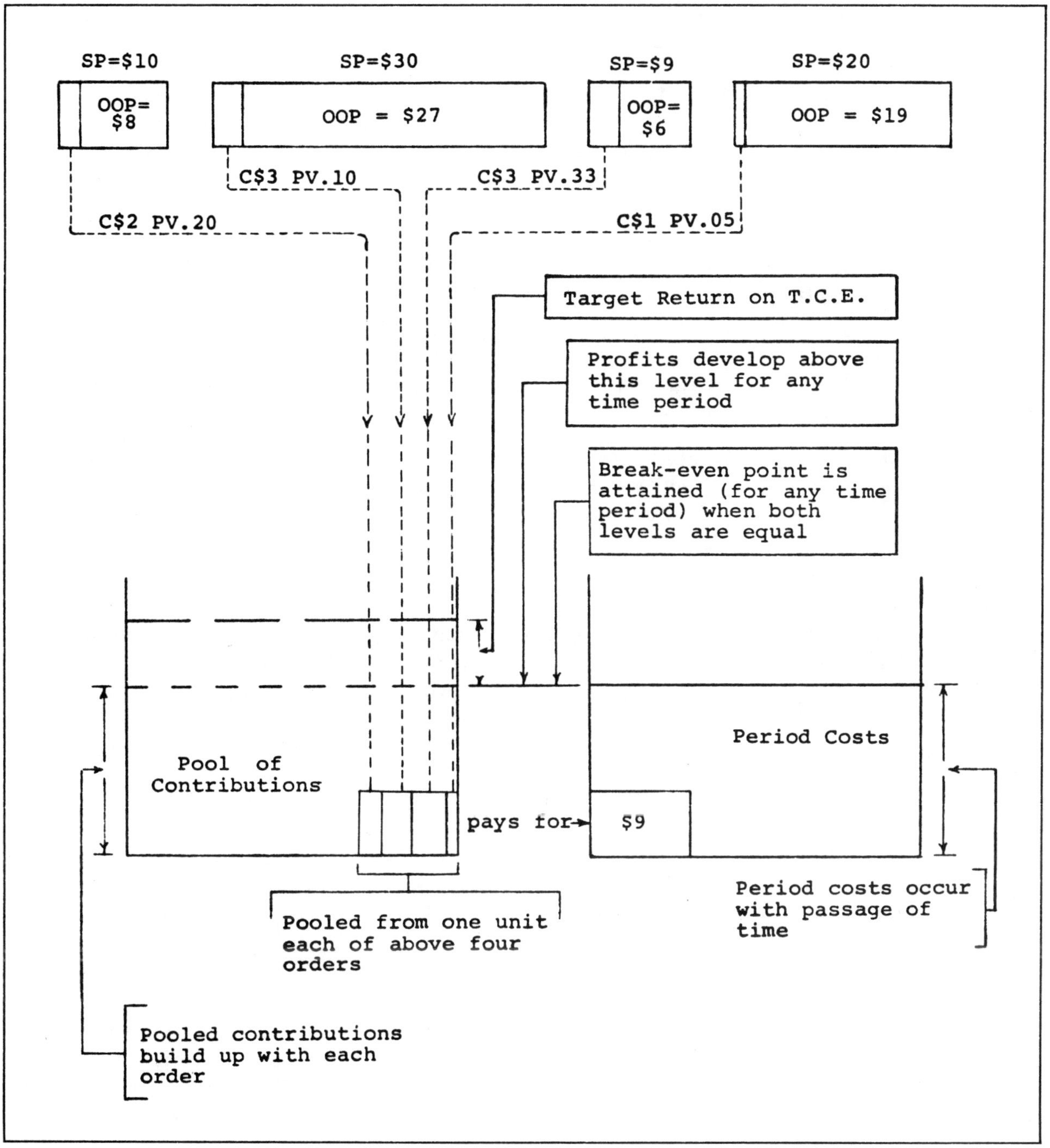

EXHIBIT 21-2: The Contribution Pool

The pool concept is a vital tool in pricing because, in any period, profits are the difference between the contributions pooled in the period and the fixed expenses *prorated* (not allocated) to the period under measurement. Thus, if annual fixed expenses are $240,000 and monthly contributions pool to $25,000, profit for that month is the $25,000 less the prorated fixed expenses of $20,000 ($240,000/12), or $5,000. Of course, when the pooled contributions equal the fixed expenses *for any period,* the company is at its break-even point *for that measurement period.*

With these data available, management can see that the sale of one of Product 2 contributes four times as much as the sale of one of Product 1, even though the latter sells for one-third more revenue. Obviously, a judicious direction of the product mix will cause the level of pooled contributions to build up at a faster rate. But it is one thing to want a favorable product mix and another to be able to get it. The activity which has to be directed towards this management goal is the sales effort. But as long as management continues to employ the classical method of basing sales compensation on sales revenue, it will have no assurance that the favorable mix will be generated. This type of plan only encourages the inflow of revenue dollars. In many client engagements where sales compensation plans were involved, *a plan based on applying commission directly on contribution dollars* has paid rich profit rewards to the company.

Exhibit 21-3 shows the relationship of oop costs, fixed costs, contribution, revenue, and profit.

SUMMARY CONTRIBUTION

When contribution data are available on specific selling prices, management can use this information in various ways:

1. To price individual products and/or orders.
2. To target prices for desired PV to classes of customers, for end markets, etc.
3. To identify characteristically the most profitable products, customers, end markets, etc.
4. To disclose which products need attention.
5. To select and improve the product mix.
6. To determine the pricing floor.
7. To evaluate proposals to increase profits by increasing prices and/or increasing volume.
8. To clarify the understanding of costs by management people responsible for pricing.
9. To get all departments to speak a common language in talking about profits.
10. To provide an easier way to predict profits available in future proposals.
11. To provide a better reward-for-performance basis of compensating the selling effort.

By having the contribution measurement, management has an absolute basis for evaluating the effect of price change on profits. Perhaps this simple example will help to dramatize the point: If a product is priced at $30 and has an oop cost of $29, its contribution is $1. If this product's price is increased just $1 to $31, the contribution is doubled ($2) and the booking at that slight price increase has the same effect on profit as if double the quantity of that product ($60) was sold at the $30 price.

BASIC PRICE DATA

The most basic and essential single piece of economic data for pricing is a knowledge of the oop cost of a product or order. Then the pricer can measure contributions from meeting competitive prices and/or he can establish selling prices of his own based on specific contribution targets. Selling prices practically determine the volume of business that can be generated in all the company's products. Because of the influence of competitive and demand factors, pricing cannot be considered apart from volume. The pricing task might be to find the most profitable combination of volume and price for a product, or it might be to find how much an increment in volume of a certain product at a given price will add to volume. Hence, the pricer must estimate the profit that can be obtained from alternative price-volume combinations through the company's line of products.

In traditional "full"-cost data used for pricing, the getting of a specific order in itself affects the cost of filling it. Each time a new price-volume proposal is at hand, the accountants must go through the laborious task of recomputing the spread of fixed costs in order to present

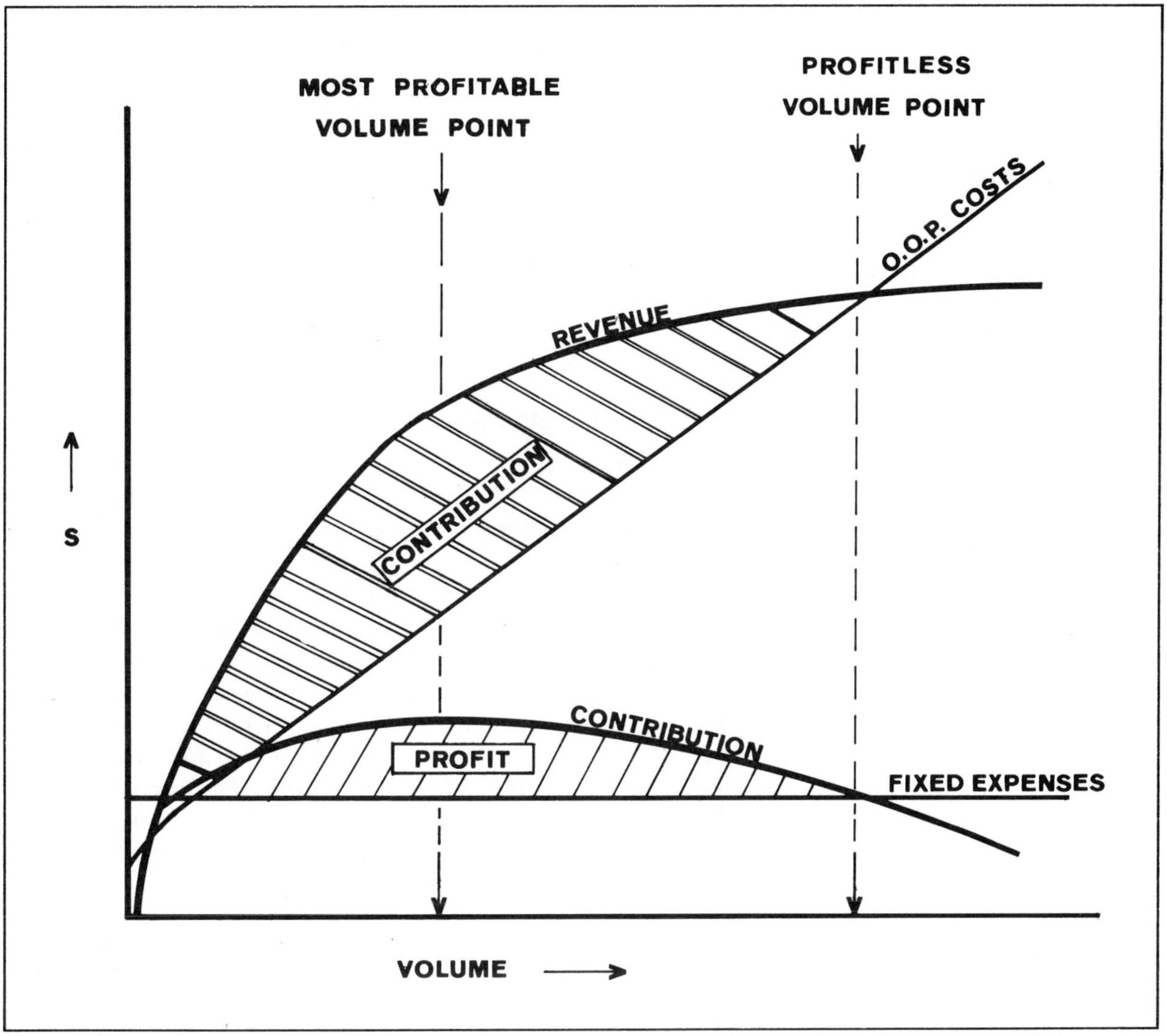

EXHIBIT 21-3: **Contribution vs. Volume**

management with a "unit cost" figure. Not only is the approach invalid, but pricing decisions often have to be made promptly; otherwise an opportunity can be lost if the price is delayed by accounting gyrations and endless recalculations.

With the basic contribution pricing data, management can make immediate decisions on price and volume because the oop costs are incremental and have practically no effect on period fixed costs. Just as important, it provides management with an objective measurement of the real economic benefit of an order.

PRICE LEADING OR FOLLOWING

Where there are established market prices for products, an individual company may not have the ability to take independent action with respect to the prices it would like to get. In this case, product costs are useless in *setting* prices because the company can only sell at the "going" price or withdraw. The company's oop costs are essential to show what contribution would be available if the "going" price were met. In this sense, oop costs are used to *analyze* a price structure, not to *establish* a price structure. Out-of-pocket costs and contribution measurements also allow the company to improve overall period profit by revising its mix in order to obtain the maximum amount of contribution dollars in a period, consistent with the least amount of revenue, employment of capital, and use of facilities. That is, the company is able to determine how much oop cost can be incurred without sacrificing profit. In following prices set by industry leaders, the company is more concerned with what products to make and what orders to take than with how to price them.

However, when a company is a price leader in its industry or offers products uniquely different from others, then it may be able to price independently and use its costs as a basis for selling prices. In terms of numbers of businessmen in the United States, most companies do not fall into this category.

THE COMPETITOR'S PRICE

Management usually becomes informed of competitive price levels through its sales force. However, there are many inaccuracies, purposeful or otherwise, which arise between the buyer's representative and the seller's representative. In this human transaction questions of personality and business ethics crop up.

Questions which arise when a competitive price is reported to the selling management are: Which salesman reported the price? What kind of a man is he? Is he more interested in commission and would he book any type of revenue for the sake of that commission? Or is he a selective salesman who tries to sell the best kind of work for his company? Is his report the only one or are there other corroborating reports? Is the purchasing agent on a "fishing expedition" attempting to get information to use against another one of his suppliers? Is the purchasing agent telling the truth in telling the seller's salesman what the going price is? Or is the purchaser trying to set one supplier against the other hoping to drive prices down in a retaliatory spiral? If the competitor's price is lower on an order, is it for this order only or is it part of a general price reduction?

BEFORE MEETING A COMPETITIVE PRICE

Before the decision is made to meet a lower price (after measuring contribution, etc.), the seller should know the habits and practices of his customers and competitors. Are competitors quoting on the same product specifications? Does the buyer know if there are any differences? What kind of value does the buyer's representative place on the product? Is it the same as the seller's or his competitors? Which of the buyer's representatives is making the judgment of value? This decision can range from the president down to the shipping clerk. Does the buyer buy solely by price without reference to value? Is he afraid of paying more for the seller's product even though he knows that there is proportionately greater value in that product than represented by the higher price? Does the buyer buy what he wants even though it is not at the lowest price? Has the buyer been told to buy always at the lowest price?

Pricing in a competitive market is an exercise in tactics and strategy. Thus, price actions should be based on some kind of *intelligence system.* Not that undercover espionage is being recommended, but through a careful collecting of pertinent data involving financial statements, credit reports, trade association participation, behavior in the marketplace, information from former employees, and the like, a composite image of the competitor can be constructed. If the competitor is offering lower prices, ask these questions: Does he believe that volume is a panacea for profit? Have his prices dropped immediately after he bought a new expensive machine? Is he pricing desperately in an effort to generate enough volume to keep the new machine busy? Is his price low one day and high the next? Does he steer away from small orders? How well does he pay his bills?

How are his collections? Is he making a profit? On all product lines? How long is he producing the product line which he is selling below your prices? Has he evaluated the market elasticity and is he trying to get it to pay off for him at a lower price level? Does he know the effect on his profit structure of lower prices and what a burden this will impose on his break-even point? Has he laid off some of his workers recently where other sellers have not? Is he pricing low because his backlog is low, and is he trying to cover fixed costs? Is this lower price an exception? Is he trying to "get his foot in the door" with an important customer? Has he followed suit when other competitors have raised prices? Is he just trying to gain technical experience on a new facility and is pricing to obtain the activity? Is he in for the "long pull" or is he an opportunist looking for fast profits? Is he actively interested in solidly promoting his good name and reputation? What do reports say about the quality of his output?

Usually, the oop costs, such as labor, material, and supplies, are more similar among competitors than the various elements of fixed costs. The oop costs reflect the product characteristics, whereas the fixed costs represent the individual company's ideas of how the business should be managed and administered. Thus, by plotting estimates of a competitor's profit and sales for several periods, the seller finds it possible to arrive at an estimate of his average PV. The more segments of his business which can be involved in this analysis, the better. This analytic effort can not only guide the seller in his day-to-day pricing problems but can give him a new viewpoint in competitive relations by answering some of the aforementioned questions.

These and many more questions have to be answered in order to get some idea of the strengths and weaknesses of the opposition. But, of course, it will pay the seller to be introspective about himself and the image he gives to competitors and customers. A seller might believe his company to project a fine image in the minds of his regular customers, but it might be evaluated differently in the minds of prospective new customers with whom the seller had no previous contact.

MEETING A COMPETITIVE PRICE

Here are the possible consequences of meeting a lower price. For one thing, the lower price can set a dangerous precedent in the market which will take major surgery to remove. While the value of the product has not changed by virtue of the lower price, some competitors may be so irresponsible as not to care, and it takes just one lower price (from perhaps a poor businessman) to get other sellers thinking about it. The chain reaction in price reductions sets in like panic selling in the stock market. It does take guts sometimes not to meet a competitive price. Then again, lowering prices even temporarily runs the risk of changing the products' values in the minds of the customer. Customers become accustomed to lower prices and the entire price level drops, stays there, and perhaps gets worse. Prices sometimes get so low that sellers withdraw one by one from booking orders so poorly priced. Then one competitor decides to return to higher levels and all follow suit until the next time when someone decides to cut prices and the vicious cycle starts all over again.

Sometimes lower prices allow greater market penetration, opening potential which was not available before. But again, will the combination of contribution-volume produce more profit than before such market penetration was attempted? Or will the lower prices permit a deeper penetration into the layers of demand? In the latter case, new classes of customers may become interested in buying the product. The perfect example is the limited edition $50 book which skimmed the top prestige layer of the market. When that layer had been exhausted, the cost of the book was successively reduced and its form and price successively changed as each next lower layer of the market was exhausted until it was offered in a $1.95 soft cover edition to the deepest layer of demand in tremendous volume.

There is also the possibility that the lowering of prices may cause the product to be withdrawn from its present market, thereby causing changes to be made in the internal operations of the sellers. And perhaps in the period during which prices were spiraling downward, the sellers left themselves a legacy of the continuous obligation to provide some form of service after the sale.

Perhaps a major consequence of blindly meeting lowered prices is the effect this action will have on the quality of sales service which had been more than simply order taking. A company could be enjoying adequate sales activity on a product priced somewhat higher than competitive levels because of the reputation and reliability of the company and perhaps because of the loyalty of customers. Under pressure from salesmen to reduce price to generate more volume, the seller takes on the appearance of his competitors and part of the company's image is lost. Now he is in the same boat with all other competitors and has to fight to hold his previous share of the market. Salesmen become order takers, and the combination of lower price and volume severely deteriorates their profit position.

Chapter 22

The Contribution Method in Pricing

When we think of price, we are naturally thinking about the dollars to be asked for a product. At the same time, we may be thinking about the price that others are selling it for. Therefore, since the asked price and the final price may be different, management must measure what contribution it would get if it met the competitive, market, or "going" price. If this contribution is acceptable to management, it will book the order at that "going" price.

As we have discussed, the out-of-pocket (oop) cost is the floor on prices. Out-of-pocket costs are considered incremental because, if the product is not made, the oop costs can be saved. If the product is made, the increment in cost incurrence is the oop cost. However, a company does not stay in business very long selling its products below oop costs, except when such sales help to sell other products which make a large enough contribution to offset the below-oop prices. On the other hand, the recovery of fixed costs in selling prices presents a complex problem because most of the fixed costs usually cannot be specifically identified with products or orders. The reason for this fact is that facilities (production, sales, administrative, technical, etc.) may be shared in common by the entire mix of products. So when a company accepts an order below oop cost, it is left with fewer dollars than it would have had if the order had not been produced. Whereas, if an order is priced above oop costs, it is making a contribution to the payment of the fixed expenses and leaves the company with more dollars than it would have had without the sale.

PV CHARACTERISTICS OF PROFIT SEGMENTS

Products and orders can contribute differently to the pool out of which fixed expenses are paid and profit made available, and these differences may change from time to time. The reasons for these differences lie in the differences in customer demand, competitive intensity, local attitudes towards certain types of products, local availability of substitute products, feeling of status, etc. Thus, neglecting the direct product costs, such as freight delivery costs to point of destination, enables one product to produce a different contribution rate in each of four sales territories in which it is sold because of the aforementioned reasons. If this is the case, then sales territories should be considered a separate profit segment for evaluation. When a seller's product is used by several different end-user markets, that same product can yield different PV's in each of those markets because of the specific characteristics of the end-market itself. Thus, it would be rewarding also to establish the end-user market as a profit segment.

Obviously, in computing PV's, we are interested in the percentage that the contribution bears to the selling price. Contribution requires only that the oop costs and selling price be known. Adding an allocated fixed cost to profit-segment analyses only distorts the inherent PV characteristic of that profit segment and could mislead management into making wrong decisions. An allocation of fixed cost is based on a calculation of the proportionate benefits a product receives from its use of the common period costs (which may be true theoretically), but it may in no way correspond to the ability of that product to contribute to the common pool of period costs which is determined by market factors. Thus, there cannot be any predictable relationship between the product's ability to contribute and its "fair share" of common fixed costs which it ostensibly uses up. Therefore, a product which receives a large share of fixed cost because it is produced on expensive facilities and requires costly technical services will not and cannot contribute in proportion to this share if it is sold into a territory or to customer classes in which the market price is low and contributes a small amount over oop cost. An attempt to equate this allocated share with a proportionate amount of contribution can price the product out of its markets. If the contribution from a "going" price is inadequate to management, means should be sought to reduce its oop cost, withdraw the product from the market, or investigate other alternatives.

In those rare circumstances where a uniform selling price is acceptable in various territories, then the PV of the product will vary only to the extent of the specific oop costs associated with each territory. These are usually the selling and the freight costs. However, there are some interesting variations that could take place. One Midwest manufacturer set up stock programs for his many products which he sold to jobbers located all over the United States. Several times a year, jobbers placed their orders with this manufacturer, and orders were shipped at prices which included all delivery costs. The mix of products and volume levels of each product ordered by jobbers were all substantially different and reflected the market served by the individual jobber. Until a product-mix and profit-segment analysis was made, the management thought that because it had to absorb the delivery costs, the contribution of the jobber located 2,000 miles away was less than the contribution of a jobber located in the same city as the manufacturer. What the manufacturer overlooked was the composite contribution that was generated by the specific product mix ordered by an individual jobber. The differences in the PV's of the various mixes were much greater than the delivery cost differences, so it was entirely probable for the combination of the contribution of the mix and the diluted contribution caused by prepaying freight cost to give a higher net contribution from jobbers who were located at great distances. From this analysis, jobbers were set up as profit segments and ranked according to their net PV—after the consideration of all contribution factors. Thus, management had a basis for future pricing, negotiating, and concession making, which was keyed to the *realistic* appraisal of its individual jobbers. Exhibit 22-1 shows how a comparative analysis was made between two jobbers, one located 200 miles from the manufacturer and one located 2,000 miles away.

PRODUCT-LINE PROFITABILITY

The calculation of contribution as the difference between the seller's oop costs and the competitive prices makes it easy to measure the relative profitability of products and other profit segments of the business, such as markets, customers, territories, etc. This knowledge of the relative rates of contribution among the various segments helps the company to decide which segments need emphasizing, which ones need attention for profit improvement, which ones yield a

Item	per M S.P.	per M Contrib.	Jobber A: M's purch'd	Jobber A: Revenue Gener.	Jobber A: Contrib. Gener.	Jobber B: M's purch'd	Jobber B: Revenue Gener.	Jobber B: Contrib. Gener.
			ORDER FROM JOBBER A, 2000 miles from plant			ORDER FROM JOBBER B, 200 miles from plant		
	$	$		$	$		$	$
A	10	4	40	400	160	0	---	---
B	48	11	0	---	---	10	480	110
C	31	17	60	1860	1020	25	775	425
D	18	3	100	1800	300	200	3600	600
E	12	7	50	600	350	0	---	---
F	20	2	20	400	40	100	2000	200
G	64	14	0	---	---	5	320	70
TOTALS			270M	$5060	$1870	340M	$7175	$1405
Less: o.o.p. delivery					175			25
Net order contribution					$1695			$1380

Effect of old policy (re: 2000-mile delivery) requiring minimum order of $7500 for no-charge delivery: Jobber A refused to pay delivery charges and company lost contribution of $1695. Ironically, Jobber A contributes more than B even though B's piece volume and revenue are substantially greater than A's, with a delivery cost 1/7th as much as A's.

COMMENT: A delivery-charge policy (or any other, for that matter) based on piece, revenue and/or machine-hour volume, ignores economic values and can adversely affect annual profit.

EXHIBIT 22-1: Comparing the Relative Values of Two Jobbers (Evaluating a Delivery-Charge Policy)

low return on capital, which ones can advantageously be replaced. While there is no defensible method of obtaining the net profit of each segment because of the arbitrary allocation of common fixed costs, it is possible to determine the rate at which each segment contributes to the net profit from all segments combined. As long as the common fixed costs are not changed by a pricing decision, these common fixed costs have no bearing on such decisions and need not be allocated to the products being priced. However, contribution and PV are relevant to pricing decisions because both oop costs and revenues do change with changes in prices and unit volume.

Exhibit 22-2 shows a typical statement of product-line profitability combining both the results of pricing and operating. First, the inherent PV of each product line is calculated by subtracting the respective oop costs. This PV typically shows the gross amount of contribution in each product line's sales dollar before the application of programmed period costs which are directly associated with, and traceable to, each. If there were no specific period costs necessary to support annual activity in each line, Product line B would rank highest with Product line C second and Product line A last. (Note this ranking is not in proportion to sales revenue.) However, after the $3 million specific programmed costs are assigned to each product line on the basis of the specific use of these costs, the ranking is changed. Now Product line A, which ranked last, is first, with Product line B second and Product line C last. Not only is Product line C last, but it shows a direct loss of $100,000; even if an attempt was made to arbitrarily allocate the common period costs, Product line C could not improve its profits and could only make the situation worse. So while a PV of .454 is indeed a rapid rate of contribution in this company, an inordinately excessive amount of specific programmed cost is required to support it, thereby making it a candidate for elimination. (Again this ranking is out of proportion to sales revenue.) Notice that there is no attempt to distribute the common period costs because they are shared in common with all lines and would not change with activity in any of the lines.

When the *allocation* of period expenses is made to product lines, the results can be most misleading. The usual practice is to distribute these expenses on the basis of sales revenue. If this distribution were attempted with the $3,500,000, the results would be as follows:

Item	Product lines		
	A	B	C
Gross contribution	$ 800,000	$1,700,000	$1,500,000
Fixed expenses distributed on the basis of sales revenue	1,050,000	1,166,667	1,283,333
Pretax profit	$ (250,000)	$ 533,333	$ 216,667

This approach would mislead management into believing that Product line A, which is really its most profitable line, is producing a large loss and that Product line C, which is actually a direct loss before the application of common costs, is generating almost one-half the profits of the enterprise. Any decision based on this wrong information could actually deprive the company of profits if the company eliminated Product line A and retained Product line C. In addition, decisions involving future planning of these lines would most probably further limit the company's profits. Some of these actions could involve increasing prices of Product line A to improve its profit, reducing prices of Product line C in the expectation of more volume, spending more for advertising and distribution for the wrong product lines, expanding into markets where distribution costs are higher, offering additional services to customers, etc.

The product-line profitability statement may be used as the format for projecting the expected product mix. Mix is as important as volume when it comes to selective selling. Rarely will all of a company's lines earn the same profit on sales and the same return on invested capital. When the PV's become known, as afforded by this type of analysis, the company can engage in special promotion and/or greater sales emphasis to attain the desired return.

PRICING FOR DESIRED CONTRIBUTION

1. When capital and period fixed costs are directly associated with a specific product, the price can be determined based on a given rate of return. In the following data:

Unit oop cost	$12
Specific fixed cost	$75,000
Specific capital employed	$200,000
Desired rate of return	30%
Number of annual units	20,000

PROFIT STRUCTURE	ANNUAL TOTAL	PRODUCT LINES A	B	C
Sales Revenue	$9,000,000	$2,700,000	$3,000,000	$3,300,000
O.O.P. Costs	5,000,000	1,900,000	1,300,000	1,800,000
GROSS CONTRIBUTION	4,000,000	800,000	1,700,000	1,500,000
Operating PV	.444	.296	.567	.454
Specific Programmed Period Costs	3,000,000	200,000	1,200,000	1,600,000
ADJUSTED CONTRIBUTION	1,000,000	600,000	500,000	(100,000)
Adj. Annual PV	.111	.222	.167	(.030)
Common Period Costs	500,000			
Pre-Tax Profit	$ 500,000			

EXHIBIT 22-2: Analysis of Product-Line Pricing & Profitability

Gross annual contribution desired from this line of products is $75,000 + (.30 × $200,000), or $135,000. To obtain the target selling price, we must find the unit contribution. Obviously, this is $135,000/20,000 or $6.75. Price is the addition of oop cost and contribution, and the target selling price would be $12.00 + $6.75, or $18.75. Note that this would give a PV of $6.75/$18.75, or approximately .35.

If it is desired to price other products in the line (for which the period costs and capital employed are still specific), simply divide the oop cost of the product by the complement of the PV:

$$\text{Price to yield a desired PV}^{1} = \frac{\text{oop cost}}{(1 - \text{desired PV})} = \frac{\$12.00}{(1 - .35)} = \$18.75$$

2. Basically, in pricing for a target rate of contribution, the same formula applies, namely, price

1 See also Chapter 20.

equals the oop cost divided by the complement of the desired PV. Most of the time in pricing, there are oop cost factors which are not known or applied until the selling price becomes known. Typical examples of these factors are sales commissions, various discounts to dealers and distributors, royalties, and the like. Since the PV is a direct rate on selling prices, these price-based additives can be anticipated and included in advance to provide for the seller his net desired contribution if he books the order. For example, let's assume that the seller wishes to net a PV of .35 on an order after paying a 5 per cent sales commission. The seller's oop costs are \$15 each. The procedure is to add to the net PV desired the additional costs, which are expressed as a percentage of the unknown selling price. Thus,

$$\text{Target selling price} = \frac{\$15}{(1 - .35 + .05)} = \frac{\$15}{.60} = \$25$$

Testing this price:

Selling price	\$25.00
oop cost	15.00
Gross contribution	\$10.00
Less: 5% sales commission	1.25
Net contribution	\$ 8.75

$$\text{Seller's net PV} = \frac{\$8.85}{\$25} \quad \text{or } .35$$

It should be borne in mind that this approach to target pricing, based on obtaining a target PV, uses the oop cost as a base without considering what may be very different elements comprising the oop cost. For example, one product's oop cost may be dominated by a heavy raw material content—perhaps one which is made by hand and doesn't require the use of expensive facilities. Such an oop cost turns over material investment in which there is typically less at stake than the capital represented by expensive capital facilities. Another product's oop cost may have a much smaller material content, but the product may be made on expensive equipment. Such a product uses more of the company's capital investment. Yet the oop costs for both products could be the same.

This method of target pricing does not recognize the varying contents of the oop cost and the price which is based on the target PV. In effect, this method marks up material cost as much as conversion costs, putting the seller in the unrealistic position of asking the customer to pay dearly for a converting service simply because the materials may be high; at the other extreme, it does not price high enough because of the lower material content. Neither one makes good business sense, does it?

Pricing for desired PV on total oop should be used only when the relationship between materials and conversion costs remains rather fixed throughout the company's product lines. In this case, if the materials-to-conversion cost ratio is high, the PV is targeted uniformly lower than if the materials-to-conversion cost ratio is low.

PRICING FOR TARGET PROFIT

In some businesses, it is possible to hold a given target selling price over much of the range of the company's capacity. This pricing situation is true in some industries that make standard products where competitors are few. Yet some of these businesses are often confronted with proposals for "special price" volume. Especially in these cases, special-price business should never be allowed to crowd out regular-price business. However, when this possibility exists, management must have the means to deal with these proposals properly and profitably.

Suppose, in the following example, management sets its profit goals as follows:

Plant capacity	1,000 units
Fixed costs	$100,000
Unit oop costs	$200
Normal volume	800 units
Target profit	$30,000

At normal volume:

Fixed cost	$100,000
oop cost (800 x $200)	160,000
Total annual cost	$260,00
Total unit cost	$325.00

Unit selling price to attain target profit:

Unit profit ($30,000/800)	$ 37.50
Normal unit selling price	$362.50

Obviously, if the 800 units were booked for sale early in the operating period, 200 additional units could be sold during the year at any price over the $200 unit oop costs for a profit. Since the mixture of regular-price and special-price business may start at the very beginning of the period, management must have current information to guide its pricing decisions. Specifically, it must know what mixture of target-price and special-price business will meet the profit requirement of $30,000 for the period.

If all 1,000 units can be sold, the normal unit selling price can be reduced:

Fixed costs	$100,000
oop costs (1,000 x $200)	200,000
Total annual costs	$300,000
Total unit cost ($300,000/1,000)	$ 300
Desired unit profit ($30,000/1,000)	30
Unit selling price at maximum capacity	$ 330

To find quickly the average unit selling price versus the required amount of units that have to be sold, use the following formula:

$$\text{Required volume} = \frac{\text{fixed cost} + \text{target profit}}{\text{average price} - \text{unit oop cost}}$$

Thus, an average selling price (representing the mixture of regular-price and special-price business) of $350 would require a volume of

$$\frac{\$100{,}000 + \$30{,}000}{\$350 - \$200} = 866.67 \text{ units}$$

to provide the target profit. The reader will recognize the denominator in the above formula as the unit contribution figure.

Std. Price List		CONVERTER A				CONVERTER B				CONVERTER C			
Quan	Price	OOP Cost per M	Contr. per M	PV	Order Contrib.	OOP Cost per M	Contrib. per M	PV	Order Contrib.	OOP Cost per M	Contrib. per M	PV	Order Contrib.
	$	$	$		$	$	$		$	$	$		$
1M	14.10	12.15	1.95	.14	1.95	47.92	(33.82)	(2.40)	(33.82)	17.50	(3.40)	(.24)	(3.40)
2½M	12.70	9.75	2.95	.23	7.38	22.72	(10.02)	(.80)	(25.05)	11.50	(1.20)	(.10)	(3.00)
5M	12.00	8.95	3.05	.25	15.25	14.32	(2.32)	(.19)	(11.60)	9.50	2.50	.21	12.50
10M	11.30	8.55	2.75	.24	27.50	10.12	1.18	.10	11.80	8.50	2.80	.25	28.00
15M	9.90	8.42	1.48	.15	22.20	8.72	1.18	.12	17.70	8.17	1.73	.17	25.95
20M	9.90	8.35	1.55	.16	31.00	8.02	1.88	.19	37.60	8.00	1.90	.19	38.00
25M	9.20	8.31	.89	.10	22.25	7.60	1.60	.17	40.00	7.90	1.30	.14	32.50
50M	8.50	8.23	.27	.03	13.50	6.72	1.78	.20	89.00	7.70	.80	.09	40.00
100M	8.10	8.19	(.09)	(.01)	(9.00)	6.34	1.76	.20	176.00	7.60	.50	.06	50.00
250M	7.80	8.17	(.37)	(.05)	(92.50)	6.09	1.71	.22	427.50	7.54	.26	.03	65.00
500M	7.60	8.16	(.56)	(.07)	(280.00)	6.00	1.60	.21	800.00	7.52	.08	.01	40.00
1MM	7.40	8.15	(.75)	(.10)	(750.00)	5.96	1.44	.20	1440.00	7.51	(.11)	(.01)	(110.00)

CAUTION: An industry published price list is not capable of making the same contribution to all converters who are capable of producing the order. All converters typically will have different o.o.p. costs. As shown above, these different o.o.p. costs will generate different contributions against this one price list. Low quantities should not necessarily be considered unprofitable; nor do high quantities guarantee high profits.

EXHIBIT 22-3: Effect of Meeting Published Prices on Industry Price List
(Don't meet list prices blindly!)

THE MARKET PRICE LIST

In many industries, leading manufacturers issue a published, catalog-type price list for their products. Most of these lists give varying prices for a given product for different quantities, or one price is published and discounts are given for higher quantities. Buyers usually purchase from these lists; if competing sellers wish to quote these buyers, they are generally asked to follow the price schedule on these lists. While it is recognized that a given product will not make the same contribution to all companies capable of producing it, it is important to realize that there are contribution variances which the *same product* can make to the *same seller* by virtue of the quantity of the order booked.

Thus, while a given quantity of Product X contributes at a certain PV rate at a certain quantity, the contribution of the same product at a different quantity can be considerably different because of the change in the published selling price for that quantity and the effect of the seller's preparatory costs. Exhibit 22-3 shows the effects which published prices of the identical product have at varying quantities for three competing companies.

While these data are of just three companies, it is surprising to see how the profitable quantity ranges move around the published price list for all competing companies in the same industry. A general plotting of unit contribution and quantity against an established price list is sketched in Exhibit 22-4. While the dangers of volume selling without a control of contribution have been

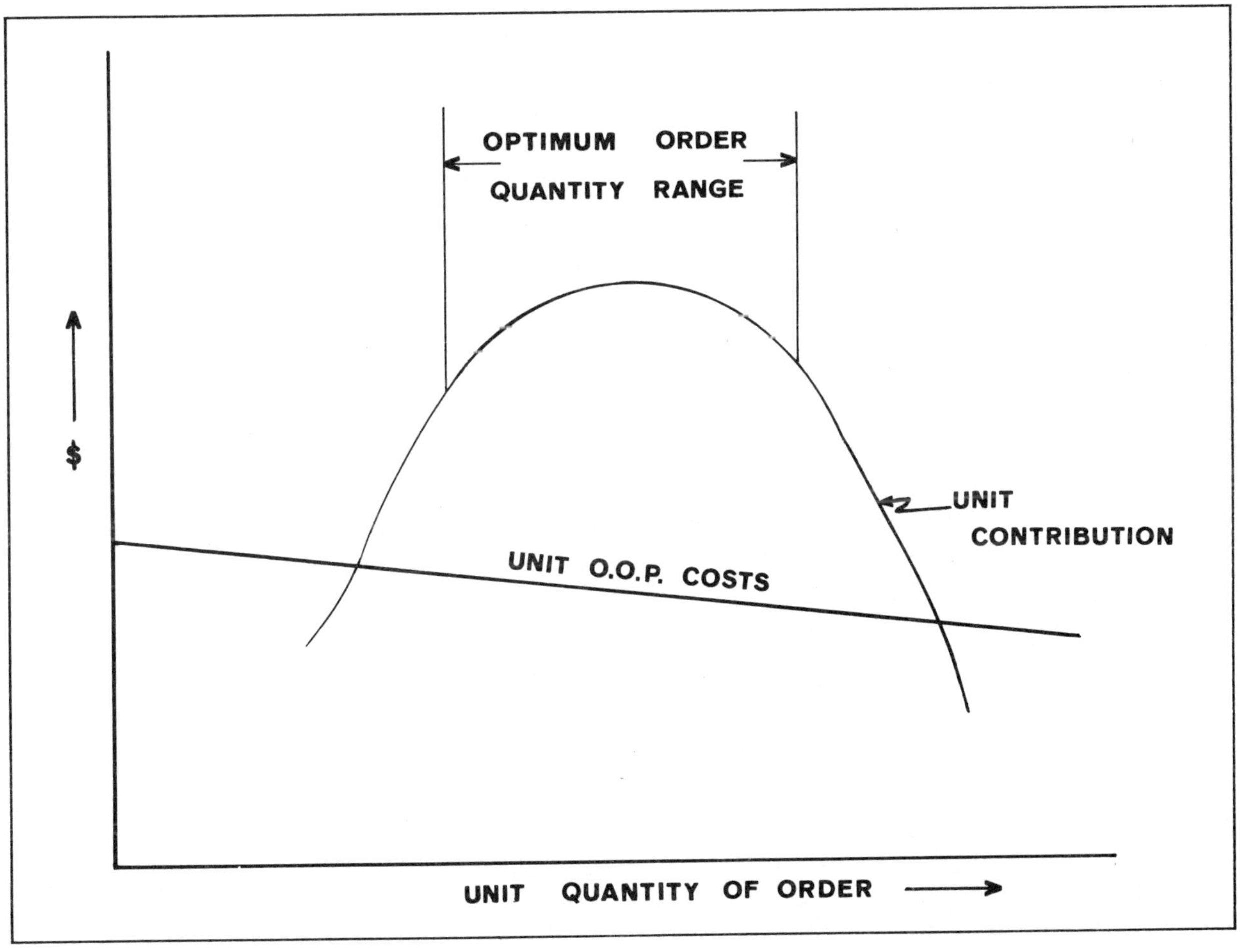

EXHIBIT 22-4: **Profitable Quantity of Product vs. Market Price List**

discussed earlier, it must be emphasized that the results can be even more disastrous when applied blindly in an industry where prices are guided by the published price list.

A published price list usually starts as a reflection of the price leader's costs and then over the years is modified by buyer reaction and expectations. *No established, published price list can ever account for the individual profit structure differences among different competing companies.* Failure to show contribution levels for different quantities can lead to selling below-out-of-pocket costs because of the mistaken belief that volume will compensate for a low price. Even though a seller's "full" cost shows a considerably higher figure than a published price for a large quantity, the belief still persists that if the quantity is high enough, the seller somehow will make money from it.

CONTRIBUTION VERSUS PV:

Many people make the common error of confusing dollar contribution with PV. They believe that as contribution money increases, so does the PV. This may or may not be so as the following tabulation indicates:

Item	Order					
	A	B	C	D	E	F
Selling price	$10	$11	$14	$20	$40	$70
oop cost	8	9	12	18	38	68
Contribution . . .	$ 2	$ 2	$ 2	$ 2	$ 2	$ 2
PV	.20	.182	.144	.10	.05	.028

In this case, the same contribution money is generated for each order, but when such money is related to the sales revenue, the PV changes quite dramatically. Obviously, the most favorable condition in this instance is an order which provides the highest PV together with the largest contribution.

Exhibit 22-5 shows the interrelationship of the variables under different conditions of pricing.

Often large contracts are given out for bid to several large suppliers who must agree to provide products at specific prices for different quantities. Under these circumstances it is essential that a subcontracting seller bid on the order size most profitable for him. Maximum volume is not necessarily the answer. Data are shown in Exhibit 22-6.

Exhibit 22-7 is a sketch showing the effect of the nonlinear relationship between PV and total order contribution imposed by inconsistent sliding-scale prices on quantity differentials. The PV is shown to be dropping constantly, but the contribution can be at a maximum. This allows management to optimize order volume to achieve maximum contribution.

CONTROL OF CONTRIBUTION

Product mix means more than the existence of several products made by one firm. The mixture of products and their effects on profits refer also to the different prices at which each is sold, the typical order quantities for each member of the product line, the characteristic PV's available for each at different volumes as reflected by both the internal out-of-pocket costs to make and sell, the characteristics of the markets and territories into which each is sold, the varying use of facilities needed for producing and selling, and the variations in the invested capital levels of each.

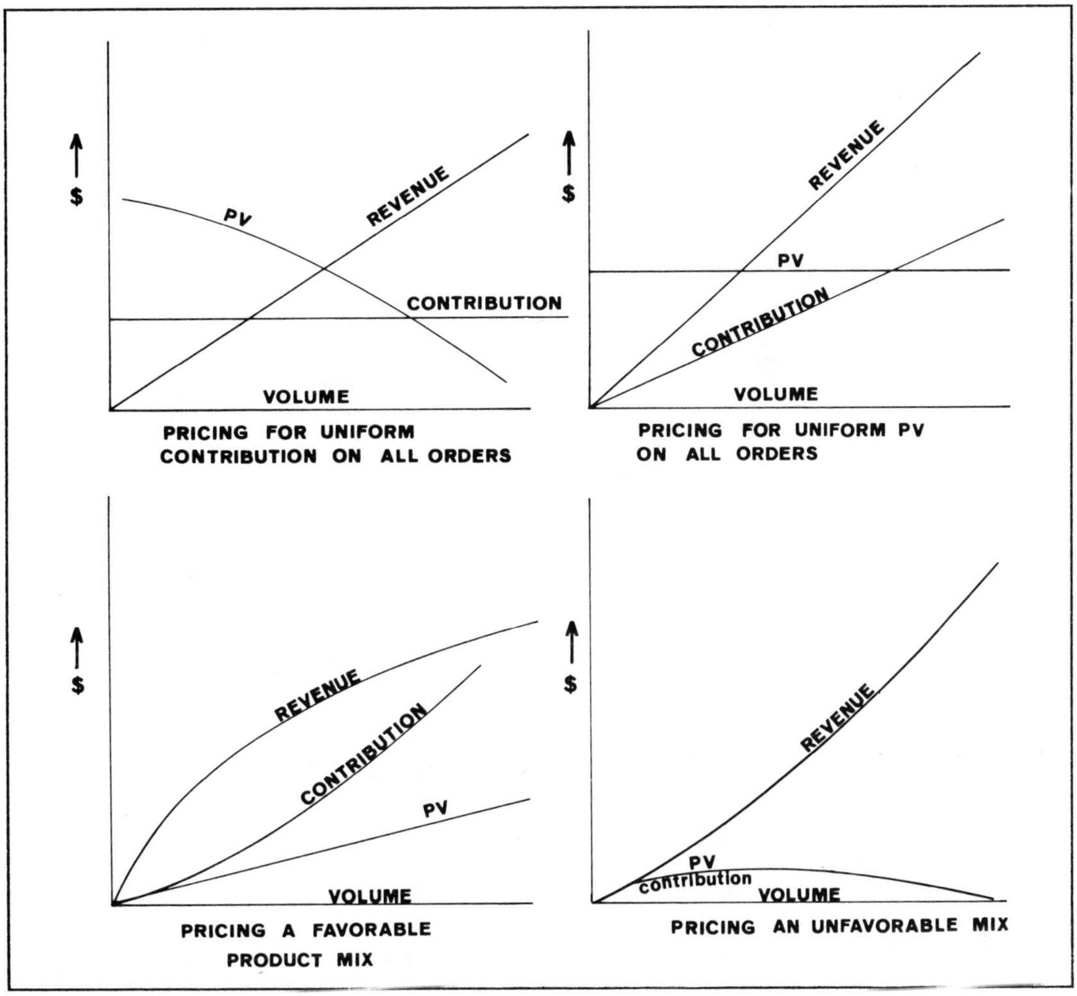

EXHIBIT 22-5: Interrelationships of PV, Contribution and Revenue

ORDER SIZE	CONTRACT UNIT PRICE	CONTRACT SELLING PRICE	SELLER'S O.O.P. COST	SELLER'S CONTRIBUTION	SELLER'S PV
1,000	$1.00	$ 1,000	$ 600	$ 400	.40
5,000	.88	4,400	2,900	1,500	.34
10,000	.74	7,400	5,600	1,800	.24
20,000	.645	12,900	11,100	1,800	.14
40,000	.5925	23,700	22,100	1,600	.067
100,000	.555	55,500	55,200	300	.005

EXHIBIT 22-6: Order Size for Maximum Contribution

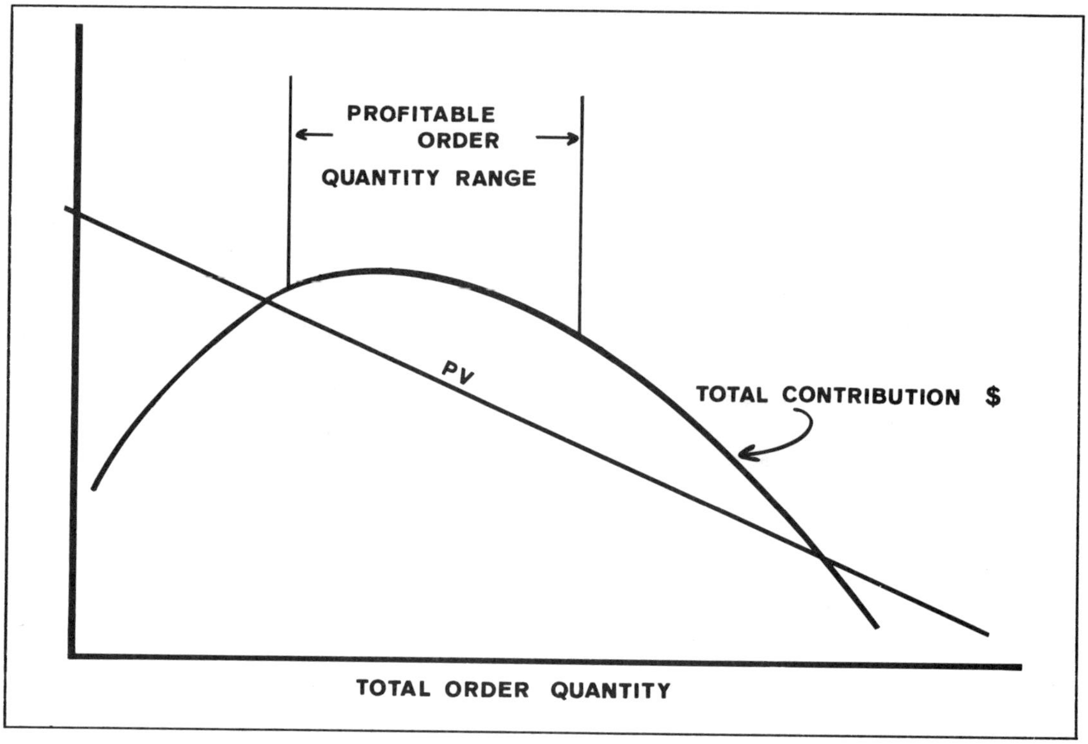

EXHIBIT 22-7: Selecting the Most Profitable Order Quantity

In pricing, management must first measure what contribution is available from meeting a competitive price or from its own set price and then relate that proposal against the use of facilities and capital which must be committed in filling the order. At the same time, management must have a control of what contributions have been booked to date and what contributions are expected to develop in the future. Then it must stack up contributions generated in a period against what period fixed expenses are for the same time interval. When contributions for a period have equaled the prorated (not allocated) fixed expenses for the same interval, the company is at the break-even point for that period.

As indicated earlier, the formula in pricing and profit planning is:

Period profit = period contribution – period fixed expenses

The period contribution is that amount which has been "deposited" in the imaginary contribution pool by the different orders booked in that period. To guide management in policing the build-up of that pool and as an aid to it in its future pricing, a Contribution Log is used. An example is shown in Exhibit 22-8. A Contribution Log is a record of pricing transactions during a period. Since entries are made at the time of booking the orders, the data are necessarily estimated rather than actual. As such, the Contribution Log reports on the *results and quality of pricing* and acts as an advance heralding of profits if actual operating performances are at least as good as the estimates.

The conventional operating statement reports profit without being able to trace its sources—it reports profit as a mixture of the results of operating meshed in with the quality of pricing. Management must have crystal-clear indication of where its profits are coming from. Low profits in a period can be the result of excellent pricing plus poor performance, or vice versa.

If each entry in this chronological log is codified and identified with other information relating

MONTH OF May PRODUCT LINE A-22

ORDER NO.	BOOKED S.P.	TOTAL O.O.P.	CONTRIB.	PV	CUMULATIVE CONTRIB.
6706	$ 9,120	$6,170	$2,950	.324	$ 2,950
6707	5,150	3,080	2,070	.402	5,020
6708	4,970	4,230	740	.149	5,760
6709	10,510	5,860	4,650	.442	10,410
6748	8,740	8,020	720	.082	79,818
6749	11,360	7,115	4,245	.374	84,063
6750	7,390	6,112	1,278	.173	85,341

SUMMARY

Total Sales Booked in Month	=	$404,873
Booked Contribution	=	85,341
Average PV	=	.21
Less: Pro-Rated Period Expenses[1]	=	55,000
Pricing Profit	=	$ 30,341

[1] Annual Fixed Period Expenses = $660,000

EXHIBIT 22-8: Contribution Log

to each transaction, such as codes for customer, location, end market involved, facility, salesman, product, product line, channel of distribution, lot quantity, etc., contribution data may be sorted by each of these parameters. When enough data have been collected and summarized, the relative profitability of each of these profit segments is ranked and exposed for managerial emphasis and action.

Besides showing the contribution rankings among the various profit segments of the firm, these data are useful for establishing future prices of these segments by pricing for a target PV as previously discussed. In this sense, *this log becomes an important source of market intelligence.*

HOW MUCH CONTRIBUTION IS ADEQUATE?

The acceptance of an amount of contribution available from meeting a competitive price is a highly personal matter to the seller. The pricing problem depends on finding for each product in the line the most profitable combination of volume and price—actually volume and unit contribution. When a seller agrees to a price after measuring contribution, he is really saying that the price of that product together with its unit volume (gross order contribution), plus the gross contributions of previous bookings in the operating year to date, plus the expected gross contributions of expected future work, will pool together to cover period fixed expenses and will leave over a profit to support the target return on capital.

This approach could be highly academic since a competitor's capital base and desired return may combine to a target return much smaller than the seller's. The competitor's lower requirements for gross annual contribution may result in a lower price. In this case, there are other guideposts open to the seller: he may employ the technique of attempting to price by maintaining a PV consistency of similar work, a PV consistent with the specific customer, a PV consistent with the class of customer of which the immediate customer is a member, or a PV consistent with the contribution the seller obtains from the use of his facilities; or he may mark up his materials and conversion costs separately for a desired return. These methods will be discussed later.

One point to watch is that while a seller's price provides adequate contribution for *his* goals, it is not so low as to provoke price retaliation from competitors. This, in the eyes of competitors, is price-cutting, regardless of the motives of the seller; this inadvertent price-cutting is as bad as purposeful price-cutting in its effect on spoiling the market.

LIMITATIONS OF THE METHOD

This chapter has discussed the relative contribution figure as one tangible piece of pricing information. Contribution is developed from subtracting the total out-of-pocket cost from the selling price. No means were used to qualify or analyze the specific ingredients of the oop cost, whether it consisted largely of materials cost or of conversion cost. Thus, the contribution could not be related to the invested capital supporting the oop cost. Surely a given amount of contribution on a specific selling price is not enough basis for evaluating the equity of a price. If that same contribution was for an order which required little invested capital to produce, the judgment of price must be necessarily different than if that contribution applied to an order in which the invested capital was high. Thus, once a target price based on the return desired on the various elements of invested capital is established, then besides the measurement of order contribution, management has the additional yardstick of measuring how far below or above booked contribution deviates from target contribution.

Additionally, the measurement of contribution alone as a basis for evaluating the quality of pricing is shallow unless there is some reference to the use of facilities required in generating the contribution. While the booked contribution of an order may be considered high, the number of facility-hours required to produce it may also be high. Booking this kind of work continually will cause the company to run out of available capacity before it can generate contribution sufficient for its desired target earnings.

The following two chapters will discuss facility-hour pricing and pricing for return on product investment.

Chapter 23

The Facility Pricing Method

Industrial facilities used by manufacturers are those which convert a raw material into a saleable state. Often, joint or common facilities are employed to produce various product lines. Thus, many different products may pass through some or all of a manufacturer's machines on their way to completion. Facilities are not restricted to machines or equipment alone. Often, common facilities refer to creative or design functions, selling and administrative services, warehousing, and in some cases, to special critical materials which are necessary in the manufacture of products.

Not all products make the same use of facility time per dollar of revenue or oop cost.

In accepting or agreeing to meet competitive prices, consideration must be given to the degree to which such orders will use up available facility time in a period. Otherwise, the manufacturer might find that in order to obtain a desired level of contribution, he is short of the necessary facility capacity. In setting target prices, a seller may aim for a specified amount of return for each facility hour he commits and this may be done effectively even though the PV of a given order may be below what he otherwise thought was acceptable.

ORDER CONTRIBUTION VS. FACILITY TIME

The acceptance or pricing of orders solely on their gross order contribution or PV may ultimately load facilities to the point where there are not enough facility hours available in which to obtain the target annual contribution. For example, the following two orders have the same revenue, contribution and PV, but there the resemblance ends:

	Order A	*Order B*
Selling Price	\$5,000	\$5,000
OOP Cost	4,000	4,000
Contribution	1,000	1,000
PV	.20	.20
Facility Hours Required	10	50
Contribution per Hour	\$100	\$20

If management depends solely on contribution pricing and aims at a minimum PV of .20, then it will randomly book orders like A and B without evaluating contribution-per-hour. If by accident, the bookings trend toward the Order B type, then irrespective of PV, this company will require 5 times the amount of facility time to produce the same contribution than the Order A type of work demands. In this event, and if the company does not have enough capacity to meet these requirements, the overall annual contribution will be considerably reduced. For example, if the company can only accommodate one-half the capacity that the Order B type of work requires, the annual contribution generated will not exceed one-half of what Order A type of work could generate. And under these circumstances, the PV could still remain at .20!

PV, CONTRIBUTION AND FACILITY TIME

As we see, the PV does not provide a clue to the loading of facility time, as the following example demonstrates:

	Order C	*Order D*
Selling Price	$10,000	$10,000
OOP Cost	8,000	6,000
Contribution	2,000	4,000
PV	.20	.40
Facility Hours Required	20	50
Contribution per Hour	$100	$80

Even though Order D contributes twice as much as Order C to the "pool," it requires a disproportionately greater number of hours to generate. Where facility hours are in very short supply, measurement of *contribution-per-hour* becomes an important pricing yardstick. For example, if both Orders C and D are competing for the same slot of facility time in a period where facilities are almost fully loaded, it is possible that Order C should be taken in preference to Order D even though the latter can provide twice the order contribution. If, under these conditions, there are only 20 hours available, then management would want to book Order C and get the $2,000 of contribution. If management mistakenly took Order D and was permitted to produce only a portion of its order, then the contribution generated would be 20 x $80 or $1,600. If 50 facility hours were available, then management might want to book Order D and obtain the $4,000 of contribution. However, if management was allowed to take a portion of Order D, its best course of action would be to book all of Order C and 30 hours of Order D. Their total contribution under those circumstances would be:

Order C:	20 hours x $100	= $2,000
Order D:	30 hours x $80	= $2,400
	Total Contribution	= $4,400

MAXIMIZING PROFIT AT FULL CAPACITY

Exhibit 23-1 is an inquiry log of all orders which could have been booked by a company in a month. The capacity of a critical, bottleneck facility (Press #7) through which all of these orders may be run is 500 hours per month. Where a company does not state its contribution in terms of its short-run limiting factor (in this case, facility time), it would book orders chronologically, providing the PV was acceptable. Using gross order contribution and/or PV as the sole acceptance factor could cause the company to run out of facility time before it had a chance to generate an acceptable level of contribution, thus reducing its return-on-capital goal. Where facility time is not limiting but plentiful, the criterion for acceptance should be gross contribution. This condition usually occurs when business is slow and management has a greater need for contribution to pay

Maximum capacity of Press #7 = 500 hours per month

Available work at the beginning of the month Order No.	ESTIMATED			
	Gross Order Contrib.	Gross Order PV	Hours Required on Press #7	Contribution per Press #7 Hour (C.P.H.)
1	$5,800	.36	290	$ 20
2	7,200	.24	120	60
3	3,840	.44	320	12
4	2,800	.22	40	70
5	2,600	.26	20	130
6	5,600	.34	280	20
7	7,200	.18	60	120
8	5,000	.26	50	100
9	2,500	.40	100	25
10	7,200	.20	80	90

EXHIBIT 23-1: Selecting Orders by CPH (scarce factor)

its period costs. Under these conditions, maximizing CPH is academic. At or near maximum capacity, CPH is crucial to profit.

The point is easily demonstrated by Exhibit 23-1 in solving three problems under the constraints that only whole orders are to be selected:

1. What is the maximum monthly contribution if orders are booked unselectively and chronologically (i.e., as they arrived)?

SOLUTION: Orders 1 + 2 = 410 hours and that's all that can be booked before exceeding the maximum capacity of 500 hours per month. *Monthly contribution = $13,000*

2. What is the maximum monthly contribution if Order 1 is rejected and bookings then proceed chronologically?

SOLUTION: That means that starting with Order 2 we may book until 500 hours are reached.

Orders 2 + 3 + 4 + 5 = 500 hours and this is where we must stop. *Monthly contribution = $16,440*

3. What is the maximum monthly contribution if orders are booked selectively according to CPH?

SOLUTION: There is more than one combination that will produce this same figure. One mix is: Order 2 + 4 + 5 + 7 + 8 + 9 + 10 = 470 hours. *Monthly contribution = $34,500*

Maximum period profit does not necessarily result from booking orders of maximum contribution. Maximum period profit is the result of maximum period contributions generated within the limits of machine capacity. The scarce factor approach to profits is one of the most effective non-pricing devices available to management.

SELLING THE SCARCE FACTOR

When the volume of products that can be sold exceeds the productive capacity of the firm, the largest contribution (and therefore the greatest profit) results from using the capacity to produce those products and orders which generate the greatest contribution per facility hour. And, as was shown previously, this doesn't necessarily mean selling those products which have the greatest PV. This is especially true where various products made on the same equipment have to be processed at different rates of speed. Usually, the most common factors which cause bottlenecks or which limit output are machines and equipment. But other factors in the company may be considered scarce. In some companies, insufficiency of highly skilled labor may be a limiting factor and so the most profitable course of action would be to use the available skilled labor to produce only those items which generate the highest contribution per hour of skilled labor. In other companies where critical materials are in short supply, management may elect to produce only those items which generate the highest contribution per unit of material.

In most industrial applications, the scarce factor is usually *time.* To illustrate the point a little differently, suppose an individual was permitted to enter a room in which the following coins were laying on the floor:

$1,000	in pennies
700	in nickels
400	in dimes
300	in quarters
200	in half-dollars
100	in silver dollars

He was told that he could keep whatever coins he could pick up *in one minute.* Obviously, the man would first pick up the silver dollar pieces irrespective of the fact there were fewer of these coins than of any other. He knows that he would wind up with more money at the end of the minute pocketing the silver dollars than if he started to pick up the pennies just because there was 10 times the amount of money in pennies. Of course, if he was permitted unlimited time, he would pick up all the coins. But where time is the limiting or scarce factor, he necessarily will pick up those coins which maximize his money intake per unit of time.

This is analogous to the comparison between gross order contribution and contribution per facility hour. The largest amount of "contribution" are the pennies and this can be obtained only if there is enough time. The smallest amount of "contribution" are the silver dollars but more value from these can be obtained per unit of time.

PRICING THE SCARCE FACTOR

In manufacturing, it is not unusual for different products to be fabricated on the same machine, each requiring a different cycle time and each carrying a different rate of contribution. Under these circumstances, the unit contribution of the product must be adjusted by the speed of output. Suppose there are two products in the line which run through the same machine:

	Product X	*Product Y*
Unit Selling Price	$3.30	$5.80
Unit OOP Cost	2.80	4.90
Unit Contribution	$.50	$.90
PV	.151	.155
Output Speed per Hour	100	50
Contribution per-Machine-Hour	$50	$45

If it is desired to increase the price of Product Y so it provides the same contribution per hour of Product X, we must calculate as follows:

	Product Y	
Desired Contribution per Hour	$50	
Output Speed per Hour	50	
Desired Unit Contribution ($50/50)		$1.00
Unit OOP Cost		$4.90
New Unit Selling Price		$5.90

Pricing to equalize contribution per hour is also demonstrated in the following example:

	Order E	*Order F*
Selling Price	$19,000	$16,000
OOP Cost	15,000	13,000
Gross Order Contribution	4,000	3,000
PV	.21	.19
Facility Hours Required	100	60
CPH	$40	$50

Order E has the higher revenue, gross contribution and PV, but since the facility hours it requires are disproportionately higher, the contribution-return it obtains per hour is not as attractive as that provided by Order F. In effect, Order E compared to Order F requires a 2/3 increase in facility time to obtain a 1/3 increase in contribution money. This is not important if excess capacity is available and if the bookings of large order commitments will not displace more profitable work in the future. Where no consideration is given to the selective selling of facility time, the annual contribution level attained is usually less than what could be obtained, as it represents the unplanned cumulative total of all orders booked solely on a gross contribution or PV basis.

The CPH approach can be very effective in target pricing to establish an acceptable and consistent return for the use of facilities. For example, management might wish to accept Order E providing it yielded the same return per hour as Order F. Using the basic pricing formula:

$$\text{Selling Price} = \text{Contribution} + \text{OOP Costs}$$

and amending it to:

$$\text{Selling Price} = (\text{Facility Hours} \times \text{CPH}) + \text{OOP Costs}$$

and using the CPH of Order F to produce the target selling price of Order E:

$$\text{Selling Price of Order E} = (100 \times \$50) + \$15{,}000$$
$$= \$20{,}000$$

Exhibit 23-2 shows four situations and in each, management has to make a choice between two orders when capacity is scarce. In Situation I, the pair of orders have equal revenue and equal contributions and PV's. In Situation II, revenue is equal but contributions and PV's are different. In Situation III and IV, revenues are unequal and the larger contribution and PV is produced from the smaller revenue. For each situation, the facility hours required sometimes follows the contribution and in other cases is opposite to the contribution. Regardless of these variables, the order to take where capacity is limited is the one with the greater CPH.

The bottom of this exhibit shows the target selling price for the order with the smaller CPH which would equate its CPH with the other order in each situation.

PRICING FOR SPECIFIC CPH

Even where a company is not operating at its maximum capacity, the use of the CPH approach is valuable in establishing price consistency to customers, for setting up minimum target prices for product lines made on the facilities, for targeting into certain end-markets or territories, etc. Some examples of various applications follow:

1. CPH on List Prices: As was mentioned in an earlier chapter, published list prices in an industry cannot possibly make the same contribution to all competing companies who are able to produce the work. Even for one specific type of product, there can be great variations from quantity to quantity, from company to company. That is, each company can find the lot quantity range which is best for it because of the published quantity differential prices which do not make the same contribution to each company at each given lot quantity. In most of these cases, it is helpful to the company to find out the extent to which taking uneconomical quantities can deprive them of needed facility time. This can have the effect of displacing facility time for more profitable work in the future.

In the following case, a company measures the effect on CPH which list prices have on three different lot quantities for the same item:

	LOT SIZE		
	500	5,000	50,000
Unit Selling Price	$10.00	$9.00	$7.00
Unit OOP Cost	8.00	7.75	6.75
Unit Contribution	2.00	1.25	.25
Lot Contribution	$1,000	$6,250	$12,500
Facility Hours Req'd	20	200	2000
CPH	$50	$31.25	$6.25

While the seller may wish to take orders in the 5000 lot quantity, he certainly should think twice about committing his equipment to lots which provide a return barely more than a tenth of what the 500 lot generates. Strategically, taking the 50,000 lot quantity is equivalent to loading up one machine for one year on a one-shift basis. Devoting this time to work which produces a $50 CPH would provide annually for that machine a contribution of $100,000 instead of $12,500. Perhaps the answer, if capacity was not fully loaded, would be to take the 5000 lot order which would provide $6,250 of contribution. This would leave a balance of 1800 hours open for other work which could produce more than a CPH of $6.25.

A price for the 50,000 lot which would give the same CPH as the 500 lot and which would recognize the savings in oop costs due to higher quantity runs would be:

	SITUATION I		SITUATION II		SITUATION III		SITUATION IV	
ORDER →	A	B	C	D	E	F	G	H
Selling Price	$10,000	$10,000	$5,000	$5,000	$18,000	$12,000	$8,000	$7,000
O.O.P. Costs	8,000	8,000	4,000	4,500	16,000	9,000	7,000	5,000
Contribution	2,000	2,000	1,000	500	2,000	3,000	1,000	2,000
PV	.20	.20	.20	.10	.111	.25	.125	.286
Facility Hours Req'd	50	20	30	10	25	60	40	20
CPH	$ 40	$ 100	$33.33	$ 50	$ 80	$ 50	$ 25	$ 100
Selling Price of order of lower CPH to equal Selling Price of order of higher CPH:								
1) Hours Req'd	50	---	30	---	---	60	40	---
2) Higher CPH	$100	---	$50	---	---	$80	$100	---
3) 1) x 2)	$5,000	---	$1,500	---	---	$4,800	$4,000	---
4) Plus O.O.P. Costs	8,000	---	4,000	---	---	9,000	7,000	---
5) Equalizing S.P.	$13,000	---	$5,500	---	---	$13,800	$11,000	---

EXHIBIT 23-2: Pricing to Equalize CPH

$$\text{Selling Price}[1] = \frac{(\text{Facility Hours} \times \text{CPH}) + \text{OOP Costs}}{\text{Lot Quantity}}$$
$$= \frac{(2000 \times \$50) + (50{,}000 \times \$6.75)}{50{,}000}$$
$$= \$437{,}500/50{,}000$$
$$= \$8.75$$

2. CPH Pricing of Quantity Differentials: A suggested way of pricing inquiries for various quantities of the same product is to maintain a uniform CPH. This method still recognizes the customer's valid expectation that he receive lower prices for higher quantities, because of the spread of certain constant preparatory and transaction costs. But this method does not dilute the target or desired CPH required by the seller.

In the following example, a manufacturer has quoted a unit price of $9.25 for a 400-piece lot and is now being asked to quote a unit price for an 800-piece lot. He first prepares his estimate on the 400 pieces and then by employing the same CPH, he obtains the unit price for the 800-piece lot:

	For 400 pieces
Material Cost at $3.25 each	$1,300
Equipment setup cost (12 hours)	67
Machine running cost (111 hours)	416
Total OOP Cost	$1,783
Revenue at $9.25 Unit Selling Price	$3,700
Order Contribution	$1,917
CPH ($1,917/123 hours)	$15.58

To make sure that he prices the 800-piece lot quantity so as to get the same return for the usage of his equipment, and recognizes the valid price break which the customer expects, the manufacturer applies the hourly contribution of $15.58 to the larger quantity as follows:

	For 800 pieces
Desired CPH	$ 15.58
Facility Hours Required for 800 pieces: 12 + (2 x 111)	234
Order Contribution Required: 234 x $15.58	$3,645.72
OOP Costs: Material at $3.25 each	2,600.00
Conversion, $67 + (2x$416)	899.00
Selling Price of 800 pieces	$7,144.72
Unit Selling Price	$8.93

This price does not insure that the customer will find it attractive nor does it say that the manufacturer couldn't get more. The price of $8.93 is simply the price which will provide the same CPH as the 400-piece quantity—considering the more effective use of preparatory costs.

3. CPH Product Profitability and Pricing: Exhibit 23-3 is an analysis of the three products which comprise Product-Line B of Exhibit 22-2 of the previous chapter. Notice that the analysis for each product is not carried below the operating PV point. Since the specific programmed period costs cover such expenses as advertising, research and development, etc., and are incurred for the entire line in total, no defensible allocation among products is possible. The operating PV shows the

1 See also Chapter 20.

PRODUCT-LINE B	TOTAL	PRODUCTS I	PRODUCTS II	PRODUCTS III
Sales Revenue	$3,000,000	$500,000	$1,000,000	$1,500,000
O.O.P. Costs	1,300,000	200,000	350,000	750,000
GROSS CONTRIBUTION	1,700,000	300,000	650,000	750,000
Operating PV	.567	.60	.65	.50
Specific Programmed Period Costs	1,200,000			
ADJUSTED CONTRIBUTION	500,000			
Adj. Annual PV	.167			
Machine Hours	17,800	3,600	8,000	6,200
C.P.H.	$95.51	$83.33	$81.25	$120.97

EXHIBIT 23-3: Analysis of Product Profitability and Facility Usage

speed at which each product's sales dollar generates contribution money, but again is no indication of how each product loads the manufacturing facilities.

Product II with the highest PV provides the lowest CPH, and Product III with the lowest PV yields the highest CPH. Management's job in pricing is to sell their facilities selectively so as to provide a realistic balance between the loading of their facilities and their needs for contribution.

The characteristic CPH shown for each product may be used in pricing of future orders if management wishes to adopt each CPH as a target. For example, suppose management is quoting on an order for Product II as follows:

Estimated OOP Cost of Order $3,653
Estimated Facility Hours Required 15.3

then:

$$\begin{aligned}\text{Selling Price} &= (\text{Facility Hours x CPH}) + \text{OOP Costs}\\ &= (15.3 \text{ x } \$81.25) + \$3{,}653\\ &= \$4{,}896.13\end{aligned}$$

This pricing technique is most valuable where management has limited knowledge of the

	TOTAL PRODUCT II	TERRITORIES			
		NEW YORK	CHICAGO	CLEVELAND	DALLAS
Sales Revenue	$1,000,000	$200,000	$300,000	$300,000	$200,000
O.O.P. Costs	350,000	75,000	100,000	125,000	50,000
Gross Contribution	650,000	125,000	200,000	175,000	150,000
Operating PV	.65	.625	.667	.584	.75
Machine Hours	8,000	1,600	2,500	2,100	1,800
C.P.H.	$81.25	$78.12	$80.00	$83.33	$83.33

	TOTAL PRODUCT II	END-MARKETS			
		FOOD	HARDWARE	COSMETICS	GIFT
Sales Revenue	$1,000,000	$250,000	$100,000	$350,000	$300,000
O.O.P. Costs	350,000	75,000	50,000	75,000	150,000
Gross Contribution	650,000	175,000	50,000	275,000	150,000
Operating PV	.65	.70	.50	.786	.50
Machine Hours	8,000	2,000	700	2,800	2,500
C.P.H.	$81.25	$87.50	$71.43	$98.21	$60.00

EXHIBIT 23-4: Profit Segments and CPH Pricing

"going" or competitive market price. If these data were available, they could measure what contribution would be provided by meeting that price, and then could reduce the information to CPH and make their decision. For example, if the going price on the above order was found to be \$3,956, the contribution generated by meeting that price would be \$3,956 – \$3,653, or \$303. For 15.3 facility hours, this would provide only a CPH of \$19.80, far below the average annual CPH for Product II. However, where competitive prices are not known, management may use the product's average annual CPH as a yardstick for pricing.

CPH PRICING OF PROFIT SEGMENTS

As was stated earlier, profit is not a single-faceted function of time or revenue. Every business consists of a number of profit segments, each of which has a characteristic PV, each of which contributes to the "pool" from which profits ultimately develop. Thus, profit is multi-faceted and is the result of the pooled contributions flowing in from all profit segments. Profit segments constitute management's knowledge of their sources of profits. Profit segments are developed by segregating total sales by customers, customer classes, geographic territories, end-market users, salesmen, machines, products and product-lines, channels of distribution, etc.

Once this sorting has been accomplished, a characteristic PV will emerge. In much the same way, it may be possible to identify and rank profit segments in terms of their characteristic use of facility time. This information is valuable for specific pricing for a particular profit segment. Exhibit 23-4 shows a sorting of the activity of Product II into three profit segments: territories, end-markets and customers. Territorially, the analysis shows that Cleveland and Dallas both provide the highest CPH in spite of the fact that Cleveland has the lowest PV and Dallas the highest. Because of the relative closeness of the variations in CPH, it would be difficult to consider that territories actually had a characteristic CPH for the selling company.

However, in the end-market sorting, there are some definite CPH patterns which are generated as a function of the end-user specifics. Sales to the cosmetic market provide the highest PV as well as the highest CPH. This indicates up to this point, that new sales to the cosmetic market can be targeted around the \$100 CPH level with possibly some slight modification for territory. However, data by market is a composite contribution of all customers within that market and therefore, it would be helpful to know the rankings of customers. This is shown in Exhibit 23-5 which is a sorting of all customers sold in the cosmetic market.

While the dynamics of the PV variations are not great among the six customers, the large variances in the CPHs indicate the characteristic mix purchased. Even though this analysis still applies to a portion of Product II's annual sales, it must be remembered that there are variations in mix within the same product. This, in terms of order quantity, size and shape of product, etc. So while customer A has the highest PV ranking, it ranks fifth in CPH. And while Customer E ranks highest in CPH, it ranks fifth in PV. And when facilities are limited, Customer E's work is to be preferred.

Once such an analysis is prepared, management is in an enviable position to direct their pricing and profit planning. When quoting an order to Customer E which might constitute a slight modification of Product II, and for which no market price can be determined, management's safest course of action is to price based on a target CPH which is related to experiences with that customer. Thus, if an inquiry for price from Customer E (for a similar product as Product II) has an estimated oop cost of \$2,317 and the machine time for processing is estimated to be 10 hours, the target price is:

$$\begin{aligned}\text{Selling Price} &= (\text{Facility Hours x CPH}) + \text{OOP costs}\\ &= (10 \text{ x } \$148.57) + \$2{,}317\\ &= \$3{,}802.70\end{aligned}$$

	TOTAL COSMETIC MARKET	CUSTOMERS IN COSMETIC MARKET					
		A	B	C	D	E	F
Revenue	$350,000	$40,000	$45,000	$50,000	$65,000	$70,000	$80,000
O.O.P. Costs	75,000	6,000	12,000	10,000	12,000	18,000	17,000
Contrib.	275,000	34,000	33,000	40,000	53,000	52,000	63,000
PV	.786	.85	.733	.80	.816	.743	.787
Mach. Hrs.	2800	400	360	580	530	350	580
C.P.H.	$98.21	$85	$91.67	$68.96	$100	$148.57	$108.62
PV RANKING		1	6	3	2	5	4
CPH RANKING		5	4	6	3	1	2

EXHIBIT 23-5: CPH by Customers in Specific End-Market

PRICING THE ANNUAL PROFIT PLAN WITH CPH

Once management has sufficient data on CPH from all of their profit segments, they can use this information in designing a future profit plan. Unlike the classical variety of profit planning which starts with unqualified sales revenue, this type of planning targets a desired CPH by product lines, products or other profit segments, and then builds the supporting costs up to the planned revenue as the last step. A profit plan which starts with revenue dollars unqualified by the specifics of contribution and facility usages is shallow and usually becomes a fact only by accident.

Exhibit 23-6 shows how a profit plan is built up using desired CPH and expected hours of usages. Actually the revenue figures need never be inserted in such a plan unless the company wishes to show the PV by product lines, which is purposely omitted in this exhibit. This profit plan is built on the product line segment, although if the costs are more closely identified with another segment, such as end-market or classes of customers, then that segment should be the basis for the plan.

In forward pricing, management can then develop variances from plan based on booked-to-target CPH and can police continuously the loading of hours together with the build up of cumulative contribution so that necessary remedial action can be taken while the facts are alive rather than after they've become ancient history.

EXPANDING THE CONTRIBUTION LOG

Exhibit 23-7 shows the Contribution Log, originally shown in Exhibit 22-8, now expanded to

	PRODUCT LINES				
	1	2	3	4	TOTAL
Target CPH	$ 30	$ 40	$ 65	$ 95	
Planned Activity Hours	6000	12000	2000	4000	
Planned Contribution	180,000	480,000	130,000	380,000	$1,170,000
Budgeted Programmed Period Costs	80,000	170,000	100,000	120,000	470,000
Budgeted Common Period Costs	---	---	---	---	200,000
Target Pre-Tax Profit	---	---	---	---	$ 500,000
Budgeted O.O.P. Costs	$420,000	$520,000	$270,000	$120,000	$1,330,000
Planned Sales Revenue	$600,000	$1,000,000	$400,000	$500,000	$2,500,000

SUMMARY

Planned Sales Revenue		$2,500,000
Budgeted O.O.P. Costs	$1,330,000	
Budgeted Programmed Costs	470,000	
Budgeted Common Costs	200,000	
Total Costs		$2,000,000
Target Pre-Tax Profit		$ 500,000

EXHIBIT 23-6: Pricing the Profit Plan with CPH

include information on the use of facilities. This supplementary information is used to guide management in the build up of contribution as it relates to the loading of facilities. Where more than one facility is involved in the production of orders, the facility used is the major facility or the one within which bottlenecks are likely to occur to cause the primary scarce factor to emerge. As in Exhibit 11-10, the Contribution Log may be designed for the entire company, for major product lines, or for major facilities irrespective of product lines. The criterion for segmenting a Contribution Log is generally the degree to which oop costs and major facility hours can be identified with the chronological transactions, so it becomes an identifiable and measurable source of profit (contribution).

A REFINEMENT OF THE TECHNIQUE

Many converting businesses will find it worthwhile to employ the CPH method, but with a refinement which will make the information more meaningful. Before explaining this method, a rationale of the contribution approach is in order: When we speak of the contribution money in an

MONTH OF May PRODUCT LINE A-22

ORDER NO.	BOOKED S.P.	TOTAL O.O.P.	CONTRIB.	PV	CUMULATIVE CONTRIB.	FACILITY UTILIZATION HRS.	CPH	CUMUL. CPH
6706	$ 9,120	$6,170	$2,950	.324	$ 2,950	52	$57	$57
6707	5,150	3,080	2,070	.402	5,020	29	71	62
6708	4,970	4,230	740	.149	5,760	24	31	55
6709	10,510	5,860	4,650	.442	10,410	48	97	68
6748	8,740	8,020	720	.082	79,818	31	23	49
6749	11,360	7,115	4,245	.374	84,063	93	46	48.50
6750	7,390	6,112	1,278	.173	85,341	38	34	48

SUMMARY

Total Sales Booked in Month	=	$404,873
Booked Contribution	=	85,341
Average PV	=	.21
Less: Pro-Rated Period Expenses [1]	=	55,000
Pricing Profit	=	$ 30,341
Facility-Hours Committed	=	1780
Average CPH	=	$48

1 Annual Fixed Period Expenses = $660,000

EXHIBIT 23-7: Contribution Log

order, we mean the difference between the selling price and the oop costs specifically identified with that order or product. However, with what we do identify the contribution money itself? Up until now, we have identified contribution money only with the revenue. Obviously though, the contribution is also identified with the oop costs but only a total oop cost basis. If the total oop costs are divided between oop material costs and oop conversion costs, then how much of the total order contribution is attributable to each?

In a converting business, the primary function of that enterprise is to convert raw materials, and to add conversion skills and the associated capital invested in those converting facilities which increase the values of these materials to the ultimate purchaser. A converting enterprise is in the business of selling the time of its facilities profitably and not to act as a jobber of someone else's raw materials. Therefore, the removal of the material cost figure from CPH calculations can provide a more sensible comparison among orders, products, customers, end-markets, etc.

LIMITATIONS OF THE METHOD

This chapter has discussed the use and loading of facilities caused by the booking of order contributions. As such, it provided one more dimension in the task of analyzing the equity of a price. Gross order contribution and usage of facilities solely give the impact that pricing has on the operating structure,but they do not evaluate or consider the capital employed in orders. Thus, while management may be satisfied with the selling price of an order based on the level of contribution it provides and the reasonableness of the amount of facility time committed to it, it really cannot evaluate how equitable that price is until it knows the specific capital invested in that order and what return on that capital the selling price will provide.

Once these data are available, management can police its pricing in terms of the target return on capital as well as providing a target price when no market price is in existence. The latter use of the technique is especially valuable when the selling company is an innovator. Such is the subject of the next chapter.

Chapter 24

Pricing for Target Return on Product/Order Investment

The ultimate objective of a business enterprise is to earn a satisfactory rate of return on all the capital employed in its operations. This objective is the basic reason for the formation of the enterprise and for the confidence which creditors place in its management. Stated goals of a return on sales or a profit on total costs are not significant until the profit has been compared with the amount of capital resources that are required to generate it. For while profit on sales may be considered high, it cannot be accepted as satisfactory unless the profit percentage on total capital is adequate and at least higher than what management could get if it invested its capital in another enterprise.

A 10% profit on sales of $2,000,000 may not be considered an adequate return for the use of capital, if $10,000,000 is the total capital employed in the company. The pre-tax return on capital in this case would be 2%, far less than what could be earned by the capital if it was invested in a blue-chip security, or even in a savings account.

The pricing function should consider the desired rate of return on capital as it applies to how products make different uses of the various elements of capital employed in their manufacture. Especially in market-product situations where no competitive price level exists, the target return approach will at least state a more rational price than one which is set by the classical "10% markup." Its use also provides a more logical ranking of prices among the various product lines of the company. This approach is also helpful when introducing a brand-new product.

COMPOSITION OF CAPITAL

Capital can refer to one or several elements on the balance sheet. But first we must understand some basic facts. Total capital is composed of current assets, also known as current, circulating, or variable capital, and fixed assets or fixed capital. Total capital employed is comprised of variable plus fixed capital. These are the assets which keep the enterprise moving and show the present location of the borrowed and owned capital. On the other side of the balance sheet are the liabilities and net worth amounts. Liabilities are borrowed capital; the net worth shows the owned capital or the equity of the stockholders. This shows where the money came from that financed the fixed and variable (assets) capital. The capital equation can be expressed in several ways:

1. Total capital employed = Liabilities + Net Worth
2. Variable + fixed capital = Borrowed capital + Owned capital
3. Total assets = Creditors' interests + stockholders' interests
4. Where the money is now = Where the money came from

Fixed capital represents the value of the machinery, equipment, land and other capital facilities which are used in producing the company's output. These do not vary with changes in output but decrease by time period to the extent of the depreciation. Variable capital on the other hand, represents cash in bank, accounts receivable and the inventories involved in the operation of the business. These elements do change with changes in output, hence the term variable capital.

SELECTING THE CAPITAL BASE

Many refer to return-on-capital pricing as *return on investment.* We avoid this term because it is confusing and may be interpreted to mean that profits are being compared with equity instead of with total capital employed. The return on equity is primarily a guide for investors and serves more as a measure of financial management than of operating management. The ultimate measure of management accomplishment requires the total capital base. Investment in the broad sense must include all assets used in making and selling a product, irrespective of whether they were provided by equity or debt. A company should use a dollar of credit just as effectively as it uses a dollar from a stockholder. A business which borrows money should increase its operating profit from the use of these funds to get a return which is greater than the cost of interest on this borrowed money.

The use of equity as the base for return on capital measurements can be quite deceptive. For example, let's assume the following operating and financial data in a company at the end of an operating period:

Pre-Tax Profit = $100,000
Total Liabilities — $600,000
Net Worth = $400,000
Return on Equity = 25%

During the next period, the quality of financial management weakens; profits are also off somewhat:

Pre-Tax Profit = $ 80,000
Total Liabilities = $800,000
Net Worth = $200,000
Return on Equity = 40%

In this weakening of financial management during the second period, there was no change in the total capital employed—it remained at $1,000,000 but the mix of the capital sources changed and became more highly leveraged. That is, a smaller amount of equity now controlled the total assets. Relating profit to equity could mislead some into believing that this second period showed an improvement. But whereas the return on equity showed an increase from 25% to 40%, the return on total capital approach showed a decrease from a return of 10% to a return of 8% in the second period.[1]

---

1 For additional financial ratios see *Successful Managerial Control by Ratio-Analysis,* by Spencer A. Tucker, Mc-Graw-Hill Book Co.

MARKUP ON DIFFERENT PRODUCT COSTS FOR SEPARATE RETURNS ON VARIABLE AND FIXED CAPITAL

Where it is possible to clearly apportion fixed capital to different products or product lines, the return-on-capital pricing approach can be used to provide prices which while differing in markups on the products' costs can still provide the same return on capital. In order to provide such differing markups, the specific characteristics on each product's employment of variable capital must be known. The following shows the different cost and capital data for two product lines:

	Product-Line A	*Product-Line B*
Unit Cost	$20.00	$30.00
Annual Quantity	30,000	40,000
Annual Cost	$600,000	$1,200,000
Variable Capital Employed:		
Cash	5% of Sales	4% of Sales
Receivables	18% " "	11% " "
Inventories	38% " "	24% " "
TOTAL V.C.E.	61% " "	39% " "
Specific Fixed Capital Employed:		
Fixed Assets	$650,000	$750,000
Desired Return on Total Capital Employed	20%	20%

1. To obtain the selling price which will provide a 20% return on the total capital employed in Product-Line A, we start out with the basic profit formula:

$$\text{Revenue} = \text{Profit} + \text{Cost}$$

and amending it to read:

$$\text{Revenue} = \text{Return on T.C.E.} + \text{Cost}$$

and then substituting the known values, letting x equal the unknown revenue, we have:

$$\begin{aligned}
x &= \text{Desired Return (Fixed Capital + Variable Capital)} + \text{Cost} \\
x &= .20\ (\$650{,}000 + .61x) + \$600{,}000 \\
x &= \$130{,}000 + .122x + \$600{,}000 \\
.878x &= \$730{,}000 \\
x &= \$730{,}000/.878 \\
\text{Revenue} &= \$831{,}435 \\
\text{Price/Unit} &= \$831{,}435/30{,}000 \\
&= \$27.71 \\
\text{Return on Sales} &= \$7.71/\$27.71 \\
&= 27.8\% \\
\text{Markup on Cost} &= \$7.71/\$20.00 \\
&= 38.5\%
\end{aligned}$$

Thus, the cost of products in Product-Line A would have to be marked up 38.5% to arrive at a selling price which would provide a 20% return on the specific elements of capital invested in it.

To prove this method:

Variable Capital Employed, 61% x $831,435	= $507,175
Fixed Capital Employed	= $650,000
TOTAL CAPITAL EMPLOYED	= $1,157,175

Desired Return, 20% x \$1,157,175 = \$231,435
Return = Revenue − Cost
= \$831,435 − \$600,000
= \$231,435

2. To obtain the selling price which will provide a 20% return on the total capital employed in Product-Line B, we use the same basic formula and make the appropriate substitutions:

x = Desired Return (Fixed Capital + Variable Capital) + Cost
x = .20 (\$750,000 + .39x) + \$1,200,000
x = \$150,000 + .078x + \$1,200,000
.922x = \$1,350,000
Revenue = \$1,464,208
Price/Unit = \$36.61
Return on Sales = 18.1%
Markup on Cost = 22%

Comparing these data on both product lines:

	Product-Line A	*Product-Line B*
Unit Cost	\$20.00	\$30.00
Unit Selling Price	\$27.71	\$36.61
Return on Sales	27.8%	18.1%
Markup on Cost	38.5%	22%
Return on Capital	20%	20%

The basic fallacies of this method are:

1. While distinctions are made for the specific capital employed in each product line, all products within each line are assumed to carry capital investments in the same proportions.
2. It is assumed that the mix of the two products, used as the basis of obtaining balance sheet data will remain as indicated, ignoring the market acceptance of the respective formula-ized prices.
3. No distinction is made in cost for materials and conversion.
4. *The markup was based on total or fully-allocated costs,* introducing the distortion that may possibly result from a shift in the activities of the various facilities within each line. No oop cost was developed and thus contributions resulting from a price lower than target, cannot be measured.

PRICING FOR CONTRIBUTION AND CAPITAL RETURN

Measuring gross contributions of booked orders for "go or no-go" pricing decisions are vital for planning profits in a period; cumulative contributions compared to period fixed expenses show the profit trend. Relating gross order contributions against facility time is valuable to show the effectiveness with which the converting facilities are being marketed. However, neither of these methods give consideration to what return on capital is being provided by the selected prices. So while we may have an order for \$10,000 at a PV of .30 or a total order contribution of \$3,000, we are also able to determine that the order would provide a CPH of \$30 if it took 100 facility hours to produce. Questions to be answered are, "Is the PV of .30 acceptable?" "Is the contribution of \$3,000 enough?" "Does the CPH of \$30 represent a fair return on the capital we have invested in the different cost elements of the order?"

The ultimate goal in pricing is to establish a selling price for an order or product that returns an amount of contribution which produces a desired return on the specific capital invested in that order. Such a selling prices is a *target selling price* representing both the seller's specific investment levels and his concept of what a fair return should be for him. Since this target is an expression of a specific figure and a desire for return, a target price is no guarantee of market acceptance—as is no other formula price. Just as the Contribution Log measures the cumulative period flow of contributions against period expenses, the target selling price provides a yardstick which tells management the trend of their pricing in relation to their desired return on capital.

The decision involving meeting a competitive price integrates: total order contribution, contribution per facility-hour and the variance between the "going" price and the target price. Sound pricing involves a balancing among these three variables. Where the company innovates a new product, or where no competitive price benchmarks exist for a product, pricing for return on capital is the starting point. Then the strategic elements like: skimming, penetrating, prestige and demand pricing factors are added.

As we have seen so far, pricing for return on capital is practiced in industry on the basis of "full" costs. This is just as misleading as cost-plus pricing. The procedure simply shifts the base from the return on sales to the return on annual capital employed and applies it to orders on an average basis.

The following method shows how prices are established by separately marking up each major element of identifiable product cost in direct relation to their specific capital investment elements without the distorting effects of facility hours or "full" cost.

PRICING FOR INVESTMENT IN PRODUCT

Basically, manufactured products contain two major cost elements which can be separated and identified with capital investments. One is raw materials cost; the other is all other direct manufacturing cost. Raw materials cost generally represent a lower investment from the standpoint of risk, than the operating facilities do. Raw materials turn over faster, are more liquid and can be discontinued in low periods. Operating facilities costs consist of elements which cannot be readily adjusted to varying sales levels and represent a long-term investment which cannot be easily discontinued. This is why a dollar's worth of raw materials investment is not expected to earn as much return as a dollar's worth of operating facilities capital.

For example, here are two products both of which have the *same out-of-pocket cost:*

	Product A	*Product B*
Materials Cost	$10.00	$ 5.00
OOP Mfg. Cost	2.00	7.00
SAME Total OOP Cost	$12.00	$12.00

Since both of these products have the same oop cost, each would provide the same contribution if both are priced the same. If Product A is priced at $14, the contribution would be $2. But if Product B was priced at $14 just because the oop cost is the same, this is tantamount to agreeing that the capital invested in Product B is the same as that invested in Product A. Even though Product B contains one-half the materials cost of A, the capital invested in Product B would generally be higher (in most industries) because it has three and one-half times the amount of facility cost than Product A. Discounting the competitive and market factors for the moment, if both products were priced the same because of their identical oop costs, Product B would be underpriced if Product A's price was right, or Product A would be overpriced if Product B's price was right.

When orders are priced in a way which makes no distinction for the different capital elements, customers are being asked to pay very dearly for a manufacturing or converting service simply because the materials happen to be a high percentage of total oop cost (as in Product A), or customers are being given partial gifts of the manufacturing service when materials happen to comprise a lower portion of total oop costs (as in Product B). Where no capital distinction is made, orders loaded with mostly material cost are difficult to sell, while highly converted products requiring a small portion of material move fast but provide a smaller return.

Even though the contribution concept must be maintained because of the necessity for knowing the cost floor and for measuring the benefits available if a price must be booked below the target price, the specific cost elements which comprise the oop cost must be separated and marked up individually to reflect the investment differences. This means that materials should be marked up separately from conversion cost and (generally) at a lower rate. If the selling prices are to reflect these differences in capital investment, then Product B will be priced above Product A.

DEVELOPING THE MARKUP FACTORS

Essential for developing separate markups is the projection of an annual profit plan. The profit plan is the foundation of operation in the progressive company and is designed to reflect the planned product mix, the PV's of each that are expected to develop, and the facility times for each. While such a plan may be adjusted during the operating year, a first rough projection sets the business ship on the right general heading and gives the markup tools to work with.

1. First, is the statement of capital and desired return:

Total Capital Employed	$2,000,000
Desired Return (Pre-Tax)	15%
Target Earnings	$ 300,000
Annual Fixed Expenses	$ 400,000
Target Contribution[2]	$ 700,000

2. Second, the operating plan:

Planned Sales		$3,000,000
OOP Costs:		
Direct Materials	$1,200,000	
Direct Mfg.	1,100,000	
		$2,300,000
Contribution		700,000
Less: Fixed Expenses		400,000
Planned Profit		$ 300,000

To develop the markup on material cost and the markup on manufacturing or conversion cost, we proceed as follows:

A. *Materials Cost Markup:* This markup is obtained by dividing the desired percentage return by the number of turns per year of capital employed for material. Assuming this turnover is 3 times, the markup on material would be: 15%/3, or 5%. Thus, as each turn of material provides a 5% return, the three turns during the year will provide the desired 15% return.

Thus, the selling price of annual material cost would be $1,200,000 x 1.05, or $1,260,000.

2 In multi-product progressive profit management, the gross revenue approach to budgeting has given way to the use of budgeting annual contribution.

B. *Manufacturing or Conversion Cost Markup:* If the selling price of annual material cost is subtracted from the planned revenue, the difference would be the selling price of every other cost involved in the planned sales. This figure would be \$3,000,000 - \$1,260,000, or \$1,740,000. In order to avoid the compounding distortion of marking up "full" costs and to provide a basis for marking up just the identifiable portion of order or product cost (the oop costs), the selling price of every other cost but materials is divided by the direct manufacturing or conversion cost to get the markup factor, as follows:

$$\frac{\$3,000,000-\$1,260,000}{\$1,100,000}$$

or 158.2%.

Thus, the selling price of direct manufacturing cost would be \$1,100,000 x 1.582, or \$1,740,000. Note that the "selling price of everything else," the *markup margin* of \$1,740,000, covers the fixed expenses on an annual basis, even though just the oop cost is the only cost being marked up.

Marking up both elements by their respective factors would produce the planned sales level, viz: \$1,260,000 + \$1,740,000 = \$3,000,000.

PRICING WITH SEPARATE MARKUPS

Applying these separate markups to the previous two Products A and B produces these selling prices:

Product A:

Cost Element	*Cost* x	*Markup* =	*Selling Price of Cost Element*	
Materials	\$10.00	1.05	\$10.50	
OOP Mfg.	2.00	1.582	3.16	
SELLING PRICE TO PROVIDE A 15% RETURN				\$13.66

Product B:

Materials	\$ 5.00	1.05	\$ 5.25	
OOP Mfg.	7.00	1.582	11.07	
SELLING PRICE TO PROVIDE A 15% RETURN				\$16.32

These are the target selling prices which will return to the seller a 15% return on the specific elements of capital invested in each product in spite of the fact that at these target selling prices, the contribution levels and PV's of each are considerably different, viz:

Product A		Product B	
Target Selling Price	\$13.66	Target Selling Price	\$16.32
OOP Cost	12.00	OOP Cost	12.00
Contribution	\$ 1.66	Contribution	\$ 4.32
PV	.122	PV	.265

Clearly, Product A earns the same return on total capital employed as B at a lower contribution and PV.

PV AND CPH NOT CONTROLLING

Generating a high PV, a large amount of order contribution and/or a large CPH is no guarantee that the selling prices producing those data are near, at, or above the target selling prices, because these factors of measurement do not include the consideration of the measurement of the desired return on the two major elements of capital invested in the order. Thus, it is possible to achieve the desired return on capital from a selling price which has a low PV, contribution and CPH. And conversely, it is possible for a high PV, contribution and/or CPH from an order to provide considerably below the return on capital.

In the first instance, a low-PV priced order of say .06 can provide the desired return on capital if the converting costs are low and production equipment used on an order is at a minimum. In this event, the return would be generated by the presence of a large amount of material cost, in which case the .06 PV may be acceptable. In the second instance, an order priced to provide a PV of .43 can provide less than the desired return on capital if the converting costs and usages of production equipment are large but where the price is not proportionately high enough for the amount of conversion applied.

In the example of Product A and Product B, the contribution of Product B is more than two and one-half times that of Product A, and yet with the same oop costs, both products generate exactly the same return on the capital employed in their respective products. Let's say that Product B will be sold for $1 less than its target price, or $15.32. Its contribution is thus $3.32, exactly twice the contribution of A and yet in spite of this greater contribution, Product B's selling price will not be earning as high a return on capital as Product A. This difference is caused obviously by the fact that in the Product A type of transaction, mostly material is being turned over. Whereas Product B is the type of work which enables the manufacturer to merchandise effectively his manufacturing facilities, which is the fundamental function in his business.

Exhibit 24-1 shows the typical relationships among PV, contribution and target selling prices that could exist for one converter-manufacturing company. The markup factors used are 10% on

Order	*Booked S.P.*	*Est. OOP Costs*		*Total OOP Costs*	*Contrib.*	*PV*	*Target S.P.**	*Revenue Variance*
		Material	*Conversion*					
6214	$4,300	$ 600	$2,500	$3,100	$1,200	.279	$4,410	$(110)
6471	4,400	2,000	1,200	3,200	1,200	.273	4,000	400
7318	7,860	1,300	4,100	5,400	2,460	.313	7,580	280
7340	7,800	5,000	1,800	6,800	1,000	.128	8,200	(400)
7460	10,400	8,600	600	9,200	1,200	.115	10,360	40
7753	7,520	300	4,840	5,140	2,380	.317	7,590	(70)
7872	6,840	**	4,560	4,560	2,280	.334	6,840	----

NET PRICING VARIANCE $140

*Markup on Materials Cost is 10%, or 1.10; markup on OOP Conversion Cost is 50%, or 1.50, to obtain desired return.

**Job on which customer supplied material.

EXHIBIT 24-1: Comparison of Contribution, PV and Target Prices

materials cost and 50% on oop conversion cost, or 1.10 and 1.50. Compare the first two orders, both selling at close to the same price and producing similar PV's and contribution amount. Order No. 6214 has been booked at a price below the target price and therefore is not providing the desired return on the capital employed in its order. Whereas Order No. 6471 has been booked at a price higher than its respective target price, thereby yielding a return above the desired return. While from a contribution-flow standpoint, both orders are adequate, it seems ovvious that the price of Order No. 6214 has not rewarded the company sufficiently for the large investment it has made in that order. This could be the result of the "going" market price which the company has decided to meet. And on the other hand, the large contribution from Order No. 6471 can be the result of the market price, which of course, does not necessarily have any direct relationship with the invested capital characteristics of this one particular seller.

In comparing the next two orders, we find a reverse effect. Here, Order No. 7318 is priced to recognize (and the market has permitted this to happen) the higher investment costs in the converting facilities. And Order No. 7340, even though it turns over far more material than conversion cost, is booked at a price which fails to get the full return on this low-investment element.

In Order No. 7460 we have a PV which is far below Order No. 7340 but whose selling price provides a return above target and far above 7340. Even at a PV of .115, Order No. 7460 obtains more than the desired return on capital. Obviously, the answer is the fact that the return is being generated principally on the turnover of materials in which the company has a far lower investment than they have in their converting facilities.

Order No. 7753 has the highest PV logged to date, but still because of the high proportion of conversion cost which is not fully reflected in the booked price, it has a small unfavorable variance to the target price. Order No. 7872 is typical in some converting operations in instances where the customer supplied the raw material to be converted. Since the company has no investment in the material portion of the order (all handling as well as converting being included in the oop cost), the markup applies just to the conversion cost.

At the end of a period, usually one month or one week, a net variance is shown which reports on the quality of the pricing function in the period and is not an indication of the results of operating. The results of operating are produced from the actual contribution figure less the period fixed expenses. The actual contribution figure is obtained by applying the different variances (performance, spending, material price and usage, etc.) to the estimated contribution amounts shown on this log. The revenue variance maintained on a cumulative basis shows the extent to which, and the likelihood of, the company's attaining its desired return on capital.

EXPANDING THE CONTRIBUTION LOG

Exhibit 24-2 shows the Contribution Log, originally shown in Exhibit 22-8 and expanded for CPH in Exhibit 23-6 is now further enlarged to show the target prices and the revenue variances between booked and target selling prices. In this form, the Contribution Log is the basis of management information reports regarding the quality of pricing and the results obtained in a period. Refinements can be made to this Log which can improve its usefulness. For example, when a column showing cumulative target selling prices versus cumulative booked selling prices, or a pair of columns showing estimated contribution versus target contribution, management can police the extent to which their pricing is attaining the desired return. Of course, the basis for this evaluation is estimated oop costs, so while these data show the direction and speed of the profit trend, the final profit results cannot be obtained until the aforementioned variances are applied to the estimated oop costs.

As shown, the Log is established for a particular product line. However, in some businesses, it may be more practical to set up the Log for the entire company. And in other cases, the Log may be subdivided into individual products or individual facilities. The criteria for making these various

Month of: May 19x1

Order No.	Booked S.P.	Total O.O.P.	Contrib.	PV	Cumula. Contrib.	MAJOR FACILITY UTILIZA. Hrs.	CPH	Cum. CPH	ROC Target SP	Revenue (Pricing) Variance	Cumula. Revenue Variance
6706	$ 9,120	$6,170	$2,950	.324	$ 2,950	52	$57	$57	$ 8,940	$180	$180
6707	5,150	3,080	2,070	.402	5,020	29	71	62	5,970	(820)	(640)
6708	4,970	4,230	740	.149	5,760	24	31	55	6,210	(1240)	(1880)
6709	10,510	5,860	4,650	.442	10,410	48	97	68	8,190	2320	440
6748	8,740	8,020	720	.082	79,818	31	23	49	8,960	(220)	(12629)
6749	11,360	7,115	4,245	.374	84,063	93	46	48½	10,980	380	(12249)
6750	7,390	6,112	1,278	.173	85,341	38	34	48	7,210	180	(12069)

S U M M A R Y

Total Sales Booked in Month	=	$404,873
Target Sales Revenue	=	416,942
Revenue (pricing) Variance	=	(12,069)
Booked Contribution	=	85,341
Composite Period PV	=	.21
Less 1/12 Annual Period Exp.	=	55,000
Booked Pricing Profit	=	$30,341
Facility Hours Committed	=	1780
Average C.P.H.	=	$48

NOTES:

*1. Additional horizontal coding required for sorting into business segments, i.e., customers, product-lines, end-use, etc.

2. Composite Period PV useful only for indicating monthly inflow of expected contribution. Not valid for price evaluating and acceptances.

3. Revenue Variance polices target return on TCE for profit plan.

4. PV by business segment (not period) has market intelligence in terms of booked business.

EXHIBIT 24-2: Contribution Log
(Basic: by Period. Sortings by: Customer, Product-line, Salesman, End-use, Territory, etc.)*

COST AND CAPITAL	TOTAL	APPLICABLE TO: Material Markup	Conversion Markup
Planned Costs:			
O.O.P. - Material	$300	$300	0
Conversion	100	0	$100
Total O.O.P. costs	400	300	100
FIXED - Selling	40	0	40
Admin.	20	0	20
R & D	30	0	30
Total fixed costs	90	0	90
TOTAL COSTS	$490	$300	$190
Planned Capital:			
VARIABLE:			
Inventory - Raw Materials	80	80	0
In-process	40	30	10
Finished	30	20	10
Total Inventory	150	130	20
Accounts Receivable	100	40	60
FIXED:			
Fixed Assets	40	0	40
TOTAL INVESTMENT	$290	$170	$120
Desired Return	20%	20%	20%
Target Earnings	$ 58	$ 34	$ 24
Planned Sales Revenue	$548	$334	$214

A. Material Markup = S. P. of Material/Material Cost
= $334/$300
= 1.11

B. Conversion Markup = S. P. of Conversion/O.O.P. Conversion Cost
= $214/100
= 2.14

EXHIBIT 24-3: Developing Separate Markup for Specific Product Line Product With High Material Content

segregations is *identifiability.* That is, if products are traceable to specific facilities and to specific elements of capital, characteristic CPH's, rates of return on capital and revenue variances can be determined.

Notice that in all of the Logs shown so far, the fixed expenses are treated as a period amount and no attempt is made to show the recovery of fixed expenses which have been allocated to and "carried" by each order. If this were done, then due solely to the accident of specific order bookings, the "recovered" fixed expenses allocated to each could be either above or below the prorated period amount. This could deceive management that their profit trend was either better or worse than it actually is and the measurement of the results of pricing would be distorted by "under-" and "over-absorption" of fixed costs.

DEVELOPING SEPARATE MARKUPS FOR INDIVIDUAL PRODUCT LINES

Earlier in this chapter, we presented a method for developing separate markups for pricing materials and conversion costs. This method was developed from annual capital data as well as annual operating data and applied to all products manufactured by the company. Where it is possible to identify portions of variable and fixed capital directly with individual product lines, separate materials and conversion markups can be developed for each product line. This method is useful where large variances exist in the use of various elements of capital for different product lines. One line of a company's products may be made entirely by hand, requiring little or no capital equipment. And another may be made entirely on expensive, fully-automated facilities. Other distinctions between product lines are their characteristically-different amounts of the elements of variable capital used. For example, one product may require large inventories and have fast collection characteristics. Another, may be just the reverse. By reflecting the differences in these elements in a pricing plan, a set of specific markups can be developed for a product line which targets prices in conformity with the company's overall desire for a uniform return.

Exhibits 24-3 and 24-4 show how separate markups are developed for two different product lines, each of which targets prices for a 20% return on total capital employed. Exhibit 24-3 is a markup plan for a product with a high material content. We assume that there is nothing distinctive about raw material about to be converted, and therefore, we have attributed all of the fixed costs to the major function of the enterprise: conversion. The same is true of the way fixed capital is applied. Where the main characteristic of the product manifests itself is in the employment of variable capital. Here, the nature of the product shows that a fairly high level of raw materials inventory must be carried, which increases the variable capital investment for that product. Conversely, finished goods move rather quickly and collections are made promptly making those variable capital elements lower in investment cost. For this particular product, a 1.11 markup on materials and a 2.14 markup on oop conversion costs are required to obtain the target 20% return on the specific capital invested.

In Exhibit 24-4, a markup plan is shown for a different product which has a high conversion cost content compared to the previous one. Besides the specific identification of the fixed costs associated with the product, the variable capital characteristics of the product are shown to be different than for the previous product. Here, for the same oop costs of $400 for both products, the variable capital for the first one is $250 and $370 for the second. Adding the fixed capital shows that the total investment for the second product is twice that of the first, thereby requiring double the target earnings at the same rate of return. For this product, a 1.18 markup on materials and a 1.73 markup on oop conversion costs are required to obtain the target 20% return on the specific capital invested. Notice how different these markups are from the first product, and yet these are used within the same company.

The aim of this and the previous markup plan is to provide a way of distinguishing between the investment levels in a product's material and conversion cost to avoid overpricing items of high material content and/or underpricing products of low material content.

COST AND CAPITAL	TOTAL	APPLICABLE TO: Material Markup	Conversion Markup
Planned Costs:			
O.O.P. - Material	$100	$100	0
Conversion	300	0	$300
Total O.O.P. costs	400	100	300
FIXED - Selling	50	0	50
Admin.	30	0	30
R & D	40	0	40
Total fixed costs	120	0	120
TOTAL COSTS	$520	$100	$420
Planned Capital:			
VARIABLE:			
Inventory - Raw Materials	30	30	0
In-process	60	10	50
Finished	90	20	70
Total Inventory	180	60	120
Accounts Receivable	190	30	160
FIXED:			
Fixed Assets	210	0	210
TOTAL INVESTMENT	$580	$ 90	$490
Desired Return	20%	20%	20%
Target Earnings	$116	$ 18	$ 98
Planned Sales Revenue	$636	$118	$518

A. Material Markup = S. P. of Material/ Material Cost
= $118/100
= 1.18

B. Conversion Markup = S. P. of Conversion/O.O.P. Conversion Cost
= $518/$300
= 1.73

EXHIBIT 24-4: Developing Separate Markups For Specific Product Line Product With High Conversion Content

Chapter 25

The Target Pricing Plan

In previous chapters and sections, we have presented target pricing plans which are designed to mark up materials and conversion costs separately and differently in order to develop a target price which, if booked, is aimed to provide the company with its desired return on the various elements of capital invested in a specific order or product. The approach that was used yielded a flat, uniform, or level markup on all oop conversion costs, regardless of the specific nature of the converting facilities on which the oop costs were incurred.

LIMITATIONS OF THE LEVEL MARKUP

If an order had \$1,000 worth of oop conversion costs and the markup factor was 1.9, the selling price of that order conversion cost was targeted at \$1,900. No discrimination was made for the mix of the specific investments in that \$1,000 oop conversion cost. Conceivably, that cost could be the result of an order made mostly by hand compared with an order which required expensive facilities. Yet, under the *level markup* approach, each dollar of oop conversion cost would carry the same markup and same selling price per oop conversion-cost dollar.

When products are converted on joint but rather homogeneous facilities (from the standpoint of facility investment), the level markup approach is an adequate guide to target prices. However, when orders are processed on a variety of alternate facilities whose investment costs vary widely, obviously the level markup acts as an averaging of the target price.

It must be mentioned again that target selling prices developed from any kind of markup scheme are an expression of the return on capital which the company desires and has no reference whatever to the marketplace. As such, it is an internal financial tool to determine to what extent prices are meeting the capital-return objective. If orders are booked below such TSP's, it does not mean that such resulting contribution is poor, and if booked above the TSP level, it doesn't necessarily follow that such pricing decisions are good. The primary pricing benchmark against which pricing quality is measured is the level of market prices. Obviously, if management doesn't keep its eye on this fact of life but pursues its *financially-oriented* target prices, it can price below market levels on the one hand and price itself out of its markets on the other.

THE DIFFERENTIAL MARKUP

To remove the inequity of the level markup which raises all oop conversion cost dollars to target price dollars by the same amount regardless of the respective underlying facility investment levels, we must develop a differential approach. In such a method, the amount of markup imposed on the oop MHR of a facility is proportionate to its investment and planned usage.

To demonstrate this technique, we will start with a profit plan which develops the *level* markup as shown in Exhibit 25-1. This is an expanded version of the simple plan shown in Chapter 24 following the heading "Developing the Markup Factors." In this exhibit, a distinction is made between the planned sales revenue and the target sales revenue to account for additional non-volume contribution required to meet the target return on total capital employed. As the reader

```
                    Total Capital Employed = $3,500,000
                    Target Return = 40%    =  1,400,000 (pre-tax)
-----------------------------------------------------------------------------
  I. Planned Sales Volume                                $5,360,000
     Projected OOP Costs:
         Material                       $2,094,000
         Conversion                      2,283,000
     Total OOP Costs                                      4,377,000
     Planned Annual Contribution                            983,000(Planned PV = .183)
     Less: Period (Fixed) Costs                             645,000(B-E PV = .12)
     Planned Pre-Tax Profit                              $  338,000
     Target Return                                       $1,400,000
     Add'l Contribution(Pricing Revenue)Req'd             1,062,000
     Target Sales Revenue (same volume)                   6,422,000
     Target Contribution                                  2,045,000(Target PV = .318)
                                                              ^
 II. Reconciliation:                                          |
     Target Return                      $1,400,000            |
     Plus: Period (Fixed) Costs            645,000            |
     Target Contribution                $2,045,000<-----------

III. At a 10% markup on materials cost, the annual materials
     contribution is $209,400, and conversion contribution =
         Target Contribution                            $2,045,000
         Less: Materials Contribution                      209,400
         Target Conversion Contribution                 $1,835,600

 IV. Level Markup on OOP Conversion Cost:
```

$$= \frac{\text{Selling Price of OOP Conversion Cost (SPOOP)}}{\text{OOP Conversion Cost}}$$

$$= \frac{\$2,283,000 + \$1,835,600}{\$2,283,000} = 1.80$$

```
     NOTE: Deficiency of level markup is that each dollar of OOP conversion
           cost is marked up exactly the same (i.e. to 1.80) irrespective
           of the investment value of the facility at which the OOP
           conversion dollar is incurred.

  V. Differential markups are developed by distributing annual conversion
     contribution to facilities in proportion to their investment (capital)
     value as shown in following exhibits.
```

EXHIBIT 25-1: Summary of Profit Plan (Preparatory to Differential Markups)

knows, this increase must come from an improvement in pricing quality rather than additional volume from unimproved prices. New terms are also introduced, e.g., conversion contribution, selling price of oop conversion cost, SPOOP, and materials contribution. Target revenue = selling price of oop conversion cost + selling price of materials cost. The selling price of oop conversion cost (SPOOP) = oop conversion cost + conversion contribution. Similarly, for materials.

In this exhibit, the target *conversion* contribution of $1,835,600 is used to develop the level markup of 1.80. In the differential approach, this same contribution, instead of being distributed evenly based on oop conversion cost dollars, will now be assigned on the basis of facilities values and respective usages.

To show the technique in simple form, turn to Exhibit 25-2 for a complete analysis and worksheet. Note that we are still keeping the basic profit-planning approach, e.g., Price = Oop cost + Contribution. Since the differential approach is applied to facilities, we alter this format to: Selling Price per Hour of a Facility = Oop MHR + Contribution per Hour. Since the only cost that concerns us is oop cost, the formula is simplified to: SPOOP = MHR + CPH. But this is a different CPH than discussed in Chapter 23. That measurement was *gross* CPH, i.e., *gross* contribution, which included material contribution, divided by major facility hours. In this refined technique, materials contribution has been excluded because we are distributing only the target *conversion* contribution. Therefore in this exhibit, SPOOP = amounts in columsn D + E. The result is CCPH. And instead of using the gross PV, which suffers from the same deficiency, we develop in the last column the CPV. This PV measurement removes the distorting effect of the presence of materials contribution and provides a more direct measurement of the contribution return on each facility.

Exhibit 25-3 shows how the CCPH's and SPOOP rates are developed from the profit plan shown on Exhibit 25-1.

BREAK-EVEN AND MINI-SPOOP

Often, after management has worked with SPOOP rates for a period of time, they wish to know the "floor" rate on each facility, i.e., the conversion contribution per hour about MHR which would establish a break-even condition. Such break-even SPOOP rates, *at the assigned-hour rate,* would generate just enough annual contribution to equal the fixed expenses. Since the projection of hours cannot be guaranteed, this measurement can act only as a guide. Sometimes, price lists are constructed using break-even SPOOP as one of the factors.

In similar situations, management wishes to know how much more contribution per hour at each facility will provide them not with the target return, but with a *minimum acceptable* return on their capital employed. So whereas a company may target a 40% pre-tax return on their capital, they may deem 20% as an acceptable minimum. Normally, this figure is established by considering the current cost of borrowings and the alternate uses of the same capital. This mini-SPOOP is valuable in building price lists and in some instances to set the practical price floor where salesmen are required to give prices on the spot. Also, mini-SPOOP can be the starting point in new sales compensation plans, where one commission is paid for bookings *between* mini- and target SPOOP, and a higher rate *above* target SPOOP.

PROFIT PLANNING WITH SPOOP RATES

To show how these lower SPOOP rates are developed, and to demonstrate a different approach in profit planning, Exhibits 25-4, 25-5 and 25-6 are presented. Exhibit 25-4 is another and more expanded approach to projecting a profit plan. The planned revenue is shown for each product line together with its characteristic PV. (This latter measurement, in its more refined use, can be expressed in CPV terms together with the characteristic material usages in each line.) Because of the different levels and risk elements in fixed and variable capital to be employed in each product line,

Prod'n Center	No. of Units	Total PMV[1] for Center	(A) Basic[2] CCPH/ Unit	(B) Annual Assigned Hours[1]	Basic[3] Annual Contrib. (A x B)	(D) Target (Convers.) C.P.H. (A x C)	(E) OOP MHR[5]	SPOOP (TSP/hr) (D + E)	Target Annual Convers. Contrib.	M.U. on OOP C.C.[7]	Convers. PV[8]
A	1	$20,000	$2.00	1,000	$2,000	$12.50	$9.20	$21.70	$12,500	2.36	.576
B	3	30,000	1.00	1,500	1,500	6.25	6.60	12.85	9,375	1.95	.486
C	2	15,000	.75	2,000	1,500	4.69	7.30	11.99	9,375	1.64	.391
D	1	30,000	3.00	1,000	3,000	18.75	8.05	26.80	18,750	3.33	.700
Annual Contribution Totals					$8,000				$50,000		

$$\text{Target Factor} = \frac{\text{Target Conversion Contribution}^{4}}{\text{Basic Annual Contribution}} = \frac{\$50{,}000^{6}}{\$\ 8{,}000} = 6.25\ (C)$$

COMMENT: This technique produces TCPH's which are in direct proportion to respective PMV's per unit. Thus, the Basic CCPH's of $2.00 and $1.00 and the Target CCPH's of $12.50 and $6.25 are in direct proportion to the unit PMV's of $20,000 and $10,000 for Centers A and B, respectively, unaffected by the respective OOP MHR's.

NOTES:

1. From MHR's Converting Facilities Classification Sheet (CFCS).
2. PMV per unit factored down by 10,000 for ease of handling.
3. Trial amount.
4. From an Annual Profit Plan, assume $50,000.
5. From MHR's Expense Assignment Worksheet (EAW).
6. From the Profit Plan.
7. Used to show deficiency of level markup.
8. PV of conversion contribution only, without the distorting inclusion of materials cost and direct-order charges.

EXHIBIT 25-2: Worksheet for Basic Differential Markup (Conversion Contribution per hour by facility) to obtain TCPH and SPOOP by Individual Machine

Production Center	Basic CCPH/ Unit*	Annual Assigned Hours	Basic Annual Contrib.	Per Unit TCPH	M. H. R. OOP	M. H. R. SPOOP	SPOOP/OOP Ratio
Adj.Die Cutters	$ .380	5,570	$ 2,117	$ 1.86	$11.72	$13.58	1.1587
Solid " "	.270	16,425	4,435	1.33	9.42	10.75	1.1411
PHP " "	3.000	5,780	17,340	14.75	10.78	25.53	2.3682
Guillotines	2.050	3,870	7,934	10.08	10.84	20.92	1.9298
Printers: P2	.045	4,925	222	.22	9.16	9.38	1.0240
" 18Q	1.100	10,740	11,814	5.41	7.41	12.82	1.7300
" 18M	1.410	18,920	26,677	6.93	7.41	14.34	1.9352
" S4	.450	815	367	2.21	11.16	13.37	1.1980
" 20F	2.100	5,440	11,424	10.32	11.54	21.86	1.8942
" 10E	3.000	3,750	11,250	14.75	12.12	26.87	2.2169
Small Jets	.600	1,810	1,086	2.95	12.43	15.38	1.2373
Large Jets	.700	1,100	770	3.44	12.68	16.12	1.2712
Offset Jets	1.800	2,040	3,672	8.85	12.79	21.64	1.6919
Multi- #1250	.650	1,875	1,219	3.20	16.10	19.30	1.1987
Mgd Printer	.700	3,680	2,576	3.44	18.13	21.57	1.1897
Heidelberg-LP	.230	240	55	1.13	10.96	12.09	1.1031
SO Folders	1.100	14,870	16,357	5.41	10.86	16.27	1.4981
LO "	2.400	13,660	32,784	11.80	11.15	22.95	2.0582
MO "	4.400	3,895	17,138	21.63	13.38	35.01	2.6165
Bindery Equipt.	.105	9,950	1,045	.52	5.98	6.50	1.0869
Auto. Clasp	.650	510	332	3.20	9.10	12.30	1.3516
" Str.&Butt.	.850	510	434	4.18	6.11	10.29	1.6841
Patch	.750	465	349	3.69	7.88	11.57	1.4682
Insert. Mach.	.540	1,270	686	2.65	4.06	6.71	1.6527
Hand Fold	.040	3,875	155	.20	3.71	3.91	1.0539
WR-STD Folders	1.400	18,770	26,278	6.88	10.53	17.41	1.6533
WRW "	2.000	38,110	76,220	9.83	12.87	22.70	1.7637
RW "	4.500	7,560	34,020	22.12	14.42	36.54	2.5339
Mark IV "	8.000	8,000	64,000	39.32	14.85	54.17	3.6478
Window Punch	.125	5,335	667	.61	7.88	8.49	1.0774
			$373,423				

Target Factor = $\frac{\$1,835,600^{**}}{\$\ 373,423}$ = 4.9156

*obtained by dividing unit PMV by 10,000

**from Profit Plan of Exhibit 14

EXHIBIT 25-3: Derivation of TCPH and SPOOP (based on Summary Profit Plan of Exhibit 25-1)

Product Line	Characteristic PV	Planned Sales Revenue	Total Capital Employed	Target Return*	Target Profit
1. Gravure Ptd, extruded-laminated stock	.42	$1,500,000	$1,400,000	34 %	$476,000
2. Flexo Ptd, rolls and bags	.31	1,800,000	1,100,000	30 %	330,000
3. Plain bags, from tubing	.11	1,100,000	600,000	22 %	132,000
	.2975	$4,400,000	$3,100,000	30.25%	$938,000

I. Planned Sales Volume			$4,400,000
Projected OOP Costs			
1. Material		$1,949,245	
2. Conversion			
2.1 C.C.T.	$ 418,700		
2.2 D.C.B.	108,840		
2.3 A.B.	189,000		
Total Conversion		716,540	
3. Non-investment			
3.1 Freight out	85,215		
3.2 Commissions	340,000	425,215	
Total OOP Costs			3,091,000
Planned Annual Contribution			1,309,000
Less: Period (Fixed) Costs			397,000
Planned Pre-tax Profits			912,000
Contribution (Revenue) Deficiency			26,000
Target Profit (pre-tax)			$ 938,000
Target Revenue (same volume)			$4,426,000
II. Target Return	$ 938,000		
Plus: Period (Fixed) Costs	397,000		
Target Contribution	1,335,000		
Less: Materials Contrib. @10%	194,925		
Target Conversion Contribution	$1,140,075		

III. Summary

	OOP Cost	Contribution	Sales Revenue
Materials	$1,949,245	$ 194,925	$2,144,170
Conversion	716,540	1,140,075	1,856,615
Non-Investment	425,215	0	425,215
	$3,091,000	$1,335,000	$4,426,000

*not uniform because of the proportions of variable and fixed capital

EXHIBIT 25-4: Development of Profit Plan (Flexible Packaging)

Production Center	No. of Units	PMV	Basic CCPH/ Unit*	Annual Assigned Hours	Basic Annual Contrib.	Per Unit			SPOOP / OOP Ratio
						TCPH	M. H. R.		
							OOP	SPOOP	
Dilts Extruder-lamin.	1	$350,000	$35.00	6,000	$210,000	$66.39	$20.37	$86.76	4.2592
8c-30" Champlain Grav.	2	625,000	31.25	8,000	250,000	59.28	32.69	91.97	2.8133
Mounter-Proofer	1	3,000	.30	2,000	600	.57	4.95	5.52	1.1151
Acraplate Molder	1	10,000	1.00	2,000	2,000	1.90	5.75	7.65	1.3304
6c-42" H-S Flexo	1	150,000	15.00	4,000	60,000	28.45	17.00	45.45	2.6725
5c-30" Kidder Flexo	1	60,000	6.00	4,000	24,000	11.38	14.50	25.88	1.7848
Cameron Sl-Rew.	2	80,000	4.00	8,000	32,000	7.59	8.78	16.37	1.8644
Stanford Sl-Rew.	1	12,000	1.20	2,000	2,400	2.28	8.28	10.56	1.2753
Schjeldahl 40" side-weld bag machine	3	60,000	2.00	9,000	18,000	3.79	11.54	15.33	1.3284
42" Beck Sheeter	1	10,000	1.00	2,000	2,000	1.90	7.20	9.10	1.2638
					$601,000				

$$\text{Target Factor} = \frac{\$1{,}140{,}075}{\$\ \ 601{,}000} = 1.896963$$

*factored down by 10,000

EXHIBIT 25-5: Construction of TCPH and Hourly SPOOP Rates (Flexible Packaging)

Annual	T.C.E.	Target Return	Target Profit	Target Contrib.	Target Conversion Contrib.[2]
Target Plan	$3,100,000	30.25%	$938,000	$1,335,000	$1,140,075
Minimum Plan	3,100,000	16 %[1]	496,000	893,000	698,075
Break-Even Plan	3,100,000	0 %	0	397,000[3]	202,075

Production Center	Basic CCPH/ Unit	Annual Assigned Hours	Basic Annual Contrib.	Per Unit Machine Hour Rate				
				OOP	Break-Even		Mini	
					TCPH	SPOOP	TCPH	SPOOP
Dilts Extruder-lamin.	$35.00	6,000	$210,000	$20.37	$11.77	$32.14	$40.65	$61.02
8c-30" Champlain Grav.	31.25	8,000	250,000	32.69	10.51	43.20	36.30	68.99
Mounter-Proofer	.30	2,000	600	4.95	.10	5.05	.35	5.30
Acraplate Molder	1.00	2,000	2,000	5.75	.34	6.09	1.16	6.91
6c-42" H-S Flexo	15.00	4,000	60,000	17.00	5.04	22.04	17.42	34.42
5c-30" Kidder "	6.00	4,000	24,000	14.50	2.02	16.52	6.97	21.47
Cameron S1-Rew.	4.00	8,000	32,000	8.78	1.34	10.12	4.65	13.43
Stanford S1-Rew.	1.20	2,000	2,400	8.28	.40	8.68	1.39	9.67
Schjeldahl 40" side-weld bag machine	2.00	9,000	18,000	11.54	.67	12.21	2.32	13.86
42" Beck Sheeter	1.00	2,000	2,000	7.20	.34	7.54	1.16	8.36
			$601,000					

$$\text{Break-Even Target Factor} = \frac{\$202{,}075}{\$601{,}000} = .33623$$

$$\text{Mini-Target Factor} = \frac{\$698{,}075}{\$601{,}000} = 1.1615224$$

NOTES:
1. Policy decision
2. Less materials contribution
3. Equal to period (fixed) costs

EXHIBIT 25-6: Developing Break-Even SPOOP and Mimi-SPOOP Rates (Flexible Packaging)

different amounts are shown for each together with varying percentages of return goals. This approach is practical where separable facilities are used, i.e., where machines are not used in common with each product line.

Note also that the separate MHR ingredients of oop conversion costs are shown as well as the non-investment elements of oop costs. This format can form the basis of a *direct-cost operating profit and loss statement* for internal managerial use. Getting a CPV for the plan, we derive from the basic PV = Contribution/Revenue: CPV = Conversion Contribution/Conversion Revenue = \$1,140,075/\$1,856,615 = .614. There is quite a difference between the CPV and the gross PV of the plan: \$1,335,000/\$4,426,000 = .30. Obviously, the difference between the rates of contribution is the level of planned annual material cost and its markup.

Exhibit 25-5 shows the construction of the target SPOOP rates along the same lines developed on Exhibit 25-3. In Exhibit 25-6, the requirement for a minimum acceptable return is stated as 16% pre-tax, and of course, the return for break-even conditions is an amount of contribution equal to the planned period costs. These two additional capital return requirements use two different target factors to generate two levels of CCPH. Since there is no change in oop MHR's, the respective CCPH's add to produce the break-even and mini-SPOOP's.

SPOOP AND "FULL" COSTS

Occasionally, people confuse the SPOOP rates with "full" cost MHR's. "Full" cost rates are a hodge-podge of mixtures: costs of different behavior characteristics; various indefensible allocation bases; projections of hourly usages based on tradition; etc. If costs are expressed solely in their "full" content, oop costs are obscured and it becomes impossible to measure to what extent the booking of an order will contribute or subtract from company profit. The arbitrarily unitized fixed expense package, even if separated from the group of direct costs, consists of fixed costs having nothing to do with production equipment, such as: executive salaries, taxes, etc., but these wind up in the "full" rates anyway.

SPOOP rates contain the underlying and separable oop MHR which is essential for the measurement of contribution. The difference between SPOOP and oop MHR is the CCPH. *This is not a cost figure, does not affect cost measurement and does not affect contribution measurements.* The CCPH (conversion contribution in total order terms) is a target figure only and does not distort any economic measurement of order benefits. CCPH is related solely to present machinery value and expected usages. Regardless of how usages are manipulated or projected with serious errors, it can never change the oop MHR, which is the basis for contribution measurement and the primary determinant of go-no-go decisions. The hours then, are used as a goal for annual facility contribution and never affect cost the way hours do in "full" MHR development.

PURIFYING CONTRIBUTION MEASUREMENTS

A manufacturing enterprise which uses productive machinery in generating its output is interested in what "profit" the equipment is making for the company. The management buys raw materials and converts them into the sold product and may earn a profit on the materials simply because he may hedge against a price increase by purchasing larger quantities in advance. This is a "trading" profit and has nothing to do with what gains or losses he is generating on his converting equipment. As a matter-of-fact, the company may survive simply because it is more of a trader than a manufacturer, e.g., earning enough by this activity to more than compensate for the losses in manufacturing.

Even where trading is not a factor in profit, it is important that the presence of materials be removed from contribution measurements. Material cost is incidental and accidental to the generating of profit and distorts the true contributing value of facilities. Exhibit 25-7 demonstrates

JOB A (LOW CONVERSION ORDER)

Basic Contribution Measurements

Order Selling Price	$7,400	
" OOP Cost	6,000	
" Contribution	1,400	(Gross Order Contribution)
" PV	.189	(GPV)
Major Facility Hours	8	
Overall CPH	$ 175	

Conversion Contribution Measurements

Element	OOP Cost	Contrib.	S.P.	Contribution Rates PV's	CPH's
Materials	$5,000	$ 500	$5,500	MPV = .091*	NA
Conversion	1,000	900	1,900	CPV = .474	CCPH = $112.50
Totals	$6,000	$1,400	$7,400	GPV = .189	CPH = $175.00

JOB B (HIGH CONVERSION ORDER)

Basic Contribution Measurements

Order Selling Price	$7,400
" OOP Cost	6,000
" Contribution	1,400
" PV	.189
Major Facility Hours	40
Overall CPH	$ 35

Conversion Contribution Measurements

Element	OOP Cost	Contrib.	S.P.	Contribution Rates PV's	CPH's
Materials	$1,000	$ 100	$1,100	MPV = .091*	NA
Conversion	5,000	1,300	6,300	CPV = .206	CCPH = $32.50
Totals	$6,000	$1,400	$7,400	GPV = .189	CPH = $35.00

COMPARATIVE DATA

Job	S.P.	OOP Cost	Contrib.	PV	Conv.Contr.	CPV	CCPH
A	$7,400	$6,000	$1,400	.189	$ 900	.474	$112.50
B	7,400	6,000	1,400	.189	1,300	.206	32.50

*Based on 10% markup. Generally remains constant for major product or product line.

EXHIBIT 25-7: Purifying Contribution Measurements (Conversion Contribution; CPV and CCPH)

the point. Here we see two different jobs, both with the same selling price, oop cost, gross contribution and gross PV. But there the similarity ends. If we were to use solely the GPV to evaluate the economic benefit given to the company, we would have to conclude that both orders contribute equally. While this is true with respect to the speed of paying fixed expenses, it obscures the relative contributions of the facilities. Using the gross contribution of Jobs A and B the GPV's are both .189 and CPH's $175 and $35. When the material revenue is removed, the CPV's are .474 and .206 and the CCPH's $112.50 and $32.50. Obviously, in Job A, the CPH gave an artificially high figure due to the presence of a high material cost content which furnished 35.7% of total contribution. Job B required 5 times the facility usage of Job A to produce the same CCPH. This shows up in its lower CPV of .206.

Exhibit 25-8 is a group of 3 sample batches of orders that show the interplays of the variables. Sample B has left blank the columns: conversion revenue, CPV and CCPH with the suggestion that the reader perform these calculations. The correct answers will show that in spite of the great variations among these four orders, the CPV and CCPH of each of them will remain the same, thus purifying the measurement of facility economy. This exhibit can also form the basis of a more refined Contribution Log.

COMPUTING TSP'S OF ORDER INQUIRIES

We have discussed two methods of "backing into" a target selling price using 1) the desired PV and 2) the desired CPH. And we have said that both methods produce prices which have a large degree of market intelligence. The reason being that both are taken from cumulative bookings data of current work which states in effect what customers have been willing to pay for products. These are the practical floors in pricing.

We also discussed a target selling price which produces a price related to the company's internal financial needs only, having no reference to the marketplace. These prices come from separate but level markups on materials and oop conversion cost.

Once conversion contribution becomes part of the company's profit planning, these three TSP's can be expanded as follows:

1. TSP (based on a desired CPV) =
   Oop Conversion Cost/(1 − desired CPV) + S.P. of Materials + DOC's.
2. TSP (based on desired CCPH's) =
   (Hrs_a x $CCPH_a$ ..... + Hrs_n x $CCPH_n$) + Oop Conversion Cost + S.P. of Materials + DOC's.
3. TSP (based on desired return on capital) =
   ($Hrs._a$ x $SPOOP_a$ ..... + Hrs_n x $SPOOP_n$) + S.P. of Materials + DOC's.

The reader will note that the last two expanded TSP's are the same in effect: a merging of facilities and investment.

Exhibit 25-9 shows the application of SPOOP rates and the target selling price approach in a job inquiry calling for 100,000 pieces. In this estimate, we have shown how other DOC's are listed. To explain some of the items: Make & Hold is a capital finance charge reflecting the manufacturer's employment of his capital in the customer's finished goods inventory. This is an experience figure stemming from previous transactions with that specific customer. This kind of figure is arrived at by estimating the length of time the manufacturer will probably have to hold his customer's products before being paid for it, the value of the money tied up, and the current cost of capital. These data are combined into a figure we call dollar-months. That is, $10,000 worth of finished oop cost held three months is equal to $5,000 held six months. Both are evaluated as 30,000 dollar-months; transaction cost consists of a flat $27 plus the variable component, which in this case is $10.

The standard hours extend both the oop conversion cost and the SPOOP for each operation and are totalled to total conversion oop cost and target conversion revenue (TSP). Direct materials are also expressed in oop and TSP terms. The Target GPV and CPV apply to targeted revenue only.

On the lower left, the bookings data are inserted. The first step is to consult the Contribution Log representing the class of work being estimated to obtain the cumulative CPV. This tells what *this* type of customer in *his* specific market for *that* particular product has been currently paying

Order No	Booked S.P.	OOP COSTS Total	OOP COSTS Mtls	OOP COSTS Conver	BOOKED CONTRIB Gross	BOOKED CONTRIB Conver	GPV	Fac Hrs	Gross CPH	Booked Conver Rev	Booked Conver PV	Booked Conver CPH	TSP (ROC)	Pricing Var	Var % on TSP	CSP/BSP Ratio
SAMPLE A: $																
6214	4,300	3,100	600	2,500	1,200	1,140	.279	70	17.14	3,640	.313	16.28	4,410	(110)	(2.5)	.847
6471	4,300	3,100	2,500	600	1,200	950	.279	20	60.00	1,550	.613	47.50	3.650	650	17.8	.360
7318	7,860	5,400	1,300	4,100	2,460	2,330	.313	140	17.57	6,430	.362	16.64	7,580	280	3.7	.818
7340	7,860	5,400	4,100	1,300	2,460	2,050	.313	40	61.50	3,350	.612	51.25	6,460	1400	21.7	.426
8961	7,000	6,000	5,900	100	1,000	410	.140	15	66.67	510	.804	27.33	6,640	360	5.4	.073
5412	6,300	4,330	300	4,030	1,970	1,940	.313	210	9.38	5,970	.325	9.24	6,375	(75)	(1.2)	.948
3698	5,800	4,200	2,400	1,800	1,600	1,360	.276	20	80.00	3,160	.430	68.00	5,340	460	8.6	.545
4116	5,580	4,200	1,800	2,400	1,380	1,200	.247	25	55.20	3,600	.333	48.00	5,580	0	-	.645
6741	5,340	4,200	2,400	1,800	1,140	900	.213	50	22.80	2,700	.333	18.00	5,340	0	-	.506
2918	4,650	3,100	-	3,100	1,550	1,550	.333	220	7.05	4,650	.333	7.05	4,650	0	-	1.000
3142	4,650	4,227	4,227	-	423	-	.091	-	-	-	-	-	4,650	0	-	
SAMPLE B:																
387	10,600	6,000	1,000	5,000	4,600	4,500	.434	40	115.00	.....	....	.....	10,600	0	0	.896
422	7,400	6,000	5,000	1,000	1,400	900	.189	8	175.00	.....	....	.....	7,400	0	0	.257
194	9,000	6,000	3,000	3,000	3,000	2,700	.333	24	125.00	.....	....	.....	9,000	0	0	.633
518	11,400	6,000	-	6,000	5,400	5,400	.474	48	112.50	.....	....	.....	11,400	0	0	1.000
341	6,600	6,000	6,000	-	600	-	.091	-	-	.....	....	.....	6,600	0	0	-
SAMPLE C:																
1641	10,000	8,000	6,000	2,000	2,000	1,400	.200	24	83.33	.....	....	.....	10,000	0	0	.34
1888	8,750	7,000	5,250	1,750	1,750	1,225	.200	21	83.33	.....	....	.....	8,750	0	0	.34
1416	30,000	24,000	18,000	6,000	6,000	4,200	.200	72	83.33	.....	....	.....	30,000	0	0	.34
1789	4,690	2,900	400	2,500	1,790	1,750	.382	30	59.67	4,250	.412	58.33	4,690	0	0	.906
1313	8,210	6,100	3,600	2,500	2,110	1,750	.257	30	70.33	4,250	.412	58.33	8,210	0	0	.518
1544	21,850	18,500	16,000	2,500	3,350	1,750	.153	30	111.67	4,250	.412	58.33	21,850	0	0	.195

EXHIBIT 25-8: Measuring Economic Quality of Orders with CPV & CCPH (Eliminating Distorting Effect of Materials)

the manufacturer. Using the *characteristic* CPV as a guide, we back into a target price of $17,322 which is the *practical pricing floor.* The order was booked by inching somewhat above this level at $17.50/M or $17,500. This booked price yielded an estimated contribution and an estimated booked PV to generate an *unfavorable* pricing variance of $666.

This is not to say that the $17.50 price is necessarily an unfavorable one. This variance whether favorable or unfavorable simply shows the amount by which the booked price departed from a *financially* targeted selling price. Once again, the PV or CPV is the real evaluator as it reflects the market price levels. This type of variance is logged on a period basis and for any time period indicates to what extent the company's cumulative pricing experiences are attaining the capital return targeted in its profit plan.

MARTIN & TUCKER, INC.
ENGINEERS

	Standard Hours	Machine-Hour Rate OOP	Machine-Hour Rate SPOOP	OOP Cost	Target S. P.
Preparation:					
A	6	$24	$54	$ 144	$ 324
B	10	21	68	210	680
C	4	23	94	92	376
Run:					
A	70	24	54	1,680	3,780
B	42	21	68	882	2,856
C	15	23	94	345	1,410
D	38	28	32	1,064	1,216
E	22	11	13	242	286

Booking Data		OOP Cost	Target S. P.
	Total Conversion	$4,659	$10,928
	Direct Materials*	5,720	6,292
1. Characteristic CPV of product segment = .538			
	Other DOC's:		
2. TSP (CPV .538) = $17,322	Commissions	710	710
3. Booked S.P./M = $17.50	Freight Cost	110	110
4. Est. Contribution = $6,175	Make & Hold	89	89
5. Booked PV = .353	Transaction Cost ($27 + $10)	37	37
6. Pricing Variance = ($666)	TOTALS	$11,325	$18,166
	Per M	$11.33	$18.17
	Target GPV		.377
	Target CPV		.574

*Target Markup = 10%

EXHIBIT 25-9: Sample Estimate (1,000,000 pcs.)

Chapter 26

Measuring the Quality of Pricing and the Results of Operations

When the construction of the Machine-Hour Rates is completed, obviously it should be immediately used for current cost-estimating and price evaluating. At this same time, there are other areas in which MHR's should be used to disclose information about other vital activities, viz: What are the company's break-even characteristics? Which are the best sources of profit? Which are the most profitable facilities, customers, end-use markets, territories, product lines, etc.? Which jobs have been previously booked at prices less than oop costs? Which prospective repeat jobs should be earmarked for price adjustments? Which of the current bookings not yet produced have been accepted inadvertently below oop cost? Which quotes that were previously rejected under the traditional cost-estimating system can be revived now that adequate contribution is disclosed the new MHR system? Etc.

THE BACKTESTING CONCEPT

Assuming the existence of an equitable set of engineered production standards, the application of new MHR's to previously booked jobs can reveal to management more than they ever knew about their company; information which they can exploit immediately and profitably. There is however, much resistance to performing this detailed element of the installation because it is time consuming. Yet, it is basically a clerical task, if properly organized. Let the reader be advised that the backtesting procedure is one of the most crucial steps in the profit-planning concepts presented in this book.

If backtesting is not performed, it's like saying that there's no point having Contribution Logs and segmental sorting of contribution sources. What no backtesting implies is that MHR's are to be used solely for cost estimating of new job inquiries. If that becomes the case, how will the company know:

.. How to price the order?
.. How much contribution is adequate?

.. How the priced job ranks with the customer's previous orders?
.. What the comparative CPH is in that product line?
.. How to decide on any concession the customer may request?
.. How the job ranks within its product line?
.. Whether the job is priced up to market levels?
.. Whether the job will displace more profitable work previously booked but not run?
.. To what extent the priced job is a fair balance between facility hours to be used vis-a-vis the period break-even contribution needs?

In the backtesting procedure, we want to know basically what and who the company has been and is, i.e., where we have been, where we are now and where we are going. Then, a new job can be priced rationally taking into consideration the internal and external variables.

THE BACKTESTING PROCEDURE

When we apply the new MHR's (and the same production standards, DOC's, etc.) to a previously-booked job which has been estimated using irrational or traditional cost-estimating methods, we are able now to determine what the estimated contribution was at that previous date. That result could make us happy or sad, depending on what the calculations show us now. We might discover that the contribution level was in fact high and more than adequate. On the other hand, it might show us that contribution was so minimal so as to return to us an inordinately low level of CPH on a major, expensive facility. Or worse yet, it might be that the previous job was inadvertently accepted at a price below our oop cost. Surely, this is critical information for considering repeat orders at the same price. If the order was priced below oop in the past, then we know not to accept it in the future regardless of volume. Or, we know by how much to raise the price if we can obtain it. If the past order was very contributing, we know to be aggressive about booking more of the same, and in fact, perhaps considering a small reduction in price to attract an increase in volume if it will more than compensate for the price drop.

More importantly, when we backtest a *representative sampling* of the mix of the company's products, and then sort the elements of the transaction by customers, products, product lines, territories, major facilities, channels of distribution, markets, etc., we can build a profile of the contribution characteristics of each of these business segments. These characteristcs tell us the price levels that customers are ready and willing to pay, and as such, provide us with one of the most effective sources of market intelligence. If we discover that Produce E, sold to Customer B, using Facility Y has been providing the company with a characteristic (cumulative) PV of .35 (revealed only after backtesting), why should a new inquiry from that customer for the same product to be made on the same facility be priced below the PV .35 level? Thus, if a new job, which falls into the foregoing constraints, carries an oop cost of $13/M, we know we are in the ballpark if we start off pricing it at $20/M. (TSP[PV .35] = $13/.65 = $20.)

BACKTESTING ILLUSTRATIONS

Exhibit 26-1 shows a summary of jobs after the backtesting was completed. Column 1 shows the sorted out one year's previously-booked revenue by customer, ranked in order of the amount of revenue generated from each customer. Column 7 shows the "profit" that was calculated at the time the orders were estimated and booked. "Full" cost was used in measuring this "profit" against each job's selling price. The total of that column led management to believe that they earned a profit of $108,905 for the year on booked sales of $1,089,048.

Backtesting these jobs yielded the re-estimated oop cost, shown in column 2, and the contribution, PV, facility hours, and CPH in the next four columns. These four columns provide instant intelligence, viz: whether the contribution was good, marginal or negative; what its rate

Cust Ident	(1) Previous Booked Sales	(2) Re-Estima OOP Cost with New OOP MHR	(3) Contrib.	(4) PV	(5) Major Facility Hours	(6) CPH	(7) Assumed "Profit" When Priced
ECS	$ 154,120	$143,689	$ 10,431	.067	813	$ 12.83	$ 15,412
EMC	114,421	106,389	8,032	.070	791	10.15	11,442
WHL	98,760	73,940	24,820	.251	510	48.66	9,876
RBS	97,410	101,512	(4,102)	(.042)	494	(8.30)	9,741
STN	92,879	80,408	12,471	.134	355	35.13	9,288
STS	84,312	91,123	(6,811)	(.081)	320	(21.28)	8,431
CBD	68,455	72,575	(4,120)	(.060)	311	(13.25)	6,846
APN	51,412	29,595	21,817	.424	284	76.82	5,141
SCE	46,544	35,792	10,752	.231	232	46.34	4,654
CPR	34,820	28,413	6,407	.184	221	28.99	3,482
RGT	31,117	25,609	5,508	.177	162	34.00	3,112
PTO	30,841	8,663	22,178	.719	329	67.41	3,084
OGA	28,336	14,164	14,172	.500	318	44.57	2,834
MLB	23,611	26,539	(2,928)	(.124)	267	(10.97)	2,361
DGY	22,970	18,123	4,847	.211	338	14.34	2,297
PES	20,417	13,945	6,472	.317	187	34.61	2,042
RBT	18,009	19,522	(1,513)	(.084)	264	(5.73)	1,801
CML	17,420	8,344	9,076	.521	118	76.92	1,742
GCL	16,990	20,201	(3,211)	(.189)	294	(10.92)	1,699
NHJ	14,392	5,239	9,153	.636	251	36.47	1,439
HYL	11,640	8,218	3,422	.294	277	12.35	1,164
KOC	10,172	8,331	1,841	.181	141	13.06	1,017
TOTALS	$1,089,048	$940,334	$148,714	.1365	7277	$ 20.44	$108,905

Pres Pricing Profit=$148,714-Period (Fixed) Expenses of $120,000 = $ 28,714

EXHIBIT 26-1: Backtesting Analyses & Results

was; how heavily or lightly the orders loaded critical facilities; and what return the orders were providing per facility-hour. The net evaluation showed that the contribution that was generated in that year was $148,714, at a rate of .1365—a PV inordinately low for this particular industry. Instead of a formula-ized "profit" of $108,905, the amount was $28,714. (Profit = Contribution – Period Expenses).

Looking through the customer listing shows many losers and winners, viz: ECS and EMC, the largest customers (in terms of revenue) were among the poorest contributors and the greatest users of major facility time. (With good customers like these, who needs enemies?) We also note that six jobs were sold at prices below oop costs. How much more profit would the company have earned had those six been rejected? (Hard as it is to accept, that would have meant a higher profit on less total sales revenue.) APN, PTO, OGA, CML, NHJ are obviously "good" customers. Besides high speed of contribution flow, hours are not too loaded and more or less in proportion to PV. APN is below OGA in PV but above him in CPH. This can show different proportions of oop

I. Results, if new MHR were in effect and orders priced below OOP were not accepted:

	(1)	(3)	(4)	(5)	(6)	(7)
TOTALS	$780,172	$171,399	.2196	5327	$ 32.18	$ 78,017*

Pricing Profit = $171,399-Period (Fixed) Expenses of $120,000 = $ 51,399

A N A L Y S I S

27% FEWER CUSTOMERS (16)	28% LESS SALES REVENUE	15% GREATER CONTRIBUTION	1950 ADDL HRS AVAILABLE (27%)

AND PRICING PROFIT INCREASED 79%

II. Results, if the company rejected first 2 customers' orders:

	(1)	(3)	(4)	(5)	(6)	(7)
TOTALS	$511,631	$152,936	.2989	3723	$ 41.08	$ 51,163*

Pricing Profit = $152,936-Period (Fixed) Expenses of $120,000 = $ 32,936

A N A L Y S I S

12.5% FEWER CUSTOMERS (14)	34.5% LESS SALES REVENUE	10.8% LESS CONTRIBUTION	1604 ADDL HRS AVAILABLE (30.2%)

PRICING PROFIT INCREASED 15% over original conditions

EXHIBIT 26-2

conversion cost vs. materials cost between the two customer characteristics. Or, it may be that APN's work runs faster on the same set of facilities.

What about a customer like NHJ who has a PV of .636? Shouldn't we be aggressive (now that we know what the score is) about programming more sales effort to develop more business from him? Yes, but within certain limits. There's no question that he has a high rate of contribution and this is especially good when facilities are not expected to be loaded. However, the drive for contribution must be balanced against how much machine time must be used for his account in order to generate said contribution. If facility time was not a consideration, then the higher the PV, the better the account. CML looks like a real winner: a good PV and high CPH, indicating that the company can generate contribution at a high rate without giving up too much facility time. And if we knew what we now know about RBS, we would have added $4,102 to profit and saved 494 facility hours.

Exhibit 26-2 shows two hindsight analyses made for the same company. I shows the consequences of booking only orders priced above oop cost (if this information was available). This would have raised profits from $28,714 to $51,399, an increase of 79%. Of course, under traditional evaluations, "profit" would show a drop from $108,905 to $78,017 and would not be considered. The net result of identifying and dropping below-oop customers is a profit increase of 79% on a revenue decrease of 28%. Vital to this evaluation is the fact that 27% more facility hours would have become available on which to have earned even more money.

II shows what the results would have been if the below-oop customers were identified and eliminated and if in addition, customers ECS and EMC were eliminated, even though still contributing marginally. Profits would have increased 15% instead of 79%, *but* now 3554 (1950 + 1604) facility hours would have become available. If facilities were not loaded, the first analysis would be selected. However, if machine time was scarce with many orders competing for the same use of facility time, then the second analysis should be the plan for the company.

This is shown on Exhibit 26-3 together with possible models of action the company could have used in selling the 3554 facility hours. Obviously, the number of models which can be tested are infinite. But the point to remember is that contribution cannot be generated without machine time unless the company is jobbing its raw materials and not converting.

Exhibit 26-4 shows the backtested sample taken in a large financial printing company by product lines, PV ranges and percentages of sales for each PV category. The overall PV of the sample was .346, quite low for this kind of business. Believing that the $416,018 sales sample was a representative one, we recommended some "turnarounds." Management then got rid of the marginal jobs, inched up some of their lower-priced work, and placed their sales emphasis on the higher contributing lines. Prior to this, they put more sales effort into the larger transactions.

Exhibit 26-5 shows the results three months after the new system was installed: an increase in composite PV from .346 to .575, or 66%, with the same proportionate increase in contribution

III. SUMMARY:

a. If major facility hours are not scarce, I is followed for maximum profit.

b. If major facility hours are well loaded, II is followed, if some or all of the liberated 3554 facility hours (1950 + 1604) can be modelled as follows (or in other variations):

	MODELS					
	1	2	3	4	5	6
	3554 hrs sold @ MIN CPH of $10.15	3554 hrs sold @ AV CPH of $20.44	3554 hrs sold @ AV CPH of $32.18	3554 hrs sold @ AV CPH of $41.08	2000 hrs sold @ MIN CPH of $10.15	1500 hrs sold @ AV CPH of $32.18
Add'l Contrib	$ 36,073	$ 72,644	$114,368	$145,998	$ 20,300	$ 48,270
Contrib from 1st 3723 hrs	152,936	152,936	152,936	152,936	152,936	152,936
Total Contrib	189,009	225,580	267,304	298,934	173,236	201,206
Less Period Costs	120,000	120,000	120,000	120,000	120,000	120,000
Pricing Profit	$79,009	$105,580	$147,304	$178,934	$ 53,236	$ 81,206

EXHIBIT 26-3

PV Range	Product Line	Previously Booked Sales	OOP Costs	Contrib.	PV	% of Total Sales
0-	Misc.legal firms	$ 2,150	$ 1,973	$ 177	.082	
.10	Misc.acctg firms	81	168	(87)	(.107)	
	Printed stationery	1,594	1,544	50	.031	
	TOTALS	3,825	3,685	140	.037	.9%
.10-	Offering circulars	1,532	1,254	278	.182	
.20	Railroad financing	2,735	2,215	519	.190	
	Munic.finan.-underwr.	1,006	896	110	.109	
	Stock & bond certificates	680	551	129	.190	
	Briefs,records,wills	10,086	8,595	1,490	.148	
	Engraved stationery	2,303	1,934	369	.160	
	Publica & booklets	55,288	44,549	10,739	.194	
	Commercial binding	1,433	1,187	246	.172	
	Other comm'l jobs	20,893	17,932	2,961	.142	
	Loss leaders	5,811	5,183	628	.108	
	TOTALS	101,767	84,296	17,469	.172	24.5%
.21-	Munic.finan.-misc.docum.	1,540	1,174	366	.238	
.30	Annual reports	67,842	49,888	17,954	.265	
	Legal & partnership agree.	3,598	2,596	1,002	.279	
	TOTALS	72,980	53,658	19,322	.265	17.5%
.31-	Listing applications	2,012	1,270	742	.369	
.40	Doc.accomp. proxy statem.	27,398	18,999	8,399	.307	
	Quart.& semi-ann. reports	4,017	2,628	1,389	.346	
	Stockholder mailings	5,479	3,687	1,792	.327	
	Other legal documents	3,356	2,167	1,189	.354	
	TOTALS	42,262	28,751	13,511	.320	10.2%
.41-	Misc.doc.filed w/reg.statements	9,729	5,211	4,518	.464	
.50	" " for underwriters	7,000	3,963	3,037	.434	
	Loans & purchase agreements	6,678	3,427	3,251	.487	
	Indentures & mortgages	15,593	9,158	6,435	.413	
	Munic.finan. & official statem.	2,003	1,096	907	.453	
	Notices & proxy statements	72,542	41,230	31,312	.432	
	Other finan. documents	8,050	4,539	3,511	.436	
	Private financing	26,210	13,218	12,992	.496	
	TOTALS	147,805	81,842	65,963	.446	35.5%
.51- .60	Registration statements	47,379	19,794	27,585	.582	11.4%
	TOTALS FOR SAMPLE TESTED	$416,018	$272,026	$143,990	.346	100.0%

EXHIBIT 26-4: Backtest Sample: Financial Printer

dollars. Having identified and ranked sources of profit, we experimented to see whether a valid PV characteristic existed by virtue of the size of the revenue. This resulted in the grouping at the bottom of this exhibit, after the unwanted jobs were eliminated or improved. Sure enough, there it was: increasing PV with increasing transaction size. This is not to say that every financial printer's economy will respond in this same way. In another financial printing company, we found that most of them showed a maximum PV in the middle revenue range. This shifting of maximum PV, as the reader will recall, is a function of the seller's specific oop cost within the same market.

Exhibit 26-6 shows what the author likes to call a Quotation Mortality Log, showing data only for unbooked or lost work due to their pricing above exisiting market levels. In other words, had

Product Code	Description	No. of Jobs	Sales*	Contrib	PV
1101	Industrial,negotiated	8	$ 200,465	$ 114,508	.572
1102	Secondary, "	1	9,260	5,095	.550
1103	Ind. subscrip."	3	69,031	43,945	.636
1104	Utility, competitive	7	112,949	64,479	.570
1105	" , negotiated	4	88,013	46,739	.531
1106	" , subscription	2	156,443	109,161	.697
1110	Underwritten, foreign	6	126,624	71,240	.562
1112	Form S-4	2	19,924	10,482	.526
1115	Foreign, no registration	6	139,989	79,770	.569
1117	Exchange offers	1	7,950	4,172	.524
1118	Employee Plan - new	4	35,995	17,664	.490
1119	" " - repeat	7	68,749	36,241	.527
1121	Private financing	1	8,316	4,639	.557
1126	Industrial revenue	6	93,470	59,193	.633
1127	Form S-5	3	125,805	72,867	.579
1129	Municipal	1	12,404	6,158	.496
1194	Selling Stockholder,negotiated	2	21,185	12,818	.605
1195	Private financing-foreign	2	24,877	14,019	.563
1196	Utility, general	1	23,477	11,855	.504
1198	SEC, not defined	1	18,803	10,273	.546
1199	Other financing, not defined	1	11,334	8,402	.741
1200	Stockholder mailing	30	296,756	138,381	.466
1200	" "	1	44,126	27,727	.628
1300	Legal	2	14,308	7,850	.548
1400	Commercial	1	6,208	3,145	.506
1500	Mergers	6	224,653	146,938	.654
*jobs above $5,000	TOTALS	109	$1,961,114	$1,127,761	.575

And by Sales Ranges:

Range	No. of Jobs	Sales	Contrib	PV	% of Total Sales
$ 5,000-$10,000	45	$ 330,376	$ 167,245	.506	12.8%
10,001- 25,000	45	711,807	386,400	.543	27.6%
25,001- 40,000	11	367,212	214,744	.584	14.2%
40,001- 65,000	5	239,532	145,457	.607	9.3%
over $65,000	3	312,185	213,913	.685	12.1%
TOTALS	109	$1,961,114	$1,127,759	.575	76 %
Not Analyzed- under $ 5,000		611,353	187,712	.307	24 %
TOTAL COMPANY		$2,572,467	$1,315,471	.511	100 %

EXHIBIT 26-5: Profit Profile: Financial Printer, 3 Months Later

the company been using rational cost-estimating data, they may have agreed to meet many of the prices offered to them. On those jobs marked YES, they would have booked $137,950 of revenue (which contributed adequately to them) out of the $211,610 revenue offered. This would have provided them with an additional contribution of $39,375 which they otherwise would not have had. This is a classical illustration of marked-up "full" cost depriving a company of available contribution.

Exhibits 26-7 and 26-8 show two types of backtest forms used for making the foregoing analyses. Basically, a backtest form is similar in format to a form used for current estimating. Each can be altered to fit a company's specific needs.

Quoted SP	"Full" Cost	"Going" Market SP*	Re-Estima OOP Cost with new OOP MHR	Available Contrib in"Going" SP	Potential PV in "Going" SP	Acceptable Based on Contrib & Class of Work?	Lost Contrib
$ 5,342	$ 4,856	$ 4,800	$ 4,120	680	.16	YES	$ 680
1,255	1,141	940	1,020	(80)	-	NO	-
1,968	1,789	1,850	1,234	616	.33	YES	616
7,860	7,145	6,800	6,641	159	.02	NO	-
6,570	5,973	6,000	4,975	1,025	.17	NO	-
7,093	6,448	5,850	5,040	810	.13	YES	810
2,762	2,511	2,300	2,419	(119)	-	NO	-
2,294	2,085	2,100	1,287	813	.38	YES	813
6,389	5,808	5,750	4,290	1,460	.25	YES	1,460
6,732	6,120	6,220	5,995	225	.03	NO	-
16,393	14,903	12,500	9,740	2,760	.22	YES	2,760
21,754	19,776	19,000	18,200	800	.04	NO	-
10,608	9,644	7,250	6,148	1,102	.15	YES	1,102
3,719	3,381	3,400	2,266	1,134	.33	YES	1,134
7,409	6,735	7,000	6,184	816	.11	NO	-
21,918	19,925	17,000	18,420	(1,420)	-	NO	-
2,763	2,512	2,500	1,880	620	.24	YES	620
37,197	33,815	26,500	18,610	7,890	.29	YES	7,890
51,959	47,235	37,000	26,880	10,120	.27	YES	10,120
1,173	1,066	1,000	940	60	.06	NO	-
2,661	2,419	2,200	2,290	(90)	-	NO	-
2,587	2,352	2,300	2,190	110	.04	NO	-
3,651	3,319	3,200	2,872	328	.10	YES	328
4,613	4,194	4,000	2,677	1,323	.33	YES	1,323
1,190	1,082	900	972	(72)	-	NO	-
11,963	10,875	10,250	6,420	3,830	.37	YES	3,830
13,641	12,401	11,000	5,111	5,889	.53	YES	5,889
2,451	2,228	2,000	2,040	(40)	-	NO	-

TOTAL REV OFFERED $211,610

CONTRIB REV LOST $137,950 = 65.2% of Total $39,375

(AVER. POTENTIAL PV = .285)

NOTE: If OOP MHR data were available, company could have added $137,950 to revenue (65.2% of quoted and lost business) and increased contribution by $39,375.

*Price suggested by customer/prospect

EXHIBIT 26-6: Lost Contribution

EVALUATING PRESENT SOURCES OF PROFITS

If estimates representing present commitments are sorted according to product line or any other of the company's profit or business segments, profitability determinations in each of these segments can be made. Exhibit 26-9 shows how such an analysis is made by major product lines. Exhibit 26-10 shows how this analysis is carried down to the products which constitute a single product line. And Exhibit 26-11 shows the analysis by end-use categories.

An even more dramatic analysis is shown in the data of a large commercial printing firm. This firm produces a wide variety of product lines—from "toothpicks to Cadillacs." Prior to the installation of a proper profit-planning and pricing system, the company measured the performance in each line on the basis of arbitrary gross profit with no measurement of contribution. One of its major lines was the printing of decorative calendars. Because of the economies effected in printing,

Client:______________________ Date Tested:__________ MARTIN & TUCKER ENGINEERS

M. H. R. BACKTEST FORM
(Profile of estimate of previously booked order)

Customer Name & City:______________________ Quantity Booked:__________

Date Booked:__________ Previous Estimate No.:__________ Other Data:__________

Salesman Code	___	Product-Line Code	___	Sq. Ft. Code	___	Printing Type Code	___
Territory Code	___	Unit S. P. Code	___	Qty. Range Code	___	Major Facility Code	___
Distribution Code	___	Style Code	___	Ink Code	___	Operation Code	___
Customer Code	___	Product Type Code	___	Ink Coverage Code	___	Product Size Code	___
Type of Sale Code	___	Material Code	___	Glueing Code	___	Special Features Code	___
Market Code	___	Thickness Code	___	End-Use Code	___	Flute Code	___
Commission Code	___	Grade Code	___	Industry Code	___	Laminating Code	___
Product Code	___	Test Code	___	No. of Colors Code	___	Blank Size Code	___

C O N V E R S I O N

From Previous Estimate: PRODUCTION CENTER	Est. Hours Req'd	M. H. R. OOP	M. H. R. SPOOP*	Est. OOP Cost	T.S.P.*	Target Contrib	SPOOP/OOP Ratio	Common Hours
PREP:								
RUN:								
*used with differential markups							T.C.Hrs=	5

ANALYSIS OF ECONOMIC VALUE

Level Markup Data:
-Markup on OOP Conv. Cost =
-T.S.P. = $
-Major facility hours =
-TCCPH = -BCCPH =

T. Pricing Perf. = $\frac{2}{1}$ = %

T.S.P. Variance = $\frac{3}{4}$ = %

TCHC = $\frac{1}{5}$ =

BCHC = $\frac{2}{5}$ =

Current CPV =

	Data	OOP	T.S.P. / B.S.P.	B. Contrib. / T. Contrib.	GPV / CPV
TARGET:	Conversion Totals			1	
	Prev. Mtls. Est.				
	Prev. Est. DOC's				
	Totals for Order		4		
BOOKED:	Revenue				
	Var. to Target			3	
	Conv. Contrib.			2	

EXHIBIT 26-7

MARTIN & TUCKER, INC.
ENGINEERS

M.H.R. BACKTEST FORM

(profile of previous estimate)

CLIENT ______
DATE TESTED ______
BOOKED ______
QUOTED ______

CUST. NAME & CITY ______ EST. OR JOB NO. ______ QTY. EST. ______
OTHER DATA ______

CUSTOMER CODE	___	PRODUCT CODE	___	PRINTING TYPE CODE	___	___
END-USE CODE	___	PRODUCT-LINE CODE	___	PRODUCT SIZE CODE	___	___
SALESMAN CODE	___	UNIT S. P. CODE	___	MAJOR FACILITY CODE	___	___
TERRITORY CODE	___	QTY. RANGE CODE	___		___	___
MATERIAL CODE	___	NO. OF COLORS CODE	___		___	___

CONVERSION

from previous estimate:		STD. ALLOWED HOURS	M. H. R.		EST. OOP COST	STD. OOP COST	STD. T.S.P.*
PRODUCTION CENTER	ALLOWED HOURS		OOP	SPOOP*			
PREP:							
RUN:							

*used with differential markups

LEVEL MARKUP DATA:				
. . ON OOP CONV. COST =	CONVERSION TOTALS			
. . ON D. MTLS. =	MTLS. PREVIOUSLY EST.			
. . T.S.P. =	OTHER DOC'S PREV. EST.			
. . TARGET CONTRIB. =	ORDER/QUOTATION TOTALS			
. . TARGET G.P.V. =	BOOKED/QUOTED TOTAL S.P.			
. . BOOKED QUOTED CONTRIB. =	BOOKED/QUOTED TOTAL CONTRIBUTION			
. . CONTRIBUTION VARIANCE =	BOOKED/QUOTED G.P.V.			
	MAJOR FACILITY HOURS			
	G. CPH			

EXHIBIT 26-8

PROFIT STRUCTURE	Totals	PRODUCT LINES			
		Litho Process	C & C only	LP	Litho Solids
	$	$	$	$	$
Sales Revenue	4,000,000	1,400,000	800,000	800,000	1,000,000
O.O.P. Costs	2,500,000	700,000	640,000	560,000	600,000
Gross Contrib.	1,500,000	700,000	160,000	240,000	400,000
Operating PV	.375	.50	.20	.30	.40
Spec. Programmed Period Costs	700,000	260,000	120,000	140,000	180,000
Net Contrib.	800,000	440,000	40,000	100,000	220,000
Net PV	.20	.314	.05	.125	.22
Common Period Costs*	400,000				
Pre-tax Profit*	400,000				
Profit %*	10%				
Total Capital Emp	2,500,000	1,200,000	450,000	350,000	500,000
Return on T.C.E. (before common costs)	32%	36.7%	9%	28.6%	44%
Return on T.C.E.* (after common costs)	16%				

*not separable nor identifiable with product lines; such data are allocated by arbitrary methods only.

EXHIBIT 26-9: Period Analysis of Product-Line Profitability

ANALYSIS of Litho Process Product Line from Exhibit 26-9	Totals	PRODUCTS R.T.E. Bl Sulph	Tuck-end Krcote	Auto. Lock Bottom
	$	$	$	$
Sales Revenue	1,400,000	800,000	200,000	400,000
O.O.P. Costs	700,000	440,000	60,000	200,000
Gross Contribution	700,000	360,000	140,000	200,000
Operating PV	.50	.45	.70	.50
Specific Programmed Period Costs*	260,000			
Net Contribution*	440,000			
Net PV*	.314			
Major Facility Hours	8000	4800	1100	2100
C. P. H.	$87.50	$75.00	$127.27	$95.23

*not separable nor identified with products; such data are allocated by arbitrary methods only.

EXHIBIT 26-10: Period Analysis of Product Profitability

the line was thought to be very profitable before the separation of fixed and direct expenses—especially those oop costs specifically identified with the sale of calendars. Because of this lack of separation, the company had little idea of the amount of specific variable capital that was required to support the calendar line.

Calendars were printed in very large quantities and placed in stock. Orders were received in small quantities from real estate offices, barber shops, insurance brokers, and other people who handed them to their customers as giveaways. Each time one of these orders was received, a small quantity of calendars were withdrawn from stock by the company and imprinted with the name of the customer. Before the separation and application of the costs of the specific people involved in

ANALYSIS of Reverse Tuck-End Product from Exhibit 26-10	Totals	END-USE CATEGORIES*			
		Frozen Food	Hardware	Cosmetics	Gift
	$	$	$	$	$
Sales Revenue	800,000	120,000	180,000	290,000	210,000
O.O.P. Costs	440,000	46,600	133,200	75,400	184,800
Gross Contribution	360,000	73,400	46,800	214,600	25,200
Operating PV	.45	.61	.26	.74	.12
Major Facility Hours	4800	1100	900	1600	1200
C. P. H.	$75.00	$66.73	$52.00	$134.13	$21.00

*can also be applied to total company operations as a product-line analysis using format of Exhibit 26-9.

EXHIBIT 26-11: Period Analysis of End-Use/Product Profitability

these tedious transactions, the PV of the calendars was .52, a most respectable contribution rate. However, when the twenty-two people in the sales service and imprinting departments were recognized and treated as a specific cost and a direct charge to the calendar line, the PV dwindled to .06. Add to that the fact that since the calendars remained in stock for long periods, the cost of its variable capital averaged $0.62 per dollar of sales, whereas most of the other product lines required an average of $0.23. Imagine the company's chagrin when it learned that its major item was barely contributing and in addition required an inordinately large amount of variable capital support. Exhibit 26-12 shows the product-line analysis of the company.

The overall results are rather appalling—a 1.3 per cent return on total capital employed. To improve the performance of the company, the identifiability test was applied, namely, if the calendar line, the line on which the company had built its image and original reputation, is eliminated, would the specific, traceable costs also disappear? The answer was yes; the line was discontinued.

DATA PROCESSING OF PROFITABILITY SEGMENTS

Profitability determinations in various segments of the company's profit structure are not done for academic interest. Such evaluations made with the methods suggested in this book will tell management more about its company than it even knew before. To get the most out of its new-

Item	Total	Commercial	Catalogs, brochures, and books	Checks and money orders	Calendars	Posters and maps	Can, wine, and liquor labels	Displays	Christmas cards	Stationery	Direct mail and premiums
Revenue	$3,088,104	$1,012,322	$228,316	$184,218	$978,732	$147,645	$371,198	$62,412	$31,714	$42,941	$28,606
Contribution	$ 985,807	$ 228,785	$ 34,476	$ 60,424	$508,941	$ 27,019	$104,678	$ 8,363	$ 5,423	$ 3,092	$ 4,606
PV	.319	.226	.151	.328	.520	.183	.282	.134	.171	.072	.161
Less: specific transaction costs	192,410	24,632	8,410	4,218	128,780	16,818	8,410	1,142			
Less: commission and royalties	346,500	30,370	11,416	....	291,134	....	11,136	1,872	....	....	572
Less: inventory-carrying interest costs	47,873	8,231	1,857	228	30,341	322	4,876	128	791	119	980
Net contribution	$ 399,024	$ 165,552	$ 12,793	$ 55,978	$ 58,686	$ 9,879	$ 80,256	$ 5,221	$ 4,632	$ 2,973	$ 3,054
Adjusted PV	.129	.163	.056	.304	.060	.067	.216	.084	.146	.069	.107
Less: common period fixed costs	375,500										
Pretax profit	$ 23,524										
Variable capital employed	$1,097,897	$ 274,380	$ 46,420	$ 11,415	$606,814	$ 16,112	$108,360	$ 6,420	$15,818	$ 2,378	$ 9,780
Vairable capital of sales, %	35.5	27.2	20.3	6.2	62.0	10.9	29.2	10.3	49.9	5.5	34.2
Fixed capital	654,000										
TCE	$1,751,897										
Return on TCE (pretax), %	1.3										

EXHIBIT 26-12: Product-Line Analysis of Commercial Printer

CONTRIBUTION BY TERRITORY

SEPTEMBER 19____

DISTRICT CODE	TARGET PV	ACTUAL PV	CONTN PER HR	BOOKED SP	TARGET REVENUE	CONTR	TARGET CONTR
1	185	212	086	4886	4721	1040	875
2	152	230	096	8797	7994	2025	1222
3	162	200	040	9369	8946	1880	1457
5	131	124	034	26129	26332	3249	3452
6	095	125	070	50150	48519	6278	4647
7	187	206	035	11293	11033	2330	2070
8	123	151	039	43641	42223	6616	5198
10	189	240	051	51738	48493	12440	9195
17	228	076	022	6679	7990	512	1823
20	135	263	121	141092	120229	37199	16336
21	119	154	098	9563	9193	1473	1103
22	097	121	046	8545	8324	1035	814
23	1,22	208	091	26741	24123	5575	2957
40	216	244	041	2896	2795	707	606
	139	205	069	401519	370915	82359	51755

SEPTEMBER TO DATE 19____

DISTRICT CODE	TARGET PV	ACTUAL PV	CONTN PER HR	BOOKED SP	TARGET REVENUE	CONTR	TARGET CONTR
1	202	163	032	20130	21117	3285	4272
2	149	191	074	61806	58770	11829	8793
3	148	196	036	50525	47629	9949	7053
5	139	171	050	83992	80819	14436	11263
6	118	147	072	77797	75230	11474	8907
7	187	183	042	32786	32948	6008	6170
8	178	147	044	84905	88061	12563	15719
10	164	235	058	268644	245901	63302	40559
17	228	130	030	21682	24434	2840	5592
20	128	227	155	390579	346377	88697	44495
21	105	154	148	45799	43292	7071	4564
22	154	179	058	25522	24786	4569	3833
23	141	198	060	57751	53881	11476	7606
40	210	249	044	4835	4595	1208	968
	149	203	067	1226753	1147840	248707	169794

EXHIBIT 26-13: Printout of Contribution by Territory

SALESMAN'RUN THRU 06/02/YEAR

PRODUCT LINE	BOOKED REVENUE	CONTRIB	PV	LP HOURS	OFFSET HOURS	CPH	TARGET REVENUE	PRICE VARIANCE
14 FRANK GREENE								
			CURRENT PERIOD					
LP	98,767	24,454	.248	625		39	93,769	4,998
OFFSET	39,252	12,231	.312	12	88	122	37,903	1,349
NO PRTG	248	62	.250				242	6
TOTAL	138,267	36,747	.266	637	88	50	131,914	6,353
			CUMULATIVE					
LP	434,600	112,059	.258	2,834	3	39	412,219	22,381
OFFSET	97,101	30,254	.312	34	261	102	96,086	1,015
NO PRTG	4,453	1,351	.303				4,002	451
TOTAL	536,154	143,664	.268	2,868	264	45	512,307	23,847
16 HARVEY CROSS								
			CURRENT PERIOD					
LP	3,340	1,466	.439	15		97	2,577	763
OFFSET	28,868	12,069	.418		52	232	25,195	3,673
NO PRTG			.000					
TOTAL	32,208	13,535	.420	15	52	202	27,772	4,436
			CUMULATIVE					
LP	33,567	9,973	.297	225		44	31,325	2,242
OFFSET	48,974	20,347	.415		152	133	47,138	1,836
NO PRTG			.000					
TOTAL	82,541	30,320	.367	225	152	80	78,463	4,078

EXHIBIT 26-14: Printout of Contribution by Salesman

END USE LISTING — THRU 06/02/YEAR

PRODUCT LINE	BOOKED REVENUE	CONTRIB	PV	LP HOURS	OFFSET HOURS	CPH	TARGET REVENUE	PRICE VARIANCE
132 SPORTING GOODS & TOYS								
CURRENT PERIOD								
LP	4,962	1,077	.217	27		39	4,838	124
OFFSET			.000					
NO PRTG			.000					
TOTAL	4,962	1,077	.217	27		39	4,838	124
CUMULATIVE								
LP	112,766	32,166	.285	872		36	104,827	7,939
OFFSET	40,479	11,682	.289	24	52	153	39,005	1,474
NO PRTG	1,365	463	.339				1,208	157
TOTAL	154,610	44,311	.287	896	52	46	145,040	9,570
187 HARDWARE & AUTO SUPPLIES								
CURRENT PERIOD								
LP	1,491	396	.266	8		49	1,380	111
OFFSET			.000					
NO PRTG			.000					
TOTAL	1,491	396	.266	8		49	1,380	111
CUMULATIVE								
LP	195,852	43,575	.222	904		48	194,908	944
OFFSET	9,950	2,985	.300		22	135	10,032	- 82
NO PRTG	6,579	1,277	.194				6,320	259
TOTAL	212,381	47,837	.225	904	22	51	211,260	1,121

EXHIBIT 26-15: Printout of Contribution by End-Use

found knowledge, management must be equipped to act on these data quickly in order to capture the profit potential revealed by each of the profit segments. While these analyses can be prepared manually, the timing for management becomes slowed down. Of course, there is no substitute for doing it by hand initially, for this technique often debugs much of the format to be used in the future. However, once the formats have been refined, management should seriously consider processing these data automatically, either by using an outside service bureau or by using its own captive electronic data processing facilities.

It may be helpful to the reader to see just how these reports are issued. Exhibit 26-13 is an actual IBM run of territorial profitability for the commercial printer. The following three exhibits are partial weekly IBM runs of a folding-carton manufacturer. Exhibit 26-14 shows the contribution run by salesman, Exhibit 26-15 shows the contribution run by end market, and Exhibit 26-16 shows the contribution run by customer.

JOB PERFORMANCE

Previous profitability determinations have dealt with period data, i.e., results attained in any time period without being able to obtain specific job characteristics. This is unavoidable due to the timing differences between the opening and closing of a time period and the start and stop of any specific job. This is due to the fact that within any practical time measurement period: jobs start but do not finish; jobs finish which started in a previous period; jobs are in process during the entire period having started in a previous period and ending in a future period; and some jobs which start and stop within the period.

Useful is an analysis of only jobs which closed out (finished) in a period together with their variances. In Exhibit 26-17 we have a monthly report which lists by product lines variances in: pricing; manufacturing productivity (conversion performance); material usages; spoilage and rejects; and methods changes. Thus, in this month, the "litho" line showed an unfavorable pricing

CUSTOMER RUN								THRU 06/02/YEAR
PRODUCT LINE	BOOKED REVENUE	CONTRIB	PV	LP HOURS	OFFSET HOURS	CPH	TARGET REVENUE	PRICE VARIANCE
0871 AMERICAN CHEM								
			CURRENT PERIOD					
OFFSET	17,071	7,340	.430		28	262	14,353	2,718
			CUMULATIVE					
LP	37,428	9,539	.255	179		53	36,544	884
OFFSET	40,900	16,895	.413		113	112	31,196	9,704
TOTAL	78,328	26,434	.337	216	113	80	67,740	10,588
3240 INDUSTRIAL SUP								
			CURRENT PERIOD					
LP	2,592	544	.210	11		49	2,592	
			CUMULATIVE					
LP	112,478	32,627	.290	910		35	104,512	7,966
OFFSET	40,479	11,682	.289		52	153	39,005	1,474
NO PRTG	1,365	463	.339				1,208	157
TOTAL	154,322	44,772	.290	934	52	45	144,725	9,597
8721 SKELLY PROD								
			CUMULATIVE					
OFFSET	132,061	38,573	.292		430	89	143,189	-11,128

EXHIBIT 26-16: Printout of Contribution by Customer

Month of 10/7x	PRODUCT LINES			Total
	Litho	LP	C & C only	
No. of Jobs Closed	18	54	16	88
Target Sales Revenue	$513,184	$269,618	$113,468	$896,270
Actual Sales Revenue	499,699	263,430	115,720	878,849
Revenue Variance	(13,485)	(6,188)	2,252	(17,421)
Var.	(2.62%)	(2.29%)	2.0%	(1.94%)
Estimated Contribution on Actual Sales Revenue	140,486	84,722	12,961	238,169
PV	.284	.322	.112	.271
Actual Contribution on Actual Sales Revenue	116,743	82,756	14,078	213,577
PV	.234	.314	.122	.243
Change in Contribution	(23,743)	(1,966)	1,117	(24,592)
Sources:				
1.Conversion Performance	(22,407)	3,781	1,016	(17,610)
2.Materials Performance	1,987	(1,867)	287	407
3.Spoilage	(2,632)	(3,992)	(186)	(6,810)
4.Methods Changes	(691)	112	0	(579)

EXHIBIT 26-17: OOP Variance Summary of Closed Out Jobs (in the Month)

variance of $13,485 at the booking point, a "marketing variance." From this point on, the four operating variances shown under "Sources" apply to the booked or actual sales revenue. It shows that productivity was lower than estimated which boosted oop conversion cost by $22,407 thus lowering contribution by the same amount. It revealed that yield from materials was better than planned by $1,987. Spoilage and rejects exceeded the amount estimated by $2,632. And it cost the company $691 in lost contribution due to having to run the order differently than the way they estimated it would run. This is sometimes called a facility-change variance.

MANAGEMENT INFORMATION REPORTS

Management information reports should give the manager hard-hitting, condensed facts on which he can take immediate action without painstaking analyses and prolonged explanations. Reports relating to the activity and quality of pricing should show the direction which pricing is taking and should be used for evaluating the various profit segments in the company's profit structure. Reports for the pricing function should answer questions such as these: How much

Period Ending June 30

	LINE A	LINE B	LINE C	TOTAL
Booked Revenue	2,611,224	608,018	265,520	3,484,762
Contribution	709,826	100,522	73,909	884,257
PV	.272	.165	.278	.254
Target Revenue	2,579,264	622,396	270,851	3,472,511
Revenue Variance	31,960	(14,378)	(5,331)	12,251
Variance %	1.2%	(2.3%)	(1.9%)	.35%
Major Facility Hrs. Sold	12,690	7,638	2,587	---
Contribution Per Hour of Major Facility	$55.94	$13.16	$28.57	---
Period Fixed Expenses	312,786	71,574	84,684	469,044
Period Profit	397,040	28,948	(10,775)	415,213
Profit % to Sales	15.2%	4.7%	(4.1%)	11.9%
Target Ret. on Capital Employed[1]	265,746	59,166	65,754	390,666
Return % on Capital Employed	22.4%	7.3%	(2.4%)	15.9%

[1] All lines have a target % return on total capital employed of 15%.

EXHIBIT 26-18: Summary of Pricing Results

PERIOD ENDING June 30

	Year-to-date Thru MAY			Month of JUNE			Year-to-date Ending JUNE 30		
	PRODUCT I	PRODUCT II	PRODUCT III	PRODUCT I	PRODUCT II	PRODUCT III	PRODUCT I	PRODUCT II	PRODUCT III
Booked Revenue	1,149,357	854,925	47,461	371,527	112,148	75,806	1,520,884	967,073	123,267
Contribution	289,987	261,281	9,838	101,422	33,790	13,508	391,409	295,071	23,346
PV	.252	.306	.207	.273	.301	.178	.257	.305	.189
Target Revenue	1,109,211	872,433	45,421	361,352	115,528	75,319	1,470,563	987,961	120,740
Revenue Variance	40,146	(17,508)	2,040	10,175	(3,380)	487	50,321	(20,888)	2,527
Press Hrs. Sold	7,586	2,581	---	1,969	554	---	9,555	3,135	---
Contribution Per Press Hour	38.22	101.23	---	51.50	60.99	---	40.96	94.12	---

Summary of Above Detail

	Year-to-date Thru MAY	Month of June	Year to Date
Booked Revenue	2,051,743	559,481	2,611,224
Contribution	561,106	148,720	709,826
PV	.273	.266	.272
Target Revenue	2,027,065	552,199	2,579,264
Revenue Variance	24,678	7,282	31,960
Variance %	1.2%	.8%	1.2%
Press Hrs. Sold	10,167	2,523	12,690
Contribution Per Press Hour	55.19	58.95	55.94
Period Fixed Expenses	260,655	52,131	312,786
Period Profit	300,451	96,589	397,040
Profit % to Sales	14.6%	17.3%	15.2%
Target Return on T.C.E.	221,455	44,291	265,746
Return % on Capital	20.4%	32.7%	22.4%

EXHIBIT 26-19: **Summary of Pricing Results**
Detail of Line A Revenue Dollars

contribution has been accumulated to date? Are we on target considering how much time has passed in the operating year? Do we have enough facility-hours available to attain our target? Which is our best customer? Our best salesman? Our best territory? Our best end market? Are the sales of an important customer in proportion to the contribution he provides and the capacity he requires?

1. *Pricing results company-wide:* Exhibit 26-18 shows the results of pricing in all the company's product lines during a certain period. All the basic information is shown: booked revenue, contribution, PV, target revenue, revenue variance, facility-hours sold, contribution per facility-hour, *prorated* (not allocated) fixed expenses, period pretax profit, target return on employed capital, and the actual return on said capital. The data shown are cumulative data from the start of the operating year. The total pricing results show that to date the company has accomplished .9 per cent more than its target of 15 per cent return on total capital employed. Whether this trend can be maintained is not only a function of the pricing quality but also a balancing between the available capacity remaining for the year and the amount of contribution necessary to achieve the year-end target. If capacity is not scarce, management need not intensively police the build-up of facility-hours committed, but instead it may devote its attention to booking contribution with a watchful eye on the commitment of working capital. This latter item of capital may become scarce as the company drives towards attaining its target.

2. *Pricing results by product line:* Exhibit 26-19 shows the details of the pricing results of Product line A shown first in the previous exhibit. Three products constitute this product line. Pricing results are shown for the period up to but not including the current month, the current month, and finally, the year to date. Notice that fixed expenses are not allocated to individual products because of the use of joint facilities and common fixed expenses incurred by the product line as one total.

3. *Charting of data:* Exhibits 26-20 and 26-21 show the pricing performances company-wide and for Product line A, respectively. These charts show the cumulative comparison between the contribution booked to date against the target contribution prorated evenly throughout the year. This latter figure is represented by the "Path of proportionate contribution." As we have discussed throughout the book, no one period can be charged with generating a given amount of sales or contribution, for this action would deny the pressures of the market and the presence of competition. The proportionate contribution line is provided as a yardstick against which the trend of cumulative booked contribution may be measured. The degree of target attainment can be realistically measured only at the end of the operating year. However, if the actual booked contribution departs too seriously from the path after a considerable portion of the operating year has passed, management should either question its original target set out in its profit plan or investigate the performance of the sales department or both. Again, these data have nothing whatever to do with production performance. This information shows what prices have been booked and what the revenue it represents is estimated to provide in contribution dollars.

4. *Pricing results by customer:* Exhibit 26-22 shows how pricing information is sorted to provide a ranking of customers by PV ratio as well as by contribution dollars. Because of the size of the typical sales transaction, only those customers which purchased a minimum of $4,000 in the period were used in this tabulation. The ranking by PV is valuable for evaluating the characteristic PV's of customers, owing to their purchasing habits, to the end market of which they are members, to the specific territory in which they are located, or to a combination of all three. While Mohaje Hardware has the largest booked PV and shows a most favorable PV variance compared to its target PV, the sales booked for it must be low as shown by its contribution ranking in the contribution tabulation. PV alone should not be the sole guide to customer quality. On the other hand, Beautycraft, which ranks low in PV and has an unfavorable PV variance, ranks on top of the

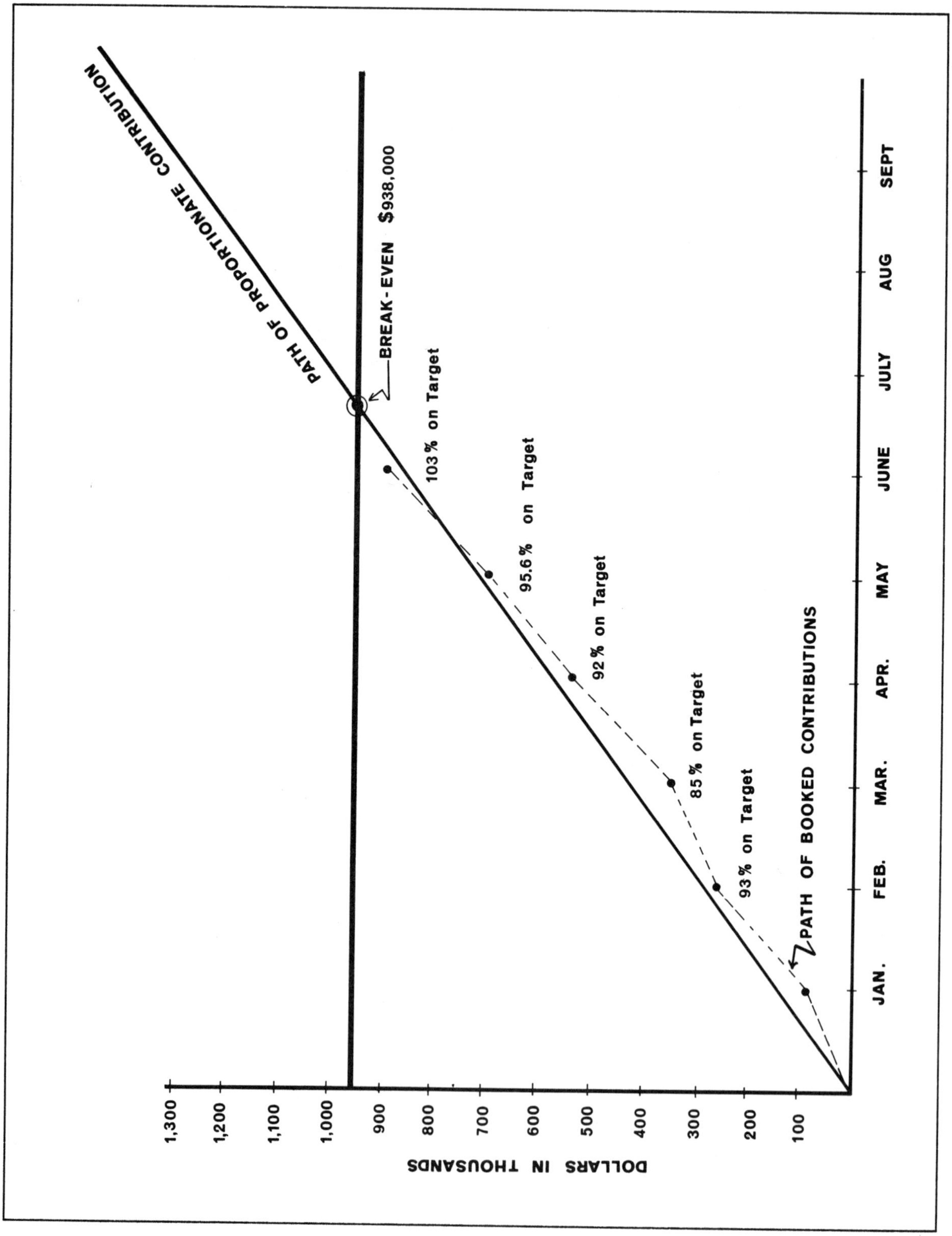

EXHIBIT 26-20: Company-Wide Pricing Results

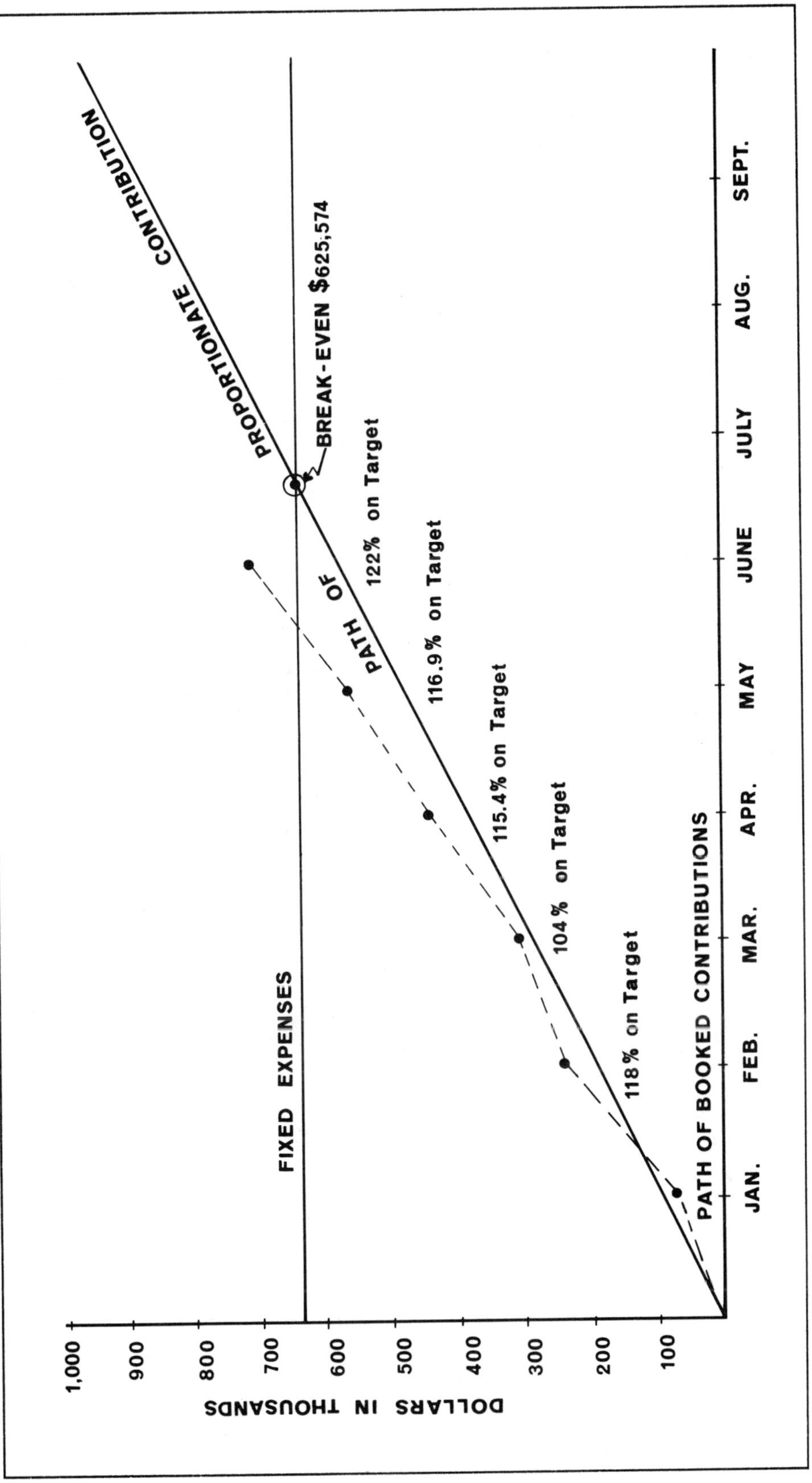

EXHIBIT 26-21: Product-Line A: Results of Pricing

Management Report
For Period Ending June 30
Customer Ranking by PV & Contribution
(Booked Sales)

PRODUCT LINE A

Customer Ranking by PV
(Min. Sales of $4,000)

Customer	*Booked P. V.*	*Target P. V.*
MOHAJE HARDWARE	.444	.314
LESTUR	.385	.355
WESTON-SMITH	.347	.328
HELENA FOX	.341	.308
CLYDE CO.	.337	.292
FEMINA	.324	.287
SHASTER	.321	.242
RONTAR	.318	.294
IND'L BRUSH	.318	.297
FERN LEATHER	.307	.270
SEMPLE	.300	.306
RON ELECTRIC	.296	.233
ASSOC. HARDWARE	.293	.244
DEWAR'S	.290	.266
AMER. HARDWARE	.287	.330
V. S. SOAP	.287	.255
BANGOR, INC.	.287	.246
TESTRON	.283	.217
HOME INDUSTRIES	.280	.272
DIMILTO-STAR	.279	.239
AMER. ENTERPRISES	.276	.251
S. W. & T.	.269	.187
GENERAL METALS	.264	.316
ALBANY PROD.	.262	.222
JENER MFG.	.261	.236
ASSOC. DRUG	.261	.277
BEAUTYCRAFT	.257	.280
JONTIL DRUG	.255	.255
HARTLEY ELECTRIC	.253	.225
LAFE PHARM.	.230	.184
FREDERICK ELECTRIC	.218	.242
BEACH WEAR, INC.	.215	.180
BRILL, INC.	.207	.211
BRETON	.202	.183
LOCKLAND	.087	.201

Customer Ranking By Contribution Dollars

Customer	*Booked Contrib.*	*Target Contrib.*
BEAUTYCRAFT	$137,686	$154,478
AMER. HARDWARE	57,210	69,084
ASSOC. HARDWARE	46,876	36,637
CLYDE CO.	44,121	35,770
BRILL, INC.	32,521	33,310
DIMILTO-STAR	30,259	24,632
SHASTER	29,829	20,155
LESTUR	28,510	25,020
JONTIL DRUG	25,589	25,589
LAFE PHARM.	22,227	16,681
HARTLEY ELECTRIC	22,068	18,940
V. S. SOAP	19,937	16,984
FREDERICK ELECTRIC	19,888	22,716
FEMINA	17,413	14,556
BANGOR, INC.	16,744	13,568
AMER. ENTERPRISES	16,688	14,661
FERN LEATHER	15,778	13,141
GENERAL METALS	15,013	19,270
HELENA FOX	14,160	12,165
WESTON-SMITH	13,020	11,931
HOME INDUSTRIES	11,270	10,790
MOHAJE HARDWARE	7,648	4,398
RONTAR	6,495	5,811
S. W. & T.	6,306	3,932
IND'L BRUSH	6,060	5,485
DEWAR'S	5,897	5,234
BRETON	5,102	4,521
TESTRON	3,374	2,370
BEACH WEAR, INC.	3,001	2,403
SEMPLE	2,985	3,067
LOCKLAND	2,406	6,389
ALBANY PROD.	1,975	1,591
JENER MFG.	1,926	1,686
ASSOC. DRUG	1,859	2,015
RON ELECTRIC	1,782	1,285
Totals	$693,623	$660,265

Favorable Pricing Variance = $33,358

EXHIBIT 26-22:

contribution tabulation. The value of cumulatively showing the booked and target PV for each customer provides rough boundaries for future pricing.

However, some kind of additional analysis is required to evaluate the worth of a customer. In this analysis, it is important to include the relationship of booked contribution to committed facility-hours to ensure that the constant booking of low-PV, high-sales business will not cause the company to exhaust its capacity before the end of the operating year. Obviously, without an analysis, the seller would have a difficult task selecting the better of the following two customers:

Customer X: Provides 10 per cent of the firm's annual sales.
Gives only 2 per cent of the firm's annual contribution needs.
Uses up 30 per cent of the annual capacity of the firm.

Customer Y: Provides 8 per cent of the firm's annual sales.
Gives 12 per cent of the firm's annual contribution needs.
Uses up only 9 per cent of the annual capacity of the firm.

Exhibit 26-23 shows how to realistically evaluate customers using five of the company's largest customers.

5. *Pricing results by salesman:* Exhibit 26-24 shows how pricing data are sorted to give rankings by salesman. The tabulations show the data by PV and contribution. Here again, one must be guided more by contribution than by PV. Of course, PV does show the type of work for which a salesman aims and can be used as some evaluation of his quality, but his productivity together with the PV of the work he gets determine the contribution results. So while Mr. Brown has the highest PV, he produces only one-half of the contribution which Mr. Thompson generates. Further evaluations are available from examining the degree to which each salesman gets the target prices. The chances are good that Thompson is a better salesman than Fuller over and above what the contribution and PV data show. Since their PV's are very close, Thompson's increase in contribution over Fuller's is more the result of aiming for better prices than for volume. The spread in revenue variance of $36,136 between these two men confirms this judgment.

6. *Pricing results by end market:* Exhibit 26-25 shows how pricing data are used to determine the sources of profit by end-use markets. Again, rankings are prepared both by PV and contribution. The PV measurement enables an evaluation of the PV characteristic of the marketplace. In many cases, this sorting is carried out to include the territories constituting each of the end markets. Even though cosmetics have a lower than maximum PV, the volume generated by the various customers in this classification is great enough to rate it highest by far in contribution over any other. Notice that the sales figure is not used in any of these measurements of pricing results because obviously that figure is meaningless unless we know the specific economic ingredients of the sale.

MEASURING THE RESULTS OF OPERATING

Conventional profit-and-loss statements combine the effects of pricing quality and internal performance with the results of inventory change. The "bottom line" is a jumble of positive and negative events from which management cannot unscramble an evaluation of any one. Such an "absorption" statement can show figures which are "in the red" in spite of high pricing quality and volume with sterling internal performance simply because there is a drop in inventory value in that period. Managements may act on this "loss" by attempting to raise prices and wind up with a genuinely negative situation as they price themselves out of their markets. Conversely, pricing quality and volume can be down with production performance mediocre in another period and management sees a profitable bottom line. This could be the result of an increase in inventory during that period. Nonetheless, management becomes complacent and believes they are doing a

Customer	Ranked by Sales Volume	PV	Contrib. Generated	Facility Hours Committed	ANALYSIS % of Total Sales	% of Total Contrib.	% of Capacity Used	C.P.H.
C	$400,000	.07	$28,000	4200	27.4	13.9	26.6	$6.67
E	340,000	.13	44,200	3600	23.3	21.9	22.7	12.27
A	320,000	.11	35,200	1700	21.9	17.4	10.8	20.70
D	220,000	.21	46,200	4100	15.0	22.8	26.0	11.27
B	180,000	.27	48,600	2200	12.4	24.0	13.9	22.14
Totals	$1,460,000	.138*	$202,200	15800	100	100	100	$12.79*

*Averages obscure the mix, and hide the real winners and losers.

EXHIBIT 26-23: Realistic Customer Evaluation

SUMMARY

Salesman	Booked P. V.	Target P. V.
Brown	.284	.255
Henry	.280	.322
Thompson	.264	.234
Fuller	.263	.277
House Accts.	.252	.257
Hapway	.228	.227
Harlow	.227	.229
Grant	.201	.183
Myer	.099	.113

Salesman	Booked Contrib.	Target Contrib.	Variance
Thompson	$195,369	$167,361	$+28,008
Fuller	162,074	174,202	-12,128
House Accts.	141,524	145,135	-3,611
Hapway	118,064	117,575	+489
Brown	103,290	89,330	+13,960
Harlow	95,644	96,971	-1,327
Henry	61,043	74,419	-13,376
Grant	5,102	4,521	+581
Myer	2,147	2,492	-345
Totals	$884,257	$872,006	$+12,251

EXHIBIT 26-24: Management Report Salesmen's Ranking By PV & Contribution Dollars Period Ending June 30

fine job. Worse yet, they may start to make undue price concessions to customers and even reward goldbricking productivity in manufacturing. Then, even with no change in inventory from period to period, a plus or minus in pricing quality can be offset by a minus or plus in internal operating performance and management is frustrated in its attempts to manage.

DIRECT-COST STATEMENTS

There is no substitute for a direct-cost operating statement which shows the pricing quality attained separate from the volume factor and surely apart from internal performance and inventory change. These statements are meant for internally reporting to management and *not* for external use, such as income tax purposes. Of course, to be believable to management, at the start of the new method, such direct-cost statements can be reconciled to the company's conventional income and expense reporting.

Unlike the conventional absorption statement, there are seven generically different forms of direct-cost statements, each one designed to use different types of data, depending how the system was set up in the company. For example, in measuring the contribution from billed sales, either the estimated oop cost of sales or the estimated oop costs incurred in the period can be used. One would require different treatment of the oop value of the inventory change in adopting one or the other. Oop variances can be either those related directly to the billed sales or those generated during the period, etc. To give the reader some exposure to the subject, two radically different forms are presented, both of which are in current usage.

Exhibit 26-26 starts out with target or planned sales followed by the actual revenue billed. Using the standard oop cost from another schedule, line 3 lists the standard contribution. The actual marketing contribution, which is caused by the market and not internal operating, is separated

FOLDING UNIT

End Use	Booked P.V.	Target P.V.	End Use	Booked Contrib.	Target Contrib.
Miscellaneous	.290	.254	Cosmetics	$451,611	$440,655
Sporting Goods	.285	.239	Medicinal	108,297	96,078
Textiles	.283	.257	Hardware	56,775	54,383
Medicinal Products	.280	.257	Sporting Goods	48,552	38,340
Cosmetics	.278	.274	Textiles	16,639	14,565
Food-Dry only	.264	.316	Food-Dry only	15,013	19,270
Hardware	.229	.221	Soap	7,063	7,370
Beverages	.194	.337	Miscellaneous	4,081	3,408
Soap	.155	.161	Beverages	1,795	3,797
			Totals	$709,826	$677,866

EXHIBIT 26-25: Management Report For Period Ending June 30
Rating of End Use Classification By PV & Contribution

(000)omitted			PV	Revenue Variance	Contrib. Variance
1. Planned Divisional Sales		$ 3,200			
2. Actual Divisional Sales		2,850		$(350)	
3. Std. Contribution		1,280	.40		
4. Actual Marketing Contribution		1,083	.38		
a.±Mix Variance:$2850 x (.02)	$(57)		(.02)		$(57)
b.±Volume " :$(350) x .40	(140)				(140)
5. ±OOP Cost Period Prod'n Variances:					
a.Performance	13				
b.Labor rate	(4)				
c.Crew change	(19)				
d.Non-chargeable labor	(6)				
e.Subsidy	3				
f.Overtime	5				
g.Method/facility change	(26)				
h.Spending: DCB	11				
i.Variable Mfg.Overhead	(5)				
j.Material price	31				
k. " usage	(4)				
l.Waste and spoilage	(1)				
m.(Overruns)Underruns	(87)				
n.Delivery	38				
Total OOP Variances		(51)			(51)
6. Actual Net Contribution for Period		1,032	.36		
7. Less:Period Variable Mfg. OH Cost		382			
8. Direct Mfg. Profit		650			
9. Less:Specific Programmed Period Cost		140	actual(Var.on sep.schedule)		
General " "		80	actual(" " " ")		
10. Direct Division Profit, before Corporate Common Costs		$ 430			

EXHIBIT 26-26: Direct-Cost P & L Statement

between that caused by shifts in the planned product mix and that caused by changes in volume. Methods of making those two calculations are shown at a and b. These unfavorable contribution variances reduce the standard contribution of $1,280,000 to $1,083,000 providing the company with its marketing (external) PV of .38.

This is the PV which has been generated from the outside and it now remains to be seen how the internal operation either enhanced or diluted it. The internal operation is evaluated by the use of 14 different variances, each separate and distinct and ready for managerial action. Some are positive and some are negative. The net result is an unfavorable contribution variance of $51,000 or a drop in PV from .38 to .36. Instead of a jumble of events and results, management now knows

	Month of 3/197x			Month of 4/197x		
a. Net Billings			$212,806			$362,201
b. Less: Material Costs			51,794			94,583
c. Balance of Revenue			161,012			267,618
d. Conversion Costs:						
OOP		$147,076			$139,039	
Fixed Mfg. Overhead		23,843			23,976	
"Full" Conversion Costs		170,919			163,015	
e. Beginning W-I-P	$284,871			$347,908		
Ending W-I-P	347,908			298,206		
+Decrease (-Increase)		(63,037)			49,702	
f. Total Manufacturing Costs			107,882			212,717
g. Manufacturing Profit			53,130			54,901
h. Sales, Gen'l & Admin. Expense			44,086			42,102
i. Operating Profit			9,044			12,799
j. ± Non-Operating Income (Expense)			(6,923)			(6,779)
k. Pre-Tax Profit on Billings			$ 2,121			$ 6,020

Data to Reconcile with and Convert to Direct-Cost P & L

	Month of 3/197x	Month of 4/197x
D. Change in W-I-P*	20,759	(16,950)
l. (17) Pre-Tax Direct Profit	$ 22,880	$(10,930)

*from Exhibit 26-28.

EXHIBIT 26-27: Conventional Operating Statement

where to take objective action to improve, correct and capitalize on gains. From this point on, expenses which are incurred by the time period are subtracted to yield the direct manufacturing profit and then the direct profit for the division.

Where such a statement is drawn for a division of a multi-divisional corporation, any corporate charge or allocation must be introduced only after the direct divisional profit. If it is inserted earlier it will obscure and distort the inherent profitability of that division.

Before presenting the next direct-cost statement format, which is far more sophisticated, we show the results of that company first in conventional form in Exhibit 26-27. Some data usually not shown on this type of statement is expanded to aid the reader to reconcile it with the direct-cost approach shown in the next exhibit for the same two months. First are the billed sales from which are deducted material cost, "full" conversion costs with the change in inventory to get manufacturing profit. So far we cannot tell anything about pricing quality and/or internal performance. Then all other period costs are deducted to give operating profit and we still cannot separate any causative event on which to take managerial action. The bottom of that statement shows how these data are reconciled to the direct-cost statement of the next exhibit.

Exhibit 26-28 shows an advanced approach to statement reporting purposes on a direct-cost basis. This format shows all results and conditions against target selling prices and all variances are then equated against targets. If PV's are inserted at each line of cost, one could then trace the proportionate progression of favorable and unfavorable events, i.e., where the contribution is being gained and/or lost. It will be helpful to run through each of the lines on the statement for a more complete understanding:

Line 1. This is the actual amount of sales volume at actual prices.
Line 2. This is the variance from TSP on the actual billed sales volume.
Line 3. Target = Actual ± variance.
Line 4. TSP of materials = Material costs + target contribution.
Line 5. When the TSP of materials is subtracted from the gross target revenue, the remainder is the conversion revenue of the billed sales at target.
Line 6. Since we are dealing with target information, we apply the work-in-process inventory change at TSP. Such data are valued from SPOOP rates X hours used plus the TSP of materials.
Line 7. In the month of 3/197x, the inventory increased thereby crediting income with another $83,796 and adjusting the billings to a higher conversion revenue for production *at target.*
Line 8. Since we are dealing only with *conversion* revenue, we subtract the oop *conversion* cost. Then we apply all of the variances of oop conversion cost *in the period* to get the actual oop conversion cost of production. (This is the inventoriable amount.)
Line 9. When this actual oop conversion cost is subtracted from the conversion revenue, we get the conversion contribution. And when the target contribution of materials is added (from line 4), we get the total production contribution, including the pricing variance.
Line 10. This line shows the period manufacturing overhead costs and its variance to adjust it to actual. *This amount is charged to the period and not to inventory.*
Line 11. This is the difference between total target production contribution and actual period manufacturing overhead to give the production profit, including the pricing variance.
Line 12. Then selling, general and administrative expenses are charged to the period, consisting of both the oop and fixed costs.
Line 13. Subtracting line 12 from 11 gives the operating profit of production at TSP, including the pricing variance.

	Month of 3/197x		Month of 4/197x	
1.Billed Sales at Actual Prices		$212,806		$362,201
2.Pricing Variance, + Unfav.(-Fav.)		13,796		46,874
3.Billed Sales at Target Prices		226,602		409,075
4.Less: Actual Material (etc.) Costs	$ 51,794		$ 94,583	
Target Contribution	5,179		9,458	
Material TSP		56,973		104,041
5.Conversion TSP of Billings		169,629		305,034
6.Beginning W-I-P at TSP	365,627		449,423	
Ending W-I-P at TSP	449,423		382,771	
+ Increase (-Decrease)		83,796		(66,652)
7.Conversion TSP of Production		253,425		238,382
8.Standard OOP Conversion Cost	165,720		156,661	
+ Unfav.(-Fav.) Variance	(18,644)		(17,622)	
Actual OOP Conversion Cost of Prod'n.		147,076		139,039
9.Conversion Contribution		106,349		99,343
Material Contribution		5,179		9,458
Total Contribution of Production		111,528		108,801
10.Budgeted Mfg.Overhead Period Costs	24,068		21,620	
+ Unfav.(-Fav.) Variance	(225)		2,355	
Actual Mfg. Overhead		23,843		23,975
11.Production Profit		87,685		84,826
12.Period Sales, Gen'l & Admin.Expense		44,086		42,102
13.Operating Profit of Production at TSP		43,599		42,723
14.± Non-Operating Income (Expense)		(6,923)		(6,779)
15.Pre-Tax Direct Profit of Production at TSP		36,676		35,944
16.± Pricing Variance		(13,796)		(46,874)
17.Pre-Tax Direct Profit of Production at Actual Prices		$ 22,880		$(10,930)
Data to Reconcile with and Convert to Conventional Absorption P & L:				
A.+Decrease (-Increase) in W-I-P at TSP	$(83,796)		$(66,652)	
B.+Increase (-Decrease) in W-I-P at OOP Cost	54,659		(42,126)	
C.+Increase (-Decrease) in W-I-P Mfg.Overhead	8,378		(7,576)	
D.Change in W-I-P		(20,759)		16,950
18.Pre-Tax Absorption Profit on Billings (k)		$ 2,121		$ 6,020

EXHIBIT 26-28: Direct-Cost Operating Statement (using TSP data)

Line 14. This is the typical non-operating income and expense, which should always be separated from conversion results.

Line 15. This is the result of applying line 14 amount to line 13 to get the pre-tax direct profit of production at TSP, including the pricing variance.

Line 16. This line recalls the pricing variance from line 2 and adjusts line 15 to obtain the direct production profit at *actual* prices.

Note that data of two months are provided to give the reader the opportunity of seeing how the information ties together. The information on the bottom of this statement shows the data by which this direct-cost statement can be converted to and/or ties in with the conventional absorption statement shown in the previous exhibit. For a few words of clarification:

Line A: Amount comes from line 6.
Line B: Costs the change in inventory in oop costs instead of SPOOP.
Line C: Is the change in inventoried period manufacturing costs.
Line B + Line C equals the amount on line e of the previous exhibit.
Line D: Shows the net change in work-in-process obtained from applying the Line B + Line C amount to Line A.
Line 18: Comes from applying the change in work-in-process to Line 17, to obtain the pretax absorption profit on billings. This should be the same amount shown on line k of the previous exhibit.

While providing the maximum effectivness for internal managerial control, this type of statement should not be attempted until there has been substantial experience gained in all other facets of the MHR system.

INVENTORIABLE COSTS

This is a term referred to in the last exhibit and requires some explanation. Inventoriable costs are those costs which enter into the valuation of the products in inventory. In external reporting for income tax purposes, these costs are generally "full" factory costs and exclude such typical items as selling, general and administrative expenses. On a direct-cost statement for internal managerial use, such inventoriable costs are just the *direct* factory costs, excluding the *direct* selling, general and administrative expenses. This calls for some adjustment in the oop MHR's for this purpose, as follows:

Oop MHR "A": This is the type of rate developed in this book consisting of all direct conversion costs, viz: CCT + DCB + Direct Manufacturing Overhead + Direct Warehousing & Receiving + Direct Selling, General & Administrative Expenses.
Oop MHR "B": This the inventoriable rate, used for calculating the standard direct cost of sales, as on line 8 of the last exhibit and used as the basis for obtaining the standard contribution on line 3 of Exhibit 26-26. This rate is derived from all direct *factory* conversion costs, viz: CCT + DCB + Direct Manufacturing Overhead + Direct Warehousing & Receiving Expenses. Both direct and period Selling, General & Administrative Expenses are charged to the period under measurement, and not included in this type of MHR.

Even though the direct-cost statement, which uses the "B" rate, is not to be used for external income tax reporting, we eliminate the direct Selling, General & Administrative costs from the rate and charge it to the period in order to avoid activity distortions in measuring the standard contribution of sales, which would defeat the aims of direct-cost income reporting.

Obviously then, the "A" rate is used for cost estimating and order price evaluations, leading to a more conservative measurement of contribution. If the "B" rate is used for this purpose (a mistake common among some accounting people), contribution would be overstated and management or others would take this as a license to price-cut.

SECTION VI
INSTALLATION FORMS

The fifteen forms included in this Section may be used as models by the reader in installing the system presented in this book.

As an alternative, the author will supply, at a charge of $25. postpaid, a bound printed book of professional installational forms, as used in Martin & Tucker, Inc. client engagements, consisting of 103 forms. Included in this package is a summary of all construction steps extracted and condensed from this text for convenient reference. For this service and convenience, send check to Martin & Tucker, Inc., The Chase Manhattan Bank Building, Little Neck, NY 11362.

Form:	Cross References to Page Nos.
Converting Facilities Classification Sheet	88, 97, 132, 140, 151, 179
Production Center Derivation Sheet	187
Crew Composition Table	89, 105, 133, 141, 142, 143, 152, 153, 154, 180, 181
Gross Hourly Cost Sheet	188, 189, 190
Direct-Charge Budget	111, 136, 144, 155, 182
Expense Classification Worksheet	83
Allocable Budget: Mfg.	91, 115, 134, 145, 156, 183
Allocable Budget: Non-Mfg.	91, 116, 135, 146, 157, 184
Derivation of Annual Chargeable Standard Hours	147, 159, 185
Expense Assignment Worksheet	92, 123, 137, 148, 160, 186
Direct-Order Charges Worksheets	161, 162, 163, 164, 165, 166, 167, 168, 169, 170, 171, 172, 173, 174, 175, 176, 177
MHR Backtest Forms	326, 327, 328, 329, 332, 333
Production Standards	196, 197, 198, 199, 200, 201, 202, 203, 204, 205, 206, 208, 209, 210, 211, 212, 213, 214, 215, 216, 217, 218, 220, 221, 222, 223, 224, 225, 226
Estimating Sheets	229, 231, 233, 235, 238, 239, 240, 241, 242, 323
Contribution Log	281, 296, 307

MHR Construction: 1

MARTIN & TUCKER
ENGINEERS
THE CHASE MANHATTAN BANK BLDG. LITTLE NECK 62, N. Y.

Summary* Converting Facilities Classification Sheet (CFCS)

P. C. No.	Production Center	No. of Units	Hp. per Unit	FOR PRODUCTION CENTER			
				Working Space Occup. sq. ft.	Present Market Value in M's	Annual Assigned Hours	Hp-hrs. in M's

*Use detailed derivative sheets to develop specific composition of each center.

P.C. No.__________

MARTIN & TUCKER, INC.
ENGINEERS

Production Center Derivation

Operation	UNITS	HP Per Unit	Total HP	Space Occupied Per Unit	Total Space Occupied	Present Market Value	Annual Assigned Hours	Run Ratio
TOTALS								

MARTIN & TUCKER
ENGINEERS
THE CHASE MANHATTAN BANK BLDG. LITTLE NECK 62, N. Y.

Summary* Crew Composition Table (CCT)

Production Center	Std. Crew per Unit	H O U R L Y				
		Base Pay per Unit	N/C Cost per Unit	Cost of Sub-Std. Prod'y	O. T. & F.B. per Unit	Crew Pay per Unit

*Use detailed derivative sheets to show specific unit and fractional manning.

MARTIN & TUCKER, INC.
ENGINEERS

DERIVATION OF EMPLOYEE GROSS HOURLY COST

CLIENT:________ DIVISION:________ LOCATION:________ DATE:________

Name:________ Dept:________ Clk #:____ Prod Ctr:________

Job Title:________ Mach.#____ Shift:___ Shift Hrs:___ Est. Prod'y:_____%

Subsidy:____% Entitled Vaca. Days:____ Holidays:____

Hrly. Base Rate: Current $_____ ; Projected $_______

Annual Item	Annual Hours	Annual Cost	Annual Excess Cost
1. Regular paid clock hours		$	$
2. Planned overtime clock hours			
3. Gross paid clock hours			
4. Overtime premium cost			
5. Paid holiday hours			
6. Entitled vacation hours			
7. Other paid time off, in hours			
8. Expected non-chargeable hours*			
9. Sub-total: (5+6+7+8)			
10. CHARGEABLE CLOCK hours (3-9)			
11. Expected performance subsidy (% x 10)			
12. CHARGEABLE STANDARD hours (10-11)			
13. Non-hourly costs:			
13.1 Fed. payroll taxes, FICA, etc.			
13.2 State, city, etc. taxes			
13.3 Workmen's compensation			
13.4 Group, accident, sickness insur.			
13.5 Hospital'n, major medical plans, etc.			
13.6 Pension, union welfare, etc.			
13.7 Bonus, gifts, C.O.L. adj.			
13.8 Uniforms, special benefits			
13.9 Profit-sharing costs			
13.10 Other			
14. Sub-total: (13.1 thru 13.10)			
15. Excess costs (4+9+11+14)			

16. EXCESS hourly rate (15/12) $________

17. Projected hourly base rate $________

18. Effective GROSS HOURLY COST (16+17) $________

19. Increase in hourly base rate (16/18) ________%

* Include only those hours (washups, etc.) which are not part of any other MHR schedule or not included in production standards.

NOTE: Do not include incentive premium costs on this sheet.

MARTIN & TUCKER
ENGINEERS
THE CHASE MANHATTAN BANK BLDG. LITTLE NECK 62, N. Y.

Summary* Direct-Charge Budget (DCB)

Production Center	Repairs, Mainten., Supplies, Parts & Outside Service	Special Items	Direct Power			Annual Direct Ch'ges	Annual Assign. Hours	Direct Charges per Hour
			Elec.	Gas	Other			

*Use detailed derivative sheets to back up specific charges for each machine.

EXPENSE CLASSIFICATION WORKSHEET (ECW)

ENDING

EXPENSE ACCOUNT			
ACCT. NO.	PRESENT NAME	M / S	TOTAL AMOUNT
	TOTALS		

EXPENSE CLASSIFICATION WORKSHEET (ECW) (CONT'D)

ALLOCABLE BUDGET OVERHEAD CATEGORIES (MHR)								
MANUFACTURING COSTS					NON MANUFACTURING COSTS			
SPACE *A*	POWER *B*	MACHINERY *C*	INDIRECT *D*	F.B. *E*	R.W.D. *F*	SELLING *G*	ADMN. *H*	F.B. *I*

EXPENSE CLASSIFICATION WORKSHEET (ECW) (CONT'D)

MARTIN & TUCKER, INC.
ENGINEERS

PAGE OF

ALLOCABLE BUDGET EXCLUSIONS					
CCT	DCB	DIRECT-ORDER CHARGES			P & L NON-CONV.
		MATERIALS		OTHER	
		PREP	PRODN		
J	K	L	M	N	O

MARTIN & TUCKER
ENGINEERS
THE CHASE MANHATTAN BANK BLDG. LITTLE NECK 62, N. Y.

Summary* Allocable Budget (AB)

Projected Expenses	Period	Direct	Total
MANUFACTURING COSTS:			
Space:			
Power:			
Machinery:			
Indirect:			
Fringe Benefits:			
TOTAL MFG. COST	______	______	______

*Use detailed derivative schedules of projected costs for each entry on the AB and enter summary totals. If this is client's first two-part MHR development, back up with Chart of Accounts converted into ECW. Include on backup sheet, list of non-conversion expenses not to be included in MHR.

MARTIN & TUCKER
ENGINEERS
THE CHASE MANHATTAN BANK BLDG. LITTLE NECK 62, N. Y.

Summary* Allocable Budget (AB) (continued)

Projected Expenses	Period	Direct	Total
NON-MANUFACTURING COSTS:			
Whse. & Del:			
Selling:			
Administrative:			
Fringe Benefits:			
TOTAL NON-MFG. COST			
from p. 1: TOTAL MFG. COST			
ANNUAL BUDGETED OVERHEAD COST			

*same as on p. 1

MARTIN & TUCKER, INC.
ENGINEERS

Derivation of Annual Std. Charg. HRS

P.C. No.	Production Center	Gross Annual * Clock Hrs.	N/C		Annual Charg. Hrs	Subsidy		Annual Std. charg. Hrs
			%	Hrs		%	Hrs.	

* From analysis of required facility hours per sales forecast.

MHR Construction 5: EXPENSE ASSIGNMENT WORKSHEET (EAW)

UNITS	PRODUCTION CENTER	MANUFACTURING COSTS									
		Space		Power		Machinery		Indirect		F. B.	
		Period	Direct	Period	Direct	Period	Direct	Period	Direct	Period	Direct
	Totals										
	Allocation Factors										
	Allocation Fractions										
	Allocation Ratios										

MARTIN & TUCKER
ENGINEERS
THE CHASE MANHATTAN BANK BLDG LITTLE NECK 62, N. Y.

MHR Construction 5: EXPENSE ASSIGNMENT WORKSHEET (EAW)(CONT'D)

TOTAL MFG. OVERHEAD		NON-MFG. OVERHEAD		TOTAL ANNUAL OVERHEAD COSTS		M.H.R. OVERHEAD ONLY		H O U R L Y		TOTAL M.H.R.	
Period	Direct	Period	Direct	Direct	Total	OOP	"Full"	DCB	CCT	OOP	"Full"

MARTIN & TUCKER, INC.
ENGINEERS

PAGE ______ OF ______

ANALYSIS & SUMMARY OF DIRECT ORDER CHARGES (DOC)

Chart No. ______________

MATERIAL: ______________________________

CLIENT COMPANY: ______________ DATE ISSUED: ______________ REVISION DATES: ______________

DIVISION/PLANT: ______________ M. & T. ENGINEER: ______________

SUPERVISORY ACCEPTANCE: ______________ M. & T. APPROVAL BY: ______________

#411

CLIENT ____________

DATE TESTED ____________

BOOKED ____________

QUOTED ____________

M.H.R. BACKTEST FORM

(profile of previous estimate)

MARTIN & TUCKER, INC.
ENGINEERS

CUST. NAME & CITY ____________ EST. OR JOB NO. ____________ QTY. EST. ____________

OTHER DATA ____________

CUSTOMER CODE	____	PRODUCT CODE	____	PRINTING TYPE CODE	____	____
END-USE CODE	____	PRODUCT-LINE CODE	____	PRODUCT SIZE CODE	____	____
SALESMAN CODE	____	UNIT S. P. CODE	____	MAJOR FACILITY CODE	____	____
TERRITORY CODE	____	QTY. RANGE CODE	____		____	____
MATERIAL CODE	____	NO. OF COLORS CODE	____		____	____

CONVERSION

from previous estimate:		STD. ALLOWED HOURS	M. H. R.		EST. OOP COST	STD. OOP COST	STD. T.S.P.*
PRODUCTION CENTER	ALLOWED HOURS		OOP	SPOOP*			
PREP:							
RUN:							

*used with differential markups

LEVEL MARKUP DATA:				
	CONVERSION TOTALS			
.. ON OOP CONV. COST	MTLS. PREVIOUSLY EST.			
.. ON D. MTLS.	OTHER DOC'S PREV. EST.			
.. T.S.P.	ORDER/QUOTATION TOTALS			
.. TARGET CONTRIB.	BOOKED/QUOTED TOTAL S.P.			
.. TARGET G.P.V.	BOOKED/QUOTED TOTAL CONTRIBUTION			
.. BOOKED/QUOTED CONTRIB.	BOOKED/QUOTED G.P.V.			
.. CONTRIBUTION VARIANCE	MAJOR FACILITY HOURS			
	G. CPH			

#413

STD. NO. ________

CHART NO. ______

PRODUCTION STANDARD

MARTIN & TUCKER, INC.
ENGINEERS

PAGE ______ OF ___

MACHINE NO. ________________ DESCRIPTION: ________________________________

OPERATION: ________________________________ ELEMENT: ________________

CLIENT COMPANY: ________________ DATE ISSUED: ________ REVISION DATES: ________

DIVISION/PLANT: ________________ M. & T. ENGINEER: ________________

SUPERVISORY ACCEPTANCE: ________________ M. & T. APPROVAL BY: ________________

THE STANDARDS CONTAINED HEREIN ARE APPLICABLE TO THE MACHINE OR OPERATION AND METHODS EMPLOYED AS OF ________ AND ARE SUBJECT TO REVISION PENDING ANY ALTERATION OR CHANGE IN METHODS OR EQUIPMENT.

SHEET No.____________

METHODS SHEET

MARTIN & TUCKER, INC.
ENGINEERS

PAGE ______ OF ______

MACHINE No.______ STD. No.______ DATE WRITTEN______

PROD. CTR. No.______ CHART No.______ BY______

NAME OF OPERATION______

NAME OF ELEMENT______

DESCRIPTION OF METHODS

LIMITATIONS, QUALIFICATIONS, CONSTRAINTS

CLIENT COMPANY:______ MANAGEMENT OK:______

DIVISION/PLANT:______ M & T OK:______

The methods, procedures, layout, etc., described refer specifically to the production standard captioned above, as of the date written. Any alteration in said methods must be reported to enable revision in the production standard, if required.

#410

Contribution Log

(Basic: by Period. Sortings by: Customer, Product-line, Salesman, End-use, Territory, etc.)

Month of: ____________

Order No.	Booked S.P.	Total O.O.P.	Contrib.	PV	Cumula. Contrib.	MAJOR FACILITY UTILIZA.			ROC Target SP	Revenue (Pricing) Variance	Cumula. Revenue Variance
						Hrs.	CPH	Cum. CPH			

S U M M A R Y

Total Sales Booked in Month =
Target Sales Revenue =
Revenue (pricing) Variance =
Booked Contribution =
Composite Period PV =
Less 1/12 Annual Period Exp. =
Booked Pricing Profit =

Facility Hours Committed =
Average C.P.H. =

MARTIN & TUCKER, INC.
ENGINEERS

Index

T

U

V

W